Japan and Global Migration

Foreign Workers and the Advent of a Multicultural Society

Edited by Mike Douglass and Glenda S. Roberts

 University of Hawai'i Press

HONOLULU

First published 2000 by Routledge
Paperback edition published 2003 by the University of Hawai'i Press
© 2003 Mike Douglass and Glenda S. Roberts for selection and editorial material
© 2003 Mike Douglass and Glenda S. Roberts for the preface to the paperback edition
All rights reserved
Printed in the United States of America
08 07 06 05 04 03   6 5 4 3 2 1

Library of Congress Cataloging-in-Publication Data

A record of this book is on file.
ISBN 0–8248–2742–2

University of Hawai'i Press books are printed on acid-free
paper and meet the guidelines for permanence and
durability of the Council on Library Resources.

Printed by Versa Press

In memory of Morita Kiriro–scholar, mentor and friend

Contents

PART I
Global and historical perspectives on migration to Japan

PART II
Livelihood and living in Japanese workplaces and communities

Figures

Tables

Contributors

Mike Douglass is a Professor in the Department of Urban and Regional Planning at the University of Hawaii. He holds a Ph.D. in urban planning from UCLA. He has been a Visiting Scholar at Tokyo University, a Research Associate at the UN Centre for Regional Development in Nagoya, and taught at Doshisha University in Kyoto. He recently co-edited *Culture and the City in East Asia* (1997) and *Cities for Citizens – Planning and the Rise of Civil Society in a Global Age* (1998) and authored "The New Tokyo Story: Restructuring Space and the Struggle for Place in a World City."

John Lie is Head of the Department of Sociology, University of Illinois at Urbana-Champaign. He received his Ph.D. in Sociology from Harvard University. His publications include *Sociology of Contemporary Japan* (special issue of *Current Sociology* 44: 1 1996). He is currently completing a book on multicultural Japan.

Takashi Machimura is an Associate Professor of Sociology at Hitotsubashi University in Tokyo. He is completing his Ph.D. in Sociology at Tokyo University and has been a Fulbright Visiting Scholar at UCLA. He is author of *The Structural Change of Global City: Urban Restructuring in Tokyo* (in Japanese), and articles about global cities and international migration.

Stephen Murphy-Shigematsu is an Associate Professor at the University of Tokyo. He teaches and practices in clinical psychology. He holds a Ph.D. in Education from Harvard University. His research interests are in mental health and ethnicity. His recent publications include, "American-Japanese Ethnic Identities" and "Representations of Amerasians."

David Pollack is Professor of Japanese and Comparative Literature, University of Rochester. He holds a Ph.D. in Chinese Literature from the University of California at Berkeley. He is the author of *Zen Poems of the Five Mountains* (1985), *The Fracture of Meaning: Japan's Synthesis of China from the Eighth through the Eighteenth Centuries* (1986), and *Reading against Culture: Ideology and Narrative in the Japanese Novel* (1992). Current research includes the construction of the cultural body in Edo Japan, and representations of power and spectacle in Edo Japan.

Glenda S. Roberts is an Associate Professor at the Institute of Asia-Pacific Studies at Waseda University. She received a Ph.D. in anthropology from Cornell University and is the author of *Staying on the Line: Blue-Collar Women in Contemporary Japan* (1994). She is on the editorial board of *Social Science Japan Journal*. She is currently engaged in teaching and research on gender, family, and work in Japanese society. She has begun to study female migrant workers in China's coastal regions, and is also engaging in research on work/life policies in multinational corporations in Japan.

Katherine Tegtmeyer Pak received her Ph.D. in Political Science from the University of Chicago and is Assistant Professor at the New College of the University of South Florida. Her dissertation, *Outsiders Moving in: Identity and Institutions in Japanese Responses to International Migration*, investigates the role of the Japanese government in maintaining the dominant understanding of Japanese national identity.

Katsuko Terasawa is a practicing attorney in Osaka and lectures part-time at Osaka City University. She has been Chairperson of the Human Rights Committee of the Osaka Bar Association (1989) and Vice Chairperson of the Human Rights Committee of the Japan Federation of Bar Associations (1990). Her books include *The Rights of Part-timers* (1987), *Foreign Workers' Human Rights* (1990), and *The Empowerment of Women* (1996).

Michael Weiner is Reader in Modern Japanese History and Director of the East Asia Research Centre at the University of Sheffield. He is also Managing Editor of *Japan Forum*, the journal of the British Association for Japanese Studies. His publications include *The Origins of the Korean Community in Japan* (1989), *The Internationalization of Japan* (1992), *Race and Migration in Imperial Japan* (1994), and *Japan's Minorities: The Illusion of Homogeneity* (1996). Current research interests include the formation of Japanese diasporan communities, and the history of eugenics in modern Japan.

Keiko Yamanaka is a Research Associate with the Institute for the Study of Social Change and a Visiting Lecturer in the Department of Comparative Ethnic Studies at the University of California, Berkeley. She received her Ph.D. in Sociology at Cornell University, specializing in population studies. Her current research is on legal and illegal immigrant labor in Japan. Recent publications include: "Return Migration of Japanese-Brazilians in Japan" and "Return Migration of Japanese Brazilian Women"

Keizo Yamawaki is an Assistant Professor in the School of Commerce at Meiji University. He received a master's degree in international affairs from Columbia University and was previously a research associate at the International Peace Research Institute at Meiji Gakuin University. He is the author of *Kindai Nihon to Gaikokujin Rôdôsha* (Modern Japan and Foreign Workers) and co-editor of *Kankoku Heigo Mae no Zainichi Chosenjin* (Koreans in Japan before the Annexation of Korea to Japan).

Acknowledgements

We would like to thank the Center for Japanese Studies of the School of Hawaiian, Asian and Pacific Studies at the University of Hawaii at Manoa, the East–West Center, the Japan Endowment Fund of the Center for Japanese Studies, and the Social Science Research Council, for funding the initial conference organized by Glenda S. Roberts on "Foreign Workers in Japan: Gender, Civil Rights, and Community Response." Appreciation is extended to Duke University Press for allowing us to reprint Chapter 6 by David Pollack, which was originally published as "Revenge of the Illegal Asians: Aliens, Gangsters and Myth in Kon Satoshi's *World Apartment Horror*" in *Positions* 1:3 (Winter 1993) pp. 677–714. James Niermann and Chad Raymond receive our lasting gratitude for their fine assistance in editing and formatting the manuscript.

Mike Douglass and Glenda S. Roberts

Preface to paperback edition

Japan and global migration in the twenty-first century

The forces accelerating the migration of labor to Japan assessed in the following chapters continue to prevail into the new century. While Japan's economic downturn has temporarily dampened the explosive growth in the employment of foreign workers that occurred during the bubble economy a decade ago, key underlying factors sustaining the demand for these workers have become even more pronounced over the past few years. Among the most important is *shōshika,* the turn toward below-replacement fertility, with 2006 being the year in which Japan's population will begin to exponentially decline. This demographic event decisively shifts the discourse about foreign workers in Japan from debates about how to solve a temporary phenomenon to the question of how to accommodate a long-term, chronic demand for labor. The salient demographic indicators for the twenty-first century include:

- Japan's population will peak at 128 million in 2006, with the subsequent decline being as steep as the increases in the twentieth century. The total population is projected to fall to 100 million by 2050 (NIPSSR 2002).
- By 2025 Japan will have the world's oldest population, with the share of people aged 65 or over doubling to 36 percent by 2050 (NIPSSR 2002). Of the age 65-plus population, 60 percent will be over 75 years old.
- The number of children below 15 years of age now accounts for only 14 percent of Japan's population. Along with Italy, this is the lowest share in the world and foretells a severe reduction of the future labor force.

These factors underlie a fundamental crisis in Japan's society and economy. Ever higher numbers of the aged population will depend on fewer workers, domestic consumer markets are likely to shrink, savings rates are expected to plummet, and small and medium-size enterprises that are the backbone of the economy and depend upon ready supplies of low-wage labor will be unable to survive (MFA 2002). Without immigration of foreign workers to offset the labor force decline outcomes will be debilitating.

- By 2050 there will be only 1.5 working people for every person over age 65

(NIPSSR 2002). This contrasts with the already troubling level of 3.6 in 2002 (Kajimoto 2002).

* Monthly contributions to national social security funds will have to increase to 35 percent of a worker's salary, compared to 17 percent now (NCPA 2002). Japan's social security system is already paying out more than it is taking in and will be exhausted by 2025 unless new sources of revenue are tapped from the economy.

To avoid such outcomes by maintaining Japan's working population at the present level would require an annual entry of at least 610,000 immigrants into the labor force over the next fifty years (*Asahi Shimbun* 2002). This compares to the total of 700,000 foreign workers estimated by government to be in Japan in 2002. This represents equally profound implications for a society that views itself to be racially and culturally homogenous and has been designing policies to limit rather than encourage the entrance of foreign workers into the country.

International worker migration will continue to respond to these trends by providing greater numbers of workers to Japan. Not only is the demand growing in Japan, but key migrant-sending countries in the region are also becoming increasingly dependent upon their workers abroad to sustain their economies. International migration, which in 2002 included 175 million people living in countries where they were not born (UN 2002), has generated a new regional focus of migration among East and Southeast Asian countries. Japan, which has become a key migrant-receiving country since the late 1980s, had a total of nearly 1.8 million registered foreigners in 2001, which was an increase of more than 222,000 over 1999 (MOJ 2001). Among this number, increases in legally employed foreign workers were also experienced for the ninth straight year. As concluded by ILO Tokyo Office (2001), these increases reflect the wide wage gaps between Japan and other Asian countries and Japanese workers' unwillingness to take manual jobs. In many ways the recession has boosted the demand for foreign workers as a means for small businesses to keep costs down in a time of falling real prices for commodities and services in Japan.

Yet, excluding special residents, who are mostly Koreans with linkages from Japan's colonial times, only 184,000 of foreigners living in Japan have permanent resident status (*Migration News* 2002). Those without residence but who are in higher skill occupations have other appropriate working visas, including some of those in the sex industry. But for low-wage foreign workers, the government's policy of no legal entry except for those of Japanese descent or those classified as "trainees" ensures that half or more of their estimated 700,000 numbers are illegally contributing to the economy (Matsubara 2002). With passport forging on the increase, smuggling at an estimated rate of 30,000 people per year, new immigration laws making workers without proper visas even more careful to avoid detection, and the very limited capacity of immigration authorities and police to effectively monitor unauthorized foreign workers, the actual numbers are surely much higher.

At the same time that demographic changes in Japan are becoming more pronounced, shifts in the composition and conditions of foreign workers are occurring. Four trends stand out: the changing composition of the foreign worker population; changes in legal status and vulnerability of foreign workers; the increase in international marriages and family formation; and growing efforts of migrants and Japanese NGOs to politically mobilize support to improve migrant working and living conditions.

Changing patterns

The government's attempt to maintain racial purity in immigration by allowing only workers of Japanese ancestry to come to Japan has run its course. The number of available *Nikkei* migrant workers has reached a plateau of around a quarter of a million—only a fraction of the anticipated future labor demand. The relative decline of *Nikkeijin* is partly due to the shift of labor demand from manufacturing and assembly, the main occupations of *Nikkeijin*, to urban services, which are much more open to irregular labor recruitment. A new wave of offshore production moved to China is sweeping through the Japanese industrial establishment, making export-oriented manufacturing even less viable in Japan now than it was a decade ago (Mastsubara 2002).

The fastest growing and largest source of foreigners in Japan is China, which, according to government figures, accounted for 332,000 migrants in 2001 (*HNK* in *GKMK* 2002:68-69). While at 145,000 in number in Japan, Filipinos continued to constitute a substantial share of foreign workers, and although such countries as Korea continue to supply migrants, China is set to become the major supplier of especially low-cost labor to Japan for many years to come (Yamawaki 2002). China has already become a major source of trainees, migrant smuggling, false passports, and workers entering Japan under student visas (Konuma 2001). A trend toward long-term settlement of Chinese people in Japan is also discernable (Tajima forthcoming).

Partly as a result of barriers to legal settlement in Japan, transnational migration patterns of repeated temporary sojourns for work are also emerging. This has long been the pattern among sex workers, some of whom are given only short-term entertainer visas that cannot be renewed in Japan, and is now appearing among *Nikkei* Brazilians. Tsuda (1999: 716-717) concludes that the migration of *Nikkei* Brazilians to Japan is becoming one of structurally embedded circular migration, wherein "they have become a permanent part of Japan's population of temporary migrants." Other migrant groups are likely to follow this emergent global pattern of transnational migration, with migrants seeing themselves as belonging to two or more societies, making the question of national citizenship and migrant rights increasingly complex.

Status and security of work and living

A twofold, seemingly contradictory response to the growing number of foreigners is occurring: increasing permanent residence and naturalization for some, and closing doors with less security for most low-wage workers. The numbers of people granted permanent residency have grown steadily over the past decade to total 184,071 in 2001 compared with 45,229 in 1992 (HNKK, 2001, in *GKMK,* 2002: 67). Foreign permanent residents are gaining important rights such as local voting rights by some local governments, and a foreign-born (Finnish) natural-ized citizen has been elected to the Diet for the first time. Naturalization is also increasing, with approximately 16,000 people being permitted to naturalize in 1999, which, though small in number, is more than twice the 1990 figure (Yamawaki et al. 2001). "Oldcomer" North and South Koreans comprised 60 percent of newly naturalized citizens in 1999. All of these numbers point to a perceptible softening toward a multicultural future for those who can gain per-manent resident status.

Yet while selected segments of the foreign population are being regularized as residents and even citizens, insecurity is on the rise among the lower tiers of foreign workers. First, the prolonged stagnation of the Japanese economy has dampened demand for legally employed *Nikkeijin,* who are now increasingly subject to "indirect" rather than "direct" hiring by firms. Between 1997 and 2001 the number of *Nikkeijin* directly hired by employers fell nearly 20 percent (Kashiwazaki 2002); 40 percent of these workers are now employed by labor contractors and dispatched to production lines, with wages being cut back and contract periods limited to three months or less. A government survey on Japanese-Brazilian workers in 2001 found one-quarter were unemployed and one-third unable to send money home to Brazil; 40 percent said they were not adequately covered by social welfare programs, including health insurance (Matsubara 2002).

Second, to keep the pretense of no migration of non-*Nikkei* workers into the country, the government is allowing increasing numbers of companies to hire them as "trainees." The trainee system was put into place in 1993, ostensibly as a system to offer technical transfer to people from developing countries. In prac-tice the system is used principally as a mechanism to recruit foreign labor at below-market wages for firms in sectors officially categorized as suffering from severe labor shortages (*GKMK* 2002:71; Yamawaki et al. 2001). The number of sectors has continued to increase, rising from 17 in 1993 to 55 in 2000 (MOJ 2000: 10). Approximately 59,000 workers came into Japan as trainees in 2001, more than three times the 1993 level of 17,000 (JITCO 2002; Hanai 2001).

The majority of the trainees are from China, followed by the Philippines and Indonesia. These workers are not protected by labor standards and receive "allowances" that are significantly lower than the wages for even indirectly hired authorized foreign workers. Like the authorized workers, they too have found their wages cut back due to a series of deductions unilaterally imposed by employers (JITCO 2002). The Study Group on the Problem of Foreign Workers' Employment concludes that the current trainee system needs to be overhauled to ensure that it reflects the original goals of technical transfer (*GKMK* 2002:55).

The greatest barrier to gaining security and equity in employment is the immigration law, which results in most workers being in Japan illegally. Asian people make up the majority of those who are apprehended for this criminalized immigration status. Most of the 33,000 arrested in 2001 were visa overstayers

(HNKK 2002: 4). Although women, the great majority of whom are recruited for the sex industry, comprise half of foreign workers, most of those apprehended are men. While the majority (70 percent) work in greater Tokyo, and others are mostly found in major cities along the Tōkaido belt to Nagoya and Osaka, they are found in all prefectures (HNK 2002:21). Since only about 20 percent of illegal migrants are discovered and even fewer are apprehended, actual patterns are likely to vary significantly from these profiles.

While openings for trainees are being expanded, immigration laws and penalties for other workers are being toughened. In early 2000 illegal entry into Japan became a criminal act, with fines and three-year prison sentences, abolishment of the statute of limitations on trying illegal entrants, and a ban on returning to Japan for at least five years after deportation (Asakura 2000). An extreme example of the implementation of this policy is the case of a refugee fleeing Afghanistan under the Taliban who, in 2002, was found guilty of illegal entry, fined ¥300,000, and scheduled for deportation instead of being granted asylum (*The Japan Times* 2002). Arrested foreigners can now be held in immigration detention centers without trial for six months; some have languished in them for two years. Jails and detention centers are already full and are unable to manage language and other difficulties in processing cases.

Tougher penalties are reported to be fuelled by an observed trend toward less tolerance of foreign workers, who are often blamed for taking jobs from Japanese citizens and are portrayed as criminal elements (*Asahi Shimbun* 2001:3). A survey by the Cabinet *(Naikakufu)* in November 2000 on the problem of foreign workers found half of the Japanese respondents agreeing that unauthorized workers should be summarily sent back to their homelands, a sixteen-point increase over a similar survey in 1990. Another survey in 2001 found only 16 percent of the Japanese respondents saying that Japan should grant visas to unskilled foreign workers (Ando 1999; Matsubara 2002).

International marriages and family formation

Marriages with and among foreign workers are on the increase in Japan, confounding the logic of disallowing migrants to assume blue-collar jobs. While non-*Nikkei* male workers are prohibited from entering Japan, in rural areas local governments are now sponsoring searches for Asian brides for Japanese farmers. A record 28,326 marriages between Japanese men and foreign women were registered in 2000 (Asakura 2002). The majority of the brides were Chinese, Filipina, Korean, and Thai. In addition, the number of people with a visa for "spouse of a Japanese" reached an all-time high of 280,436 in 2001, a total increase of 77,267 since 1992.

Even in the realm of marriage, the government is expanding its prerogatives over the rights of foreigners. At the end of 2002 a Supreme Court judgment overturned a 1988 ruling that had upheld the right of a foreign spouse to maintain her spousal visa even though her Japanese husband had abandoned her to live with another woman. This decision gives priority to the convenience of the

Immigration Office to rule on sham marriages. Terasawa (author of Chapter 10 in this volume) feels this judgment will have a substantial impact on pending immigration policy cases, and will be deleterious to the human rights of foreign spouses.

Families form among migrants as well, and the increasing presence of spouses and children creates new challenges for local school districts, where educators are hard pressed to teach in a multi-cultural, and often multi-lingual, classroom (*Asahi Shimbun* 2001). In locales such as Hammamatsu in Shizuoka, where many *Nikkei* Brazilians work in the auto-related industries, educators are particularly concerned about the high truancy rates of 30 to 50 percent due to lack of language and other support (Yamawaki 2002). With regard to children, another Supreme Court judgment made at the end of 2002 denied the recognition of Japanese nationality at birth for a child born to a Filipina-Japanese couple before they had married (Terasawa, personal communication Dec. 2002). This bodes ill for securing rights to citizenship for children from international marriages. Currently there are more than 1,000 stateless children born in Japan without citizenship in either their parents' home country or in Japan (Ami 2002).

The issues related to marriage and families of foreign workers open broader discussions on social discrimination in housing, access to public services and amenities, and treatment of foreign customers by shop owners as well as government laws and regulations. Currently there is very little legislation to protect foreigners against discrimination in housing. However, migrant workers are beginning to successfully challenge discrimination by shopkeepers and in accessing amenities such as public swimming pools.

Migrant organization, NGO support and local governments

A prominent theme running through the chapters of this book is that, while some quarters of government and society persist in acting as if migration to Japan is both harmful and temporary, other more realistic and positive sources of migrant support are also emerging. In the past, most of this support has come from Japanese and international NGOs, local governments, and scholars. Now migrants are collectively empowering themselves as well. In 1999, a group of undocumented overstayers from Iran with almost ten years of residence in Japan successfully appealed to the Tokyo Immigration Office for permission to reside legally in Japan. Civic groups initiated a signature campaign on their behalf domestically and internationally. In February 2000, some of the group were granted their request, an unprecedented event for foreigners without Japanese relatives (Yamawaki et al., 2001; *Japan Watch* 2002). In the same year a group of 250 foreign workers and supporters walked from Ginza to Hibiya Park with banners saying, "We are not criminals" and "We want to stay in Japan legally" (*The Japan Times* 2000). While other foreign groups, notably permanent Korean residents, have long histories of mobilizing their communities to assert their claims to government, the self-organization of newer, much more vulnerable unauthorized foreign workers opens a new chapter in the politics of worker immigration to Japan.

NGOs also continue to emerge in ever greater numbers in support of foreign workers. Such groups as the National Network in Solidarity with Migrant Workers (Asakura 2000), Asian People's Friendship Society (APFS), Hand-in-Hand Chiba, and many other advocates offer counseling and legal aid and provide assistance in housing, schooling, day care for children, and other services (*Asahi Shimbun* 2002). Although many labor unions still oppose the entrance of unskilled workers, others show support, and a Labor Union for Migrant Workers was established in November 2002 as the first union for foreign workers in Japan (Matsubara 2002). The Foreign Workers branch of the Zentoitsu Workers Union (see Roberts, Chapter 12) currently enrolls 1,822 foreign workers, up from 1,594 in 1999.

Issues of exclusion and inclusion

Japan is simultaneously facing crises of exclusion and inclusion. By adopting more stringent laws to exclude foreign workers, it faces tremendous difficulties in coming to terms with its demographic future of diminishing population and labor force. Yet because these laws invariably become less effective in stemming the entrance of foreign workers as both Japanese enterprises and recruitment networks find new ways to circumvent them, it also perpetuates a system of illegal migration. While perhaps convenient to enterprises wishing to pay very low wages, this risks an equally problematic crisis of inclusion of foreign workers into everyday life accompanying the advent of Japan as a multicultural society.

The crisis of how to socially prepare for a multicultural society is mirrored by an equally profound crisis of keeping foreign workers out of Japan under current race-based and trainee program policies. Japan is not the only nation facing these crises; several European countries are also on the brink of rapid population decline as well. Japan is, however, moving ahead of almost all other nations on the curve of population decline. Its labor force is shrinking faster than the population as a whole; Japanese women are already shunning the positions being taken by foreign workers; and the elderly cannot do most of the "dangerous, dirty, and difficult" jobs taken up by foreign workers. As stated by a senior member of the Japan Trade Union Confederation *(Rengo)*, foreign workers are now indispensable for small and midsize businesses across Japan (Okada 2002).

Positive contributions are also emerging, especially at local levels of government and social mobilization. While some are now calling for a new social consensus among Japanese people about who they want themselves to be and what kind of nation they envision for the future (*GKMK* 2002:16-18), the reality is that trends show a decisive deepening of foreign worker presence in all spheres—economic, social, and political—of society in Japan. This opens the discussion to Hirowatari's (1998: 106) declaration that "it is time to wrap up our history as a 'monoethnic society'. . . but that will not be an easy task."

Mike Douglass and Glenda S. Roberts
January 2003

References

Ami, H. (2002) "Despite Being Born in Japan, 7-Year-Old Is Deemed Stateless," *The Japan Times* (2 February).

Ando I. (1999) "The Fate of Foreign Workers as Japan Enters the 21st Century," *Social and Pastoral Bulletin*, 91, 1 (15 August).

Asahi Shimbun (2002) "Editorial: Foreign Workers' Plight" (26 August).

Asahi Shimbun (2001) *"Gaikokujin no Fuhōshūrou 'yokunai' 49 percent Naikakufu no Yoronchōsa"* (Cabinet survey finds 49 percent say illegal work by foreigners "not good"), 3 (4 February).

Asahi Shimbun (2001) *"Hoikuen ha tabunkashakai, kotonaru shūkan, rikai he shikkōsaku-go teijūka nado haikei"* (Daycare centers trial and error over multi-cultural society, different customs, understanding: Increasing residence, etc. in the background), 21 (23 October).

Asahi Shimbun (2002) "Foreign Workers' Plight: Social Programs Should Offer Better Protection," 24 (27 August).

Asakura Takuya (2000) "New Immigration Law Misunderstood, Experts Say," *The Japan Times* (7 February).

Asakura, T. (2002) "Fixed International Marriages Often Disappoint", *The Japan Times* (8 January).

GKMK (Gaikokujin Koyō Mondai Kenkyūkai) (2002) "Gaikokujin Koyō Mondai Kenkyūkai Hōkokusho" (Report of the Study Group on the Problem of the Employment of Foreigners), Tokyo: Ministry of Health, Labor and Welfare.

Hanai, K. (2001) "Fairness for Foreign Workers," *The Japan Times* (22 January).

Hirowatari, S. (1998) "Foreign Workers and Immigration Policy," Junji Banno, ed., *The Political Economy of Japanese Society* (Oxford: Oxford University Press), 81-106.

HNK (Hōmushō Nyūkokukanrikyoku) (2002). "News Scope Heisei 11 nen ni okeru nyūkan hō ihan jiken" (Incidents of violations of the immigration law in 2001) in *Kokusai Jinryū* (July): 19-21.

HNKK (Hōmushō Nyūkokukanri Kyoku Keibika) (2002) "Fuhō taizai gaikokujin mondai no genjo to nyūkoku kanrikyoku no Torikumi" (The current status of the problem of illegally staying foreigners and actions taken by the Bureau of Immigration) in *Kokusai Jinryū* (June): 2-6.

ILO (International Labour Organization, Tokyo Office) (2001). "News Flash," (December).

Japan Watch (2002) "Movement for Residence Rights of Undocumented Workers Begins." http://www.twics.com/anzu/Japanwatch/Labor/Undocumented3.html.

JITCO (Japan International Training Cooperation Organization) (2002) "Statistics on Trainees and Technical Interns," http://www.jitco.or.jp/eng/index.htm.

Kajimoto, T. (2002) "Cloud of Population Decline May Have a Silver Lining," *Hawaii Hochi* (November 16):1.

Kashiwazaki C. (2002). "Japan's Resilient Demand for Foreign Workers," *Migration Information Source,* May 22, http://www.migrationinformation.org/Feature/display.cfm? ID=8.

Konuma, M. (2001) "Immigration Woes Threaten Fates of College, Chinese Students," *The Japan Times* (20 December).

Matsubara. H. (2002) "Economic Gloom Just Adds to Illegal Workers' Plight: Government, Devious Employers Seek to Reap Benefits without Legal Responsibilities," *The Japan Times* (27 June).

MFA (Ministry of Foreign Affairs) (2002) "Social Security in Japan: Toward a Japanese Model of the Welfare State," http://www.mofa.go.jp/j_info/japan/socsec/maruo/maruo_4.html

Migration News (2002) "Japan," 9:10 (October).

MOJ (Ministry of Justice) (2000). "Introduction—Social Changes and Immigration Control" in *Major Issues and Guidelines on the Immigration Control Administration, http://www.moj.go.jp/ENGLISH/IB/IB2000/ib03.html.*

MOJ (2001) "Statistics on the Foreigners Registered in Japan" (Tokyo).

NCPA (National Center for Policy Analysis) (2002) "Japan's Looming Social Security Crisis," http://www.ncpa.org/pi/congress/socsec/socsec12.html.

NIPSSR (National Institute of Population and Social Security Research) (2002) *Population Projections for Japan: 2001—2050, with Long-range Population Projections, 2051—2100* (Tokyo).

Okada, T. (2002) "Importing Cheap Labor Has Its Price," *The Japan Times* (July 10)

Tajima, J. (forthcoming) "Chinese Newcomers in the Global City Tokyo: Social Networks and Settlement Tendencies," *International Journal of Japanese Sociology.*

The Japan Times (2000) "Overstayers March in Plea for Resident Permits" (1 May).

The Japan Times (2002) "Court Fines Asylum Seeker 300,000 Yen" (21 September).

Tsuda, T. (1999) "The Permanence of 'Temporary' Migration: The 'Structural Embeddedness' of Japanese-Brazilian Immigrant Workers in Japan," in *The Journal of Asian Studies* 58 (3): 687-722 (August).

UN (United Nations) (2002) "Number of World's Migrants Reaches 175 Million Mark — Migrant Population Has Doubled in Twenty-five Years" (New York: Press Release POP/844) (28 October).

Yamawaki, K. (2002) "Gaikokujin seisaku: Tabunkakyōsei he kihon hō seitei wo" (Toward enacting a basic law for a multicultural-coexistent (society): Policies on foreigners), 13 (6 November).

Yamawaki, K., A. Kondo and C. Kashiwazaki (2001) "Taminzoku kokka: Nihon no kōsō" (Japan's design for a multicultural nation), *Sekai* (July).

Part I

Global and historical perspectives on migration to Japan

1 Japan in a global age of migration

Mike Douglass and Glenda S. Roberts

Introduction

Long thought to be immune from the globalization of labor migration, Japan has over the past decade begun to experience quantum increases in the numbers of women and men who have not simply come to work and quickly returned home, but are also bringing families, forming new households with Japanese nationals, and residing in neighborhoods in cities and regions throughout the country. Many government representatives and citizens continue to believe that this is a temporary phenomenon, occasioned by acute labor shortages in low-wage occupations, which will be overcome through factory automation and off-shore relocation of corporate Japan's labor-intensive industries. However the country's impending population decline, rapidly aging society and growing low-wage service sector, along with widening income disparities between Japan and most of the world, point to a greater certainty that the global age of migration has come to stay.

Foreign workers and households continue to fit uncomfortably into the Japanese setting. Tightening immigration control, in a situation of continuing demand for these workers in Japan, has led many workers to endure illegal migrant status and the insecurities it entails, while others, even with proper visas, face institutionalized discrimination in finding housing and effectively utilizing legal and other services. Migrants from some parts of the world, such as those of Japanese descent from Latin America, fare better than others in terms of legal status and acceptance at the workplace and in the neighborhood. Personal attributes, choices and circumstances which add to the variety of situations produce a rich diversity of experiences rather than an archetypal experience. Yet government policies and public attitudes share a common perspective: they see the presence of foreign workers as a phenomenon to be tightly controlled and kept at arms' length from the routines of Japanese life, rather than one that is to be accepted, which will bring about a new Japanese society that provides for a "co-existent citizenship" (Hirowatari 1998) of peoples from many ethnic and cultural heritages.

Insecurity, vulnerability and other factors such as feelings of isolation lead many, including those caught in government campaigns to crack down on illegal migration, to exit Japan and abandon thoughts of becoming long-term residents. Among these, a significant number, including tens of thousands of women in the sex and entertainment industry who are given short-term "entertainment" visas, routinely return to work in Japan, becoming part of transnational migration streams of people who chronically move among countries according to life-cycle events and job opportunities. While not finding a permanent footing in Japan, many of them have come to hold a certain attachment to living and working there and have learned how to construct a transnational existence bridging their countries of birth with Japan, and possibly other countries as well. Although these people are statistically counted as short-term stayers, the reality is much more complex as many begin to form long-term relationships, including marriage to and having children with Japanese nationals, which spill over national boundaries, immigration categories, and have an effect on future generations.

Trends suggest that, despite highly restricted immigration policies, increasing numbers of foreign workers and their families will end up staying in Japan for their lifetime, even though Japanese citizenship might never be afforded them. As the title of Chapter 6 by Yamanaka poignantly indicates, many migrants have an idea in their mind that they will return home but they are not certain when that will happen, and in the meantime they form relationships and develop new personal identities in Japan which make returning home awkward and difficult.

Whether they are short-term stayers, transnational migrants, or life-long residents of Japan, foreign workers and households are having a substantial impact on Japan's economic, social and political landscape. In some sectors of the Japanese economy they have become indispensable to small- and medium-sized enterprises, and future demand for low-wage labor in many emerging service activities, ranging from restaurant dishwashers and busboys to workers in health care for the aged, is likely to be filled by foreign workers. In the sex industry, foreign women are now found in every prefecture of the country. In areas where they are concentrated, foreign workers are creating their own economy of food stores, restaurants and shops. Where enough of them gather, they are organizing their own festivals that also attract Japanese citizens in very large numbers.

Even when labor demand levels off, as in the recession of the 1990s, migrants still come from abroad to find niches in the job market or to stay with friends from their home country as they engage in lengthier job searches. The great majority of foreign workers prove themselves to be hard working, responsible residents. Instead of being included in the daily life of Japanese society and receiving equal treatment under the law, however, they continue to face severe problems of exclusion and discrimination. Whether against "old-comers" from Japan's past colonization of Taiwan and Korea or the "newcomers" of the bubble economy era (November 1986–December 1991), barriers to regular employment, housing, and social services are commonly encountered by foreign workers in Japan (Komai 1995, Itoh 1996, Tsuda 1997, Morita and Sassen 1994).

Discrimination against migrants is hardly exclusive to Japan. Most societies have problems in creating and sustaining peaceful multi-ethnic co-existence. Immigration tends to exaggerate racism, xenophobia, and ethnocentrism and, all too often, becomes the focus of socially-divisive political agendas. At the same time, voices rising among Japanese citizens are championing the rights of foreign workers to be treated equally with Japanese labor at the work place and with Japanese citizens in the community. Contemporary Japan has people and organizations whose stance on this issue covers all points of the compass. They range from an official from the Ministry of Justice who, in response to deliberations on the UN Declaration of Human Rights, declared that "the treatment of foreigners is totally up to the discretion of the Japanese government . . . We can do with them as we please" (quoted in Hirowatari 1998: 88) to workers in non-profit organizations dedicated to ensuring that the rights obtained by Japanese citizens are also given in law and in practice to foreigners.

National and local governments also move in different directions with regard to foreign workers. Some local governments are in the forefront of efforts to provide social services to foreign workers. They even allow foreigners to work as civil servants. Most recently, the municipality of Tokyo has established a foreign residents' council to act as an advisory board to the mayor. Nearby Kanagawa Prefecture has established committees comprised solely of foreign residents for the purpose of having their opinions reflected in local government policies (*Japan Times* 1997, Yoshida 1998).

Beyond the specific responses of governments and citizen organizations to the situations facing migrant labor from abroad, Japanese cities and regions are not only beginning to register the presence of foreign workers and households as co-workers and neighbors, but also becoming exposed to a variety of different cultural practices. Ethnic neighborhoods are appearing in cities, and urban as well as rural areas are seeing an influx of foreign brides who bring along their own cultural heritage and lifestyles.

The challenge for Japan is to decide whether the response to the increasing presence of foreign workers and families will be one of trying to marginalize these alternative expressions of social and cultural identity through, for example, an implicit policy of containing foreign workers in ghettos or one of creating the political and social atmosphere for a multicultural society to flower. Signs of both possibilities exist, and it is as yet uncertain which tendency will win out. In the short-run, however, it appears that a '*sakoku*' (secluded country) attitude remains strong, buttressed by the myth of a pure Japanese culture (Itoh 1996, Lie ch. 4).

Migration to Japan in the contemporary world economy

Although in this volume the focus is on people from other countries coming to work and live in Japan, it is important to understand that, throughout most of its modern period since 1868, Japan has been a net sender of international migrants. Following Japanese government involvement in international agreements millions of Japanese people emigrated to settle permanently in other countries.

Migration up to the early post Second World War years

We return to the question of migration of foreigners to Japan. Records show Chinese migrants living in Japan in the seventeenth century, with their numbers increasing until the cession of Taiwan to Japan in 1895. By the end of the Second World War there were about 28,000 Taiwanese in Japan, of whom 14,000 elected to remain. Together with mainland Chinese who remained, they numbered 34,000 in 1948 (Vasishth 1997: 131).

By far the largest foreign presence in contemporary Japan is that of Koreans. Korea was colonized in 1910, and Korean workers subsequently came in increasing numbers as recruited workers as well as forced labor. By 1938, approximately 800,000 Koreans resided in Japan, compared to 30,000 in the 1920s (Yamawaki 1996 and this volume). During the Second World War, Koreans were brought to Japan in three phases: company-directed recruitment (1939–41), government assisted recruitment (1942–4), and forced draft (1944–5) (Weiner 1994: 194). By 1945, there were 2,100,000 Koreans residing in Japan (ibid.: 198). Even after repatriation of colonized peoples living in Japan following the Second World War, several hundred thousand Koreans continued to live in Japan.[1] In 1996, the number of permanent residents registered in Japan included 572,564 North and South Koreans, 30,376 Chinese and 23,100 others. In total, Koreans make up 91.5 percent of Japan's permanent resident aliens (JIA 1997a: 14).

In April 1947, under a new Alien Registration Ordinance, Korean and Taiwanese residents were deemed aliens. This Ordinance became the Alien Registration Law when the San Francisco Peace Treaty took effect in 1952, and Korean and Taiwanese residents became disenfranchised of the Japanese nationality they had held during colonial rule (Hirowatari 1993). This excluded them from many social welfare benefits and kept them from public sector employment (Vasishth 1997). At the same time, processes for becoming a Japanese national were severely assimilationist, requiring naturalized citizens to assume Japanese surnames and cease to use their own. As a result, many people who would have naturalized refused to do so, while many of those who did met with ostracization from their kindred. Due to strong pressure from Korean and other citizen's groups, the naturalization procedures have become somewhat less constraining in recent years (Hicks 1997, Murphy-Shigematsu ch. 9), perhaps partly because of this, more people are now seeking naturalization.[2]

With a vast supply of returning soldiers and rural labor reserves available to provide cheap labor power for Japan's recovery and stellar economic rise, migration to Japan from all countries was minimized after the Second World War up to the late 1970s (Morita and Iyotani 1994). This distinguished Japan from Western Europe, which was already highly urbanized. In 1950 almost half of the Japanese labor force was in agriculture. In less than two decades Japan subsequently experienced an accelerated urban transition which had taken almost a century in Europe.

The 1970s and 1980s

While Europe was massively recruiting immigrant "guest workers" in the 1960s, Japan was still able to use rural migrants as its pool of low-wage labor (Morita 1992). But this was changing rapidly. By the mid-1970s, less than 1 percent of the population lived in communities of fewer than 5,000 people. Village Japan had been decimated, and the share of national population residing in urban places had increased from a little over one-third in 1950 to more than three-quarters (Douglass 1993). With incomes and wages rising, the stage was being set for foreign migration into urban Japan. This began to be acted out in the 1980s when labor scarcities combined with the rising value of the yen against the dollar to confront Japanese employers, especially those in small to medium-sized manufacturing and construction industries, with severe problems of reducing costs to compete in foreign as well as domestic markets. Although from the 1970s Japanese women in increasing numbers began to fill low wages jobs as so-called "part-time" workers in manufacturing and services – especially married women past child-bearing age – they were not sufficient to meet the demand (Roberts 1994). The use of foreign migrant labor became Japan's next source of low-cost workers in the 1980s.

As noted, Japan remained a net international exporter of low-wage migrants until the 1960s. Trends in the worker emigration and immigration began to reverse by the 1970s and 1980s as more foreign labor began to enter Japan than Japanese workers to leave the country. The first reversal in the 1970s took the form of the recruitment of Asian women into Japan's domestic sex industry. By the 1990s, well over 50,000 women were coming to Japan annually as so-called "entertainers."[3] While the vast majority of sex workers come in shifts under short-term six-month visas, in 1992 alone 90,000 foreign women were classified as visa overstayers, with an estimated 90 percent of these coming from the sex industry (Komai 1995: 72).

Thus, unlike other high-income countries of the world, Japan's labor migration initially consisted overwhelmingly of women (Tiglao-Torres 1993). But the migration of foreign women into Japan's sex industry suddenly began to be matched from the latter half of the 1980s by the immigration of men into low-wage jobs often described as "the three Ks" (*kitanai, kiken, kitsui* – dirty, dangerous and difficult) which appeared in the context of Japan's domestic labor shortages and yen revaluation.[4] By the late 1990s, approximately 300,000 visa overstayers and more than three times that number of legal migrants with work permits were estimated to be in Japan, most of them of Japanese descent from Latin America, "trainees," entertainers, and foreigners working outside their permitted occupations.

The outcome of increased demand for male workers is an almost equal balance in the numbers of male and female workers coming to Japan in recent years. However, the specific occupations and immigration status of men and women remained quite different. Women are still recruited for the sex industry, although diversification toward other services is occurring, and some *Nikkei* as well as many Asian women are entering factory and service sector work.[5] There is also evidence that undocumented Korean women find jobs outside the sex and entertainment industry through their networks of Korean relatives who are residents of Japan (Moon 1995). Many women are also coming into Japan as spouses of foreign male workers and Japanese men. For their part, immigrant men are filling a much wider band of occupations, ranging from construction and manufacturing to hotel, restaurant and other service jobs.

Whatever the occupational profile, the increasing numbers of both men and women also bring about an increasing likelihood of family and community formation, and of children being born to immigrant households. By extension, this signals the advent of a much more multicultural society than Japan has experienced in its history.

Two key events in the early 1990s have been expected to make a profound impact on migration to Japan. The first was the revision of immigration laws which began in 1989 and was further refined in subsequent years with the intention simultaneously to open the doors to large-scale immigration of workers of

Japanese descent (*Nikkeijin*), predominantly from Latin America, and to close the doors on all other would-be migrants seeking low-wage work in Japan. The second was the burst of Japan's bubble economy, which sent Japan into a deep recession that has continued well beyond earlier optimistic predictions and is now caught up in the finance and economic crises that are heavily impacting other economies in Asia.

These two changes have worked as expected in some ways but not in others. The opening of immigration to *Nikkei* quickly resulted in more than 200,000 migrants from Latin America coming to Japan.However, closing off legal channels for immigration from other countries has been more complex. The numbers of immigrants from some countries that had enjoyed easy access previously, such as Bangladesh, Iran and Pakistan, showed drops as the Japanese government temporarily abolished bilateral visa waiver agreements in 1989, 1992 and 1989 respectively (Kashiwazaki, 1998: 240). On the other hand, the numbers of immigrants from China and Korea, as well as women from the Philippines, have continued to increase. Similarly, the effects of the recession have slowed the immigration of some groups, but overall immigration still continues at an historically very high level. The principal impact seems to have been to make foreign workers more vulnerable in job security and hours paid for work, rather than simply to curtail migration.

By the late 1990s, Japan's position in global migration had been fundamentally transformed from that of just a few decades earlier. From a net exporter of labor, it has become a net importer. It has, during the same period, become a principal capital and investment exporter, which has had the effect of changing the migration streams of Japanese emigrants from low-wage workers to managers and corporate elites. The outcome of these trends is a new pattern of north–south migration. Low-wage workers move north to Japan in response to widening gaps in income between Japan and countries in the south, while Japanese technicians, managers and administrators move in the reverse direction, under the impulses of the penetration of foreign markets by Japanese products, and direct foreign investment relocating low-technology, labor-intensive production off-shore (Low 1995).

Realities and myths about the future of migration to Japan

Sources of the increasing presence of foreign workers stem from both internal factors in Japan and external factors conditioned by an increasingly integrated global economy. Therefore the surge of foreign workers migrating to Japan is nested in a complex number of intertwined relationships which cannot simply be treated as a "border" problem. This complexity of factors, which also includes issues of basic human rights, is creating pressures of such magnitude that to continue the official policy of allowing foreign worker "entrants" but not "immigrants" will only lead to a heightening dissonance between the realities of increasing foreign settlement in Japan and the myths of Japan as a closed, single-race society.

The realities

Internally, the most salient factors underlying the demand for foreign labor are found in the way in which Japan's demographic trends are woven into its economic successes. The successes have created one of the economically richest countries in the world. From a devastated country at the end of the Second World War, Japan has seen its *per capita* incomes soar to levels which have created severe labor shortages in many low-wage sectors of the economy. In the process, the population has become highly urbanized, family sizes have decreased and birth rates fallen to such a level that, in addition to being unable to fill many low-wage occupations, the population and labor force are facing impending absolute declines due to birth rates that have fallen below replacement levels. At the same time, Japan faces an increasing economic and welfare burden on the working population owing to its rapidly aging population, which is also requiring a vast expansion of low-cost health services and health workers.

All of these factors point to the demand for labor continuing to create more opportunities for workers from abroad to come to Japan. Foreign workers in such occupations as waitresses, cooks and transportation workers are already beginning to account for increasing shares of visa overstayers. In parallel with the growth of domestic-market service occupations, there is the persistence of low-paying jobs in manufacturing and construction that cannot be eliminated through automation or off-shore relocation of production. This trend will be heightened to the extent that Japanese workers continue to decline the low-paying and low-status occupations that foreign workers have already begun to fill.

Four major external global factors bringing high levels of migration to Japan are equally powerful. First, the income gap between Japan and most other countries of the world, including its Asian neighbors, remains wide and is expected to widen in the coming years in absolute terms, even with exceptional economic performances in some other countries. The magnitude is so great that migrants with university degrees from abroad are willing to work in the most menial jobs and live in conditions of poverty and emotional deprivation in Japan to enable them to send remittances abroad to their families at levels not realizable through work in their home countries.[6]

The combination of widening income gaps and still rapidly-growing labor forces in poorer countries is producing what are, in practical terms, unlimited supplies of world immigrant labor. The financial débâcles impacting East and South-East Asia from late 1997 are expected to direct even more of this migration toward Japan. Currency devaluations have not only further widened international income gaps with Japan – in some cases, such as Indonesia, increasing them as much as fourfold – they have also lowered the propensity for workers to migrate to Korea and Taiwan which have both suffered currency devaluations. In this context, a recovery of Japan's economy would accelerate the migration of low-wage workers.

Second, coming to Japan is being increasingly routinized through a number of channels, including professional recruiters, migrant smugglers, and governments themselves. Governments have been found to be recouping substantial portions of the wages and incomes of their migrant nationals through contract labor agreements and controls over issuing of passports and other documents (Friedland 1994, Zlotnik 1995). Hence, immigration is not simply a matter of markets moving individuals over international space of their own volition or even for their own principal benefit, but is a process sustained by organized recruiters, including the state (Sighanetra-Renard 1992, Douglass ch. 5). Japanese government reports find that the recruitment of undocumented foreign workers is becoming increasingly organized and sophisticated, with growing involvement of crime syndicates based in Hong Kong, Taiwan, Thailand and the Philippines, as well as the Japanese *yakuza* (Cornelius *et al.* 1994). In this context, the gap between the number of illegal immigrants and enforcement capacity is also growing. Fewer than 2,000 immigration inspectors are authorized to check on employers in a country with millions of enterprises and a large number of labor contractors (Morita and Sassen 1994).

Third, revolutionary advances in international air transportation and instantaneous availability of information have increased access to, and knowledge about, potential destination countries to a point at which even relatively poor rural people can travel abroad in very large numbers in search of work, often through professional recruiters. The increasing ease of communications and physical movement among countries is lending itself to new forms of migration that, instead of resulting in one-way permanent migration, are multi-directional, of varied duration, and may involve several countries within a given time period (Kritz and Zlotnik 1992, Schiller *et al.* 1992). Networks among migrant groups, once established, become exceptionally difficult for governments to contain as information and skills on how to gain entry through various channels and legal loopholes becomes more readily available and sophisticated.

Finally, citizen groups and non-government organizations (NGOs) are emerging in sending as well as receiving countries to, in effect, keep doors open for immigration. In championing the causes of social justice and basic human rights for foreigners in Japan, they are challenging immigration policies, legal procedures and police practices that are oriented toward sealing off Japan's borders, and the many forms of official discrimination against migrants which keep them in the most vulnerable low-wage, high-risk situations (see Roberts ch. 12).

The dissonance between the objective conditions that will continue to bring high levels of immigration to Japan and the prevailing perception in Japan that this intrusion of foreigners has a limited time horizon can partly be attributed to a number of myths prevalent in Japan. These concern the history of immigration, the presumed power of the state over economic forces and actors, the potential for offshore investment by Japanese corporations to lead to falling demand for cheap immigrant labor, and the perceived need for prevention because immigrants impose high economic and social costs on Japan.

Myth One: Japan has no history of immigration

> *Forbes Magazine* to a Japanese official: "I'd like to know the procedures to follow to immigrate to Japan and obtain Japanese citizenship."
> Anonymous Japanese official: [complete surprise and astonishment] "Why do you want to immigrate to Japan? . . . There is no immigration to Japan."
> (Brimelow 1993: 58)

One of the most persistent beliefs held by government, citizens and even scholars alike in Japan is that the nation has no history of immigration. This belief is fundamental to current policies and debates about immigration. Because it perpetuates the idea that Japan consists of a single race of people, who have a single cultural origin and continuity without direct contribution of foreigners, it is used to justify the position that immigration is an assault on the racial purity of Japan (Denoon *et al.* 1996).

In fact, Japan is not only a product of distinct waves of large-scale immigration from different origins in ancient times, it has benefited from the influx of other peoples and cultures for a long period leading up to the present time (McCormack 1996).[7] Its world-renowned ceramics industry, for example, was greatly stimulated by the import of Korean potters in the early seventeenth century. Yet throughout all this history, the policy of government and practice of Japanese society has been to pretend that immigration was not occurring and to require foreigners either to live in officially-designated enclaves or otherwise to be contained in specific neighborhoods.[8] The Chinese and Korean residents mentioned earlier are also considered to be outside the category of immigrants.

In the late 1970s the wave of migration to Japan of female recruits for the sex and entertainment industry presented a potential confrontation to the policy of not allowing foreign workers to migrate to Japan. Gender and other biases meant that the thousands of foreign women entering Japan from this period onward were even more invisible than were the Chinese and Korean male workers who had preceded them in the earlier migration stream of the pre-Second World War period. It was only when male immigration began to increase dramatically after 1986 that the immigration of women began to receive attention (Ito 1992, Yamanaka 1994). By the 1990s an estimated 100,000–200,000 women, largely recruited through organized crime networks, were entering Japan each year to work as bar hostesses and prostitutes. This type of immigration of women for the sex trade is itself a continuation of a century-long involvement of Japan in the international organization of prostitution in Asia beginning in the late nineteenth century. During the Second World War, as many as 200,000 "comfort women" from Japan's conquered territories were forced to prostitute themselves for Japanese troops.[9]

Despite the realities of history, foreign scholars have also tended to accept the view that Japan is a country without immigrants. Sassen (1994: 63), for example, declares that "Japan has never had immigration." Such a position can only be maintained, however, by categorizing the millions of Koreans and Taiwanese coming to Japan before the Second World War and, presumably, the thousands of women who have entered Japan to work in its sex and entertainment industries as "forced labor recruitment." Such a view catagorizes immigration to Japan during this century as "forced labor," thereby denying the possibility that human agency existed even in horrific conditions and choices were made by many migrants to leave home countries and come to Japan. A more useful vantage point is to accept the reality that Japan has long used foreign workers as a source of cheap labor supplies, regardless of immigrant status. Accepting this view would make even more striking Sassen's claim (1994: 64) that Japan "lacks a belief in the positive contribution of immigration" and that "the concept of immigration does not exist in its law on the entry and exit of aliens."

Japan has had a number of waves of immigration over the past century. While small in number relative to the national population, immigrants have been recruited to provide a major source of labor in particular sectors of work and types of occupations. Moreover, as in the case of Koreans brought to Japan during colonial times, reversing immigration trends becomes increasingly difficult to effect once a certain scale of presence has been established. Recent government data show, for example, that while many observers believe that the resident Korean population in Japan essentially represents the progeny of the original colonial population remaining in Japan after over a million Koreans were repatriated following the Second World War, new Korean migration to Japan over the past decade has experienced an upsurge that has continued even with the current recession (Ministry of Justice 1997).

Looking at the contemporary scene, the still relatively small share of foreign residents in Japan perpetuates the belief that immigration is so insignificant that it is not occurring. At just over 1 percent of the total population, the presence of foreigners would appear to be incidental to Japanese society and economy. There are, however, several reasons why the presence is more prominent than the numbers might imply.

First, the share continues to increase. According to official figures the 1996 total of 1.41 million registered foreigners (1.12 percent of the total population) set a new record for Japan, both as a total number and as a percentage. Between 1986 and 1996, registered foreigners increased by 63 percent, and even in the economic downturn of the 1990s they increased by 16 percent. As a rate of growth, these increases far outstrip those of the Japanese population, which will soon experience negative growth rates.

Second, the uneven spatial distribution of foreign workers and households means that the presence is much greater in some areas than in others. As shown in Tables 1.1 to 1.3, more than 80 percent of registered foreign residents – who do not include at least 300,000 visa overstayers – reside in the three great metropolitan regions of Tokyo, Osaka and Chubu. In the city of Oizumi-cho in the Gumma Prefecture extension of the Tokyo metropolitan region, *Nikkeijin*, most of whom do not speak Japanese, now account for 12 percent of the total population, and their share is increasing. In the nearby Isezaki City they account for 5 percent of the population and have been increasing in number by about 10 percent every year (*Asahi Shimbun* 7 Jan. 1998). Oizumi appears to be becoming a national cultural center for Brazilian *Nikkeijin*. The 1997 festival there, complete with 400 samba dancers in five teams dressed in elaborate costumes, attracted 170,000 people, many of whom were Brazilians living in other areas of Japan (*Hawaii Hochi* 21 August 1997). Approximately 400 shops now orient their trade toward the 4,000 Brazilians in the town of Oizumi. Another 1,000 migrants, representing thirty-four nationalities, also reside in the town. With seventy babies born to foreign parents in 1997, one projection is that even without further immigration, foreign worker households will comprise 20 percent of the population within ten years.

Each group of foreign workers shows a different pattern of spatial concentration from the others. *Nikkeijin*, who have been largely recruited for auto and electronics sub-contracting firms, are most likely to reside in the suburbs of Tokyo where many of Japan's electronics giants have plants and sub-contractors and in the Chubu region near Toyota Motors sub-contractors (Table1.4). For most other migrant workers who, unlike the *Nikkeijin*, do not have long-term work visas, housing is found on construction sites, in factories or in dilapidated wooden row housing and apartments in downtrodden parts of the city. Choices are extremely limited both by cost and by active discrimination against foreigners. Areas that do accept foreigners and are affordable have become "*gaijin* (foreigner) houses" (Komai 1995). At least a dozen such places exist in Tokyo (Machimura ch. 8), with concentrations of Chinese near the two major entertainment quarters, South-East Asians (Filipinos, Thai, Indonesians) concentrated along the river front to the east and south of the Imperial Palace, and others filling in a "*gaijin* triangle" running from Kabukicho in Shinjuku to Okubo and Ikebukuro.

Kabukicho, the most well-known night-life entertainment area in Tokyo, has a very high concentration of foreign workers, partly because it also has a section of low-rent wooden apartments. Although the low-rent residents used to be Japanese bar hostesses, now "nine out of ten people are from the 'third rate' countries," (Komai 1995: 142), and it has come to be called "Little Hong Kong" or "Chinatown." In contrast, the Koreans and Taiwanese, with long-established presence dating from Japanese colonial times, allegedly occupy the best locations and better housing in Shinjuku.

In addition to significant concentrations of foreign households in certain urban neighborhoods, foreign workers have become indispensable in key sectors of the Japanese economy. Electric machinery, plastics and certain chemical processing industries, construction, and auto parts making have already become well-known for their reliance on foreign workers to keep wages down and carry out jobs that Japanese workers avoid. Recently, even rural regions have tapped into the availability of cheap, dependable foreign labor. The owner of a chain of hot spring hotels operating in Tochigi Prefecture reports that he began hiring *Nikkeijin* in the early 1990s as a means of coping with the outmigration of Japanese women who used to be available as low-wage part-time workers, and the aging of customers who are increasingly on low fixed incomes. The owner now states that for his business to economically survive, he is now entirely dependent upon foreign workers. But he complains that since only *Nikkeijin* are officially allowed to come to Japan as workers, the supply of foreign workers is constrained and will not be sufficient in the future (*Asahi Shimbun* 7 Jan. 1998: 1). Such comments are not uncommon and suggest that if the future needs of the economy are to be met, Japan will be home to increasing numbers of foreigners.

Given the Japanese government's reluctance to recognize Japan as a country of immigration, Berger's (1998: 320) "*de facto* country of immigration" categorization of Germany, which "continues steadfastly to maintain [its] non-immigration status," can be applied to Japan. When translated into practice in the case of Japan, immigration policies for this type of country are characteristically designed to control in-coming workers as supplies of labor rather than including them as potential citizens (Hirowatari 1998). In the law of both countries nationality is defined primarily on blood rather than on birthplace, and naturalization is considered as an exception to the blood principle and granted only in a restricted manner (Hirowatari 1993).

Table 1.1 Regional distribution of registered foreign residents by country of origin, 1996

	Total	Asia total	Korean	Chinese	Filipinos	Other Asian	Brazil, Peru	Other LDC	Europe, N. America
Tokyo metro*	552,221	399,493	169,436	128,910	44,805	56,342	85,229	14,836	52,663
Osaka metro**	379,861	349,709	294,083	41,084	5,674	8,868	14,591	3,404	12,157
Chubu metro***	233,539	122,035	83,243	20,016	11,814	6,962	101,552	3,575	6,377
Okayama	14,105	11,375	8,345	1,713	896	421	1,873	213	644
Hiroshima	26,467	20,955	14,912	3,366	1,919	758	3,958	275	1,279
Fukuoka	35,216	32,295	23,910	5,961	1,585	839	329	653	1,939
Other prefectures	173,727	124,219	63,230	33,214	17,816	9,959	31,362	3,401	14,745
Japan total	1,415,136	1,060,081	657,159	234,264	84,509	84,149	238,894	26,357	89,804

Source: Ministry of Justice, Annual report of Statistics on Legal Migrants 1997 (Dai 36 Shutsunyūkoku Kanri Tōkei Nempō, Tokyo: Ministry of Justice, Section III, Table 1.

Notes:

*   Tokyo, Ibaraki, Tochigi, Gumma, Saitama, Chiba, Kanagawa
**   Osaka, Kyoto, Nara, Hyogo, Wakayama
*** Aichi (Nagoya), Gifu, Shizuoka, Mie, Shiga

Table 1.2 Distribution of foreign residents within regions by country of origin, 1996 (%)

	All foreign residents	Asia Total	Korean	Chinese	Filipino	Other Asian	Brazil, Peru	Other LDC	Europe, N. America
Tokyo metro	100.0	72.3	30.7	23.3	8.1	10.2	15.4	2.7	9.5
Osaka metro	100.0	92.1	77.4	10.8	1.5	2.3	3.8	0.9	3.2
Chubu metro	100.0	52.3	35.6	8.6	5.1	3.0	43.5	1.5	2.7
Okayama	100.0	80.6	59.2	12.1	6.4	3.0	13.3	1.5	4.6
Hiroshima	100.0	79.2	56.3	12.7	7.3	2.9	15.0	1.0	4.8
Fukuoka	100.0	91.7	67.9	16.9	4.5	2.4	0.9	1.9	5.5
Other prefectures	100.0	71.5	36.4	19.1	10.3	5.7	18.1	2.0	8.5

Source: Ministry of Justice, Annual report of Statistics on Legal Migrants 1997 (Dai 36 Shutsunyūkoku Kanri Tōkei Nempō), Tokyo: Ministry of Justice, Section III, Table 1.

Table 1.3 Distribution of foreign residents among regions by country of origin, 1996 (%)

	All foreign residents	Asia Total	Korean	Chinese	Filipino	Other Asian	Brazil, Peru	Other LDC	Europe, N. America
Tokyo metro	39.0	28.2	12.0	9.1	3.2	4.0	6.0	1.0	3.7
Osaka metro	26.8	24.7	20.8	2.9	0.4	0.6	1.0	0.2	0.9
Chubu metro	16.6	8.6	5.9	1.4	0.8	0.5	7.2	0.3	0.5
Okayama	0.9	0.8	0.6	0.1	0.1	0.0	0.1	0.0	0.0
Hiroshima	1.9	1.5	1.1	0.2	0.1	0.1	0.3	0.0	0.1
Fukuoka	2.5	2.3	1.7	0.4	0.1	0.1	0.0	0.0	0.1
Other prefectures	12.3	8.8	4.5	2.3	1.3	0.7	2.2	0.2	1.0
Japan	100.0	75.0	46.6	16.4	6.0	6.0	16.8	1.7	6.3

Source: Ministry of Justice, Annual report of Statistics on Legal Migrants 1997 (Dai 36 Shutsunyūkoku Kanri Tōkei Nempō), Tokyo: Ministry of Justice, Section III, Table 1.

Table 1.4 Intra-regional distribution of foreign residents by country of origin, 1996 (%)

	Total	Asia total	Korean	Chinese	Filipinos	Other Asian	Brazil, Peru	Other LDC	Europe, N. America
Tokyo metro	39.0	37.7	25.8	55.1	53.0	67.0	35.7	56.3	58.6
Tokyo	17.8	19.2	14.2	30.8	19.8	25.6	3.2	24.8	37.1
Ibaraki	2.0	1.6	0.8	1.7	2.9	5.8	3.9	2.0	2.0
Tochigi	1.5	0.9	0.5	1.2	1.8	2.7	4.4	2.5	0.8
Gumma	1.9	1.1	0.5	1.1	3.4	3.2	6.0	2.7	0.8
Saitama	4.5	4.2	2.5	6.5	7.5	8.5	5.9	6.6	3.6
Chiba	4.0	4.0	2.4	5.1	8.6	8.4	3.8	5.5	4.1
Kanagawa	7.3	6.7	4.9	8.7	9.0	12.8	8.5	12.1	10.2
Osaka metro	26.8	33.0	44.7	17.5	6.7	10.5	6.2	12.9	13.5
Osaka	14.8	18.6	25.9	9.0	3.1	3.7	2.9	5.8	4.7
Kyoto	3.9	4.9	6.8	2.2	1.0	1.1	0.5	2.5	2.8
Nara	0.7	0.8	1.0	0.6	0.4	0.4	0.6	0.5	0.7
Hyogo	6.9	8.2	10.4	5.5	1.8	5.1	2.0	3.8	5.0
Wakayama	0.4	0.5	0.6	0.2	0.4	0.3	0.2	0.2	0.4
Chubu metro	16.5	11.5	12.7	8.5	14.0	8.3	42.4	13.6	7.1
Aichi (Nagoya)	8.2	6.7	7.8	4.8	6.5	3.7	16.7	6.0	3.7
Gifu	1.8	1.3	1.3	1.3	1.7	1.0	4.4	0.8	0.6
Shizuoka	3.6	1.6	1.2	1.5	4.2	2.2	13.2	3.1	1.6
Mie	1.6	1.0	1.2	0.6	1.1	0.9	4.6	2.1	0.7
Shiga	1.3	0.9	1.2	0.4	0.5	0.5	3.5	1.5	0.5
Okayama	1.0	1.1	1.3	0.7	1.1	0.5	0.8	0.8	0.7
Hiroshima	1.9	2.0	2.3	1.4	2.3	0.9	1.7	1.0	1.4
Fukuoka	2.5	3.0	3.6	2.5	1.9	1.0	0.1	2.5	2.2
Other prefectures	12.3	11.7	9.6	14.2	21.1	11.8	13.1	12.9	16.4
Japan	100.0	100.0	100.0	100.0	100.0	100.0	100.0	100.0	100.0

Source: Ministry of Justice, Annual report of Statistics on Legal Migrants 1997 (Dai 36 Shutsunyūkoku Kanri Tōkei Nempō), Tokyo: Ministry of Justice, Section III, Table 1.

Myth Two: the Japanese govenrment can effectively prevent immigration

A second myth is that the major reason why Japan was not inundated with immigrants in the past, when Europe and North America were, is that strict governmental policy effectively sealed off Japan from such migration. Following this logic, tightening immigration controls now would presumably have the same effect, even if the underlying factors bringing migrants to Japan have changed. By the late 1980s, however, these conditions had changed so radically that government policies to keep out unskilled workers became increasingly ineffectual. Labor scarcities became acute, particularly in the then-booming construction industry. Under pressure from Japanese business, particularly smaller-scale sub-contractors, government policies made a partial reversal by allowing *Nikkeijin* to come as laborers to Japan. Other immigrants not granted such ease of entry also began to come in large numbers, using tourist and study visas as pretexts for entry while working full-time.[9] Visa overstaying became a widespread practice not only of Philippine and Thai women in the entertainment and sex industry, but also of male workers from China and South-East Asia. In 1996 the government reported that Japan had almost 300,000 visa overstayers – officially illegal migrants – in the country. From 1993 there were increasing numbers of overstayers from several key countries – Korea, Philippines, China and Taiwan – after a downturn immediately following the burst of Japan's bubble economy in 1991 (Table 1.5).

Competing, sometimes contradictory, immigration policies also create avenues for immigrants to come to work in Japan, even without having an appropriate work visa. The government actively promotes the entry of tourists, students, trainees, businessmen and women entertainers. To a very limited extent, there are also provisions for political refugees. In addition, the international travel of Japanese and the presence in Japan of increasing numbers of foreigners has lead to a burgeoning of international marriages between Japanese and non-nationals. With such contradictory policies and interests, illegal immigration "is likely to emerge in Japan as a relatively viable option for persons denied access to *bona fide* migration opportunities" (Kritz and Zlotnik 1992: 11).

Lastly, the breakdown of full-time employment systems and the casualization of labor hiring in Japan, a common occurrence in almost all high-income countries, facilitates the incorporation of illegal migrants into the labor system (Sassen 1994). Among university-educated Japanese employees, jobs with bonuses, health care, housing, retirement and other benefits have long been the norm in larger companies, but part-time and temporary work has proliferated, especially for older men and women, in smaller companies, and even in large ones in such areas as custodial services and lower-status office work. The increasing casualization of employment is accompanied by an erosion in the collective monitoring of hiring practices by labor. With the increasing use of dispatch services and sub-contractors, labor finds it increasingly difficult to collectively organize to monitor its interests. And with each level of management shrugging off responsibility for hiring to another level, the undocumented hiring of illegal immigrants easily becomes routine. This is even more pronounced in the service sector, which is the least organized in terms of labor unions and which typically employs a large portion of its employees on a part-time and highly insecure basis at low wages.[11]

For the above reasons, government policy to limit immigration has been an imperfect solution to Japan's perceived threat of immigrant invasions.[12] In fact, a large increase in illegal immigration came after the December 1989 adoption and June 1990 implementation of a more restrictive immigration law which includes stiff sanctions against employers and the tightening of visa requirements. These observations are consistent with the conclusions of Cornelius *et al.* that:

> Japanese immigration policy is inchoate, with little consensus evident within the government on the basic directions of policy. . . Current policy has three major tenets: (1) admitting foreign workers, on whatever basis, should be a last resort; (2) no unskilled workers should be admitted; (3) all foreigners should be admitted on a temporary basis only. But each is being systematically undermined and disregarded both by Japanese companies and by the government itself.
>
> (Cornelius *et al.* 1994: 385–7)

In the face of tight legal restrictions, illegal entry is becoming more organized and undetected. While official figures show that the number of people turned away at regular ports of entry has fallen (though still at record high levels of 16,000 in 1997), illegal entry by sea through smaller port cities is apparently on the rise and more creative forms of circumventing regulations, such as entire group tours disappearing after entry, are being attempted.[13]

Myth Three: immigration of low-wage labor will not be needed in the future

The belief that immigration of foreign workers is temporary and historically unprecedented in Japan is deeply embedded in Japan and reiterated in Western

Table 1.5 Visa overstayers by country of origin, 1996

Country of origin	1995	1996	Change 1995–96 (%)
Korea	43,675	51,580	18.1
Philippines	36,583	41,997	14.8
Thailand	48,281	41,280	-14.5
China	34,394	39,140	13.8
Peru	14,549	13,836	-4.9
Iran	13,879	13,241	-4.6
All others	91,237	81,766	-11.6
Total*	282,598	282,840	-0.0

Source: *Honpō ni okeru fuhō zanrūysha sū* (Number of Illegal Overstay Immigrants in Japan), *Kokusai Jinryu,* 7 February 1997: 18–27.

Notes: * male = 160,836; female = 123.664.
　　　Increasing countries: Korea, Philippines, China, Taiwan.

literature. Muller, in contrasting immigration in the US with Japan, concludes, for example, that:

> Japan is the prime example of a technologically advanced nation that depends on its own population for nearly all of its workers. . . Japan's ability to maintain a high living standard with virtually no dependence on immigrant labor reflects some distinctive aspects of Japanese culture, religious philosophy, and nationalism.
>
> (Muller 1993: 287–8)

The millions of foreign workers entering Japan over the past two decades would seem to counter this view. It is so widely held that the current reality is explained away in a number of ways. First, as noted above, there is a belief that if government were to get tough on immigration, it could stem the tide. While stringent controls do undoubtedly keep migration to Japan well below the levels it might otherwise be – as do discriminatory practices in housing, social services and social relations in general – the larger question is whether such labor will be in demand in the future and how business and international migrant job searches will combine to circumvent, if not relax, even Japan's tough immigration controls.

Another argument in favour of foreign immigration being a short-term phenomenon is that the real cause of the influx was hyper-economic growth exaggerated by an artificial "bubble economy" of finance capital. This was attended by a dramatic rise in the value of the yen against the dollar and other major currencies, resulting in acute labor shortages and increased labor costs in Japan's manufacturing export engine of economic growth (Stalker 1994). Caught off-guard by these trends, sub-contractors and smaller firms turned to immigrant labor as a short-term strategy to lower production costs, and thereby assisted parent companies in staying competitive on the world market. With the burst of the bubble and the deep recession that followed, the expectation has been that the demand for foreign workers in construction and other occupations will plummet. In other words, the foreign worker influx was viewed as a necessary but undesirable response to acute crises rather than a recognition of longer-term trends.

More recent evidence does not, however, support this view. Although, for example, illegal immigration has fallen from Iran and a few other countries that, until recently, had exceptionally easy entry to Japan, as previously noted, the major sending countries that neighbor Japan – Korea, China and the Philippines – continue to show increases. Figure 1.1 also shows that illegal migration has attenuated, although it is still at levels that are several times greater than those of the late 1980s and has only been marginally subdued. Assuming a recovery of the Japanese economy, and given the new sectors in which foreign workers are finding employment in Japan today, there is every reason to expect the immigration will accelerate in pace with, or perhaps overtake, the demand for labor, as Japan's own labor force begins to precipitously decline in numbers.

Another major reason given for an expected steady decline in the demand for foreign workers in Japan is the continuing transnationalization of Japanese corporations. Official government policy has been to support the process of putting labor-intensive segments of production offshore through direct foreign investment (DFI) in manufacturing and assembly operations abroad, notably in East and South-East Asia. In the late 1980s DFI from Japan was phenomenal (Douglass 1993), and although the recession of the early 1990s dampened this outflow momentarily, recent indicators show that it is on the rise again as global economic integration continues to present a compelling need to move labor-intensive activities from high- to low-wage locations. The view is thus taken that the acute demand of the recent past for labor will be countered over time by shifting it to Japanese factories offshore. In the early 1990s only 6 percent of Japanese production was being done overseas, compared to one-fifth in the US and Europe (Sender *et al.* 1995). Thus the argument runs that, if the transnationalization of Japanese corporations were to achieve levels similar to those of the US or Europe, the need for cheap labor in Japan for export-oriented production would evaporate.

Such a position is only partially valid at best. First, the work of most migrants in Japan has no obvious relation to Japan's export economy. The majority of foreign women are in the entertainment and sex industry. Data on undocumented male migrants show that less than half are in the manufacturing sector, and even in this sector a significant share is for domestic rather than international production.[14] In total, the data reveal that only about one quarter or less of labor movement to Japan is in the export manufacturing sector. Thus, while transnationalization of production and the adoption of labor-saving technologies are sure to continue in Japan, and thereby reduce demand for simple labor in some key segments of export-oriented manufacturing, demand for low-wage labor in many sectors is not being reduced by foreign investment in labor-intensive assembly and manufacturing.

In addition, as Japanese society ages and population growth falls below replacement by the end of the next decade, the growth in the demand for personal health and other services can only be met by immigration. It is not unthinkable that, as with Europe and North America, nursing and other health care and domestic service occupations will increasingly be filled by immigrants. Recent population projections released by the National Institute of Population and Social Science Research point to a rapidly aging and shrinking population: in their "mid-line" prediction, Japan will have a population of 100 million by the year 2050, down from the current 126 million. The "low-line" scenario is 92 million in 2050, and 50 million in 2100 (Jinkō Mondai Shingikai (eds) 1997: 4).

The central concern is that the population will come to resemble an inverted triangle, with few young people to support the many elderly. In 2015, one in four Japanese will be sixty-five years of age or older, and in 2049 the rate will be one in three. The sources of this rapid graying of society are found in the plunging birthrate, which was 1.42 in 1995, along with ever-increasing life expectancies (*Nikkei Weekly*, 27 January 1997: 6). In 1997 Japan had nearly 20 million people over sixty-five years of age. By 2010 these senior citizens will account for 22 percent of the national population, 50 percent more than youth under age fifteen.

With women expected to live until eighty-seven and men until eighty, and with the number of people under fourteen expected to decline year by year, attracting Japanese labor for lower-paying jobs in services such as health care is likely to become difficult. As with the private sector call for foreign labor for construction

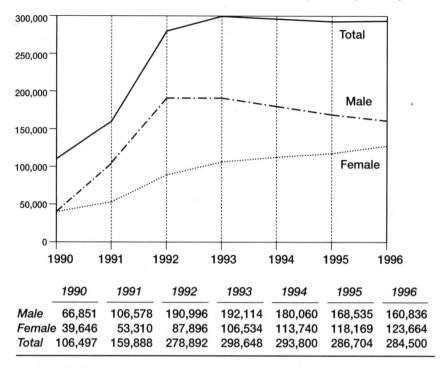

	1990	1991	1992	1993	1994	1995	1996
Male	66,851	106,578	190,996	192,114	180,060	168,535	160,836
Female	39,646	53,310	87,896	106,534	113,740	118,169	123,664
Total	106,497	159,888	278,892	298,648	293,800	286,704	284,500

Figure 1.1 Visa overstayers in Japan, 1990–6

Source: Ministry of Justice (1990–7) *Annual Report of Statistics on Legal Migrants,* various editions, Tokyo: Ministry of Justice.

and factory work in the late 1980s, the need for health care and related service workers will surely result in the government relaxing immigration controls in practice, if not in law, in the coming years so as to recruit immigrants to fill the vacancies.

While foreign investment has been placing labor-intensive production into selected lower-income economies of the world, it also paradoxically stimulates the movement of labor to Japan. Local workers in Japanese enterprises abroad are often sent to Japan for training, to learn Japanese, and to become familiar with Japanese culture and ways of doing business. This, in turn, fosters the possibility of seeking immigration into Japan to use these skills to greater advantage and for higher incomes. In this light, Figures 1.2 and 1.3 present a revealing relationship between trends in direct foreign investment and the entrance of foreigners into Japan by showing that rather than countering each other, they co-vary through time. As direct foreign investment has increased, so has immigration to Japan. Direct foreign investment by Japanese companies went from less than 40 billion dollars in 1980 to 464 billion dollars in 1995, with very large proportions invested in labor-intensive production in East and South-East Asia (Table 1.6).

By the late 1990s, a substantial amount of labor-intensive segments had been put offshore. Many labor-intensive activities, such as VCR assembly and lower quality electronic goods, have been or are being phased out in Japan. This includes even those activities carried out by small Japanese producers and sub-contractors, many of which have become managers of overseas operations rather than producers in Japan. At the same time, this investment also channels access to Japan's domestic market through Japanese corporations rather than through an open international market. The fact that, even in the late 1980s, less than 2 percent of electronic goods entering Japan bore foreign brand names shows how the domestic market is still protected against foreign competition despite – or, more accurately, because of – massive increases in direct foreign investment (Douglass 1993). This results in the continuation of some sectors of manufacturing in Japan for the domestic market in products that are otherwise not competitive on international markets and explains the persistence of the relatively high share of labor in manufacturing in Japan in comparison to other OECD countries.

Equally revealing are the statistics showing that the overwhelming number of factory jobs being created by Japanese direct foreign investment in other Asian countries are filled by women. Four-fifths or more of employees in assembly-line work in textiles and electronics, the dominant sectors of Japanese production abroad in Asia, are women. In contrast, the types of jobs that are filled by immigrants working in the manufacturing sector in Japan are almost exclusively oriented toward male labor. Parts and component making, metal and plastic, printing and binding, plating, press operating, and materials coating are the principal activities for which immigrant labor are hired (Morita and Sassen 1994). Due to quality control and other considerations, such as domestic-market orientation, these activities are among the least likely to be put offshore.

The result is a gender division of labor among immigrants in Japan that is the reverse of the practices of Japanese firms abroad. In Japan, foreign male workers are the new low-level industrial workers; abroad, indigenous women fill the assembly lines of Japanese-affiliated companies. In Japan, Japanese women continue to occupy the low-wage, insecure assembly jobs, with a majority of foreign women being brought to Japan for the entertainment and sex industry. Thus the internationalization, or more accurately the transnationalization, of the Japanese economy produces a more complex picture than the one suggesting that rising direct foreign investment causes a decline in demand for immigrant workers in Japan. While some segments of manufacturing will continue to move offshore, many others will stay and even expand in Japan. Moreover, transnationalization of business also generates a phenomenal growth of producer-related services in Japan that, at least at the lower end, are likely candidates for immigrant labor.[15]

As concluded by Hirowatari (1998: 85), the persistence of the view that the entry of foreign workers is only a temporary phenomenon is "fraught with danger" because, as experienced in Europe "the introduction of foreign workers will lead to a certain percentage settling, even if the initial period of residence is restricted." The danger arises from the deflection of attention away from the necessity of making social and legal preparations needed to absorb them into Japanese society, which will lead to a two-tier society that will "sow seeds of trouble for the future" (ibid. 106). Further, "Admission of foreign workers without such preparations is both irresponsible on the part of the receiving state and also unfortunate for the foreign workers" (ibid. 85).

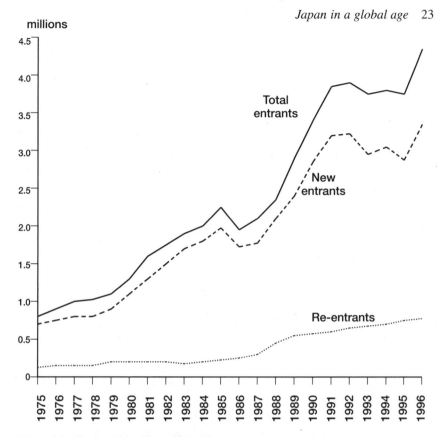

Figure 1.2   Entrants into Japan 1975–96
Source: Ministry of Justice, *Annual Report of Statistics on Legal Migrants 1997*, Tokyo: Ministry
of Justice, Section III, Table 1.

Myth Four: immigration imposes high costs on Japanese society and economy

The view that migration can be prevented is driven by the sentiment that it should
be prevented. This normative stance has social as well as economic dimensions.
Socially, immigrants are popularly associated with all kinds of ills: undermining
Japanese culture, bringing unwanted cultural practices to Japan, fostering crime
and other anti-social behavior, transmitting HIV AIDS, bringing racial impurity
to Japan, and, if in great numbers, leading to intolerable demographic pressure
on Japan's limited land resources.

   One of the more sensational media themes is that low-income foreign entrants
are responsible for new crime waves sweeping the country (Tsuda 1997). This is
revealed by a recent statement by the head of the National Police Agency, who
states that "although internationalization is good for the country's politics and
economy, it isn't any help in maintaining public peace" and that Japanese are
becoming increasingly fearful for their safety due to an increasing number of
crimes committed by foreigners living in Japan.[16]

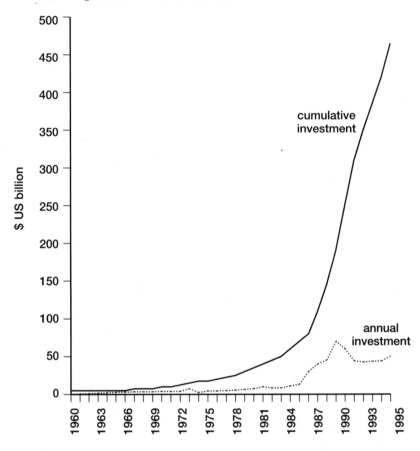

Figure 1.3   Annual and cumulative Japanese direct foreign investment, 1960–95
Source: JETRO and Ministry of Finance

Close analysis of *gaijinhanzai* (crimes by foreigners) does not support the the-sis that foreigners are more likely to be criminals than are Japanese citizens. Further, there is some evidence that some, such as visa overstayers, receive harsher sentences than Japanese citizens in order to send the message to would-be illegal migrants at large. Komai (1995: 155) cites the case of a Thai woman, convicted of injuring a Filipina in a hostess club in Nagoya who was given a three-year sentence because, according to the judge, "We must consider that she was in Japan illegally at the time of the crime, and her punishment should there-fore be heavy." Herbert (1996: 261) also notes that Asian foreigners "are criminalized collectively through the tendency of courts to give harsher sentences than are received by Japanese offenders." In most cases, illegal migrants who are arrested on suspicion of committing crimes are simply deported without a chance to defend themselves. Since criminal records are based on arrests rather than con-victions, such cases are also reported as part of the foreigner "crime wave." According to migrant support groups, these records are further exaggerated

Table 1.6 Worldwide distribution of Japan's direct foreign investment, 1990–5

Destination	1990	1991	1992	1993	1994	1995
Total	100.0	100.0	100.0	100.0	100.0	100.0
US	45.9	43.3	40.5	40.9	42.2	43.8
Europe	25.1	22.5	20.7	22.0	15.2	16.7
East Asia	12.2	14.1	18.1	18.1	22.7	23.2
Asian NIEs	5.9	5.3	5.6	6.7	7.0	6.3
ASEAN 4	5.7	7.4	9.4	6.7	9.5	8.1
China	0.6	1.4	3.1	4.7	6.2	8.8
Others	16.8	20.0	20.7	19.0	19.9	16.3
Mfg./assembly	100.0	100.0	100.0	100.0	100.0	100.0
US	41.2	45.2	37.6	36.3	33.2	37.8
Europe	29.7	21.9	20.9	18.3	13.5	10.7
East Asia	19.3	23.5	28.8	32.2	35.8	41.7
Asian NIEs	5.2	5.2	4.4	6.6	6.1	6.4
ASEAN 4	13.1	15.8	18.0	13.2	16.3	16.6
China	1.0	2.5	6.5	12.4	13.4	18.7
Others	9.8	9.5	12.7	13.2	17.5	9.8

Source: JETRO and Ministry of Finance

because non-Japanese are more likely to be arrested on suspicion of crimes than are Japanese (Friman 1996). A very large share of arrests of foreigners are for only one type of crime: not having the proper visa.

Given these biases, official data for 1995 show that, of the almost 4 million foreigners entering Japan that year, foreigners accounted for 2.4 percent of the nation's penal code offenses (mostly felonies) and 4.2 percent of its drug-related (cannabis and heroin) offenses (Tsuda 1997). More than half (52 percent) of the penal code offences involved violations of the Immigration and Recognition of Refugee Status Law. While these figures are still comparatively small in proportion to the total criminal offenses committed nationwide, they do point to another concern, namely, the absence of clear protection of human rights in the Japanese legal system (Terasawa ch. 10). Although Japan is a signatory of international covenants on standards, it has not adjusted its practices to match them. Arrest warrants are, for example, written only in Japanese, and foreigners often do not know what they are suspected of and the reasons for their arrest or detention (Tsuda 1997).

Arguments concerning the economic costs imposed on Japan by migrants are equally problematic. Many mainstream unions in Japan, like those in the US and Europe, see foreign immigrants as job stealers who both take away and lower wages for unskilled work in Japan. Evidence from research on foreign workers in Japan does not support these contentions. Low-wage foreign workers are, in the main, filling positions vacated by Japanese workers. Even in the construction industry, which employs a quarter or more of foreign male workers, the jobs done by foreigners are often the most marginal, such as cleaning up construction sites. Studies in Europe and North America also show that migrants make substantial and positive contributions to the economies of host countries (Sider 1992). Some analysts have gone further by showing that the implicit costs of raising and educating this labor in the home country are greater than the remittances of incomes and wages sent back by migrants (Berger and Mohr 1975, Castles and Kosack 1974). While remittances appear in short-term episodes, the costs to labor are spread over the life of the migrant and even beyond. As Sider commented:

> The process of working-class transnational migration is a process of sucking value out of migrants' home countries and transferring that value to the host country. It is appropriation *above and beyond* the surplus value appropriated directly from the workers in their work – it is appropriation from the migrant's kin-groups, communities, regions and countries.
>
> (Sider 1992: 232)

The xenophobia underlying exclusionary policies and public opinion follows from what Lie (ch. 4) has described as the sense of Japaneseness that sets Japan both apart and above other Asian cultures. In this context, the growing presence of foreign workers and households in cities, towns and rural Japan accentuates the self-identity of Japanese people as a distinct, socially and economically homogeneous people (Lie ch. 4, Murphy-Shigematsu ch. 9). As such, it promotes even stronger measures to limit and control the entry of foreign workers into Japan. This perception goes beyond popular media; it also works itself into scholarly discourses on migration, sometimes with avowedly good intentions. Shimada (1994: 209), for example, concludes that migration to Japan is undesirable because smooth integration of immigrants would be very difficult given that Japan is "basically a single-race nation." Komai (1995), gives the argument an unusual twist by faulting Japanese society by stating that, in the long term, migration to Japan is undesirable because, given Japan's previous track record in the poor treatment of foreigners, he does not see any possibility for harmonious co-existence.

The single-race belief has also easily found its way into government pronouncements on international relations and human rights debates. As late as 1980, the Japanese government declared that "there are no ethnic minorities in Japan" (quoted in Hirowatari 1998: 91). Although criticisms led to a revised report in 1987, which belatedly gave recognition to the *Ainu*, the 150,000 Koreans who had become Japanese citizens were not mentioned. As concluded by Hirowatari:

> Putting it another way, you could say that, in the legal sense, taking on Japanese citizenship was considered, even demanded, to be an act of becoming Japanese in body as well as soul. It is precisely for this reason that . . . Korean residents of Japan cannot but feel that taking Japanese citizenship is 'denying oneself' and 'betraying one's countrymen and women.'
>
> (Hirowatari 1998: 91)

Japan's foreign workers in global perspective

A variety of localized forces – the state, corporate interests, class and other cleavages – have joined with globally-integrating processes to organize, regulate and sustain accumulation within and across national boarders through international migration. Maintaining differentials in the spatial mobility of capital and labor is essential to the capacity of capital to subordinate labor to its needs. This is achieved by national policies to selectively restrict the international mobility of labor (Lycklama a Nijejholt 1992). Reactions of citizens reveal how race, class, culture and other deeply embedded divisions are drawn upon to lend political support and give credence to these policies. In this context, foreign and Japanese workers in Japan are part of an interpenetration of national and international divisions of labor, with the increasing presence of foreign workers underscoring how difficult it has become to separate domestic from international labor issues. They are equally part of an emerging multi-cultural reality with social, political and economic dimensions that are only just beginning to be understood and played out in neighborhoods, cities and regions of Japan.

The past three decades have witnessed the increasing ability of capital to move globally in many forms – finance, commodity, production – while labor has remained significantly less mobile, making it less able to either respond to spatial differences in income-earning opportunities or negotiations with capital on an equal footing. In this context, the role of national boundaries has changed over the past few decades from a defense and national security purpose to an increasingly economic one, particularly with regard to regulating international flows of labor. Borders are now part of the (inter-)national construction and reproduction of labor systems that are used to segment and selectively recruit labor internationally. They are also used as part of "rent-seeking" activities by sending governments, which often take significant portions of the wages of contract laborers.

This global–local process is inadequately portrayed as the working of a labor market. It is, more accurately, a part of a globalizing labor system in which only a fraction of labor is actually recruited and subject to rewards and discipline through a market-determined wage. Kept in conditions of extreme vulnerability, undocumented labor is not paid a market wage, but is instead paid well below the going rate for legal resident workers. Among foreign workers with appropriate visas, segmentation by ethnicity, gender and national origin is pronounced in Japan (Tsurushima 1993, Yamanaka ch. 6). Those at the lower end, including those married to Japanese citizens but having only spousal visas, are disciplined with isolation, discrimination, and threats of deportation (see Terasawa, ch. 10).

The combination of insecurity created by the state and by exclusion from housing and community life emanating from Japanese society has resulted in the convenience of treating foreign workers in Japan as "disposable workers" (Kobayashi 1996: 25). A case in point was the Operation White Snow campaign that the Nagano Prefectural Police launched in January 1997, a year before the opening of the Winter Olympics of 1998. Illegal workers had been employed to construct the Olympic Village, and only after their work was finished did the police carry out round-ups and deportations of the workers. A local contractor was quoted as saying that he had tried unsuccessfully to hire Japanese laborers for the job, and he could not have done it without foreign workers (*Mainichi Daily News* 1 Nov. 1997:12, *Japan Times* 4 Feb. 1998: 3).

Terasawa (ch. 10) also illustrates how the legal system is finessed by Japanese companies who use foreign workers as an employment "buffer." When times are good, employers often violate labor laws in hiring migrants, and when the economy slides, employers dismiss them or refuse to renew their contracts. Thus they form the lowest segment in the labor hierarchy, next to Japanese temporary, part-time and day laborers. Terasawa's analysis of cases shows that the marginal position of most foreigners keeps them from utilizing provisions for equal protection with the Japanese under the law.

This position of foreign workers has been underscored by the ways in which the impact of recession in the 1990s has fallen most heavily on foreign workers, including *Nikkei* workers, who are concentrated in sectors hardest hit and none of whom have ever been hired on a full-time, permanent basis (Yamanaka, ch. 6). As labor demand dropped, pervasive firing of these workers began. Wages also went down. Undocumented workers have also suffered, with reports of workers from some countries now living in parks, hotels, and movie theaters (Komai 1995).

The inevitability of increasing migration to Japan

Japan is not alone in thinking that strict border controls can stem the rising tide of international migration. Most Asian governments have similar policies. For these societies, the influx of foreign workers presents a profound shock that goes beyond public policy and strikes deeply into cultural attitudes and beliefs. Yet a number of researchers portray Japan as reaching the point at which the "objective conditions" are in place for an inevitable immigration of foreign workers (Morita and Iyotani1994, Spencer 1992). The driving processes follow the experience of the West: drastically declining natural population growth rates, increasing labor short-ages, affluence that makes menial/dangerous and dirty work unattractive; wide and growing gaps between Japan and other Asian countries. In addition, improvements in transportation and information allow heightened access to Japan from places as physically and culturally distant as Iran.

The specter of immigration coming to Japan needs, however, to be carefully distinguished from that imagined from the history of Europe in the 1960s. First, the world economy has changed substantially since immigrant workers flooded into Western Europe in the post Second World War decades. A new international division of labor and the transnationalization of capital have removed the compelling need to bring low-wage labor into advanced countries for the sake of sustaining the Fordist factory system. Second, the labor system in Japan is also rapidly changing in a manner that is making all lower segments of Japanese labor more vulnerable. To imply that Japanese labor is not connected to the in-migration of foreign labor misses the point that all segments of labor are highly integrated into the international labor system.

In other words, the Japan-follows-Europe explanation is the wrong way to view international migration. World migration is no longer a process among nations, but is instead caught up in the globalization of capital transcending national borders. In this sense, migration to Japan is not necessarily for the purposes of sustaining Japan's competitive position, but is more accurately a part of an emerging international labor system that spans national space and is as concerned with supplying labor for domestic services as it is with production for export. Somewhat paradoxically, therefore, Japan's future demand for foreign workers will increasingly be oriented toward filling jobs that cannot be exported and are, essentially, serving the domestic market. Moreover, immigration is part of a wider restructuring of the Japanese labor system away from guaranteed, full-time employment and toward "flexible" employment of part-time and even "just-in-time" workers, hired on short notice at low hourly wages and with no benefits. Foreign labor is not simply filling in a labor market gap, but is part of an on-going transformation of capital-labor relations in Japan that is character-ized by rising income inequalities and greater vulnerability of many segments of labor (*Sekai* 1994).

With the advent of a new millennium, Japanese society faces a tremendous challenge in coming to terms with the presence of what is likely to be many mil-lions of immigrant workers in its midst. By the end of 1997, the Ministry of Labor's cautious estimate of the number of legal and illegal foreign workers was 630,000 (*Asahi Shimbun* 7 Jan. 1998), an increase of 30,000 in two years (Kobayashi 1996), with almost half being in Japan illegally. Even conservative government projections, that exclude the current resident Korean population, pre-dict that 3 to 4 million people without Japanese citizenship will be living in Japan by the year 2015 (Kono 1994). More generous estimates would put the number at twice or more than the government figures.

Within Asia, the recent collapse of major industrializing economies, resulting in substantial increases in the exchange value of the Japanese yen, is likely to accentuate the focus of international migration on Japan. This revaluation is tak-ing place in a context of deepening poverty in such countries as Thailand, the Philippines and Indonesia, and the expulsion of foreign workers from such coun-tries as Korea and Malaysia. One expected outcome of all of these factors is that the widening income gaps between Japan and the rest of Asia, stricter migration controls throughout Asia, and limited possibilities of finding work for workers returning home will increase the propensity to try to migrate to Japan, even dur-ing a period of protracted recession in Japan.

The continued exclusion of foreign migrants from the level of economic, social and political life enjoyed by Japanese citizens carries a high risk. The resulting gulf, summed up as the difference between inclusion and exclusion, will inevitably raise continuing issues of social justice and basic human rights, and will create potential for social unrest. The included are those who fit into Japan's self-image of a prosperous, technologically innovative, and democratic society. The excluded, which includes Third World immigrants, are those who are necessary for the reproduction of society, but who do not fit into the imagery of the Japanese sense of identity. However, the included and excluded groups are more closely bound together than is commonly understood: the corporate elite need the illegal immi-grants as the ultimate foundation of the economy, and the middle class increasingly finds the foreign workers have become the cooks and dishwashers in the neighbor-hood restaurant and diner. Out of this contradiction and the multi-layered character of Japan's own version of the post-modern city, an enormous energy, cultural dynamism and innovative capability emerge. At the same time, co-existence carries the potential for social breakdown, conflict, repression, and violence.

Coming to terms with the inevitable requires a thorough rethinking of citizen-ship, who in Japan should have access to it, and all the rights and privileges that it assumes. Specifically, it will need a strong de-linking of conferring citizenship from a consideration of ethnic assimilation.[17] As concluded by Castles and Miller:

> The 'content of citizenship' must be de-coupled from ideas of ethnic homo-geneity or cultural assimilation. Cultural pluralism must be embraced. If ideas of belonging to a nation have been based on myths of ethnic purity or of cultural superiority, then they really are threatened by the growth of eth-nic diversity that will require major political and psychological adjustments.
>
> (Castles and Miller 1993: 273)

Earlier in this chapter, we noted that both Germany and Japan share legal struc-tures that base nationality on blood principles, and restrictive naturalization laws. But recently, Germany's Social Democratic and Green Parties have proposed to loosen the blood-principle base of nationality, by granting automatic citizenship to any third generation foreigner born in Germany and any German-born child with a parent that has lived in Germany since the age of fourteen. Dual citizenship would also be allowed (Cohen, 1998). Japan is sure to watch these developments closely.

As many writers represented in this book suggest, aside from political and psychological adjustments, a growing ethnic diversity will also require a reconsideration of "Japaneseness" in history as well as in its contemporary context. Contemporary processes of economic globalization and migration to Japan have only partially questioned this belief and, as McCormack (1996: 2) concludes, may be the source of a recent rise in an even more exclusive concept of who is and who cannot be Japanese. Yet the rise of Japan of as a world economic superpower will continue to confront Japanese society with questions about citizenship in a global age of migration. The challenge ahead has been well stated by Hirowatari:

> It is time we made up our mind to admit 'co-existent citizenship', wrap up our history as a 'monoethnic society', and begin the preparations for forming an 'open society'. Doing so could be the first step towards creating the new essence of Japanese society.
>
> Hirowatari (1998: 106)

Themes and organization of the book

The chapters in this book highlight the ways in which meeting the challenge of co-existent citizenship is both being inhibited and moving forward in Japan. As a collection, the chapters also reveal a complex picture beneath a generalized pattern of extreme vulnerability, constant legal, social and economic discrimination and low-incomes. Different immigration policies are applied to Korean, *Nikkeijin* and other would-be immigrants. Residential patterns vary among foreigners, as does the capacity for networking within the country and abroad. Employers distinguish among foreigners by offering different jobs, wages and status according to race and country of origin. This stratification of foreigners overlaps that of Japanese labor, making a clear line between foreign and Japanese labor impossible to draw. Some local governments are expanding their support services, while others continue to resist giving equal treatment to foreign workers.

Part I sets the historical and global stage for later discussions. While most of the chapters in this volume address the situations of migrant workers in contemporary Japan, their location in history cannot be perceived without reference to those migrants and forced laborers from China and Korea who preceded them, beginning in the late nineteenth century, and whose descendants now make up ethnic populations of significant stature. In Chapter 2, Keizo Yamawaki explicates their history for us, reminding us of the parallels between earlier and present migrants' treatment.

In Chapter 3, Michael Weiner situates migration to Japan squarely in the Castles and Miller pattern of contemporary world migration characterized by globalization, acceleration, differentiation and feminization (Castles and Miller 1993). In Weiner's estimation, the absence of consensus among policy makers or the public on matters of in-migration, weak administrations and the worsening recession have meant the lack of any change at the national level toward the incorporation of foreign workers. At the same time, however, economic conditions in the region, as well as continuing need in domestic small-scale manufacturing, point to the likelihood of continuing migration to Japan. Weiner suggests the creation of a regional cooperative framework to create guidelines to improve conditions for migrant workers, but he does not see any concrete movement toward this at present.

In Chapter 4, John Lie unravels the Japanese sense of unique identity that, in fusing nation, class and ethnicity into a single concept of Japaneseness continues to be drawn upon to justify a closed-door policy on immigration. He argues that the presence of foreign workers, who are assumed to be of Third World and therefore lower class origin, accentuates within Japanese society an us and them, middle-class versus lower-class, homogeneous versus multi-ethnic, and cultured versus uncouth worldview. The upper class in this scenario is cast as white Europeans and North Americans, since the Japanese upper-class itself is supposedly not visible in post Second World War egalitarian society.

In Chapter 5, Mike Douglass follows with a historical perspective on female migration from and to Japan, presenting the view that Japan's own particular patterns of female migration differ substantially from other countries of the world. This raises a number of further questions about gender relations imbedded in culture and its practices Japan. Japan's almost singular specialization in the entry of female workers into the sex industry represents a reversal of patterns initiated almost a century ago when young Japanese women were being sent to brothels in East and South-East Asia. This was repeated during the Second World War by sending "comfort women" to serve as sex slaves for Japanese soldiers. The high recruitment for the sex industry and the extremely limited entry of women for other types of work reflect both the nature of patriarchy and strong sense of unique racial and middle-class identity among Japanese people.

Part II focuses on contemporary issues related to foreign workers and households attempting to earn a living and establish themselves in Japanese communities. In Chapter 6, Keiko Yamanaka draws upon her interviews of *Nikkeijin* from Brazil to give a poignant picture of hopes realized and dreams unfulfilled by people of Japanese descent coming to Japan to not only seek economic gain but to experience first-hand how they would be welcomed to a motherland. In Chapter 7, David Pollack investigates the subtext of Kon Satoshi's *manga* (comic book), *World Apartment Horror*, which reveals, in a way that perhaps only this form of comic exposition can, how race is used to turn to justify the superiority of even junior members of the *yakuza* over university-educated women and men from other Asian countries.

In Chapter 8, Takashi Machimura investigates the variations in settlement patterns among various foreign groups in Tokyo, disclosing that each also has different levels of social network support and neighborhood formation. From this perspective, there are many types of foreign workers rather than a single generalized foreign worker in Japan. He also points to variations in responses of local governments toward foreign residents, ranging from ignorance and exclusion to attempts for more political and social incorporation.

In Chapter 9, Stephen Murphy-Shigematsu reveals through his exploration of lives of persons of multi-ethnic identity, the complexity of ethnic identification in Japan today. While formally the naturalization process does not require dissociation from one's ethnic background, in practice people are often leaned on by officials to relinquish signs of their ethnicity, such as their names. As Murphy-Shigematsu points out, one can gauge how far a society has come in accepting multiculturality by viewing to what extent it acknowledges the existence and open identity of multi-ethnic people in its midst. While the terminology used to denote multi-ethnic people has evolved over time toward less derogatory nomenclature, Murphy-Shigematsu's research indicates that Japan has some distance to go before it will fully accept Japanese nationals who are multi-ethnic, and thereby disengage blood from nationality and ethnicity.

Part III considers national and local government practices, legal frameworks, and the appearance of non-governmental organizations joining in solidarity with foreign workers. In speaking of the tremendous difficulties migrants face in making their way in Japan, they also point out positive changes underway that, if magnified throughout society, have the potential of creating an entirely different scenario that acknowledges cultural pluralism and seeks to endow foreign workers with basic rights of citizenship, if not citizenship itself.

Immigrants are often caught in bureaucratic wrangling that has produced its own set of no-win "Catch-22" contradictions, as explained in Chapter 10 by Katsuko Terasawa, a practicing attorney in Japan. The three major legs of the legal apparatus confronting foreign workers – labor law, civil law and immigration law – form a maze of often contradictory processes for even such simple matters as visa extensions for foreign women in the process of divorce from their Japanese husbands. Foreign workers, who even if illegally in the country are legally entitled to file unfair labor practice complaints to the Ministry of Labor, risk being reported to the Immigration Bureau and deported before their cases can be heard. She shows quite clearly that, without the help and advocacy of legal talent in Japan, seeking justice for foreign workers through Japan's legal system is often impossible. A number of concrete proposals are made for improving key aspects of the legal system to bring greater consistency and justice to foreign workers and residents.

In the face of tightened national immigration controls and restrictions on access to social services by foreign workers, many people have placed hope on local governments to provide more favorable treatment of foreign workers. This question is taken up by Katherine Tegtmeyer Pak in Chapter 11, who examines four cities' responses to the growing presence of foreign workers. In discovering that localities do have a significant degree of autonomy from the central government, she explores the possibility of "local internationalization" as a process for incorporating foreign workers into the fabric of Japanese society.

Glenda Roberts concludes the book in Chapter 12 by by delineating the goals, activities and impact of some of the non-government foreign worker support organizations in the Tokyo metropolitan area. As yet, these and other like-minded groups form a small minority. They have none the less directly assisted many immigrants in availing themselves of legal recourse and other forms of assistance, and as they begin to form bridges among themselves by holding joint meetings and seminars, there is hope that the growing numbers of global migrants will find their situations improving in the future.

Notes

Grateful appreciation is extended to Stephen Murphy-Shigematsu, Jim Nickum, Kathy Tegtmeyer Pak, Keiko Yamanaka and Keizo Yamawaki for their comments on drafts of this chapter.

1 For detailed historical research on the history of old-comer Koreans in Japan, see Weiner (1989, 1994, and 1997).
2 Between 1952 and 1987, 140,977 Koreans and 35,827 Chinese naturalized; between 1988 and 1992, an additional 27,479 Koreans and 7,017 Chinese naturalized (Hanami 1998: 214).
3. Herbert (1996: 30) reports that new entries of persons in entertainment went from 23,844 in 1982 to 44,989 in 1986 and 71,026 in 1988. The figure for 1996 was 53,952, a 9.8 percent drop from 1995 (JIA 1997b: 5). Men are included in these numbers, though they are estimated to make up a very small proportion of the total.
4 While such jobs are referred to in the media and popularly as "the three Ks," support groups for foreign workers feel the term disparages this sort of work as well as the workers, so the groups shun the use of the term.
5 *Nikkei,* or *Nikkeijin,* is the Japanese term for the descendants of Japanese who emigrated between 1968 and 1973. In the context of foreign workers in Japan, *Nikkeijin* workers are the deescendants, up to the third generation, of those who emigrated to South America, in particular Brazil and Peru. *Nikkeijin* of up to the third generation of descent are, under the 1989 Law of Immigration Control and Recognition of Refugees, allowed to reside in Japan for up to three years without restriction on their social and economic activities (Yamanaka 1996). By 1994, females comprised more than 40 percent of the annual arrival from Brazil. *Nikkei* women are employed mainly in factory work, hotels and hospitals, where their wages are similar to those of part-time Japanese women.
6 This, of course, is true of migrants in general, not only of those who come to Japan. Migrant workers often experience the emotional trauma of alienation from their families as they spend increasingly long periods abroad. Those left behind sometimes become so used to the remittances that they do not want the worker to return. In January 1998, a migrant worker from China who had been employed in Hiroshima, distraught at his wife's desire for him to remain in Japan, lashed out randomly at two passers-by, killing a boy and injuring a woman. He then committed suicide (*Japan Times* 31 Jan. 1998: 2).

7 The ideology of Japanese homogeneous 'natural community' has been put forth from at least the eighteenth century. According to McCormack (1996: 2), "Unlike other societies which are mixed (*o-majiri*), especially the United States . . . Japan is thought to be pure and homogeneous, and therefore to have had an easier time becoming an 'intelligent society.'" Post-Second World War political reforms directed attention to questions of individual rights and democracy, but did not question the "ethnic implications of the aboriginal inhabitants of Japan (Ainu) or other groups such as the large Korean minority; deep-rooted assumptions about 'Japaneseness' therefore survived intact."

8 Following the opening of Japan with Perry's visit, from 1859 to 1899 all foreigners were required to live in restricted settlement areas. Although Westerners were freed from this requirement in 1899, the policy stayed in effect for Chinese workers up to 1939 (Yamawaki ch. 2). In the 1880s, treaties were revised to allow both Chinese and Koreans to reside in treaty ports, but only Koreans were allowed to live outside the treaty ports. Newspapers in Japan registered a great fear of uncontrolled migration of Chinese to Japan, including the fear that they would introduce bad customs and habits, ruin public morals and marry Japanese women, thereby eroding the spirit of loyalty and discipline in Japanese society. In 1918 regulations were adopted to prohibit "destitute" (i.e. poor Chinese) people from entering Japan.

9 There is now a growing body of literature on the "comfort women," as well as social support groups that seek justice for them from the Japanese government. See Osanai (1995).

10 There are twenty-seven different types of status for foreigners entering Japan (SOPEMI 1993). The current policy was largely formulated in 1992 as part of the Seventh Basic Plan for employment measures and is designed to facilitate immigration of specialists and technicians whose presence is consistent with the internationalization of the economy and Japanese society.

11 For Japan as a whole, the share of part-time workers increased from about 7 percent to 12 percent between 1970 and 1987; for women the share went from 12 percent to 23 percent. Most part-time work is in services, but it has also increased in manufacturing (Sassen 1994).

12 In Japan, the qualifying period before immigrants can apply for naturalization is five years, but this has been reduced to three for immigrants of Japanese descent (Stalker 1994).

13 Among the more creative attempts was that of a Pakistani man who disguised himself as a member of the United Nations peacekeeping mission in the former Yugoslavia, complete with a UN emblem on his bag and a forged identification card. Visa overstayers account for about 90 percent of those deported from Japan, which totaled almost 50,000 in 1997. Smuggling migrants in by ship is thought to be increasing by as much as one-third per year as Chinese gangs link up with Japanese gangs to organize the smuggling, which is thought to occur along all the Japanese coastline (*Hawaii Hochi* 10 June 1997).

14 Cornelius *et al.* (1994) cite government data on illegal male migrants in 1993 which found half were in the construction industry. The next highest share was in manufacturing, mainly metal and plastics processing, printing and binding and small-scale electrical machinery makers.

15 Morita and Sassen (1994: 157) conclude that "As the current generation of Japanese service employees in low skill service jobs retires and young highly-educated Japanese reject these jobs, there may well be a gradual acceptance of immigrant workers."

16 *Hawaii Hochi* 27 June 1997. In 1996, the police arrested 11,949 foreigners for involvement in 27,414 crime cases, more than 40 percent of whom were Chinese. Police officials state that the trend is toward an increase in organized crime, but two-thirds of cases (7,901) were violations of immigration controls. None the less, the National Police Agency has ordered local police offices nationwide to step up

measures against crimes involving foreigners.
17 There is no officially legal racial or ethnic requirement for becoming a naturalized Japanese (see Note 12 above).

References

Asahi Shimbun (1998) "Gaikokajin Kara 'tonari bito' he" (from foreigness to 'neighbours') (7 Jan.): 7.

Berger, J. and Mohr, J. (1975) *The Seventh Man,* London: Penguin.

Berger, T. (1998) "The Perils and Promise of Pluralism: Lessons from the German Case for Japan," in M. Weiner and H. Tadashi (eds) *Temporary Workers or Future Citizens? Japanese and US Migration Policies,* London: Macmillan.

Brimelow, P. (1993) "Closed Door," *Forbes* 152, 2 (30 August): 58–9.

Castles, S. and Kosack, G. (1974) *Immigrant Workers and Class Structure in Western Europe,* London: Oxford University Press.

Castles, S. and Miller, M. J. (1993) *The Age of Migration,* New York: Guilford Press.

Cohen, R. (1998) "Germany, Long a Land of One 'Volk,' Is Becoming Many-Hued," *International Herald Tribune* 17–18 Oct.: 2

Cornelius, W. A., Martin, P. L. and Hollifield, J. F. (1994) "Japan: the Illusion of Immigration Control," in W. Cornelius, P. Martin and J. Hollifield (eds) *Controlling Immigration: a Global Perspective,* Stanford, Calif.: Stanford University Press: 395–414.

Denoon, D., Hudson, M., McCormack, G. and Morris-Suzuki, T. (eds) (1996) *Multicultural Japan; Palaeolithic to Postmodern,* Cambridge: Cambridge University Press.

Douglass, M. (1993) "The New Tokyo Story: Restructuring Space and the Struggle for Place in a World City," in K. Fujita and R. C. Hill (eds) *Japanese Cities in the Global Economy: Global Restructuring and Urban-Industrial Change,* Philadelphia: Temple University Press.

Friedland, J. (1994) "Traffic Problem; Illegal Chinese Immigrants to Japan," *Far Eastern Economic Review* 157, 31 (4 August): 20.

Friman, H. R. (1996) "Gaijinhanzai: Immigrants and Drugs in Contemporary Japan," *Asian Survey* 36, 10: 964–78.

Hanami, T. (1998) "Japanese Policies on the Rights and Benefits Granted to Foreign Workers, Residents, Refugees and Illegals," in M. Weiner and T. Hanami (eds) *Temporary Workers or Future Citizens? Japanese and US Migration Policies,* London: Macmillan.

Hawaii Hochi (1997a) "Illegal Immigrants Growing Innovative," 10 June: 1.

—— (1997b)"NPA Chief Says Faith in Safety Shaken," 27 June: 1.

—— (1997c) "Do Traditional Bon and Samba Mix? Gunma Town Struggles to Embrace Japanese-Brazilian Returnees," 21 Aug.: 1.

Herbert, W. (1996) *Foreign Workers and Law Enforcement in Japan,* London and New York: Kegan Paul Internatiunal.

Hicks, G. (1997) *Japan's Hidden Apartheid: The Korean Minority and the Japanese,* London/Brookfield Vt.: Ashtate.

Hirowatari, S. (1993) "Foreigners and the 'Foreigner Question' Under Japanese Law," *Annals of the Institute of Social Science* 35: 91–122, Tokyo: Institute of Social Science, University of Tokyo.

—— (1998) "Foreign Workers and Immigration Policy," in J. Banno (ed.) *The Political Economy of Japanese Society,* Oxford: Oxford University Press.

Ito, R. (1992) *"'Japayuki-san' Gensho Saiko"* (Rethinking The *'Japayuki-san'* Phenomenon), in t. Iyotani and T. Kajita (eds), *Gaikokujin Rōdōsha-ron* (Foreign Workers), 293–332, Tokyo: Kobundo.

Itoh, M. (1996) "Japan's Abiding *Sakoku* (Seclusion from Other Countries) Mentality," *ORBIS* 40, 2: 235–46.

JIA (Japan Immigration Association) (1997a) *Heisei 9 Nen Ban Zairyû Gaikokujin* Tôkei (Statistics on Foreign Residents, 1997 edition), Tokyo: Nyukan Kyokai.

—— (1997b) *1996 Statistics on Immigration Control,* Tokyo: Nyukan Kyokai.

Japan Times (1997) "Tokyo Begins Accepting Applications," (16 August): 4.

—— (1998a) "School Grieves Death," (31 Jan.): 2.

—— (1998b) "Illegal Aliens who Helped Build Games Sites Seen Facing Sweep," (4 Feb.): 3.

Jinko Mondai Shingikai (eds) (1997) *Shōshika ni Kansuru Kihonteki Kangaekata ni tsuite* (Basic Viewpoint on the Problem of the Trend towards Fewer Children), Tokyo: Kōseishō.

Kashiwazaki, C. (1998) *Nationality and Citizenship in Japan: Stability and Change in Comparative Perspective,* Ann Arbor: UMI Dissertation Services.

Kobayashi, K. (1996) "Illegal Labor Policy in Japan Means 'Disposable Workers'," *Migration World* 24, 5: 25–6.

Komai, H. (1995) *Migrant Workers in Japan,* New York: Kegan Paul International.

Kono, S. (1994) "International Migration in Japan: A Demographic Sketch," in W. Gooneratne, P. Martin and H. Sazanami (eds) *Regional Development Impacts of Labour Migration in Asia,* Nagoya: UNCRD Research Report Series, No 2.

Kritz, M., Lim, L. and Zlotnik, H. (eds) (1992) *International Migration Systems: A Global Aproach,* Oxford: Clarendon Press.

Low, L. (1995) "Population Movement in the Asia Pacific Region: Singapore Perspective," *International Migration Review* 29, 3: 745–64.

Lycklama a Nijejholt, G. (1992) "The Changing International Division of Labour and Domestic Workers: A Macro Overview (Regional)," in N. Heyzeer, G. Lycklama a Nijeholt and N. Weekrakoon (eds) *The Trade in Domestic Workers: Causes, Mechanisms and Consequences of International Migration,* London: Zed.

Mainichi Daily News (1997) "'Operation White Snow' falls on Olympics," (1 Nov.): 12.

McCormack, G. (1996) "Introduction," in D. Denoon, M. Hudson, G. McCormack and T. Morris-Suzuki (eds) *Multicultural Japan; Palaeolithic to Postmodern,* Cambridge: Cambridge University Press.

Ministry of Justice (1997) *Annual Report of Statistics on Legal Migrants,* Tokyo: Ministry of Justice.

Moon, O. (1995) "Migratory Process of Korean Women to Japan" in International Peace Research Institute, *International Female Migration and Japan: Networking, Settlement and Human Rights*, Tokyo: Meiji Gakuin University.

Morita, K. and Iyotani, T. (1994) "Japan and the Problem of Foreign Workers", in W. Gooneratine, P. Martin and H. Sazanami (eds) *Regional Development Impacts of Labour Migration in Asia,* Nagoya: UNCRD Research Report Series no. 2.

Morita, K. and Sassen, S. (1994) "The New Illegal Immigration in Japan, 1980–1992," *International Migration Review* 28, 1 (Spring): 153–63.

Muller, T. (1993) *Immigrants and the American City,* New York: New York University Press.

Nikkei Weekly (1997) "Latest Population Forecast Should be 'Call to Action,'" (27 Jan.): 6.

Osanai, T. (1995) "Imperial Authorization of Abduction, Detention, and Military Gang Rape," in Asia-Japan Women's Resource Center, *Women's Asia* 1 (August): 26–31.

Roberts, G. S. (1994) *Staying on the Line: Blue-Collar Women in Contemporary Japan,* Honolulu: University of Hawaii Press.

Sassen, S. (1994) "Economic Internationalization: The New Migration in Japan and the United States," *Social Justice* 21, 2 (Summer): 62–81.

Schiller, N., Basch, L. and Blanc-Szanton, C. (1992) *Towards a Transnational Perspective on Migration: Race, Class, Ethnicity, and Nationalism Reconsidered,* New York: Annals of the New York Academy of Sciences.

Sekai (1994) *Shotoku Bumpai Byodo no 'Shinwa' wa Kuzureta* (The 'Myth' of Income Distribution Equality has Collapsed), 72 (March).

Sender, H., Farilough, G., Jayasankaran, S., and McBeth, J. (1995) "The Great Escape," *Far Eastern Economic Review* 158, 13 (March 30): 54–6.

Shimada, H. (1994) *Japan's 'Guest Workers': Issues and Public Policies,* Tokyo: University of Tokyo Press.

Sider, G. (1992) "The Contradictions of Transnational Migration: A Discussion," in N. Schiller, L. Basch and C. Blanc-Szanton (eds) *Towards a Transnational Perspective on Migration: Race, Class, Ethnicity, and Nationalism Reconsidered,* New York: Annals of the New York Academy of Sciences.

Singhanstra-Renard, A. (1992) "The Mobilization of Labor Migrants in Thailand: Personal Links and Facilitating Networks", in Kritz, M., Lim, L. and Zlotnik, H. (eds) *International Migration Systems: A Global Aproach*, 190–204, Oxford: Clarendon Press.

SOPEMI (1993) *Trends in International Migration: Annual Report 1993,* Paris: OECD.

Spencer, S. (1992) "Illegal Migrant Laborers in Japan," *International Migration Review* 36, 3: 754–85.

Stalker, P. (1994) *The Work of Strangers: A Survey of International Labor Migration,* Geneva: ILO.

Tiglao-Torres, A. (1993) "Features of the Migration of Men and Women in the Philippines," Proceedings from the International Colloquium "Migration, Development and Gender in the ASEAN Region," Kuala Lumpur: University of Malaysia: 67–114.

Tsuda, M. (1997) "Human Rights Problems of Foreigners in Japan's Criminal Justice System," *Migration World* 24, 1–2: 22–7.

Tsurushima, S. (1993) "The Stratification of Foreign Workers in Japan," unpublished manuscript, Honolulu: International Seminar on Foreign Workers in Japan: Gender, Civil Rights, and Community Response, East-West Center, Honolulu, Hawaii (1–3 Dec.).

Vasishth, A. (1997) "A Model Minority: the Chinese Community in Japan," in M. Weiner (ed) *Japan's Minorities,* New York and London: Routledge.

Weiner, M.(1989) *The Origin of the Korean Community in Japan 1910–1923*, Manchester: Manchester University Press.

—— (1994) *Race and Migration in Imperial Japan,* London: Routledge.

—— (1997) "The Representation of Absence and the Absence of Representation: Korean Victims of the Atomic Bomb," in M. Weiner (ed) *Japan's Minorities: The Illusion of Homogeneity,* London: Routledge.

Yamanaka, K. (1994) "Theory versus Reality in Japanese Immigration Policy," in W. Cornelius, P. Martin and J. Hollifield (eds) *Controlling Immigration; a Global Perspective*, Stanford, Calif.: Stanford University Press: 411–14.

Yoshida Reiji (1998) "Kanagawa Gives Voice to Foreigners," *Japan Times* 14 August: 3.

Zlotnik, H. (1995) "The South-to-North Migration of Women," *International Migration Review* 29, 1: 229–55.

2 Foreign workers in Japan

A historical perspective

Keizo Yamawaki

Introduction

The growth of the foreign worker population has become a major issue in Japan since the late 1980s. When the nationwide debate on the question was at its height in 1988 and 1989, it was assumed by many commentators, both for and against the influx of foreign workers to Japan, that it was a new and unprecedented phenomenon. Since then, especially since June 1990, when the revised Immigration Control Act came into effect, popular interest in the issue has declined, and the notion that the influx of foreign workers is new to Japan has not been questioned. Any serious student of Japanese history, however, knows that prewar Japan faced a grave problem regarding Korean and Chinese immigrant workers.

In the debate, some mentioned the Korean and Chinese forced labor during the Second World War as the precedent, but failed to notice the presence of migrant workers in the 1920s and 1930s.[1] In fact, the number of Koreans in Japan amounted to over 30,000 in 1920, increased to 300,000 in 1930, and reached 800,000 in 1938, one year before the forced labor began (Morita 1968: 66). Table 2.1 shows the exact number of Koreans in the 1920s.

Table 2.1 Number of Koreans in Japan

Year	Arriving	Returning	Residents
1920	27,492	27,497	30,189
1921	38,118	25,536	38,651
1922	70,462	46,326	59,772
1923	97,397	89,745	80,415
1924	122,215	75,430	118,152
1925	131,273	112,471	129,870
1926	91,092	83,709	143,798
1927	138,016	93,991	165,286
1928	166,286	117,522	238,102
1929	153,570	98,275	275,206
1930	95,491	107,771	298,091

Source: Morita, Y. "*Senzen ni okeru Zainichi Chōsenjin no Jinkō Tōkei* (Statistics on the Korean Population in the Prewar Period)," *Chōsen Gakuhō* 48: 66, 69.

Regrettably, current debate on foreign workers in Japan refers to Japan's past experience only rarely and inaccurately. When discussing the issue of foreign workers in Japan, the nation's earlier experience must be taken into account. By focusing on the late 1890s and the early 1920s, when the question of foreign workers became a serious social concern in Japan, this chapter offers a historical perspective to the current debate about the issue.

I shall briefly summarize the evolution of Japan's immigration policy on foreign workers prior to the Second World War, which can be divided into three periods. The first period was from 1859 to 1899, when there were foreign settlements in Japan to which foreigners were restricted. The second period was from 1899 to 1939. In 1899, foreign settlements were abolished and Westerners were free to live and work anywhere in the country. At the same time, an imperial decree on foreign workers was issued, which forced Chinese workers to live and work only in the former foreign settlements. The third period ran from 1939 to 1945. In 1939, the Japanese government allowed Japanese companies to initiate large-scale recruitment of Koreans in Korea and Japan. Thus began the wartime mobilization of Korean workers. Chinese workers from northern China were also mobilized from 1941 onwards.[2]

It should be clarified at the outset that unskilled foreign workers in modern Japan were predominantly Koreans and Chinese. There were three major groups of foreigners in Japan in the period from 1859, when foreign settlements were established, to the end of the Second World War. First, there were Westerners, such as the British and the Americans, who stayed in Japan as traders and *oyatoi* (professionals), employed by the Japanese government, universities or private companies. Second, there were Chinese, who remained the biggest foreign group until the years following the annexation of Korea in 1910. Third, there were Koreans, who surpassed the Chinese to become the biggest group in around 1917.

This research focuses on the Korean and Chinese workers. There may be some objection to the inclusion of Koreans under the colonial rule among foreign workers, but I would like to defend this inclusion for the following three reasons. First, it is true that Koreans were not foreigners in a strict legal sense after Japan's annexation of Korea in 1910. They were, however, treated as *gaichijin* or those belonging to the outer territory, and their legal status was clearly different from *naichijin*, those belonging to the inner territory. For example, Korean migration to and from the inner territory was more or less controlled by the Government-General of Korea, while the migration of *naichijin* was not under such control. Another difference was that Koreans in the Korean Peninsula did not get suffrage rights even after "universal" suffrage was realized in Japan in 1925 with respect to men aged over 25. Second, Korean workers occupied the lowest position in the Japanese labor market – cheap and unskilled – because of their ethnic origin, which was similar to Chinese workers. Third, Korean residents in Japan were deprived of their Japanese nationality after the Second World War, and became the biggest foreign group in the country. In looking at the employment of foreign workers in Japan before and after the Second World War, I therefore believe it is important to regard Koreans in the colonial period as foreign workers.

Foreign workers in the late 1890s

Foreign settlements and the debate on naichi-zakkyo

The Tokugawa government (1603 to 1867), which had maintained its relative isolation from the outside world for more than two hundred years, concluded commercial treaties with the United States, the Netherlands, Russia, Britain and France in 1858, and ports were opened in Kanagawa (Yokohama), Nagasaki and Hakodate in July 1859. Ports were also opened in Hyogo (Kobe) and Niigata, in 1867 and 1868 respectively. Foreign settlements were established in designated areas of these ports where foreign merchants could settle and engage in trade (see Beasley 1987). According to extra-territoriality stipulations in the treaties, foreign residents in the settlements were outside the jurisdiction of the Japanese government and would be subject only to their own country's laws administered through consular courts.

Those who occupied the settlements were Westerners, mainly British and Americans, and the Chinese.[3] Many of the Western merchants came from China as agents of firms already trading in the Chinese ports of Canton, Hong Kong, Shanghai and elsewhere. Therefore, most of the Chinese were brought to Japan by those Western merchants as compradors, cooks, servants, and longshoremen. The Chinese were not officially allowed to reside in the settlements, but their existence in them was overlooked by the Japanese authorities because they were employed by the Westerners.

In March 1868, the newly formed Meiji government confirmed its decision to carry forward its observance of the treaties that the Tokugawa government had concluded with the Western powers. In 1871, the Meiji government concluded a friendship and commercial treaty with China, effective in 1873. It was an "equal" treaty in the sense that both sides obtained extra-territorial rights with respect to each other. The Chinese were therefore officially allowed to reside in the settlements. In 1876, the Japanese government also concluded a friendship treaty with Korea. This treaty was unequal, because Japan had extra-territorial rights in Korea, but the same rights did not apply to Korea with respect to Japan. This meant that Japanese subjects in Korea were outside the jurisdiction of the Korean government, but Koreans in Japan were subject to the jurisdiction of the Japanese government.

Thus, Japan allowed foreign, that is, Western and Chinese, merchants to live and work in the foreign settlements, such as those in Yokohama, Kobe, and Nagasaki, and did not maintain jurisdiction over them. The Koreans, however, were free to live and work in Japan outside the settlements. This contrast in legal status between Chinese and Koreans in late-nineteenth-century Japan has not received appropriate attention either from historians of modern Japan or from researchers of the Chinese and Koreans in Japan. I have carried out other research on this subject (Yamawaki 1994: 35–48), including the analysis of documents on the treatment of Koreans in Japan in the 1880s and 1890s found in the Diplomatic Record Office of the Foreign Ministry of Japan.

In 1882, preparatory meetings between Japan and the Western powers for the revision of the unequal treaties commenced. The expectation was that the treaties would soon be revised, and throughout the 1880s heated debate took place on the issue of *naichi-zakkyo*, or mixed residency by Japanese and foreigners in Japan.

The discussion hinged on whether, in accordance with international practice at the time, foreigners would be allowed to reside anywhere in the country if Japan gained jurisdiction over foreign residents within its border.

Common opinion among the mass media during this period was that Japan could not help but accept Westerners, but that it should reject the Chinese. For example, an editorial entitled "The Joy and Anxiety of Mixed Residency," in *Jiji Shinpō* on 20 February 1884 argued that there was a serious problem with Chinese workers in the United States, and that Japan would have a more serious problem if it opened its borders since it was situated much closer to China than was the United States. In 1889, the magazine *Nihon-jin* published an article titled "On Mixed Residency of the Chinese and the Japanese." It highlighted four disadvantages if the Chinese were to be allowed to stay in Japan. First, Chinese merchants would beat their Japanese counterparts. Second, Chinese workers would outdo Japanese workers. Third, the Chinese would introduce bad customs and habits and ruin public morals. Fourth, some of the Chinese would marry Japanese women, and thereby the Chinese offspring would multiply and the traditional spirit of loyalty and discipline would disappear.

In 1894, the Japanese government finally revised the unequal treaties, and, in exchange for obtaining jurisdiction over these foreigners, agreed to allow them to live and work throughout Japan from 1899. In 1899, however, Imperial Ordinance No. 352 was enforced, and Chinese workers were allowed to live and work only in the former foreign settlements. I focus now on the debate concerning the adoption of this ordinance.

Imperial Ordinance No. 352 and Chinese workers

Imperial Ordinance No. 352 came into effect on 4 August 1899. It said that those foreigners who did not have freedom of residence according to a treaty or custom could reside, move, and engage in trade and other activities outside the former foreign settlements. However, in the case of laborers, permission from the authorities was required in order to reside or work outside these former foreign settlements. This ordinance was a compromise between those who advocated the expulsion of Chinese and those who argued that Chinese, like Westerners, should be given equal treatment. The former was represented by the Ministry of Home Affairs and the latter by the Ministry of Foreign Affairs. A brief summary of the debate follows.[4]

The most heated debate between the two took place just before the adoption of the ordinance in 1899. Aoki Shūzo, then Foreign Minister, sent an appeal on 26 June to Prime Minister Yamagata Aritomo. The Chinese were restricted to foreign settlements by Imperial Ordinance No. 137 of 1894, enacted after the outbreak of the Sino-Japanese War in the same year, and Aoki believed that this restriction had to be abolished. He refuted all the main points raised by those favouring the restriction. On the point that the Japanese in China were restricted, he wrote that this was because Japan had extra-territorial rights in China. On the question of workers, he contended that Japan had a sufficient labor force and that wages were low. Regarding merchants, he asked why the Japanese should fear the Chinese when they were ready to compete against Westerners. With respect to public morals and sanitation, he said that not all Chinese had those problems, and that it was not too late to regulate once the problem occurred. In terms of why the Chinese ought to be treated like other foreigners, he argued that: first, every country granted residency to those foreigners who did not enjoy extra-territorial rights; second, Chinese were not as competitive as Westerners and that Japan should show its open-mindedness to the world; third, if China were to become the largest market for Japanese products then it was wise to show gestures of friendship; and fourth, if Japan expelled the Chinese, it would have a negative impact on the Japanese in the United States.

On 28 June 1899, Saigo Tsugumichi, then Home Minister, presented a bill to supersede Imperial Order No. 137 of 1894. He raised the following five points as to why the Chinese had to be regulated. First, on the point that Japan should follow European countries' lead and allow the Chinese to reside in Japan since China did not have extra-territorial rights, he argued that Europe did not need to restrict the Chinese as Europe was so far from China. He further pointed out that the United States and Australia did restrict the entry of the Chinese, in the same way that Germany and France restricted the entry of workers from Eastern Europe. Second, he contended that European industrialists would employ the Chinese in Japan and undercut their Japanese rivals. Third, the Japanese industrialists would soon employ Chinese workers and Japan would face a labor problem and resemble Europe, where socialist parties "poisoned" society. Fourth, on the question of public morals and sanitation, he maintained that the Chinese were not accustomed to observing laws, so that it would be impossible to regulate their behavior. Lastly, he argued that once Japan allowed mixed residency, it would be diplomatically and domestically difficult to reverse that position, because it would meet the objection of Japanese capitalists. He believed that confrontation would arise between Japanese workers, who would try to expel the Chinese, and Japanese capitalists, who would try to block expulsion. Thus he refuted the position of Foreign Minister Aoki.

After many rounds of discussion at the government level, an immigration act was adopted for the first time in the modern history of Japan. It was proclaimed on 28 July, enforced from 4 August, and called Imperial Ordinance No. 352 of 1899. The ordinance did not explicitly mention the Chinese, but it had the practical effect of regulating Chinese workers.

Imperial Ordinance No. 352 and Korean workers

It is interesting to note that Koreans were hardly mentioned in the debate on *naichi-zakkyo*. In fact, Koreans were exempted from the application of Imperial Ordinance No. 352, and were free to live and work in Japan both before and after 1899.

Most researchers maintain that the history of Koreans in Japan began in 1910, when the annexation of Korea took place, since they view the presence of *Zainichi Chōsenjin,* or Koreans in Japan, is the result of the colonization of Korea by Imperial Japan. I have no argument with this view, but it tends to emphasize the discontinuity between the pre- and post-1910 periods. Thus, almost all researchers argued until recently that Imperial Ordinance No. 352 was intended to confine foreign workers, including Koreans, in the former foreign settlements and that this ordinance ceased to apply to Koreans only in 1910. They also referred to the *Nihon Tōkei Nenkan*

(Japan Statistical Almanac), which indicated the number of Koreans in Japan in 1909 to be 790 (Morita 1968: 64).[5] As they assumed most Koreans in Japan before 1910 were students, they paid scant attention to the possible presence of Korean workers around that time. In fact, I believe that at least several hundred Korean workers were already in Western Japan before the turn of the century.

I have shown that this interpretation of the ordinance is wrong and pointed out the possible inaccuracy of the *Nenkan* (Yamawaki 1994: 35–111). I shall now look at the case of Chōja Coal Mine, which demonstrates the presence of Korean workers in Japan in the late 1890s.

Chōja Coal Mine is located in Saga Prefecture in the Kyushu region. More than 200 Korean miners were brought there in 1897 and 1898. Tojo (1991) published this information in his work, which draws on a series of articles on those workers in a local newspaper, *Moji Shinpō.* The Chōja Coal Mine was managed by a local entrepreneur named Higashishima. After the Sino-Japanese War of 1894–5, the coal industry was booming, and coal mines in Saga faced a severe shortage of labor. In December 1896, Higashishima asked the Governor of Nagasaki to allow him to employ Chinese workers, but instead the Governor recommended the employment of Korean workers. With the assistance of a labor broker from Tsushima, a Japanese island situated very near Korea, Higashishima brought about 230 Korean workers in four groups between August 1897 and February 1898. These Koreans did not seem to know that they were to work in a coal mine, and some tried to escape after working there for two months. On 22 January 1898 there was a fight between the Korean miners and the Japanese, and more than sixty Koreans escaped from the mine.

Foreign workers in the early 1920s

Chinese workers

Research on the increase of Korean workers in Japan in the 1920s has been undertaken by a relatively large number of scholars, mainly Koreans in Japan, but knowledge about this part of history is not shared by the Japanese public at large. I will return to the problem later in this chapter. I focus now on the question of Chinese workers in the 1920s, which has been subject to far less investigation than that of Korean workers in the same period.

Apart from the forced labor of the 1940s, in most accounts of Japanese history, Chinese workers are mentioned only in relation to the debate on mixed residence in the 1880s and 1890s. As explained earlier, it is relatively well documented that they were the subject of national debate as to whether Japan should allow foreign nationals to live in Japan after the abolishment of foreign settlements. It is widely believed that after this period the problem of Chinese workers did not arise until the 1940s, when forced labor was undertaken. Contrary to this view about the Chinese in pre-Second World War Japan, the question of Chinese workers was also a serious social issue in the 1920s.[6]

On 1 February 1918, Ministerial Ordinance No. 1 on the Entry of Foreigners, issued by the Home Ministry, became effective. This was the first legal regulation on the entry of foreigners in the history of modern Japan.[7] The first clause of this ordinance listed types of foreigners that were to be prohibited from entering Japan.

It included those in need of relief, such as the mentally incompetent, the mentally ill, the poor and others. This clause was later used by the Japanese authorities in justifying their rejection of the entry of Chinese workers in the 1920s.

According to Table 2.2, the number of Chinese workers found working without work permits began to increase around 1918, when the Japanese economy was booming because of the First World War. This period is known for the great influx of Korean workers into Japan. Similar increases also occurred within the Chinese worker population. In 1921, the number of Chinese workers employed without a work permit were found to have increased dramatically. In that year, for example, there were more than 1,000 Chinese longshoremen, compared to seven in 1920.

Despite such increases, there seemed to be no significant enforcement of the ministerial ordinance until 1922. On 7 January of that year, forty-seven Chinese who arrived in Kobe on board a boat from Shanghai were refused entry, and on 13 March, 170 Chinese workers in Tokyo were ordered to leave the country. On 12 October, five representatives of more than 300 Japanese longshoremen in Tokyo appealed to the Department of Foreign Affairs of the Metropolitan Police Board to expel Chinese workers from Japan. They said that they felt threatened because over the previous year, Chinese workers had invaded their workplace. They also said that there were more than 500 Chinese workers in the city and that they could not compete as the Chinese worked for a salary which was 30 percent lower.

In 1922, observing the harsh treatment of Chinese workers by the Japanese government, Chinese students in Japan put strong pressure on their Embassy to lodge a protest with the Japanese government. A first letter of protest was sent by the Chinese *chargé d'affaires* to the Japanese Foreign Minister on 4 April. This was soon followed by letters on 17 and 20 April, and 4, 17, 20, and 27 June. The protest was persistent, but the Foreign Ministry kept rejecting the Chinese claim that the "workers" whom the Japanese government was trying to control were, in fact, merchants and technicians. On 10 October, the Chinese consul in Nagasaki also went to Tokyo to appeal to the Foreign Ministry for the relaxation of the regulations on Chinese workers (Yamawaki 1994: 124–7).

Table 2.2 Number of Chinese workers without work permits

Occupation	1918	1919	1920	1921	1922	1923	1924
Carrier	0	0	3	0	31	421	475
Coolie	38	76	106	249	2,271	2,327	467
Cook	65	85	124	285	337	340	344
Barber	81	80	94	106	211	248	174
Construction	0	0	0	0	57	110	60
Clamp craftsman	36	51	55	122	460	217	51
Carpenter	0	0	0	0	0	0	45
Tailor	1	4	2	4	20	18	29
Longshoreman	0	1	7	1,012	162	517	4
Other	22	26	47	134	154	158	81
Total	243	323	438	1,912	3,703	4,356	1,730

Source: Gaiji Keisatsuhō (Report of the Police for Foreign Affairs) 25: 116–19.

On 13 February 1923, there was a fight between Japanese and Chinese workers in Yokohama. About 300 workers were involved, and twenty were injured. The fight was instigated by the Japanese workers who felt threatened by the Chinese working for less money. There were other instances of violence between the Japanese and migrant workers, but by far the most disastrous incident for migrant workers took place in the aftermath of the Great Kantō Earthquake of 1 September 1923. It is well known that approximately 6,000 Koreans were killed by the Japanese military, police and populace in the aftermath of the earthquake. The fact that Chinese were also killed received much less attention until recently. According to a recent survey, almost 700 Chinese were killed by the Japanese, mainly in Tokyo and Yokohama (Niki 1993: 85), where almost half of the Chinese workers in Japan were living in 1923 (Table 2.3). As Table 2.4 shows, more than half of the Chinese workers living outside former foreign settlement areas were "coolies". In Tokyo's Oshima district alone, where the dormitories for Chinese workers were concentrated, more than 400 Chinese were killed.

I believe that this massive killing of Chinese workers clearly demonstrates that the issue of Chinese workers in the 1920s was a serious problem. It should not be ignored by researchers working on the issue of foreign workers in contemporary Japan.

Korean workers

It is generally accepted by historians that Koreans began to emigrate to Japan around 1917 owing to the labor shortage in Japan caused by the economic boom during the First World War. Throughout the 1920s and 1930s, Korean immigration continued to grow.

In spite of the the Government-General of Korea's efforts to restrict Korean migration, the number of Koreans entering Japan began to increase rapidly in the early 1920s. The most significant event of that period was the massacre of approximately 6,000 Koreans by the Japanese in the aftermath of the Great Kantō Earthquake. This has generally been viewed by researchers as stemming from the contradiction of Japan's colonization of Korea and they have concentrated on

Table 2.3 Number of Chinese workers by region (as of August 1923)

| Region | Inside Former F. S. | | Outside Former F. S. | Total |
	With permits	Without permits		
Tokyo	0	743	1,613	2,356
Kanagawa	653	22	490	1,165
Aichi	0	21	404	425
Hyogo	664	229	293	1,186
Osaka	10	704	233	947
Kyoto	0	284	82	366
Nagasaki	111	98	0	209
Others	14	155	526	695
National Total	1,452	2,256	3,641	7,349

Source: "*Shinsaimae Shinajin Rōdōsha Chōsahyō*" (Survey of Chinese Workers before the Earthquake): *Diplomatic Record of the Foreign Ministry of Japan*: 1. 5. 2. 2–6–6: 1146.
Note: F. S. = foreign settlements.

Table 2.4 Number of Chinese workers by occupation (as of August 1923)

Occupation	Inside Former F. S. With permits	Inside Former F. S. Without permits	Outside Former F. S.	Total
Coolie	40	0	1,955	1,995
Peddler*	25	0	474	499
Barber	129	1,249	417	1,795
Cook	267	931	263	1,461
Odd-jobber	386	25	214	625
Tailor	292	1	84	377
Clamp makers	2	6	55	63
Miner	0	0	47	47
Rattan makers	36	0	44	80
Total	1,177	2,212	3,553	6,942

Source: "*Shinsaimae Shina Rōdōsha Beppyō*" (Survey of Chinese Workers before the Earthquake): *Diplomatic Record of the Foreign Ministry of Japan*: 1.5.2.2–6–6: 1147.
Notes: * Indicates a peddler who is likely to become a manual laborer.
F. S. = foreign settlements.

clarifying that the Japanese authorities were responsible for the massacre of Koreans. While I accept that view, I would like to indicate another aspect of these events, namely the antagonism of Japanese workers towards their Korean counterparts.[8]

The first large-scale conflict between Japanese and Korean workers took place on 18 November 1910, in Yamanashi Prefecture. More than 100 workers were involved in a fight in which dynamite was used and four workers were killed (Kim, 1990). This was followed by a series of small-scale conflicts. According to the Volume Eight of *Nihon Rōdō Nenkan* (Labor Almanac of Japan), published in 1927, the causes of antagonism between the Japanese and Koreans were: first, emotional friction, originating from differences in language, customs, and living conditions; second, the contempt and fear by the Japanese, the ruling people, of the Koreans, the ruled people; third, troubles originating from employment relations, involving such issues as wages not being paid. I suspect that after March 1920, when a recession began, there was a shift in the nature of the antagonism. The fear and contempt factor came to the fore, exacerbated by the image of Koreans as competitors in the unskilled labor market and by the Korean revolt in the March First Independence Movement. Most of the members of the vigilante committees who were tried for murdering Koreans were from the lower strata of society.

Yamada (1983) is one of the very few historians of Japanese-Korean relations who relates the massacre of Koreans after the Great Kantō Earthquake to the antagonism between Japanese and Korean workers. Yamada pointed out that the greatest share (40 percent) of the massacre in Tokyo Prefecture occurred on the western side of Arakawa River of South Katsushika District, an area in which many Koreans working as construction laborers and odd-job men were living. The area did not burn, and many Japanese and Koreans poured into it from the burned areas.

He further explained the background of the massacre as follows:

- Two-thirds of workers in the City of Tokyo and the neighboring five districts at the time were from the countryside, and were unskilled laborers in very small factories and household industries, while those from Tokyo became skilled workers in the heavy industries which developed during the First World War.
- The number of workers in South Katsushika District doubled from 1914 to 1921, and the ratio of factories with less than thirty workers was about 70 percent in 1922.
- Many of these unskilled workers lost jobs in the recession which began in 1920.
- The influx of Korean and Chinese workers took place in the midst of this unemployment crisis.

Yamada suspects that the earthquake took place when the discriminated emerged as rivals, rumors of rioting by Koreans spread, and Japanese underclass laborers organized the vigilante committee under the guidance of managers of factories, foremen and landlords to kill the rivals.

Tozawa Ninsaburō, who was a union leader in South Katsushika District at the time, observed the following about the antagonism of Japanese workers towards the Koreans (Tozawa 1963: 32–4):

- Before the earthquake there was a fundamental contradiction between the Japanese, especially lower-class laborers, and the Koreans.
- After the recession, Japanese capitalists were eager to employ Koreans, who worked better for lower wages than the Japanese.
- Japanese workers, who had a strong sense of contempt for Koreans, started to see them as competitors for a limited number of jobs.
- When the rumor of Korean rioting spread, Japanese lower-class workers had a stronger motive for attacking the Koreans than ordinary Japanese.

Thus, I find it very important to see the incident in light of the tensions associated with increased worker immigration, as well as in the context of Japan's colonization of Korea.

Conclusion

In this chapter, I have demonstrated that the question of how Japan deals with foreign workers is a much older one than many think. I have shown that, in the 1880s and 1890s, there was a heated debate as to whether Japan should admit Chinese workers, and that, as early as the late 1890s, Korean workers were brought in to work in a coal mine in Saga Prefecture. I have also shown that the increase of Korean and Chinese workers was a serious social problem in the early 1920s. These immigrant workers supplied cheap unskilled labor and occupied the lowest position in the Japanese economic structure. The sudden increase of Korean and Chinese workers in the early 1920s led to the most tragic incident in the history of foreign workers in Japan, the massacre of these workers in the aftermath of the Great Kantō Earthquake in 1923.

In the debate on foreign workers in the late 1980s, many Japanese scholars and journalists referred to the experience of European countries, such as Germany. Unlike the United States, neither Japan nor Germany had a formal system for accepting foreigners as immigrants, so it may make some sense to compare the cases of the two countries. It seems to me, however, that the prevalence of such comparison also reflects Japan's indifference to its own past.

Where does this indifference come from? I believe it is connected with the fact that, since the Second World War, the Japanese government as well as the Japanese people paid scant attention to its migrant – Korean and Chinese – communities. In 1952, Koreans and Taiwanese were deprived of their Japanese nationality and became foreigners by a unilateral decision of the Japanese government. Japan's record of the treatment of those foreign residents was regrettably poor. The Japanese government did not think foreigners deserved the protection of Japanese law because they did not possess Japanese nationality. Their right to live as legitimate members of Japanese society was disregarded in the name of "rational discrimination" based on nationality.[9] In other words, their existence was ignored by the Japanese government. This is all the more striking, given their special status as foreigners originating from Japan's former colonies, which suggests that they be accorded more favorable treatment than foreigners in general. The relative invisibility of the Korean presence was also owing to strong prejudice and discrimination against Koreans by the Japanese people, compelling Koreans to adopt Japanese names and, assisted by their physical similarity to the Japanese, to blend into the general population.[10]

More attention began to be paid to the Korean community in the 1970s, when they began to actively pursue their rights as members of Japanese society. By this time, second and third generation Koreans saw themselves as members of the local communities in which they lived, not as temporary residents who would ultimately return to their country of origin.[11] Grassroots movements in the 1980s to refuse finger-printing, which was required for foreigners when they registered at the local government, also appealed to the conscience of certain segments of Japanese society.

However the growth of the belief in the idea of *tan'itsu minzoku kokka,* or Japan as a mono-ethnic nation, was strengthened as Japan became increasingly dominant as an economic superpower in the world through the 1970s and 1980s (Aoki 1990). This had a negative impact on Japanese attitudes about granting foreign residents a legitimate place in Japanese society. When the influx of Asian workers attracted national attention in the late 1980s, the Korean and Chinese communities were hardly visible to Japanese society.

As for Koreans in Japan, another factor seems to be involved. Korean migration in the 1920s, 1930s, and the war period in the early 1940s, has not been seen as migration by many researchers, since Korea was a colony of imperial Japan. They think that it was a "forced" rather than a "natural" migration, whether economically or physically, and they tend to reject the comparison between Korean migration then and current Asian and Latin American migration. It is true that the political context, that is, the colonization of Korea under Japanese imperialism in which Korean migration took place, should never be disregarded, but I believe a comparison sheds light on the economic and social aspects of migration to Japan in both periods.

What can we learn from the pre-Second World War history concerning foreign workers in Japan? First, we have to be aware that the Japanese prejudice against Asian immigrants is more than a century old, and cannot be removed overnight. In May 1899, Hara, one of the most prominent political leaders in modern Japan, made the following comment on the adoption of Imperial Ordinance No. 352:

> Our civilization is mainly imported from China . . . While the Japanese paid high respect to China in ancient times, these days, many people think that Japan has moved ahead of China and tend to despise the Chinese people because of the recent import of Western civilization. After the Sino-Japanese War, this tendency became strengthened and regrettably there are some who argue that the Chinese should be expelled from the Japanese territory. While treating the Chinese in the country as the worst kind of human beings, to advocate friendship and solidarity with China is a behavior unacceptable in the world.
>
> (Hara Takashi 1899)

Hara's comment also applies today, when people from the rest of Asia face discrimination such as problems in finding housing, at the same time as many Japanese are advocating closer ties with their home countries.

Second, there seems to be some parallel between the 1920s, when foreign workers, initiated by the economic boom of the late 1910s, increased despite the subsequent recession, and the 1990s, when foreign workers, attracted by the "bubble" economy of the late 1980s, increase in spite of the recession that followed. In the early 1920s, foreign workers increased as the "Japanese-style labor market" was formed through the structural change of the Japanese economy (see Sumita 1976). This suggests that the current increase of foreign workers can be also analyzed by focusing on the internationalization of the labor market, promoted by the globalization of capital (see Kimae 1988).

Third, the Japanese who regard violence against foreigners and "ethnic cleansing" as something which happens in remote regions should remember the massacre of Koreans and Chinese in the wake of the Great Kantō Earthquake. The Japanese should not only remember it as a stain in the history of modern Japan, but also take it as a current issue. As Kato (1994: 48–52) argues, contemporary Japanese are not directly responsible for the criminal acts of the Japanese prior to the Second World War, but that if the social and psychological structures which fostered those acts still exist today, as it appears they do, contemporary Japanese are certainly responsible for overcoming those structures.

Japan does have its own experience of dealing with immigrant workers, from which it can and should learn more. A more precise understanding of Japanese history is needed, and this chapter, which focuses only on pre-Second World War history, is a small contribution to that aim. A re-examination of the Chinese and Korean communities in Japan before and after the Second World War would help greatly in formulating a framework on which an analysis of foreign workers in contemporary Japan should be based.

Notes

This chapter is an expanded version of "Two Myths regarding Foreign Workers in Prewar Japan," in *Prime*, 1 (1994). *Prime* is a biannual periodical of International Peace Research Institute, Meiji Gakuin University. I am very grateful to Professors Ishida Takeshi and Kim Eun-Young for their comments on this article.

1 Spencer (1992: 754) maintains that "[u]p until the 1980s, comparatively few foreigners had actually gone to live and work in Japan" except "[t]he Koreans and Chinese who were brought to Japan as forced laborers before and during World War II." But this account is not accurate, either. To begin with, it is not clear what he means by forced laborers before the Second World War. If he means those Korean and Chinese workers who immigrated to Japan in the 1920s and 1930s, it has to be pointed out that they were not forced to do so in the physical sense. One may well argue that they were forced to immigrate because of economic hardship under colonial rule, but I believe this should be distinguished from the physically forced labor during the Second World War.

2 For readers interested in a general history of Koreans and Chinese in modern Japan, Weiner (1994) deals with Korean migration to Japan in the whole period of colonial rule, that is, from 1910 to 1945, while Vasishht (1997) offers a broad outline of the historical formation of the Chinese community in Japan from the late 19th century to the present.

3 Before the opening of these ports, most of the foreigners in Japan, who were allowed to stay only in Nagasaki, were Dutch and Chinese.

4 For details of this debate, see Yamawaki (1994: 57–66).

5 For example, Weiner argues that:

> [u]ntil 1910 the Korean community in Japan was composed primarily of students, political exiles and consular officials. Although there may have been a small number of Koreans who were illegally in the coal mining industry before this time, the evidence is by no means conclusive.
>
> (Weiner 1989: 52)

Weiner adds that Imperial Ordinance No. 352 and its supplementary ordinance "appear to have been designed with the express purpose of preventing the entry of foreign laborers. By the act of annexation, however, these immigration laws ceased to apply to Koreans."

6 For details of Chinese migration to Japan in the early 1920s, see Yamawaki (1994: 115–95).

7 Imperial Ordinance No 352 of 1899 was a regulation on residence and work, not on the entry of foreigners.

8 For details on the conflicts between Korean and Japanese workers, see Yamawaki (1994: 273–81).

9 For the legal treatment of Koreans in post-Second World War Japan, see Tanaka (1995).

10 Koreans were ignored not only by the ordinary people but also by social scientists who specialized in ethnicity or migration. They tended to focus on the problems in the West as if there had been no such problem in Japan.

11 After the victory in the Hitachi case, in which a second-generation Korean high school graduate fought to confirm his right for employment regardless of his nationality, *Minzoku Sabetsu to Tatakau Renraku Kyogikai,* or Council to Fight against Ethnic Discrimination, was formed in 1974.

References

Aoki, T. (1990) *Nihon bunkaron no Henyō* (The Change of the Views on Japanese Culture), Chūō Kōrōnsha: 109–125.

Beasley, W. G. (1987) *Japanese Imperialism 1894–1945*, Oxford: Oxford University Press.

Hara, T. (1899) *"Shina-jin no Naichi-Zakkyo* (Mixed Residency with Chinese)," *Osaka Mainichi* (1 May).

Jiji Shinpō (1884) (20 February)

Kato, S. (1994) *"Sengo Sedai no Sensō Sekinin* (The Responsibility of the Post-war Generation for the War)", *Kamogawa Shuppan:* 48–52.

Kim, H. (1990) *"Yamanashi-ken Ryōsen-mura no Chō-nichi Rōdōsha Shōtotsu Jiken* (The Incident of the Conflict between Korean and Japanese Workers at the Ryōsen Village in Yamanashi Prefecture): 18 November 1910," Zainichi Chōsenjin Kenkyu 20: 61–75.

Kimae, T. (1988) *"Rodō Shijō no Kokusai-ka* (The Internationalization of the Labor Market)," *Kikan Rodō-hō* 149: 6–16.

Morita, Y. (1968) *"Senzen ni Okeru Zainichi Chōsenjin no Jinkō Tōkei* (Statistics on the Korean Population in the Prewar Period)," *Chōsen Gakuhō* 48: 63–77.

Nihon-ijin (1889) "Shinajin no Naichi-zakkyo wo runzu" (The Mixed Residence of the Chinese and the Japanese), 35: 1–5.

Niki, F. (1993) *Shinsaika no Chugokujin Gyakusatsu* (Massacre of Chinese at the Earthquake), Tokyo: Aoki Shoten.

Spencer, S. (1992) "Illegal Migrant Laborers in Japan," *International Migration Review* 26, 3: 754–86.

Sumita, M. (1976) *Rōdō Keizai Ron* (On Labor Economics), Tokyo: Chikuma Shobō.

Tanaka, H. (1995) *Zainichi Gaikokujin*, Tokyo: Iwanami Shoten.

Tojo, N. (1991) *"Meijiki Nihon ni okeru Saisho no Chōsenjin Rōdōsha* (The First Korean Workers in Meiji Japan)," *Keizaigaku Kenkyu* 57, 3/4: 297–315.

Tozawa, N. (1963) *"Taidan: Kantō Daishinsai ni Okeru Chōsenjin Gyakusatsu no Sekinin"* (Interview: The Responsibility of the Massacre of Koreans at the Kantō Great Earthquake), *Chōsen Kenkyū Geppō,* (October).

Vasishth, A. (1997) "A Model Minority: The Chinese Community in Japan," in M. Weiner (ed.) *Japan's Minorities: The Illusion of Homogeneity,* London: Routledge.

Weiner, M. (1989) *The Origins of the Korean Community in Japan 1910–1923,* Manchester: Manchester University Press.

—— (1994) *Race and Migration in Imperial Japan,* London: Routledge.

Yamada, S. (1983) *"Kantō Daishinsai to Chōsenjin Gyakusatsu* (The Great Kanto Earthquake and the Massacre of Koreans)", *Sanzenri* 36: 39–45.

Yamawaki, K. (1994) *Kindai Nihon to Gaikokujin Rōdōsha* (Modern Japan and Foreign Workers), Tokyo: Akashi Shoten.

3 Japan in the age of migration

Michael Weiner

The purposes of this contribution are threefold: to place current migration to Japan within an historical context; to summarize Japanese policy responses to migrant labor flows during the twentieth century; and to locate contemporary labor migration to Japan within a comparative, regional context in terms of both policy formation and the emergence of regional migration systems. Fieldwork in Japan and elsewhere in Asia was made possible through the generous support of the Economic and Social Council's Asia–Pacific Program.

Cross border migration is not an invention of the twentieth century. Nor are current levels of population movement isolated phenomena. On the contrary, like the ever increasing movement of capital, commodities and culture, improvements in transportation and the proliferation of print and electronic media, migrations are both a consequence of and a catalyst for further global integration. There is little doubt, however, that both the volume and significance of contemporary (since the mid-1980s) population movements surpasses that of earlier migrations. The potential for future and greater population flows, both within and across national borders, is of growing concern to policy makers in labor-importing countries like Japan. In China, for example, economic growth rates, impressive though they have been, are insufficient to absorb the estimated 150 million surplus workers in the rural sector (OECD (SOPEMI) 998: 73). Growing income inequalities, environmental degradation, demographic pressure, political upheavals such as those which accompanied the demise of the Soviet Union, the introduction of new production systems, and the creation of regional and sub-regional trade zones have also ensured that virtually all states will be affected by the transnational movement of labor. Castles and Miller have identified four general factors which are likely to influence population movements during the next twenty years (Castles and Miller 1993: 8):

- Globalization: increasing diversity of countries of origin and destination.
- Acceleration: quantitative growth of migration in all major regions and an increasing impact on state policies.
- Differentiation: the tendency of states to simultaneously experience multiple types of migration (e.g. labor, refugee, family reunification).
- Feminization: the increasing role of women as autonomous actors in all types of migration.

These factors certainly correspond to the situation in Asia–Pacific, where more than 50 percent of the world's population and approximately two-thirds of the global labor force are located. During the 1970s and early 1980s, Asia–Pacific international migration involved the movement of people from Asia to Australia, the Middle East and North America. Since that time, however, intra-regional migration, including both massive flows of Low Level Manpower (LLM) from low income countries with excess labor to Asian NICs and Japan, and the movement of highly skilled transient labor, has increased dramatically.

Cross-border population flows have also ensued from internal migrations generated by rapid economic, social and political transformations. Recent Hong Kong investment in the Shenzhen Special Economic Zone in southern China, for example, led to the creation of two million jobs in the local manufacturing sector and stimulated a massive rural-urban transfer of mainly female labor (Skeldon 1992: 44). Similarly since 1968, the *transmigrasi* program in Indonesia has involved the movement of an estimated 6.5 million people from Java to less-densely populated islands such as Irian Jaya (Castles and Miller 1993: 154). Some commentators have suggested that it is possible to differentiate contemporary, international migration streams in Asia–Pacific by type: labor to high income Western countries; intra-Asian labor; highly-skilled transient labor; refugee; and student; between labor importing countries (e.g. Japan, Singapore, and Taiwan) and labor exporting countries (e.g. China, the Philippines, India, Bangladesh, Indonesia, and Sri Lanka); and countries like Korea, Hong Kong, Malaysia and Thailand that export some types of labor but import others (Wickramasekara 1996: 98). These formulations, though useful, do not take full account of the enormous flows of undocumented workers, diverse migration channels, overlaps which often occur in practice between the categories, the role of governments, and the significance of social and cultural practices which affect both the decision to migrate and the employment niches occupied by migrant workers in destination countries.

Besides, while both contemporary population flows to Japan and the response of political and economic elites to the entry of foreign workers must be located within the appropriate historical context, they need also to be considered against the background of earlier migrations *within* and *to* Japan. This has added significance in view of current orthodoxies which construct Japanese national identity as racially and culturally exclusionist, and which deny the experience of accommodating foreign migrant workers in the past. But, as elaborated below, the post-1868 creation of a modern industrial state in Japan has been accompanied by the movement of people from one spatial location to another. This has involved the mobilization of both indigenous sources of labor and, during the pre-1945 period, the exploitation of labor drawn from the Chinese and Korean colonial periphery. The provinces of southern Korea, in particular, provided a virtually inexhaustible reservoir of inexpensive and mobile labor, and, by early 1945, there were approximately two and a half million Koreans resident in Japan.

In drawing parallels between current population flows and the pre-1945 movement of colonial labor to Japan, it is equally important to remember that both are aspects of a vast migration of labor from peripheral regions to the advanced industrial countries or their colonial possessions (Castles 1986: 761). This often involved the deployment of both free and 'unfree' labor (Cohen 1987). During the second half of the nineteenth century, indentured labor was deployed in more than forty countries by all the major colonial powers (Potts 1990: 63–103). Appleyard estimates that British administrations recruited in excess of thirty million workers from the Indian sub-continent for deployment elsewhere in the British Empire (Appleyard 1991: 11). Indian labor was transported as far afield as the Caribbean, East Africa and Fiji. The Dutch also recruited Chinese coolie labor for construction work in Java, while the colonial administration in Malaya imported Indian, Chinese and Indonesian labor for work in the tin mines and rubber plantations.

For Chinese and Korean workers from the colonial periphery who entered Japan before and during the Pacific War, economic function and social status were determined by a subordinate identity as colonial subjects. Although the annexations of Taiwan in 1895 and Korea in 1910 conferred a certain degree of occupational and residential mobility within Japan proper (*naichi*), the possibility of political, economic and social equality was only vaguely mentioned. On the contrary, subject Chinese and Koreans were promised assimilation, a process designed to replace their cultural heritage with an identity reflecting their status within an Asian race hierarchy. This found expression in social policies of both metropolitan and colonial administrations.

Economic deprivation and political marginalization played a part in the decision to migrate, but structural reliance on the sort of flexible labor offered by migrant workers was a far more important factor in regulating population flows. Between 1915 and 1945, the demand for cheap industrial labor remained more or less constant, and migration from the colonial periphery was self-perpetuating response to labor market conditions in Japan. Active recruitment of colonial labor was initially stimulated by the industrial boom which accompanied Japan's entry into the First World War (Chōsen Sōtokufu 1924: 412, Iwamura 1972: 11). However, Japan had many Chinese and Korean workers before this. Indeed, Chinese trading communities had existed in western Japan for several centuries, while several hundred Koreans were recruited for employment in the Kyūshū coalfields immediately before the turn of the century (Tojo 1994: 142–75). None the less, there can be little doubt that the massive migrations from Korea in particular which took place during the colonial period formed the basis of present day (1998) *zainichi* (long-term resident) communities.

In addition to the push-pull factors outlined above, the political dimension served as a further and critical precondition for migration. Until the imposition of labor mobilization programs during the Pacific War, government policies toward the entry of colonial labor were driven by contradictory and competing impulses. On the one hand, the colonial worker was initially perceived as a flexible and inexpensive source of labor whose entry and length of residence in Japan could be controlled by labor market forces. During periods of economic expansion it was expected that the presence of temporary colonial labor would benefit both employer and indigenous worker by resolving labor shortages, increasing production and creating further employment opportunities for Japanese labor. Conversely, as an employment safety valve, migrant labor was particularly vulnerable to lay-offs during recessionary periods. In 1917, for example, several thousand Chinese from Zhejiang province were recruited to alleviate temporary labor shortages in the transportation industry but, by 1922, many had returned to China. Those that remained swelled the growing pool of semi-employed day laborers in the Tokyo-Yokohama region (Vasishth 1996: 128).

On the other hand, the unrestricted entry of Koreans and Chinese, whose racial and cultural characteristics set them apart from indigenous Japanese, was regarded as a potential threat to the integrity of the Japanese polity. Such concerns notwithstanding, population flows from southern Korea, in particular, to the major centers of capital and industrial accumulation in the Kantō and Kansai regions and to the coalfields of north Kyūshū and Hokkaidō, remained relatively free from direct interference from Tokyo until late 1923. In contrast, the Government-General of Korea imposed controls on the activities of Japanese recruiters and labor brokers in 1918. A year later, at the height of the March First Independence Movement in Korea, the colonial authorities introduced the *Ryokō Shōmeisho* (Travel Certificate) system. Until the abolition of the *Shōmeisho* system in 1922, any Korean intending to travel to Japan had to obtain a travel certificate from the police. Administrative attempts to regulate the entry of *hantōjin* (peninsulars) were *ad hoc* measures driven by security rather than economic conerns. The same is true of the *Shōmeisho* system and the temporary ban on all travel between Korea and Japan introduced after the Great Kanto Earthquake in September 1923. When restrictions on the entry of Korean labor were finally introduced in 1925 (revised 1927 and 1928) they were poorly conceived and had little impact on population movement into Japan (Weiner 1994: 62–3, 120–2). This failure to generate a coherent and enforceable immigration policy contributed to a fourfold increase in the size of the Korean community between 1925 and 1938. (See Table 3.1.)

Although wage rates in Japan were substantially higher than those in Korea or Taiwan, on average migrant workers were paid a third less than indigenous workers. Regarded as suited for tasks involving physical strength alone, colonial workers were concentrated in small sub-contracting firms, heavy construction work, coal mining, and, in the case of female labor, the textile industry. Coupled with a willingness to endure inferior wages, undesirable working conditions, unsociable hours and low status, concentration in unskilled or semi-skilled occupations also ensured that the migrant worker was particularly vulnerable to

Table 3.1 Korean migration to Japan 1918–38; selected years

Year	Resident Population in Japan
1918	18,690
1922	70,187
1926	150,807
1930	419,009
1934	689,651
1938	881,347

Source: compiled from tables appearing in Weiner 1994: 63, 122.

cyclical unemployment. Their role as replacement labor, moreover, militated against trades union affiliation and when migrant workers did participate in industrial action against employers it tended to reinforce more generalized perceptions of the migrant as a political and cultural antagonist (Osaka-shi 1924: 3).

Reflective of their class position as replacement labor, the lives of migrant workers were characterized by little of the continuity associated with modern urban life. Very few were employed as permanent *shokkō* (factory operatives), while those that were tended to be excluded from large- and medium-sized firms. Economic marginalization was paralleled by exclusions from the housing market which reduced most migrants to living in flophouses, tenements, or, in the case of *hiyatoi-ninpu* (day laborers) and mine workers, work camps operated by labor contractors. Under these circumstances, sanitation and basic health care were a perpetual problem in migrant areas and this, in turn, increased their susceptibility to dysentery and other infectious diseases. With few exceptions, contemporary accounts ignored the structural origins of migrant worker poverty and disease, instead ascribing these to racially or otherwise inherent characteristics (Chōsen Sōtokufu 1924: 411).

In contrast to the systematic programs of assimilation undertaken by the colonial authorities in Korea and Taiwan, the assimilation of migrant worker communities did not emerge as a social policy issue in Japan until the mid-1920s. This was largely due to perceptions of migrant workers as temporary sojourners who would return home once the demand for their labor disappeared. Nor were the newcomers expected to develop formal associations or to shelter within mainstream Japanese political or trades union organizations. Integrationist policy initiatives, beginning with the creation of the *Sōaikai* (Mutual Care Association) in 1921 and culminating in the establishment of a national *Kyōwa* (harmonization) network in the mid-1930s, were essentially mechanisms of social and political control. They were designed to suppress political and trade union activism; regulate the entry of 'approved' migrants; and encourage those forms of social and cultural integration which acknowledged the fundamental differences between the newcomers and the Japanese majority (Pak 1979: 103, Ozawa 1977: 46–7). Responsibility for the formulation and implementation of *Kyōwa* policies were initially shared between the Welfare and Home Ministries, though the latter gradually assumed a predominant role.

Although the public objective of the *Kyōwakai* (Harmonization Association) was the integration of Japanese and *gaichijin* (literally, peoples of the outer territories: Korea, Taiwan, and later, Manchukuo) within a greater racial and cultural community, the integrationist project retained core racial assumptions which justified subordination, exclusion and exploitation. This was never more evident than during the latter stages of the Pacific War. The *Kokka Sōdōin Hō* (National Mobilization Law) of 1938 served as the basic enabling legislation which paved the way for wartime controls governing the recruitment, deployment, and management of labor. A legal framework for the collective deployment of colonial labor was agreed by the Cabinet Planning Board in 1939 and, thereafter, until 1945, annual quotas were drawn up for the importation of colonial labor (Weiner 1994: 190–8). As is clear from Table 3.2, the most significant increases were registered during the years 1942–4.

Although it was anticipated that labor quotas would be met through voluntary recruitment, by 1943 the failure of this policy had become apparent. In that year, Koreans resident in Japan became eligible for labor conscription and this was extended to the whole of Korea in 1944. Recruitment practices frequently incorporated an element of coercion or misrepresentation, while contracts, initially for a two-year period (one-year in the case of conscripted Chinese labor) were often unilaterally extended by employers. Most Chinese and Korean conscripts were assigned to work in either general construction or coal mining (Matsumura 1967: 179–81) and between 1939 and 1945 the percentage of Koreans in the national coal mining labor force increased from 6 percent to just over 30 percent (Weiner 1994: 198). In fact, approximately 60 pecent of the Koreans who entered Japan, either voluntarily or involuntarily, between 1938 and 1945 were employed in coal and metal mining. Though paid less than their Japanese counterparts, colonial mineworkers were employed almost exclusively as face workers: the most hazardous and physically arduous area of minework. Under such conditions, work-related injuries and fatalities among colonial workers were disproportionately high. Desertion rates were also correspondingly high, despite the often brutal efforts of employers and police officials to restrict the movement of conscripted labor. Although on a far smaller scale, Manchurian Chinese were also subject to labor conscription from 1942. As in Korea, recruitment quotas were only rarely filled on a voluntary basis and the authorities in Manchukuo regularly turned to conscripted labor (mainly peasants and prisoners of war) from North China. Between 1943 and 1945, approximately 42,000 Chinese were transported to Japan, of whom only 31,000 survived the war (Kato 1973: 246–9).

Migration in the postwar period: Fortress Japan

From the late 1980s, the movement of foreign workers in Japan began to generate widespread national concern. While xenophobic nationalists and liberal social scientists debated the issue of foreign labor, and while conflicting interests within and between relevant ministries prevented the formulation of a coherent and enforceable set of policies, Filipina entertainers, Iranian telephone card sellers, and Bangladeshi factory operatives gradually emerged as recognizable character

Table 3.2 Estimates of the Korean population in Japan, 1939–45

Year	Recruitment/conscription totals	Resident population	Annual increase
1939	53,120	1,030,394	—
1940	59,398	1,241,394	210,925
1941	67,098	1,469,230	227,915
1942	119,851	1,625,054	155,824
1943	128,354	1,768,180	193,126
1944	286,000	1,911,307	143,127
1945	10,622	2,100,000	188,693

Source: Weiner 1994: 198.

types in the cities of Japan. Indeed, the evidence suggests that, despite a lengthy economic crisis and unprecedented postwar levels of unemployment, particular sectors of Japanese industry have become structurally dependent on foreign labor (Iguchi 1998a: 166–81). Moreover, although usually treated as a recent phenomenon, reliance on migrant labor has been a factor of economic growth in Japan throughout the post-1945 period.

It could also be argued that the combination of economic, political and demographic factors that govern contemporary labor flows to Japan are comparable to those which determined colonial migration during the period 1919–45. Post-1945, the penetration of industrial and investment capital in developing regions has transformed peasant farmers into wage laborers within the global economy. As Sassen has observed, rather than restricting labor mobility, the internationalization of the Japanese economy has directly assisted in the creation of a highly mobile industrial proletariat within Asia (Sassen 1993: 86). As in the past, the pattern of migrant employment in contemporary Japan has been two-dimensional, with concentration in particular industrial sectors as one facet of the situation. The concentration of foreign migrant workers in largely unskilled occupations within certain industries needs to be taken into account to fully appreciate their role.

These apparent continuities also obscure a number of important differences between migration pre- and post-1945. The main difference is that, despite the existence of permissive factors which act as a precondition to cross border migration, international labor flows to Japan remained minimal throughout the high growth decades of the 1950s and 1960s. A number of factors account for this. First, during the *Izanagi* boom of the mid- to late-1960s, rapid growth in labor demand was largely satisfied through annual increases in the number of school graduates entering the job market, intersectoral labor transfers (agriculture to industry and service), and internal migration (rural to urban). In the 1960s, rural-urban migration totaled an estimated ten million persons. It was the gradual depletion of these rural sources of industrial labor in the late 1960s that led to consideration of the recruitment of foreign labor, and *Keidanren* (Japan Federation of Employers Associations) voiced support for the import of foreign labor as early as 1970. In the post-oil crisis environment of the 1970s, the recession-led decline in labor demand, coupled with an annual 1 per cent expansion in the Japanese labor force, averted the immediate need for foreign workers. Second, the migration and subsequent settlement of Koreans, and to a lesser extent Chinese, during the pre-1945 period militated against the recruitment of foreign labor. In the postwar milieu, these post-colonial others, who existed on the margins of *ippan* (normal) society, served as a bureaucratic reminder of the unforeseen consequences of labor importation. Third, the availability of alternative migrant destinations, coupled with the pre-1985 Plaza Accord dollar-yen exchange rate and relatively higher transportation costs, reduced the attractiveness of Japan as a destination country for migrant workers. Fourth, 'Japan lacked the networks and linkages with potential immigrant-sending countries that could have facilitated the formation of international migration flows' (Sassen 1993: 86). Finally, the existence of immigration and nationality laws, framed during the Cold War with the assistance of American Occupation officials, which carefully regulated the entry and residence of aliens seemed to provide an effective barrier to the employment of non- or less-skilled foreign labor.

By the mid-1980s, however, annual growth rates of 5 percent, coupled with Japan's emergence as a major source of direct foreign investment and overseas development assistance and its dominant position as a regional exporter of goods and services and culture, had altered perceptions of Japan in labor-exporting countries. Such permissive factors, which include the wide disparities in wage levels between Japan and potential sending countries, naturally provide only a partial explanation for the marked transformation which followed. Of equal significance were the structural demands for foreign labor which emerged during the *Heisei* boom years of the late 1980s. A combination of extremely low fertility rates, a decline in the number of new entrants to the labor market, the exhaustion of indigenous labor reserves, including reliance on part-time (mainly female) labor, and the degradation of employment in the manufacturing and construction industries where small and medium-sized firms predominate, were key mechanisms helping the incorporation of foreign workers (both legal and illegal) into the domestic labor market. In general, labor shortages were most acute in those industries which had historically encountered the greatest difficulty in the recruitment and retention of labor. At the height of the *Heisei* boom in 1989, the job opening rate in the construction industry, for example, had risen to an unprecedented level of 5.81 (Ijiri 1990: 35). Japanese high school graduates were also far less likely than in the past to seek employment in traditional 'dirty' industries, not so much because of low pay but because of low prestige.

Government responses to the entry of foreign labor have been generously described as a 'policy mix', involving no less than seventeen separate ministries and governmental agencies (Koshiro 1998: 157). More often than not policies have been determined by competition rather than cooperation between ministries. Neither the Prime Minister's Office nor the political parties have been central to the process though they, like the ministries directly engaged in policy formulation, have created *ad hoc* committees and study groups to consider immigration-related issues. A positive and unforeseen consequence of this failure in public policy at the national level has been a strengthening of the role of sub-national governments and NGOs, particularly in regions which support large foreign worker populations. This has been particularly evident in areas of *Nikkeijin* settlement where local authorities have adopted integrative policies to support foreign worker communities. A more accurate assessment of the national situation might also point to the failure to generate a coherent policy framework, a determination to exclude rather than incorporate foreign labor despite economic evidence to the contrary, and the failure to broaden the scope of protective legislation to include undocumented workers, particularly in the case of female labor which constitutes an increasing proportion of the total migrant labor force. The retention of policies which prohibit the employment of *hijukuren rōdōsha* (non-skilled) foreign labor, inadequate enforcement, and a legal framework which criminalizes undocumented foreign workers have all contributed to the perpetuation of a system which both discriminates against, and assists in the exploitation of, foreign labor.

Prior to revision of the Immigration Control and Refugee Recognition Law

1990, alien residence status was separated into eighteen categories, s٬ ٬f which permitted employment. The 1990 revision established twenty-eight categories for legal residence and fourteen for legal employment. Although immigration procedures were simplified and new employment categories added, pre-existing prohibitions on the employment of undocumented workers were reinforced (Rōdō Kijun Chōsakai 1997: 82–3). In fact, the basic tenets of Japanese immigration policy remained unchanged. As outlined in the 7th and 8th Basic Employment Measures Plan of 1992 and 1995 respectively, and the Economic Plan for Structural Reform of Economy and Society (1995), these rest upon the following principles:

- To reduce potential social costs, including education for the children of migrant workers, and the emergence of 'social' problems associated with immigrant settlement, foreigners should be admitted to the country on a short-term basis only.
- The admission of foreign labor should only be considered after all domestic alternatives (e.g. increased mobilization of part-time [female and the elderly] sources of labor, increased reliance on offshore production facilities among small- and medium-sized firms) have been explored.
- The admission on a temporary basis of highly skilled transient workers (e.g. academics, researchers, employees of transnational corporations, journalists) and those relatively less-skilled workers designated as company 'trainees'. Under no circumstances will the admission of *hijukuren rōdō* (non-skilled labor) be considered as a response to immediate or longer-term labor shortages.

(Rōdō Kijun Chōsakai 1997: 83)

The first and third principles refer exclusively to matters of border control. The second principle, however, suggests the existence of significant domestic labor reserves and/or sufficient alternative overseas production sites to meet labor demand well into the twenty-first century. Despite ministerial claims to the contrary, evidence suggests that increased utilization of female and elderly workers is unlikely to satisfy predicted demands for labor in terms of either quantity or quality. Labor force participation rates for both these groups are already among the highest in the industrialized world. It is, moreover, difficult to envisage a situation in which the elderly, for example, would be able to compensate for labor shortages in the transportation and construction industries – both of which are primary sources of employment for foreign workers. Similarly, offshore production and increased reliance on capital intensive facilities is an option available to only a small minority the small- and medium-sized firms that are the main employers of foreign workers.

Even before the 1990 revision came into effect, approximately 30,000 undocumented workers, mainly from Bangladesh and Pakistan, voluntarily left Japan to avoid possible arrest and deportation. Between 1989 and 1992, Japan also suspended visa exemption agreements with Bangladesh and Iran in an effort to reduce the flow of migrants from these countries. The short-term impact of these administrative actions was a sharp decline in entries from all three countries. Under the revised ICRRL, employers also risked a maximum fine of 2 million yen if they knowingly employed undocumented workers. With the exception of company trainees, students, and the descendants of Japanese nationals (up to third generation), the employment of non-skilled foreign workers was prohibited. This final category was intended to regulate the movement of LLM to meet labor requirements in undesirable but necessary areas of industry, while preserving racial homogeneity as expressed through blood lineage (Nojima 1989: 99, Kansai Dōyūkai 1989: 5). As a consequence, the number of *Nikkeijin* increased tenfold between 1988 and 1990. Between 1990 and June 1991, the *Nikkeijin* population, comprised primarily of Brazilian and Peruvian nationals, more than doubled from 71,495 to 148,700 and currently stands (1998) at more than 200,000. Brazilian *Nikkeijin* currently form the largest foreign national grouping in Japan, after Koreans and Chinese.

Larger firms have been in the best position to exploit these legislative changes and gain access to international labor markets through officially sanctioned 'trainee' programs or the employment of *Nikkeijin*. Japan's massive entertainment industry, whose association with regional traffickers in female labor is well-documented, has also successfully exploited the 'gap' which exists between laws that criminalize female sex workers and the actual demand for labor of this type. In contrast, small- and medium-sized firms, including those reliant on technologically advanced production methods, have experienced greater difficulty in obtaining access to international labor networks. The consequent failure to meet demand for LLM has, in some instances, left employers with two alternatives: factory closure or the employment of undocumented workers.

The 1990 revision of the ICRRL has been followed by a series of administrative measures designed to facilitate enforcement. These include:

- Tightening controls on language schools (1994) which, in many instances, had functioned as employment exchanges rather than educational institutions.
- Reinforcing the distinction (1996) between 'entertainers' and 'hostesses'.
- The establishment of Employment Service Centers for Foreigners (since 1993).
- An increase in the number of Immigration Bureau Inspectors.
- Expansion of company trainee programs.
- Strengthening of sanctions against employers who knowingly employ undocumented workers.

(Iguchi 1998a: 182–4)

At first glance, employer sanctions are quite severe, allowing for the imposition of large fines and/or imprisonment. Enforcement, however, is another matter and relatively few employers have been prosecuted for infringement of the ICRRL. On the other hand, the frequency with which individual or groups of undocumented workers have been apprehended at the port of entry (mainly Chinese) has recently increased. Immigration 'sweeps' are also made easy by the neighborhood *koban* (police sub-stations) system. Although often manned by only two or three officers, the police have an encyclopaedic knowledge of their patch and its inhabitants. Concealment is a virtual impossibility and undocumented workers have always resided in Japanese cities with the tacit approval of the local police. To what extent this situation has been altered as a result of the current recession is difficult to ascertain and evidence is anecdotal.

There are certainly far fewer Iranian telephone card sellers on the streets of Tokyo than eighteen months ago. Similarly, hundreds of undocumented (mainly Filipino) workers who were employed on numerous construction sites associated with the Nagano Olympics, and whose existence was well known to the local police, were unceremoniously rounded-up immediately before the opening ceremony. There may also be fewer Thai and Filipina hostesses to be found in Tokyo's entertainment districts but their place has been assumed by women from eastern Europe and Latin America. Increased levels of enforcement, as measured by the number of apprehensions under the ICRRL, moreover, have not resulted in a significant decrease in the overall number of undocumented workers (Iguchi 1998a: 174). Despite a protracted recession, during which consumption has stagnated and unemployment has reached unprecedented levels, Ministry of Justice estimates of the number of undocumented workers are constant at approximately 300,000. The rapid rates of increase which characterized the *Heisei* boom years have subsided, at least temporarily, but underlying demand for particular types of foreign labor has remained constant. Evidence suggests that demand for foreign migrant labor may no longer be sensitive to cyclical changes in the Japanese economy.

As foreign workers have become an integral feature of Japanese economic life, in the factory towns of Gunma, Shizuoka and Aichi Prefectures and in the metropolitan centers of Tokyo-Yokohama and Osaka, mass deportations might well create more problems than they would resolve. At the same time, public opinion surveys suggest considerable ambivalence towards the issue of foreign workers, particularly in terms of settlement and the potential for family reunification, while the government remains wedded to 'closed door' polices on the recruitment of non-skilled foreign labor. Recognition of the structural role performed by foreign labor is, however, increasing among private sector employers and employer federations. The most significant consequence of the growing divide between government policy and labor demand has been further labor market segmentation consisting of: indigenous full-time workers; indigenous part-time and contract workers (mainly women and the elderly); *Nikkeijin* and foreign company trainees; and undocumented foreign workers.

The tens of thousands of long-term Korean and Chinese residents whose access to both public and private sector employment remains subject to legal and informal restrictions must also be added to the picture. Reliance on 'side door', as in the case of *Nikkeijin* and company trainees, sources of temporary labor has also generated further and unforeseen difficulties. Initial take-up rates for officially-sanctioned trainee programs were low, largely due to a lack of emphasis on the acquisition of transferable skills. The 1993 changes in the format of trainee programs, which increased trainee availability for production work at the expense of linguistic and skills acquisition, have also been criticized as exploitative. *Nikkeijin* communities, whose existence were made possible by a racially informed revision of the ICRRL, have contradicted notions of an immutable Japanese identity. Although the linear descendants of Japanese emigrants, second and third generation *Nikkeijin* identity reflects multiple influences, only a minority of which are Japanese in origin.

Virtually all government and other elites engaged in policy formation oppose programs which would legalize the status of the undocumented workers currently in Japan, on the grounds that this would encourage further illegal migration. Nor does the introduction of a European-modeled 'guestworker' system, though at one time endorsed by the Ministry of Labor, elicit support (Koshiro 1998: 154–7, Iguchi 1998b: 293–316). Yet again, the concern is that supply would considerably outpace demand and encourage further illegal flows from, in particular, China.

Despite the emergence of integrationist projects at sub-national level, the absence of a clear consensus among either policy makers or the public at large, weak administrations, and a deepening economic crisis have all militated against significant change at national level. This lack of a domestic imperative, coupled with a rejection of both the European and American models, does not, however, exclude the emergence of alternative, regionally-based approaches to the foreign labor question. In the section that follows I will try to place contemporary migration to Japan and the policy responses this has generated within a regional and comparative framework.

Economic crises and international migration in Asia

In much of the relevant literature, migration to Japan is excluded from the wider economic, political and social processes taking place in Asia. When other Asian states are mentioned, Japan is seen as a potential destination country for migrant workers, and, where comparisons are drawn, the United States and Germany figure more prominently in the literature than do the nations of East and South-East Asia. To a certain extent, the absence of a regional perspective reflects Japan's historical ambivalence towards both Asia and its own identity as an Asian state. It also highlights the fact that, during the 130-year transformation from a semi-feudal state on the periphery of Asia, Japan has sought inspiration, in terms of new ideas and technologies, from Europe and the United States. This has remained relatively unchanged despite Japan's emergence, during the 1980s, as a major source of regional direct foreign investment and overseas development assistance; and the emergence of regional production systems which, coupled with rapid economic growth throughout the region during the 1980s, suggested that regional integration was just around the corner. In the current economic crisis it is easy to forget both the triumphalism which punctuated the Asian boom years and the extent to which regional political leaders associated economic development with the efficacy of Asian values. Definitions of Asian values, like their European and American counterparts, remained elusive and often obscured high levels of labor exploitation and political corruption.

Asian values can also be viewed as a discursive attempt to generate a sense of homogeneity among a heterogeneous grouping of Asian states distinguished by language, political and economic system, religion, and history. As far as migration is concerned, the current crisis has emphasized the absence rather than the presence of either an identifiable set of core values or a regional institutional framework within which policy coordination could take place.

Although international migration now affects all regional states, neither APEC nor ASEAN have undertaken a coordinating role and have left issues of border control, social and economic integration, and repatriation entirely in the hands of individual states. To an extent, this lack of multilateral coordination is entirely comprehensible since conflicting interests between sending and destination countries, compounded by political instability in some countries, continue to affect policy outcomes. As sending countries try to increase the number of out-country workers, particularly during periods of rising unemployment at home as now, receiving countries seek to lower their dependence on foreign labor. In common with economic development generally, the emergence of migration systems in Asia has not been an even or unitary process. Until relatively recently, postwar intra-regional migration was minimal and Asian guestworkers (primarily Thai and Filipino) were far more likely to be found in the Gulf States than elsewhere in Asia. Current migration streams are also multiple, involving significant flows of political refugees, non-skilled labor, and highly-skilled transients. In some instances, cross-border labor migration has been managed through bilateral agreements, whereas in others the role of independent labor brokers and/or criminal syndicates has been predominant.

In Singapore, Hong Kong, Taiwan and Malaysia specific economic and political mechanisms exist to regulate the importation of non- or less-skilled migrant workers (Kuwahara 1998: 13–14). This contrasts with the situation in Japan, where company trainee programs and the recruitment of foreign nationals of Japanese descent perform a similar function. Korea was a net exporter of labor until recently and maintains company trainee programs for foreign workers. At the same time Thailand, particularly during the high growth years of the 1980s, attracted a growing number of economic and political refugees from Laos, Cambodia and Burma (Sussangkarn 1996: 134–5). Whereas a common language may have assisted in the economic and social integration of migrant workers, as in the case of labor migration between Indonesia and Malaysia, this has certainly not been the case in Japan or Korea. With few exceptions (e.g. Indonesia, Bangladesh and the Philippines), it is no longer possible to draw a clear demarcation between labor sending and receiving countries. Equally, given the diversity of population flows, particularly betweeen males and females, conventional push-pull formulations can no longer be relied upon to provide an accurate assessment of the situation. Individuals make the decision to migrate for a multitude of reasons, only some of which can be ascribed to economic self-interest.

However, from a regional perspective, it is possible to identify certain characteristics of emerging migration systems in Asia:

- Current population flows are diverse and supported by a multiplicity of migration channels and networks.
- In the context of rapid economic growth, cross-border migration has been preceded by rural–urban transfers of labor within countries.
- The increasing feminization of labor migration throughout the region has not been reflected at the policy formation level.
- Despite increasing levels of unemployment in destination countries, the persistence of labor shortages in non- and less-skilled occupational niches has encouraged further, often undocumented, labor migration.
- The absence of regional coordination has increased the likelihood that states

will pursue narrowly defined national interests through increased reliance on border controls and other forms of enforcement, including the potential for mass deportations.

- The scale and political implications of current population flows are far greater than in the past.
- The current crisis has affected both national economies and particular industrial sectors to varying degrees, suggesting a correspondingly high level of diversity in terms of future cross border population movement.
- Although collective deportations remain unlikely in the short-term, the pay and working conditions of migrant workers are likely to deteriorate as employers seek to reduce labor costs.

The most recent estimates of the number of documented foreign workers in the region are: Malaysia 1.14 million; Singapore 560,000; Taiwan 210,000; Korea 200,000; and Thailand 316,000. Japan's foreign population, estimated at 1.4 million in 1995, that is, approximately 1 percent of the total population, is dominated by Koreans (657,000), Chinese [including Taiwanese nationals] (234,000), Brazilian *Nikkeijin* (202,000), and Filipinos (84,000). In some cases, however, the documented worker population has been surpassed by flows of undocumented workers: Malaysia 560,000; Korea 123,000; Thailand 943,000; and Japan just under 300,000. Compared with labor participation rates in Malaysia of 12 percent and in Singapore of 20 percent, documented foreign workers in Japan constitute just over 1 percent of the total labor force (Battistella and Asis 1998: 3).

The catalyst for the Asian financial crisis was the 1996 export slowdown, which raised doubts over regional economic growth, reduced the flow of international capital required to sustain current account deficits, and increased market concerns with dollar exchange rates. The Thai baht was the first currency to collapse, followed in rapid succession by the Philippine peso, the Malaysian ringgit, the Indonesian rupiah and the Korean won. Current (September 1998) attention is focused on Japan where it is hoped the Obuchi Government will succeed in reversing the decline in consumer and financial confidence and where unemployment has reached levels unprecedented since 1945.

While the causes of the crisis are beginning to be understood, there is no consensus as to either its ultimate impact or length. Within Asia, there is also concern whether the IMF rescue packages will ease or exacerbate the crisis. Some have argued that the IMF-imposed regimes, modeled on those which were successfully applied in Latin America, may retard economic recovery, increase unemployment and poverty, and generate social and political instability throughout the region. It is also widely acknowledged that Asian countries lack the social security infrastructure to withstand the impact of the rising unemployment, which is a consequence of both the crisis and the cure. Political ramifications have already emerged in Korea and Indonesia where financial and political instability forced the resignation of President Suharto.

The ability of regional states to contain the political and social consequences of the economic crisis, including border control, will ultimately depend on three interrelated factors: the managerial skills of political elites; a commitment to a fair distribution of the economic costs of recovery to all sectors of society; and multilateral cooperation either through existing fora or through the creation of new institutional frameworks. Confronted with the potential of increased emigration from sending countries, the response so far in labor-importing countries has been dominated by issues of border control and the repatriation of foreign, particularly undocumented, workers.

Among the most affected countries, Korea, Malaysia and Thailand have already instituted or intend to implement voluntary repatriation schemes. Between December 1997 and March 1998, just over 46,000 undocumented workers left Korea under an amnesty program. At the same time the redeployment of some Indonesian workers in Malaysia from the construction to the plantation sector has been coupled with plans to repatriate approximately 900,000 foreign workers during 1998. On the other hand, the first stage (May 1998) in the planned repatriation of approximately 900,000 foreign workers from Thailand was delayed by opposition from the fisheries industry and rice mill operators because of the unavailability of local labor (Battistella and Asis 1998: 3).

In the less affected countries such as Hong Kong, Japan, Singapore and Taiwan, demand for particular types of foreign labor has remained relatively constant though border controls and enforcement procedures have been strengthened in Japan and Singapore.

Migrant labor vulnerability has also varied by industrial sector. Demand for domestic labor, for example, has remained relatively stable in some labor importing countries e.g. Singapore. In Malaysia, while particular sources of migrant worker employment such as construction and manufacturing have contracted, others e.g. the plantation sector continue to absorb foreign workers. Reflecting the critical role of small- and medium-sized contractors within the Japanese manufacturing sector, demand for foreign labor has also remained constant. Although the regional data is incomplete, the evidence suggests that demand for non-and low-skilled labor in particular industrial sectors has reached structural proportions in several labor-importing countries (See, for example, Pillai 1998: 76–8).

Conclusion

As noted earlier, migrant labor employment throughout the region is two-dimensional, reflecting concentration in low-skilled, low-paying jobs in particular industrial sectors. A further generalization to be drawn is that, though avoided by indigenous workers even at times of crisis, economic development has generated further employment opportunities for foreign labor in these very sectors. The available data does not permit an assessment of whether, or to what extent, unemployed indigenous workers are likely to re-occupy jobs left vacant by departed migrant workers. If the experience of Japan and other developed economies is an example, this outcome is unlikely. In fact, the tightening of border controls suggests that the potential for further flows of undocumented labor remains significant. Calls for a tightening of immigration controls in labor-importing countries such as Japan may well be contradicted by emigration pressures in sending countries. A deterioration in wages and working conditions for foreign workers is also unlikely to act as a deterrent to further migration since the nominal value of remittances has increased as a result of exchange rates movement.

Predicting even the immediate future of international migration in Asia remains difficult, not least because unresolved structural problems within the Japanese economy may trigger a further wave of currency devaluations. This would have a direct impact on regional levels of unemployment and migration. Under such circumstances, mass deportations of foreign workers would become far more likely. The avoidance of this nightmare scenario depends on a number of factors, some of which are beyond the control of national governments. Although identification of the most appropriate forum may prove difficult, resolution of related issues such as the repatriation of foreign workers and protection of human rights, will require Asia-wide cooperation. So far, however, the Migrant Workers Convention, which would provide guidelines in this area, has only been ratified by the Philippines and Sri Lanka. Similarly, cooperation would enable individual governments to deal more effectively with labor trafficking, particularly in the case of female migrants. Rather than focusing on individual migrants, as is currently the case in Japan, cooperation would enable individual governments to target labor brokers and employers more effectively. In contrast to existing laws which regard migrants as a temporary and disposable source of labor, a regional framework, which acknowledges the structural role performed by non- and less-skilled foreign workers in labor-importing countries such as Japan, would facilitate the introduction of integrative as opposed to exclusionist legislation. As the European and American experiences have confirmed, migrants workers are more than units of production, and settlement is an inevitable consequence of migration.

References

Appleyard, R. T. (1991) *International Migration: Challenge for the Nineties*, Geneva: IOM.

Battistella, G., and Asis, M. (1998) *The Impact of the Crisis on Migration in Asia* (conference report), Manila: Scalabrini Migration Center.

Castles, S. (1986) "The Guest Worker in Europe: An Obituary", *International Migration Review*, 20, 4.

Castles, S., and Miller, M. J. (1993) *The Age of Migration; International Population Movements in the Modern World*, London: Macmillan.

Chōsen Sōtōkufu Shomubu Chōsa-ka (1924) *Hanshin-Keihin Chihōo no Chōsenjin Rōdōsha* (Korean Workers in the Osaka-Kobe and Tokyo-Yokohama Regions), Keijo [Seoul], cited in K. S. Pak (compiled 1975/6), *Zainichi Chōsenjin kankei Shiryō Shūsei* (Archival Materials Related to Koreans in Japan), vol. 1, Tokyo: San-ichi Shobo.

Cohen, R. (1987) *The New Helots: Migrants in the International Division of Labor*, Aldershot: Avebury.

Homusho (1996) *Annual Statistics on Immigration Control*, Tokyo: Okurasho Insatsukyoku.

—— (1997) *Annual Statistics on Immigration Control*, Tokyo: Okurasho Insatsukyoku.

IOM (1997) *Trafficking in Women to Japan for Sexual Exploitation: A Survey on the Case of Filipino Women*, Geneva: IOM.

Iguchi, Y. (1998a) "Country Report – Japan", in Japan Institute of Labor, *Workshop on International Migration and Labor Markets in Asia*, Tokyo: Japan Institute of Labor.

—— (1998b) "What Can We Learn from the German Experiences Concerning Foreign

Labor", in M. Weiner and T. Hanami (eds) *Temporary Workers or Future Citizens, Japanese and US Migration Policies*, London: Macmillan.

Ijiri, K. (1990) "The Breakdown of the Japanese Work Ethic", *Japan Echo* 17, 4.

Iwamura, T. (1972) *Zainichi Chōsenjin to Nihon Rōdōsha Kaikyū* (Korean Residents and the Japanese Working Classes), Tokyo: Azekura Shobo.

Iyotani, T. (1992) *"Sakerarenai Kadai; Sengo Nihon Keizai ni okeru Gaikokujin Rōdōsha"* ("The Unavoidable Problem; Foreign Workers in the Postwar Japanese Economy"), in T. Itotani and T. Kajita (eds) *Gaikokujin Rōdōsha-ron* (Foreign Workers), Tokyo: Kobundo.

Jain, P. and Mizukami, T. (1996) *Gurasurūtsu no Kokusai Kōryū* (International Exchange at the Grassroots Level), Tokyo: Hābesuto sha.

Jameson, F. and Miyoshi, M. (eds) 1998 *The Cultures of Globalization*, Durham: Duke University Press.

Japan Institute of Labor (1998) *Workshop on International Migration and Labor Markets in Asia,* Tokyo: Japan Institute of Labor.

Kansai Keizai Dōyūkai (ed.) (1989) *Habahiroi Gaikokujin Koyō no Sokushin wo* (Accelerating and Widening Employment of Foreign Workers), Osaka.

Kato, Y. (1973) *Nihon Teikokushugi-ka no Rōdō Seisaku* (Labor Polcies under Japanese Imperialism), Tokyo: Ochanomizu Shobo.

Kawamura, M. (1993) *"Taishū Orientarizumu to Ajia Ninshiki"* ("Commonsense Orientalism and Asian Consciousness"), in M. Kawamura (ed.) *Kindai Nihon to Shokuminchi; Bunka no Naka no Shokuminchi* (Japan and its Colonial Possessions; Cultural Representations of Ccolonies As), v 7, Tokyo: Iwanami Shoten.

Keisatsucho (1996) *Keisatsu Hakusho*, Tokyo: Okurasho Insatsukyoku.

Kempadoo, K. and Doezema, J. (eds) (1998) *Global Sex Workers; Rights, Resistance, and Redefinition*, New York and London: Routledge.

Komai, H. (1992) "Are Foreign Trainees in Japan Disguised Cheap Laborers, *Migration World* 20, 1.

—— (1993) *Imin Shakai Nihon no Kōzō* (The Structure of Japan as an Immigration Society), Tokyo: Kokusai Shoin.

Koshiro, K. (1991) "Labor Shortages and Employment Policies in Japan", in *Second Japan–Asean Forum on International Labor Migration in East Asia*, Tokyo: United Nations University.

—— "Does Japan Need Immigrants", in M. Weiner and T. Hanami (eds) *Temporary Workers or Future Citizens, Japanese and US Migration Policies*, London: Macmillan.

Kuwahara, Y. (1991) *Kokkyō Koeru Rōdōsha* (Workers Crossing National Borders), Tokyo: Iwanami Shoten.

—— (1998) "Economic development in Asia and its Consequences for Labor Migration", in OECD, *Migration and Regional Integration in Asia*, Paris: OECD.

Matsumura, T. (1967) *"Nihon Teikokushigi-ka ni okeru Shokuminchi Rōdōsha"* (Colonial Workers under Japanese Imperialism), *Keizaigaku Nenpo*, n 10.

Nishio, K. (1990) "The Danger of an Open-Door Policy", *Japan Echo*, 13, 1.

Nojima, T. (1989) *"Susumetai Nikkeijin no Tokubetsu Ukeire"* (Special Receiving Arrangements for Nikkeijin Proceeding) , *Gekkan Jiyu Minshu*, November.

OECD (SOPEMI) (1993) *Trends in International Migration*, Paris: OECD.

—— (1996) *Migration and the Labor Market in Asia, Prospects to the Year 2000*, Paris: OECD.

—— (1998) *Migration and Regional Economic Integration in Asia*, Paris: OECD.

Osaka-shi Shakai-bu Chōsa-ka (1924) *Chōsenjin Rōdōsha Mondai* (The Problem of Korean Workers), Osaka.

Ozawa, Y. (1977) *Zainichi Chōsenjin Kyoiku-ron* (A Study of Education for Korean Residents in Japan), Tokyo: Aki Shobo.

Pak, K. S. (1979) *Zainichi Chōsenjin Undō-shi: 8.15 Kaihō-mae* (The pre-Liberation History of the Korean People's Movement in Japan), Tokyo: San-ichi Shobo).

Pillai, P. (1998) "Country Report – Malaysia", in Japan Institute of Labor, *Workshop on International Migration and Labor Markets in Asia*, Tokyo: Japan Institute of Labor.

Potts, L. (1990) *The World Labor Market: A History of Migration*, London: Zed.

Rōdō Kijun Chōsakai (ed.) (1997) *Nihon no Rōdō Seisaku; Heisei Kyūnen-han*, Tokyo: Rōdōsho.

Rōmu Gyōsei Kenkyūjo (ed.) (1997) *Gaikokujin Rōdōsha no Shūrō, Koyō Nyūzu no Genjō* (The Employment of and Jobs Held by Foreign Workers), Tokyo: Rōdōsho Shokugyo Anteikyoku.

Sassen, S. (1993) "Economic Internationalization: The New Migration in Japan and the United States", *International Migration* 13, 1.

Shimada, H. (1990) "Now Hiring", *Look Japan*, August.

—— (1991) "The Employment of Foreign Labor in Japan", *Annals of the American Academy*, AAPSS: 513.

—— (1994) *Japan's "Guest Workers", Issues and Public Policies*, Tokyo: University of Tokyo Press.

Skeldon, R. (1992) "International Migration within and from the East and Southeast Asian Region: A Review Essay", *Asian and Pacific Migration Journal* 1, 1.

Sussangkarn, C. (1996) "Labor market developments and international migration in Thailand", in OECD, *Migration and the Labor Market in Asia, Prospects to the Year 2000*, Paris: OECD.

Tojo, N. (1994) "*Meiji-ki, Nihon ni okeru Saisho no Chōsenjin Rōdōsha*" (The First Korean Workers in Japan during the Meiji Period), in Y. D. Kim *et al.*, *Kankoku Gappei Mae no Zainichi Chōsenjin* (Koreans in Japan Before the Annexation of Korea), Tokyo: Akashi Shoten.

Vasishth, A. (1996) "A Model Minority; The Chinese Community in Japan", in M. Weiner (ed.) *Japan's Minorities; The Illusion of Homogeneity*, London and New York: Routledge.

Weiner, M. (1994) *Race and Migration in Imperial Japan*, London and New York: Routledge.

—— (ed.) (1996) *Japan's Minorities; The Illusion of Homogeneity*, London and New York: Routledge.

Weiner, M. and Hanami, T. (eds) (1998) *Temporary Workers or Future Citizens; Japanese and US Migration Policies*, Basingstoke and London: Macmillan.

Wickramasekara, P. (1996) "Recent Trends in Temporary Labor Migration in Asia", in OECD, *Migration and the Labor Market in Asia: Prospects to the Year 2000*, Paris: OECD.

Yamanaka, K. (1993) "New Immigration Policy and Unskilled Foreign Workers in Japan", *Pacific Affairs* 66, 1: 72–90.

4   The discourse of Japaneseness

John Lie

One Sunday in 1993, I took a train to Ishikawa Station, half an hour away from
where I was living in Yokohama. Walking westward from the station, I entered
Chinatown and ate in a restaurant which was remarkable for its sordid interior as
much as for its savory noodles. Walking eastward amidst Chinese-language signs
and speakers, I explored Kotobuki-chō, one of the most notorious *doyagai* (slum) in
Japan. Beyond shabby buildings and sleeping drunks – the inescapable sight and
stench of poverty – I passed people talking animatedly in various Asian tongues,
including Tagalog and Thai. Passing a Korean restaurant, I was overwhelmed by the
aroma of Korean food as well as by loud conversations in Korean.

Later in the afternoon, I went to Roppongi, one of the most fashionable areas in
Tokyo. Navigating a crowd of well-dressed people, I felt as under-dressed as I had
felt over-dressed in Kotobuki. I passed Israelis hawking cheap jewelry and Iranians
peddling telephone cards. At a fancy French café, I ordered the most expensive cup
of coffee of my life from a Bangladeshi waiter. Conversing with a Japanese friend,
I recounted my day and my inescapable impression of Japanese multiethnicity. She
begged to differ and insisted that I was mistaken. She remained unconvinced as I
talked about Ikaino, the Korean area of Osaka, and other notably multiethnic areas
of Japan such as the Chikuho region in Kyūshū (Allen 1994: 51–3). When I re-iter-
ated about the foreign workers whom I had met in Kotobuki, she said that Yokohama
had always been an exception (Torii 1977). Yokohama, Nagasaki, Kōbe, and Tokyo
were all port cities and therefore were atypical. She went on to insist that neither
Kotobuki, Roppongi, Ikaino, nor Chikuho was really Japan.

What is the real Japan? In this paper, I will try to elaborate on the discourse of
Japaneseness which insists on the ethnically homogeneous nature of contemporary
Japanese society. In discussing the matter, I will highlight its three critical assumptions about class, culture, and ethnicity. The new foreign workers are considered
diametrically opposed to the Japanese; they are the class, cultural, and ethnic others.
A major source of ideas and evidence of Japaneseness in the post-Second World War
period is *Nihonjinron*, or theories of Japanese people and culture (Yoshino 1992).

Japan as a middle-strata society

Contemporary Japan is often characterized as a middle-class society. Proponents
of this view typically cite surveys that reveal that 90 percent of adult Japanese

place themselves in the middle strata *(chū kaisō)* (Murakami 1984: 167, Mamada 1990: 24). Alternative characterizations of Japan, such as mass society *(taishū shakai)*, share the vision of Japan as a relatively affluent and egalitarian society. The belief in an affluent and egalitarian Japan is confirmed by the new foreign workers who are almost inevitably viewed as less educated and lower status than Japanese. Matsuyama Yukio (1985: 143–4) expressed his happiness at being born in Japan, which "does not have class and is an egalitarian society."

The reality of past and present inequality in Japan belies the assumption of a universal middle-class society. The rigid hierarchy, which precluded status mobility and inter-status marriage, characterized Tokugawa Japan. Although the Meiji Restoration of 1868 introduced features of formally egalitarian citizenship, Meiji Japan was far from shedding the remnants of premodern status hierarchy. Pre-Second World War Japan was a status society with a clear distinction between the strata of hereditary elite (the imperial household [*kōzoku*], nobility [*kazoku*], and gentry [*shizoku*]) and commoners *(heimin)* (Lebra 1993: 57–60). There was a definable elite in pre-Second World War Japan, which often traced themselves to the Tokugawa period (Silberman 1964: 108). If formal barriers to marriage and employment ended, informal restrictions remained significant.

Status inequality did not end with the eradication of the hereditary elite in 1947. Indeed, many Japanese scholars have described post-Second World War Japan as as an inegalitarian society, whether as a consequence of capitalism or of the Emperor system (Ōhashi 1971). Perhaps the best-known textbook on post-Second World War Japanese society in the world – Nakane Chie's *Japanese Society* (1970: 87) – delineates Japan as a "vertical society" *(tate shakai)*, characterized by "vertical stratification by institution or group of institutions." As one wag put it, however, her book may be a very astute ethnography of the University of Tokyo which is steeped in rank consciousness, vertical hierarchy, and groupism. An American scholar concurs: "The Japanese view of the world . . . is essentially hierarchical" (Greenbie 1988: 12).

Beyond facile generalizations, specialized studies underscore the considerable extent of Japanese inequality. The Japanese educational system remains inegalitarian. No-one in Japan seriously questions the university hierarchy with the University of Tokyo *(Tōdai)* and Kyoto University at its apex (Ehara 1984: 265–6). In the late 1970s, *Tōdai* graduates dominated the two most powerful state bureaucracies: 89 percent of the Ministry of Finance and 76 percent of the Ministry of Foreign Affairs (Rohlen 1983: 91; Passin 1982: 135–6). Elitism at these institutions is, as Nakane (1970) would suggest, undeniable (Takeuchi 1984: 37–63). The quality of primary and secondary schools differs widely and the access to better schools depends significantly on pre-existing social inequality (Smith 1995: chs 2 and 3). Contrary to the dominant image in the United States of the Japanese educational miracle, high schools, especially in poorer areas, are wracked by absenteeism, violence, prostitution, and drug use (Rohlen 1983: 137–41, 294–301).

Educational inequality, income inequality, and occupational hierarchy exist side by side. As Hiroshi Ishida (1998: 307) concludes: "the unequal distribution of occupational outcomes is related not only to different levels of educational credentials . . . but also to the difference by type and quality within the same level of educational credentials." Corporate hierarchy is formidable (Takeuchi 1995:

181–7, Spilerman and Ishida 1996: 338–9). Comparative analysis shows Japan to be no more egalitarian or open to intergenerational mobility than Britain or the United States (Ishida 1993: 253–7). It is possible to view Japan as a class-stratified society (Steven 1983: 319).

Furthermore, the pervasiveness of middle-class consciousness must be placed in a proper context. In a 1975 survey, 90 percent of respondents placed themselves in the middle strata (*kaisō*), but only 4 percent in the middle class (*kaikyū*); in fact 71 percent said that they were working class (Naoi 1979: 365). The language of class and the language of status are two totally different things. Most Japanese are quite clearly conscious of class differences as defined by occupational hierarchy or income inequality but this does not mean that they are class conscious. It simply means that the claim of Japan as a statusless or classless society needs to be critically examined (Katase and Tomoeda 1990: 126, Misumi 1990).

Given the considerable of inequality in contemporary Japanese society, why is there such a pervasive sense of equal status? First, the post-Second World War era saw a spate of progressive reforms. Legal distinctions based on status ended, the Emperor ideology and its concomitant hierarchy gave way to American-style democracy with its egalitarian ethos. Status equality was buttressed by lessening economic inequality. The massive land reform purged large landlords from the countryside while *zaibatsu* dissolution eroded the dominance of large capitalists.

Second, there are ideological sources of egalitarianism. In the total mobilization toward the end of the Fifteen Years War (1939–45), the organization and ideology of solidarity and sacrifice highlighted elements of egalitarianism. The post-war universalist ideologies – whether Marxism or progressive liberalism – articulated the egalitarian ethos that had existed during the Fifteen Years War. Postwar democracy confirmed the emerging predominance of egalitarian ideals.

Third, the competitive examination system underscored meritocracy: a career open to talent superseded the hereditary and entrenched elite. There is, however, a prewar continuity in the Japanese ideology of self-reliance and success (*risshin shusse*) in which school was the principal institutional route of upward mobility (Sakurai 1984: 190–2). The supposedly objective nature of entrance examinations underpinned the meritocratic educational and employment system. The system contributes to a widespread sense of a non-status, although far from classless, society because there is no status-based hindrance to educational and economic success. Meritocracy produces inegalitarian outcomes but this is not necessarily an indictment of its fair workings.

Fourth, the post-Second World War economic growth provided structural mobility and the new ideal of the middle strata in the guise of "salary man." Farmers in the countryside declined, while *sararîman* ("salary man," denoting white-collar workers) in cities increased. In 1969 when he returned to a Tokyo suburb which he had studied a decade previously, Ezra Vogel observed:

> By now all these aspirations for security, material possessions, and regular hours have been realized not only by the salary man, but by most of the population of Japan. The model and the vision that were provided by the salary man a decade ago have been essentially achieved already . . .
>
> (Vogel 1971: 271)

The salary man, or middle strata, status became the norm in postwar Japan:

> The way of life of the salary man dominates the mass media, the popular stories, the 'how to' books . . . The educational system is dominated by the spirit of the salary man.
>
> (Vogel 1971: 267)

The ideal penetrated the countryside as well:

> In some rural communities, farmers now turn over their income to the co-operative, draw it out in the form of 'sarari' (salary) and proudly claim that they are just like salary men.
>
> (Vogel 1971: 267–8)

Factory workers, in a similar vein, struggled to become ordinary Japanese (*hyōjunteki na kokumin*) (Kumazawa 1981: 71). For example, they commuted to work dressed like a *sararîman* in a suit and a tie. After about 1955, obvious status or class markers, such as clothes that distinguished occupational groups until then, disappeared (Kumazawa 1981: 73).

Finally, rapid economic growth provided a profound sense of material improvements. From the devastation of the Fifteen Years War, Japan experienced virtually uninterrupted growth until the 1973 oil crisis. Luxury goods, such as cars, color televisions, and coolers (air conditioner) became commonplace. The poverty of the immediate post-Second World War years quickly became a faded memory. In the course of a mere generation, the images of poverty and desperation captured in the 1950s films of Kurosawa Akira were superseded by the visions of plenty and playfulness in the 1980s films of Itami Jūzō.

Thus, many Japanese believe that they live in a universal middle-status, even middle-class, society. By 1990, buoyed by the bubble economy, the dominant Japanese self-image projected a society of affluence. It is not only the labor-market condition that discouraged people from assuming less-prestigious jobs. New foreign workers – employed predominantly in undesirable jobs such as manual work and the water trade – enhanced the widespread sense of Japan as a society of middle-strata, middle-class people. In other words, Japanese are middle class and foreign workers are lower class.

Some foreign workers such as refugees are poor and in desperate straits (Mainichi Shinbun Tokyo Honsha Shakaibu 1990: 20–9). However, the vast majority of them come closer to Rey Ventura's characterization of "underground" Filipino workers in Japan:

> If (he) was facing starvation . . . he wouldn't begin to be able to think of going abroad. It is only when you have some cash in hand or the ability to raise a loan that you can start thinking in those terms.
>
> (Ventura 1992: 163)

Filipina prostitutes were often well-educated (Kikuchi 1992: 182). I was constantly impressed by the fluent English, which suggested high educational attainment, of the Filipinos and Iranians whom I met in Kotobuki and elsewhere.

None the less, the Asian migrant workers' significant diversity of educational attainment or class background is ignored in the dominant Japanese view. A Bangladeshi construction worker may be a college graduate, a Filipina bar maid a professionally certified nurse, an Iranian telephone card seller a son of a medical doctor. Upper and lower class, college-educated and illiterate are all lumped into the category of foreign workers, who are inevitably associated with low-class jobs. Hence, the opposition is established between the affluent, middle-class Japanese and the impoverished and lower-class foreign workers.

Ironically, politically progressive people most clearly articulated the contrast between Japanese and the new foreign workers. Claiming to be sympathetic to their plight, one self-appointed supporter of foreign workers' struggle argued that they should be allowed to work in Japan because they are pitiful (*kawaisō*) and poor (*mazushii*). Progressive Japanese analyses therefore highlighted external, structural factors, such as poverty, rather than individual desires and initiatives (Tou 1992: 29–33). It is, of course, misleading to emphasize only the exploitation and the pathos of the new foreign workers. After all, most of them enter Japan voluntarily and consciously endure the demanding working conditions.

The *noblesse oblige* of Japanese progressives leads them to exaggerate the pathos of foreign workers. A Thai worker surprised the concerned Japanese Okabe Kazuaki (1991: i) by saying that he "felt sorry for Japanese people because there was no foreign country where they can make ten or twenty times the going wage in Japan." Additionally, the media, which is always in search of interesting copy, highlighted sensational stories of suffering. Rey Ventura writes:

> Before I arrived [in Japan] . . . I had the notion that life there was simply a matter of loneliness and exploitation and the continual pressure to remit money home. This was the way it had been written up in dozens of articles about migrant workers.
>
> (Ventura 1992:19)

The multifaceted reality of the new foreign workers cannot be described only by portraying unrelenting suffering and exploitation.

The unwanted sympathy and thinly veiled presumption of superiority lead many foreign workers to resent Japanese haughtiness. After the October 1987 death of a starved Bangladeshi student, Japanese activists launched a movement to feed foreign students. In spite of the good intention, many foreign students found the effort offensive (Tanaka 1991: 178–9). In fact, very few Japanese note the contrast between some foreign workers' upper- or middle-class background and their lower-class employment. Most Japanese were shocked to realize that some of the Asian migrants were the elites in their own country because of their college education.

Underlying the contrast between the lower-class foreign workers and the middle-class Japanese is the widely diffused belief in Japanese affluence and Third World poverty. The proposition of Japanese prosperity and Third World poverty is unassailable but, just as not all Japanese are rich, not all Third World people are poor. Class and nation are, however, fused in the prevailing Japanese social view. By ignoring inequality in their own country, many Japanese have little sense of inequalities elsewhere. The nationalist framework and the prevalent mindset mean that many Japanese ignore intra-national variations in favor of international comparisons. The ostensible class uniformity of Japan is transposed to other countries. Motoyama Yoshihiko (1991), one of the leading Japanese economists, begins his survey of developing countries with a chapter entitled "The desperate poverty of developing countries" but does not mention the significant inequality within a developing country or among developing countries. He is merely reflecting a widespread view that the third world is, simply, "desperately poor." As I have noted, many foreign workers are in fact people of relatively privileged background but that they hail from countries poorer than Japan – and that they seek employment in affluent Japan – confirms many Japanese's equation of impoverished third world countries with low-class foreign workers.

If Japanese are middle-class and the new foreign workers are lower-class, who are the upper class? In short, the old foreigners (*gaijin*) assume the role of the upper class. *Gaijin* (outsiders) in post-Second World War Japan almost inevitably referred to white North Americans and Europeans. Although Europeans and Americans may have low educational attainment and low occupational status in their own countries, they are almost inevitably regarded as superior to Japanese. Commercials that convey elegance and style, for example, inevitably use white Euro-American models.

The archetypal Japanese depiction of upper-class life is a Swiss chateau or a British country house. Hence, Japanese who wish to differentiate themselves often assume aspects of European culture. Imada Minako's fashionable school in Harajuku teaches *haut bourgeois* French cuisine, including "Diane de Poitiers' cheesecake, Ludwig II's *choux* swans and Catherine de Medici's sabayon" (Petkanas 1993: 7). Shino Rinji owns three French restaurants and built a museum in his native Wakayama Prefecture – the home of the *Burakumin* writer Nakagami Kenji – that resembled the Louvre. For his country club: "French lampposts line the driveway to the chateau-like clubhouse. . . And those who lose their way among the French rose bushes can refer to a French-Japanese guidebook" (Thornton 1995: 70). These examples of Europhilia and emulation of Western aristocratic tastes are a reflection that the cultural superiority of Europe and the United States was taken for granted. As a man in his forties paradigmatically stated: "But, of course, *gaijin* are rich. Don't they live in a large mansion, relax in a swimming pool, and eat fat, juicy beefsteaks for breakfast?" The expression can be more prosaic. Yamamoto Akira (1986: 110–12), a scholar of popular culture, recalls that the first thing he did when he arrived in the United States in the 1960s was to make himself a Dagwood sandwich. The popularity of the cartoon *Blondie*, with sumptuous sandwiches that the protagonist often concocted, projected an indelible image of American wealth and superiority.

The ubiquitous presence of white Europeans and North Americans as the personification of the upper class stems in part from the invisibility and the near absence of the domestic upper class. The remnants of the hereditary elite lead concealed lives. Beyond their small size, they are not only residentially segregated but attend special schools, shop in designated stores, and eat at exclusive restaurants (Lebra 1993: 148–55). The break-up of large family firms and the post-Second World War land reform dwindled the fortunes and numbers of the upper class. Post-war corporate elites are paid professionals and, in status if not in income, *sararîman*. The meritocratic elite do not constitute an aristocracy.

Cultural superiority

An implicit corollary of the contrast – Japanese as middle class, foreign workers as working or lower class – is that Japanese are more advanced, or better, in terms of culture and civilization than foreign workers. Class superiority is, in other words, overlaid by cultural superiority. Japanese are, to put it crudely, better than foreign workers.

Status homogeneity is matched by cultural essentialism. Most Japanese assume that the nation-state and national culture are one and the same. Not only are most Japanese comfortable in talking about *the* Japanese culture, the question of any cultural diversity is at best of secondary interest. Japanese tend to adopt an ethno-nationalist frame – or the United Nations model of the world – when they delve beyond the simple differences between Japanese and non-Japanese. Because Japan is believed to be ethnically and culturally homogeneous, almost all other countries are believed to be so as well. That Filipinos may group themselves according to their places or origin (Ventura 1992: 49–50), or that Indonesia consists of myriad different cultures does not strike most Japanese as obvious.

National cultures are unequal. The idea of a hierarchy of civilizations or cultures has been deeply entrenched in Japan. Influenced by Thomas Buckle and François Guizot, Fukuzawa Yukichi, perhaps the greatest social thinker of modern Japan, delineated a hierarchy of civilizations in his widely disseminated publications. In his view, European countries and the United States are civilized (*bunmeikoku*); Turkey, China, Japan, and some other countries are semi-civilized (*hankai no kuni*); and Australia and Africa are savage (*yaban no kuni*) (Fukuzawa 1931: 24).

The tradition of grand history – the rise and fall of civilizations and the attendant assumption of a moral hierarchy of nations – remains a popular genre in Japan which has been exemplified in the post-Second World War period by the popularity of Arnold Toynbee. Postwar intellectuals and the reading public found Toynbee's cosmopolitan spirit attractive but they also found his view of cultural hierarchy reasonable (Toynbee 1976: 21; cf. McNeill 1989: 268–70). In this regard, Ian Buruma notes: "national prejudices . . . tend to follow closely the political and economic fortunes of the countries concerned. The stereotypes are not hard to guess: Germans are industrious and disciplined, thus wholly admirable, rather like the Japanese themselves" (Buruma 1992: 186).

It has been an accepted, albeit contested, fact since the Meiji Restoration that Japan was behind the West. Catching up with the West was perhaps the pre-Second World War national mandate. The slogan *wakon yōsai* (Japanese spirit, Western technology) underestimates the extent to which Japanese political, military, business, and educational leaders acknowledged Western superiority and sought to emulate the West. The very word for culture or civilization (*bunmei*) had extremely positive connotations, and was associated above all with the West (Maruyama 1984:

15–17). Nitobe Inazō (1984: 129) observed that just as "our ancestors sought knowledge from Korea and China," the Japanese of his time "should emulate [their ancestors] and must absorb knowledge from the West." European cultural influences were decisive. The celebrated writer Akutagawa Ryūnosuke's memorable line – "My life is not worth a line of Baudelaire" – is but an exaggerated expression of this mindset.

The influence of Europe, particularly Germany, in scholarly endeavors and in cultural pursuits was pervasive in the prewar period. The project of emulating the West – the desire for cultural improvement – manifested itself in glorifying the ideal of *kyōyō* (cultural literacy, or *Bildung*) (cf. Conze and Kocka 1985). Fukuzawa Yukichi's (1931) *Gakumon no Susume* (The Encouragement of Learning) set the tone by selling 220,000 copies, one for every 160 Japanese (Koizumi 1966: 28). Ambitious pupils read the collected works of great writers; the German Reklam editions signaled intellectual seriousness. *Bunko* (small paperbacks) that are ubiquitous in contemporary Japan began when Iwanami Shoten, perhaps the leading publisher, sought to emulate the ideal of Reklam editions.

The display of *kyōyō*, or cultural capital, became a popular activity from the late nineteenth century onwards (Tsutsui 1995: 32–6). *Kyōyō* was quintessentially about acquiring Western culture. The Kyoto University professor Ashizu Takeo recalls that his college friends argued vociferously about whether Wilhelm Furtwängler's or Arturo Toscanini's rendition of Beethoven symphonies was superior (Waki and Ashizu 1984: 105–6). Postwar Japan's most celebrated intellectual Maruyama Masao wrote in his diary in 1954 when Furtwängler died:

> No event gave me more shock recently than Furtwängler's sudden death. The desire to listen in person to Beethoven's Ninth conducted by him and performed by the Berlin Philharmonic – this is 90 percent of my reason to want to go to Europe – has now finally become forever an unrealizable dream.
>
> (Waki and Ashizu 1984: 115)

Maruyama goes on to note, after an *excursus* on Maria Callas, that many Japanese are known to be Furtwängler maniacs (Waki and Ashizu 1984: 122). Regardless of the accuracy of Maruyama's impression, the lure of the West, and its place as a cultural center, is undeniable.

In spite of occasional nativist strains, postwar intellectual life continued to value European and American intellectual imports. Indeed, the power of the classics has been widely accepted, and knowledge of Western classics is widespread. Gail Bernstein (1983: 123) was surprised to discover Fumiko, "the genteel farm woman," in a peripheral farming community in Ehime: "Fumiko had read in translation a surprising number of American classics, including Louisa May Alcott's *Little Women* and some of Hemingway's novels, as well as books on race problems in America." Edward Fowler (1996: 61) encountered in the famous *doyagai* San'ya, a day laborer, who told him: "You're from the United States and teach Japanese literature! I should tell you that I'm not entirely ignorant of your field. I know the name of Donald Keene." By contrast, the contemporary American novelist Thom Jones said that Stendhal's *"The Red and the Black* is a book that many of my friends have yet to read (or have never even heard of)"

(Fried and Garvey 1997: 43). Virtually all Japanese writers – or college graduates – would find this statement shocking because Stendhal's novels are standard reading in Japanese intellectual life. The popular novelist Murakami Haruki, for example, recalls his youth as a time when he read *The Brothers Karamazov*, *Jean Christophe*, *War and Peace*, and *Quiet Flows the Don* three times each, and notes: "I thought that *Crime and Punishment* was lacking in page number" (Murakami and Anzai 1986: 144). To paraphrase Samuel Johnson, few would have wished that it were so, but Murakami's zeal is suggestive of the Japanese desire for *Bildung*.

The United States superseded Europe after 1945. The hold of Germany over Japanese high culture waned. In sociology, for example, close reading of Marx and Weber gave way to attentive perusal of Talcott Parsons or Robert K. Merton. In virtually all spheres of cultural life, whether sport or music, American influence became paramount.

In this regard English has an hegemonic hold in Japanese life. For many Japanese, to be international means to learn English (Manabe 1990: 6). To call musical instruments in Japanese was considered *déclassé* (*yabo kusai*) (Suzuki 1990: 226–7). Whatever is cool (*kakkoii*) is often rendered in English. In the 1990s, virtually all the popular rock groups not only had English-sounding names, but were also written in *rōmaji* (Roman characters). Thirty-seven of the fifty best-selling records in 1992 had *rōmaji* titles (Minoshima 1993: 45).

Alongside the lingering assumption of Western superiority is an even more widespread belief that Japan is ahead of other, particularly neighboring, Asian countries. *Datsua nyūō* (escape Asia, enter Europe) became a shorthand of modern Japanese attitude. Indeed, many Japanese still consider Japan to be not part of Asia. The ordinary use of Asia distinguishes Japan from continental Asia. Asia was written in *kanji* (Chinese characters) in the prewar period but it is now written in *katakana*, which is a script now used to denote foreign names and words. When I lived in Tokyo in the mid-1980s, several of my politically progressive friends recommended that I read *Ajia wa naze mazushii no ka?* (Why Is Asia Poor?) by Tsurumi Yoshiyuki (1982). Asia for Tsurumi and my progressive friends evidently, did not include Japan.

Japan had, of course, colonized or invaded much of East and South-East Asia in the prewar period and there is undoubtedly a remnant of cultural superiority stemming from military victories and colonial rule. Imperial Japan engaged in its own civilizing mission, spreading everything from Emperor ideology to Japanese language in East and South-East Asia (Kawamura 1994).

Needless to say, imperial ideology often asserted the unity of Japan and Asia. Okakura Kakuzō trenchantly asserted that Asia is one, although some used the same idea to justify Japanese imperialism (Ōoka 1985: 184–6). The aesthete Yanagi Muneyoshi wrote appreciatively about Korean culture (Tsurumi 1982: 163–85). Respect for classical Chinese culture never disappeared completely. The 1879 Imperial Rescript on Education stated: "For morality, the study of Confucius is the best guide" (Passin 1982: 227), and the 1943 Ministry of Education Policy on Instruction said: "Through classical Chinese, the students shall study the thought and culture of the Empire and of East Asia . . . so that they may contribute to the cultivation of our national spirit" (Passin 1982: 269).

The postwar Japanese economic miracle has once again distinguished Japan from its poor Asian counterparts. Just as Westerners represent upper class and signify cultural superiority, Asians come to stand for lower class and denote cultural inferiority. Domestic class relations can be easily transposed onto the world system of national hierarchies where Japan, quite obviously, stands near the top. It is only another step to affirm Japanese cultural and moral superiority over others. In various college cafeterias, I often overheard students discussing their impressions of poverty in other East and South-East Asian countries where they had spent their vacation. Although some lamented the poverty, others enthusiastically engaged in telling each other tales of horror which at times degenerated into comparative scatology. When even a day-laborer can go on a sex tour to Thailand (Fowler 1996: 72–73), it is not difficult to affirm Japanese prosperity and superiority.

None the less, most people were reluctant to state that Japan is number one. Indeed, very few would directly state that Japan was superior to others. Japan's defeat in the Second World War was catastrophic and, even today, few would insist on Japanese cultural superiority and outright chauvinism. Only right-wing nationalists, conservative politicians, and some younger people directly expressed any sense of self-confidence about Japanese culture. Even then, the statements were often not about Japanese superiority but about American decline. For example, Prime Minister Miyazawa Kiichi said in February 1992: "American workers have come to lack a work ethic" (Neff 1992: 33). Although many dislike Japanese subservience to the United States in political affairs, almost no one would declare Japanese cultural superiority. The critic Yasuhara Ken (1993: 3) is exceedingly critical of the United States but he is, in fact, even more critical of Japan because it continues to admire the United States.

In addition, many Japanese are sympathetic to the problems of underdeveloped nations and are wary of cultural prejudice. Whether because of political correctness or plain politeness, many Japanese rarely express an unreserved judgment about Japanese cultural superiority. The earnestness of progressive writers, such as Motoyama (1991) or Tsurumi (1982) that I have cited, is simultaneously a conscious effort to express global solidarity (Iwanami Shoten Henshūbu 1991).

Expressions of Japanese superiority, in point of fact, occur indirectly. Often stated as asides, these utterances effectively mask essentially the same sentiment as those who are ethnocentric and even chauvinistic. Two examples follow.

One common response to the new foreign workers concerned their personal hygiene. When pressed to name their distinctive feature, many Japanese whom I interviewed remarked that they are unkempt. A young man who just came back from a trip to China said that toilets in China were abominably dirty. He seemed to conclude, therefore, that many Chinese people have low hygienic standards. Such an expression of cultural superiority reveals the basic way in which social distinction is often articulated. As George Orwell noted in *The Road to Wigan Pier*:

> Here you come to the real secret of class distinctions in the West – the real
> reason why a European of bourgeois upbringing, even when he calls himself
> a Communist, cannot without a hard effort think of a working man as his

equal. It is summed up in four frightful words which people nowadays are chary of uttering, but which were bandied about quite freely in my childhood. The words were: *The lower classes smell.*

(Orwell 1937: 127)

The new foreign workers smelled and seemed dirty to many urban Japanese. A self-identified progressive, who had been working on behalf of foreign workers, said that they smell for an objective reason: according to him, they cannot afford to take baths every day like Japanese. It is worth remembering that many Western tourists complain about the poor state of Japanese toilets. An American academic told me *ad nauseam* about the disgust she felt riding a commuter train, sandwiched between a *sararîman* with halitosis and another with psoriasis.

Another displaced expression of cultural superiority, often articulated by women, was gender relations. One office worker talked at length about Arabs although she clearly meant Iranians. According to her, they come from a culture that oppresses women. Based on a television documentary which she had recently seen, she recounted in horror that women in Arab societies had to wear veil in public and lead lives of submission to their husbands. She continued that, in contrast, Japanese women are free and independent, and that she could wear a mini-skirt whenever she liked and could go out at any time of the night. It is ironic that, at least in comparison to advanced industrial societies, Japanese women lag behind their counterparts in most measures used for female advancement, such as gender equality in wages (Brinton 1993: 222–4, Osawa 1993: 110–16) or political representation (Pharr 1981: 40). In the 1970s, Joyce Lebra articulated an opinion still common among Western visitors to Japan in the late 1990s: "The majority of women in Japan, whether married or single, cling to the traditional definition of women as 'good wife and wise mother.' There has been no fundamental questioning of this traditional ideal" (Lebra 1978: 297). Furthermore, American feminists have noted that Japanese women are subservient and that their clothing caters to male tastes. The woman I interviewed, however, had no inkling that Western feminists might regard Japan in the same way that she regarded Arab societies.

In general, many cross-cultural comparisons use gender relations as a gauge of cultural hierarchy. There was, in fact, a gamut of cultural comparisons. Just as Americans derided the patriarchal Japanese, Japanese castigated the patriarchal Iranians. An Iranian man, who claimed to shuttle back and forth between Paris, Los Angeles, and Tokyo, told me about the infernal situation of American women. When I asked why he thought that the situation of women in the United States was much worse than that of Iran, he discussed the endemic violence against women in the United States. "Our women are well cared for," he said. In addition, many Japanese would agree with Sumiko Iwao's observation that: "We must question the often-heard line that Japanese women 'lag behind' women in the United States and Europe . . . Japanese women have made equality based on mutual dependence acceptable and workable" (Iwao 1993: 265). Given myriad measures that one may use to compare the situation of women, it is easy for one group to claim superiority over others based on their choice of measures. That another group may not share the same criteria is taken as another indicator of their superiority: their capacity for sound judgment. What is missing is, of course, an appreciation of not only the complexity of the issue at hand but also the widespread variation, even in one's own culture.

Some Japanese claim that their cultural superiority is based on their everyday observations of, and interactions with, the new foreign workers. The natives' superior command of language and local customs make them inevitably the teachers, hence the superiors, of their neophyte neighbors and acquaintances. Local knowledge, in other words, ensures a sense of superiority, however parochial it may be. A young Japanese woman unhesitatingly claimed that Japanese were superior because of "our fashion sense"; the migrant workers were "unfashionable" (*dasai*). A comparison with Westerners is instructive. It is not uncommon to hear Japanese talk of Westerners (*hakujin* or *gaijin*) as smart or cool (*kakkoii*). When asked why, a common response is to highlight their physique (e.g. tall) or appearance (e.g. well-dressed). In contrast, the migrant workers – usually Asian manual workers – are said to be short and shabbily dressed, as they often undoubtedly are.

In cultural expressions and practices, we observe indirectly articulated expressions of Japanese superiority. They are intimately connected with the Japanese economic power and its consequences. Although outright expressions of cultural chauvinism occur from time to time, it is more striking to see how cultural superiority is often expressed indirectly and unintentionally. Prewar legacy should not be stressed. Although older Japanese feel inferior to the West and superior to Asia, the same mix of sentiments does not exist across generations. The sources of cultural superiority, along with modes of expression, are diverse although they are united in affirming Japanese superiority over the new foreign workers.

Japan as ethnically homogeneous

A cardinal axiom about Japanese society is its ethnic homogeneity. However, like all large nation-states, Japan is ethnically diverse. None the less, as the late 1980s debate on foreign workers demonstrated, many commentators presumed Japan to be pristine and pure before the onslaught of the new foreign workers. Indeed, the debate over the new foreign workers reinforced the view that Japan has been and remains a monoethnic society.

In spite of concerted efforts by some scholars and activists to challenge the belief in Japanese ethnic homogeneity, the view that only Japanese live in Japan is deeply rooted and widely shared. After expressing his gratitude to be born in Japan after traveling abroad, a Japanese writer notes: "It is rare to find a country so unperturbed by ethnic or racial problems" (Matsuyama 1985: 143–4). Indeed, the urgency of the foreign worker debate stemmed in part from the perceived absence of any ethnic problem, or any ethnic minority, in Japan.

Most Japanese believe that Japan is ethnically homogeneous. When asked about Japan's existing minorities, many people seemed puzzled and confused. The virtual equation between the state, nation, and ethnicity (as well as class and culture) has rendered Japan as a distinctively homogeneous country. When confronted with the fact of ethnic diversity, many Japanese either ignore or deny it.

The most common acknowledgment of existing Japanese minorities was the presence of the *Ainu*. Many people sensed that they were somehow different from ordinary (*futsū*) Japanese although what exactly these differences are remained vague. Responses ranged from superficial remarks, such as the more hirsute character of the *Ainu*, to some outright racist comments, such as remarks about their savage (*yaban* or *mikai*) culture. As the Japanese government had refused to acknowledge the *Ainu* as an indigenous people, the repercussion was widespread public ignorance and prejudice (Uemura 1992: 85–99, Honda 1993). Interestingly, when asked how many *Ainu* there were in Japan, no one mentioned a figure higher than 1,000 when, in fact, some estimates are as high as 300,000. The low figures emphasised the widespread view that the *Ainu* are a virtually vanished and vanquished people.

Okinawans, in contrast, were perceived to be much closer to, or indeed part of, mainstream Japanese people and culture. Several people mentioned a recent popular television drama in which Okinawa was portrayed as a feudal domain during the Tokugawa period, like other prefectures of contemporary Japan. Okinawa is regarded as having a regional identity. However, some people whom I interviewed considered Okinawans to be an ethnic minority group. A Japanese Brazilian of Okinawa descent asserted the ethnic distinctiveness of Okinawans. This was due to her experience of discrimination in Brazil by other Japanese Brazilians. She noted, however, that Japanese people did not discriminate against her as an Okinawan, but rather as a *Nikkeijin* (Ike 1995: 202).

Burakumin also did not merit a distinctive status. In the Tokyo metropolitan area, unlike the Kansai region, education regarding *Burakumin* (*dōwa kyōiku*) is virtually non-existent. No one mentioned them as an ethnic minority group and few young people were aware of the prejudice they face. When I suggested that they should be regarded as an ethnic minority, most people disagreed strongly. For many of them, *Burakumin* status is a historical relic that holds no contemporary relevance. Even when differences were acknowledged, ethnic minority status was denied because ethnicity is a racial issue in Japan. The equivalence of the state, nation, and ethnicity renders the unity and homogeneity of Japan possible and makes for classifications based on descent. Although *Burakumin* face discrimination in employment and marriage based on their birth and status, they are not considered an ethnic minority because they are said to stem from the same racial stock as other Japanese.

Although almost all Japanese are vaguely aware of the existence of Korean and Chinese residents in Japan, the knowledge concerning them is virtually nil. One indication is the astonishment expressed by several people when I told them that many famous athletes and entertainers were in fact Korean Japanese, although they used Japanese names in public. One college student was beside himself when I told him that the actress Yasuda Narumi was Korean Japanese. According to a popular survey in 1993, Yasuda was regarded as the kind of woman that most college-aged men hoped to marry. Because of his shock, he vowed to study ethnic relations in Japan.

The assumption of Japanese ethnic homogeneity is deeply held. It is assumed that only Japanese people live in Japan, save for visitors. Indeed, on several occasions in the course of daily interaction, Japanese were shocked and even became angry when I revealed that I am not a Japanese national. A woman who cut my hair said: "Why didn't you tell me?" as if it were my obligation to identify my citizenship status before every encounter with Japanese people.

Given the dominant belief of Japan as an ethnically homogeneous country, the new foreign workers represent the potential of heterogeneity. Against the pristine simplicity of homogeneous Japan, they represent the polluted complexity of the heterogeneous world outside Japan. A small shop owner in his fifties expressed his worries about the migrant workers because he was uncertain whether they came from the mountain or the sea (*yama no mono ka umi no mono ka wakaranai*). In effect, he expressed an essential conservative vision; a change may upset his world of peace and stability. Naturally, others hope to change the homogeneous character of Japan. A college student was in favor of opening the country because he found Japan boring. His friend thought that, in the era of internationalization, Japan needed more foreigners to make Japanese more international. The salient point is, however, that both views presume Japan to be ethnically homogeneous.

Indeed, Japanese ethnic homogeneity exists in marked contrast to foreign ethnic heterogeneity. In other words, if inside denotes simplicity and purity, outside represents complexity and pollution.

The discourse of Japaneseness

The discourse of Japaneseness articulates a vision of Japan as a homogeneous society. Unencumbered by major cleavages and inequalities, class and ethnic divides that characterize most advanced industrial countries are absent in this view of Japan. Further, Japan's economic might makes them an affluent, middle-class society, unlike impoverished, lower-class societies where foreign workers come from. What renders this contrast all the more striking is the illusion of a pure Japan encroached upon by polluted outsiders, who are, by virtue of their lower class and cultural status, ultimately inimical to the Japanese body politic.

Recall Emile Durkheim's classic distinction between mechanical solidarity and organic solidarity. He argued that most primitive social solidarity was based on homology, or likeness, among individuals. The solidarity of complex societies is, in contrast, based on interdependence. Needless to say, contemporary Japanese society is a complex entity with a great deal of role differentiation, not to mention income inequalities, gender differences, regional disparities, and distinct aspirations and life goals. None the less, the discourse of Japaneseness portrays 125 million Japanese citizens as like individuals whose primary identity is Japanese. In delineating a boundary between Japanese and non-Japanese, the discourse sets the insiders against the outsiders.

The state provides the basis for this enduring form of ethnic and cultural homogeneity. By equating nation, ethnicity, and class, Japan emerges as a society of mechanical solidarity. Although Japan may experience fluctuating fortunes, the assumptions underlying the discourse of Japaneseness remains robust. What is of crucial interest is that this view denies salient social divisions as well as the country's history which shows differences and dissension.

What makes the new foreign workers distinct from earlier foreigners is that they are viewed as completely different from the contemporary Japanese characterization of themselves. Although Europeans and North Americans have served as the cultural superiors whom Japanese emulated, Koreans and Chinese, like other existing minorities in Japan, have been suppressed: either assimilating to the wider Japanese culture or eking out a living as foreigners on Japanese soil. Their features and cultural characteristics mark out the new foreign workers and place them as the opposite of contemporary Japanese.

The pervasiveness of this social vision can be gauged even from the people who are consciously attempting to speak out and act against the more xenophobic elements in Japanese society. Although progressives wish more humane treatment of foreign workers and attack the xenophobic practices of the government, their assumptions and utterances often are the same as those of their opponents. The self-proclaimed progressives regard the new foreign workers as poor (lower class), from the Third World, bringing undesirable cultural practices and beliefs (economic and cultural inferiors) into an ethnically homogeneous country (denying, except in several notable exceptions, the existence of *Ainu* or *Burakumin* as minorities). Indeed, the arrival of the new foreign workers only highlighted the view of Japan as hitherto ethnically homogeneous. Hence my friend, whom I described in the opening vignette, can endlessly accept exceptions to the hegemonic vision of Japan as an ethnically homogeneous society.

It is not surprising, then, that many foreign workers should share the same vision of Japan: as an affluent, culturally advanced, and ethnically homogeneous nation. Whether treated well or poorly, their images of Japan, as ill-informed as many of them may be, mirror those advanced by the Japanese themselves. Their judgments, as in the case of progressive Japanese, may be quite negative; charges of xenophobia, racism, close-mindedness, and other hard-hitting indictments of Japanese society were prevalent. None the less, they all share the same assumptions based on the discourse of Japaneseness.

Thus, the discourse of Japaneseness equates nation and ethnicity with the state, effacing class and other divisions as well as ignoring the past. It pits Japanese against foreign workers and provides a powerful basis for regarding Japan as a monoethnic society.

Nihonjinron *and the discourse of Japaneseness*

The discourse of Japaneseness was not, of course, spontaneously generated against the new foreign workers. When their initial influx raised the question of who they are, it also generated the question of who Japanese are and what kind of society Japan is. There was a plethora of ready-made answers to Japanese identity in the extensive writings on Japanese national character or theories of Japanese and Japanese culture (*Nihonjinron* or *Nihon bunkaron*).

All major nation-states feature writings on national identity. Whether as a state ideology to promote national integration or as a form of civil religion, there are interminable and inconclusive discussions on what it means to be a member of a particular nation-state, how it differs from other nation-states and so on.

Nationalist historical writing traces a nation-state's birth and growth, while nationalist social sciences establish the nature and characteristics of a nation and its inhabitants. Hence, books on *The Germans* or *The French* are perennial best-sellers and inform popular discussions on Germany and Germans or France and the French.

Thus, *Nihonjinron*, or writings about the nature of Japanese people, culture, and society, is merely a Japanese variant of an almost universal discourse of modern nation-states. Friedrich Nietzsche once wryly observed that what makes Germans unique is that they are obsessed by the question of Germanness. Without acknowledging its uniqueness, it is possible to claim the same about contemporary Japanese. Many Japanese eagerly purchase and peruse numerous *Nihonjinron* books and readily discuss them at offices and bars. Its popularity is such that one book even offers a way to quit being Japanese (Sugimoto 1990: 25). According to Nomura Sōgō Kenkyūsho's 1979 bibliography, about 700 books on *Nihonjinron* appeared between 1946 and 1978 (Aoki 1990: 24), and many more have appeared since then. Hence, Harumi Befu (1990: 54–67) calls *Nihonjinron* a mass consumption commodity, while Peter Dale (1986: 14) observes that it represents the commercialized expression of Japanese nationalism. *Nihonjinron*, whatever its intellectual merit, is plainly good business as many books on what it means to be Japanese become bestsellers in Japan.

There are widely divergent perspectives on *Nihonjinron*. Critics say that it functions as a conservative ideology by encouraging cultural or chauvinistic nationalism (Sugimoto and Mouer 1982, Dale 1986, Befu 1990). For others, however, it is a matter of serious scholarship. At one conference, a major theorist of *Nihonjinron* spoke scathingly of ideological critics, claiming that they do to *Nihonjinron* writings what they claim *Nihonjinron* writers do to Japanese. Brian Moeran (1989: 183–4) suggests that *Nihonjinron* is "a means whereby it can practise on the West precisely the kind of orientalism from which it has had to suffer, and to some extent still suffers, at the hands of Westerners." In other words, the Japanese discourse on Japaneseness is a form of Occidentalism, or rendering the West as the other (Aoki 1990: 149–50).

The diversity of perspectives is in part a reflection of the changing historical production. If the early *Nihonjinron* writings expressed the prevailing sense of Japanese inferiority *vis-à-vis* the West, more recent writings claimed a sense of superiority. Indeed, there is no reason to doubt that *Nihonjinron* both became more popular after the rapid economic growth of the 1960s (Hamaguchi 1982: 4–5), and that their contents became much more positive about Japanese people and culture (Aoki 1990: 82). It is not surprising that Ezra Vogel's (1979) paean to the Japanese miracle, with its propitious title of *Japan as Number One*, should have become one of the all-time best-selling non-fiction books in Japan (Aoki 1990: 123).

Furthermore, there is no uniformity of quality or of content in the Japanese writings on themselves. The most common narrative pattern is to stress one or another feature of Japanese national character or collective psychology, such as curiosity (Tsurumi 1982), relational orientation (Hamaguchi 1982), collectivism (Hamaguchi and Kumon 1982) or self-uncertainty (Minami 1983). The central conclusion and the fundamental assumption of all *Nihonjinron* writings are that

Japanese people and culture are different, even unique. The basis of *Nihonjinron* is the prominence of the category of Japaneseness; the only taboo is that Japanese are not just like other people.

Most assertions of Japanese difference or uniqueness are empirically false or unverifiable. At times they merely demonstrate the authors' ignorance and prejudice. Mori Mikisaburō (1971: 11) confesses that he thought that only Japanese called leprosy as Hansen's Disease. In 1993, I was shocked by a distinguished Japanese sociologist's assertion that only Japanese criminals cover their face because Japan has a unique culture of shame. When I pointed out that South Korean criminals act in a similar fashion, he replied that, somehow, they must be different. Such a patently non-logical or non-empirical assertion is, however, often taken as yet another characteristic of Japaneseness. According to Yamamoto Shichihei, the proponent of Japanese religion (*Nihonkyō*), Japanese place feeling over logic (Yamamoto and Komuro 1981: 1).

What are claimed to be different or unique characteristics of Japanese are, in fact, frequently shared by other East Asian, if not virtually all, cultures. Aida Yūji (1972: 17) regards a particular way of carrying a child unique to Japan until he realizes that many Chinese do the same thing. *Amae* (dependence) is an idea made popular by the Japanese psychoanalyst Doi Takeo (1973). Although widely believed to be unique to Japan, there is a similar phenomenon in South Korea. It is often asserted that Japanese care deeply about what other peoples think of Japan (Aoki 1990: 114). However, James Bowman (1992: 27) writes: "Americans have always been, more than the people of most nations, solicitous of the opinions of foreigners about their country." Others say that Japanese are notorious for apologizing constantly. Paul Barker (1996: 36) notes in this regard: "The English air is alive with the sound of 'Sorry!' London is the only capital city where the person you bump into apologizes."

If many descriptions of Japanese difference or uniqueness are problematic, then the same can be said for their cause. A commonly given explanation for Japanese difference is that Japan experienced nearly three centuries of seclusion (*sakoku*) during the Tokugawa period. Hence, the Japanese are "insular": "History and geographic isolation have been combined with this racial unity to fuel a strong sense of national identity" (Buckley 1990: 82). In fact, *sakoku* implied the state monopoly of trade and foreign relations, not complete seclusion of society from foreign influences. As Yamaguchi Keizō (1993: 41–7) argues, virtually all East Asian states featured state monopoly of trade and the Tokugawa state had extensive contact with other sovereign states. In addition, Tokugawa-era intellectuals had extensive knowledge of the world beyond the Japan, and eagerly sought Chinese and, later, Western knowledge. The very idea of *sakoku* only became popular after the Meiji Restoration to distinguish the premodern period from the modern period of enlightenment and civilization (Arano 1988: ii). Furthermore, the fact of being surrounded by ocean actually encouraged intercultural contact before the Meiji era; water transportation is, in fact, much more useful than land transportation in the rugged terrain that characterizes much of Japan.

In spite of the manifest limitations of *Nihonjinron* writings, many of the books are eagerly read by Japanese seeking knowledge of themselves and their culture. Occasionally, I found that people referred to one or another *Nihonjinron* book to substantiate her or his claim about one or another aspect of Japanese history or culture. Not surprisingly, Ruth Benedict's (1947) *The Chrysanthemum and the Sword* appeared to be something of a sentimental favorite, although people who referred to it had clearly not read the book carefully. Most were content to rehash the proposition about Japan being a culture of shame. Japanese people are, in other words, reflexive, and Western academic discourse about Japan has had an impact on Japanese view of themselves. This is, of course, not unique to Japanese people. "Apocryphal stories abound in professional folklore about the American Indian informant who, in response to the ethnographer's question, consults the work of Alfred Kroeber, or the African villager in the same situation who reaches for his copy of Meyer Fortes" (Marcus and Fischer 1986: 36).

I have argued that the new foreign workers in Japan constitute a group diametrically opposite to the dominant Japanese image of themselves. Against an affluent, universal middle-class society stands the impoverished Third World, while Japanese economic and cultural superiority is in marked contrast to the ori- originating countries of the foreign workers. Finally, a diverse range of nationalities and ethnicities are entering a pristine and pure society which is eth-. nically homogeneous. The particular social vision of Japan, as articulated in the discourse of Japaneseness, is ironically shared by progressive critics as well as by the new foreign workers themselves. *Nihonjinron* provides a ready-made repository of propositions about Japanese society.

References

Aida, Y. (1972) *Nihonjin no Ishikikōzō: Fūdo, Rekishi, Shakai*, Tokyo: Kodansha.

Allen, M. (1994) *Undermining the Japanese Miracle: Work and Conflict in a Coalmining Community*, Cambridge: Cambridge University Press.

Aoki, T. (1990) *"Nihon Bunkaron" no Henyō: Sengo Nihon no Bunka to Aidentitî*, Tokyo: Chūō Kōronsha.

Arano, Y. (1988) *Kinsei Nihon to Higashi Ajia*, Tokyo: Daigaku Shuppankai.

Barker, P. (1996) "England, Whose England?" *Times Literary Supplement* (12 July): 36.

Befu, H. (1990) *Ideorogî to Shite no Nihon Bunkaron*, expanded edition, Tokyo: Shisō no Kagakusha.

Benedict, R. F. (1947) *The Chrysanthemum and the Sword*, Boston: Houghton Mifflin.

Bernstein, G. (1983) *Haruko's World,* Stanford, Calif.: Stanford University Press.

Bowman, J. (1992) "Through Alien Eyes," *Times Literary Supplement* (12 June): 27.

Brinton, M. C. (1993) *Women and the Economic Miracle: Gender and Work in Postwar Japan*, Berkeley: University of California Press.

Buckley, R. (1990) *Japan Today*, 2nd edn, Cambridge: Cambridge University Press.

Buruma, I. (1992) "Afterword," in R. Ventura (ed.), *Underground in Japan*, London: Cape: 185–93.

Conze, W. and Kocka, J. (1985) "Einleitung," in W. Conze and J. Kocka (eds) *Bildungsbürgertum im 19. Jahrhundert, Vol.1: Bildungssytem und Professionalisierung in internationalen Vergleichen*, Stuttgart: Klett-Cotta: 9–26.

Dale, P. N. (1986) *The Myth of Japanese Uniqueness*, New York: St. Martin's.

Ehara, T. (1984) *Gendai Kōtō Kyōiku no Kōzō*, Tokyo: Tokyo Daigaku Shuppankai.

Fowler, E. (1996) *San'ya Blues: Laboring Life in Contemporary Tokyo*, Ithaca, N.Y.: Cornell University Press.

Fried, K. and Garvey, H. (1997) "Word for Word: What Writers Are Reading," *Village Voice* (7 January): 40–4.

Fukuzawa, Y. (1931) *Bunmeiron no gairyaku*, Tokyo: Iwanami Shoten.

Greenbie, B. B. (1988) *Space and Spirit in Modern Japan*, New Haven, Conn.: Yale University Press.

Hamaguchi, E. (1982) *Kanjinshugi no Shakai Nihon*, Tokyo: Tōyō Keizai Shinpōsha.

Hamaguchi, E. and Kumon, S. (eds) (1982) *Nihonteki Shūdanshugi: Sono Shinka o Tou*, Tokyo: Yūhikaku.

Honda, K. (1993) *Ainu Minzoku*, Tokyo: Asahi Shinbunsha.

Ike, S. (1995) *"Jirei 1: Burajiru de no Okinawakei e no Sabetsu,"* in M. Watanabe (ed.) *Kyōdō Kenkyū Dekasegi Nikkei Burajirujin, ge: Shiryōhen*, Tokyo: Akashi Shoten: 199–204.

Ishida, H. (1993) *Social Mobility in Contemporary Japan*, Stanford, Calif.: Stanford University Press.

—— (1998) "Educational Credentials and Labour-Market Entry Outcomes in Japan," in Y. Shavit and W. Müller (eds) *From School to Work: A Comparative Study of Educational Qualifications and Occupational Destinations*, Oxford: Clarendon Press: 287–309.

Iwanami Shoten Henshūbu (ed.) (1991) *Sinpojiumu Atarashii Sekai Chitsujo to Ajia*, Tokyo: Iwanami Shoten.

Iwao, S. (1993) *The Japanese Woman: Traditional Image and Changing Reality*, New York: Free Press.

Katase, K. and Tomoeda, T. (1990) *"Kachi Ishiki,"* in J. Hara (ed.) *Gendai Nihon no Kaisō Kōzō 2: Kaisō Ishiki no Dōtai*, Tokyo: Tokyo Daigaku Shuppankai: 125–47.

Kawamura, M. (1994) *Umi o watatta Nihongo*, Tokyo: Seidosha.

Kikuchi, K. (1992) *"Gaikokujin Rōdōsha Okuridashikoku no Shakaiteki Mekanizumu – Firipin no Baai"* in I. Toshio and K. Takamichi (eds) *Gaikokujin Rōdōsharon: Genjō Kara Riron e*, Tokyo: Kōbundō: 169–201.

Koizumi, S. (1966) *Fukuzawa Yukichi*, Tokyo: Iwanami Shoten.

Kumazawa, M. (1981) *Nihon no Rōdōshazō*, Tokyo: Chikuma Shobō.

Lebra, J. (1978) "Conclusion," In J. Lebra, J. Paulson, and E. Powers (eds) *Women in Changing Japan*, Stanford, Calif.: Stanford University Press: 297–304.

Lebra, T. S. (1993) *Above the Clouds: Status Culture of the Modern Japanese Nobility*, Berkeley: University of California Press.

McNeill, W. H. (1989) *Arnold J. Toynbee: A Life*, New York: Oxford University Press.

Mainichi Shinbun Tokyo Honsha Shakaibu (ed.) (1990) *Jipangu: Nihon o Mezasu Gaikokujin Rōdōsha*, revised edn, Tokyo: Mainichi Shinbunsha.

Mamada, T. (1990) "Kaisō Kizoku Ishiki," in J. Hara (ed.) *Gendai Nihon no Kaisō Kōzō 2: Kaisō Ishiki no Dōtai*, Tokyo: Tokyo Daigaku Shuppankai: 23–45.

Manabe, S. (1990) *Kokusaika no Ishiki Kakumei: Shinjidai e no Pasupōto*, Kyoto: Hōritsu Bunkasha.

Marcus, G. E. and Fischer, M. J. (1986) *Anthropology as Cultural Critique: An Experimental Movement in the Human Sciences*, Chicago: University of Chicago Press.

Maruyama, K. (1984) *Bunka no Fetishizumu*, Tokyo: Keisō Shobō.

Matsuyama, Y. (1985) *Kokusai Taiwa no Jidai*, Tokyo: Asahi Shinbunsha.

Minami, H. (1983) *Nihonteki jiga*, Tokyo: Iwanami Shoten.

Minoshima, H. (1993) "Yomikata Oshiete," *AERA* (3 August): 44–5.

Misumi, K. (1990) *"Kaikyū Kizoku Ishiki,"* in J. Hara (ed.) *Gendai Nihon no Kaisō Kōzō*

2: *Kaisō Ishiki no Dōtai*, Tokyo: Tokyo Daigaku Shuppankai: 71–95.

Moeran, B. (1989) *Language and Popular Culture in Japan*, Manchester: Manchester University Press.

Mori, M. (1971) *"Na" to "Haji no Bunka"*, Tokyo: Kōdansha.

Motoyama, Y. (1991) *Yutakana Kuni, Mazushii Kuni*, Tokyo: Iwanami Shoten.

Murakami, H. and Mizumaru, A. (1986) *Murukami Asahidō no Gyakushū*, Tokyo: Asahi Shinbusha.

Murakami, Y. (1984) *Shinchūkan Taishū no Jidai – Sengo Nihon no Kaibōgaku*, Tokyo: Chūō Kōronsha.

Nakane, C. (1970) *Japanese Society*, Berkeley: University of California Press.

Naoi, M. (1979) *"Kaisō Ishiki to Kaikyū Ishiki,"* in K. Tominaga (ed.) *Nihon no Kaisō Kōzō*, Tokyo: Tokyo Daigaku Shuppankai: 365–88.

Neff, R. (1992) "Japan Takes a Good, Hard Look at Itself," *Business Week* (17 Feb.): 32–4.

Nitobe, I. (1984) *Seiyō no Jijō to Shisō*, Tokyo: Kōdansha.

Ōhashi, R. (1971) *Nihon no Kaikyū Kōsei*, Tokyo: Iwanami Shoten.

Okabe, K. (1991) *Taminzoku Shakai no Tōrai*, Tokyo: Ochanomizu Shobō.

Ōoka, M. (1985) *Okakura Tenshin*, Tokyo: Asahi Shuppansha.

Orwell, G. (1937) *The Road to Wigan Pier*, New York: Harcourt Brace Jovanovich.

Osawa, M. (1993) *Kigyō Chūshin Shakai o Koete*, Tokyo: Jiji Tsūshinsha.

Passin, H. (1982) *Society and Education in Japan*, Tokyo: Kōdansha International.

Petkanas, C. (1993) "It's Not Easy Behaving Well in France, Critics Say," *International Herald Tribune* (31 August): 1.

Pharr, S. J. (1981) *Political Women in Japan: The Search for a Place in Political Life*, Berkeley: University of California Press.

Rohlen, T. P. (1983) *Japan's High Schools*, Berkeley: University of California Press.

Sagimoto, Y. and Mover, R. (1982) *Nihon wa "Nihonteki" ka: Tokushuron o Koe Tagentaki Bunaseki e*, Tokyo: Tōyō Kaiyai Shinpōsha.

Sakurai, T. (1984) *"Kindai" no Imi – Seido to Shite no Gakkō, Kōjō*, Tokyo: Nihon Hōsō Shuppan Kyōkai.

Silberman, B. S. (1964) *Ministers of Modernization: Elite Mobility in the Meiji Restoration, 1868–1973*, Tucson: University of Arizona Press.

Smith, H. W. (1995) *The Myth of Japanese Homogeneity: Social-Ecological Diversity in Education and Socialization*, Commack, N.Y.: Nova Science.

Spilerman, S. and Ishida, H. (1996) "Stratification and Attainment in a Large Japanese Firm," in A. C. Kerckhoff (ed.) *Generating Social Stratification: Toward a New Research Agenda*, Boulder, Colorado: WestviewPress: 317–42.

Steven, R. (1983) *Classes in Contemporary Japan*, Cambridge: Cambridge University Press.

Sugimoto, Y. (1990) *Nihonjin o Yameru Hōhō*, Tokyo: Hon no Ki.

Suzuki, T. (1990) *Nihongo to Gaikokugo*, Tokyo: Iwanami Shoten.

Takeuchi, Y. (1995) *Nihon no Meritokurashî: Kōzō to Shinsei*, Tokyo: Tokyo Daigaku Shuppankai.

Tanaka, H. (1991) *Zainichi Gaikokujin: Hō no Kabe, Kokoro no Mizo*, Tokyo: Iwanami Shoten.

Thornton, E. (1995) "French Links," *Far Eastern Economic Review* (23 March): 70.

Torii, T. (1977) *Yokohama Yamate*, Tokyo: Sōshisha.

Tou, N. (1992) *"Nihon ni Okeru 'Gaikokujin Rōdōsha' Rongi no Shomondai,"* in H. Momose and M. Ogura (eds) *Gendai Kokka to Imin Rōdōsha*, Tokyo: Yūshindō: 11–37.

Toynbee, A. (1976) "Civilization on Trial," in A. Toynbee, *Civilization on Trial and the World and the West*, New York: North American Library: 9–229.

Tsurumi, Y. (1982) *Ajia wa Naze Mazushii no ka*, Tokyo: Asahi Shinbunsha.

Tsutsui, K. (1995) *Nihongata Kyōyō" no Unmei: Rekishishakaigakuteki Kōsatsu*, Tokyo: Iwanami Shoten.

Uemura, H. (1992) *Senjū Minzoku: "Koronbusu" to Tatakau Hitobito no Rekishi to Genzai*, Tokyo: Kaihō Shuppansha.

Ventura, R. (1992) *Underground in Japan*, London: Jonathan Cape.

Vogel, E. F. (1971) *Japan's New Middle Class: The Salary Man and His Family in a Tokyo Suburb*, second edn, Berkeley: University of California Press.

Waki, K. and Ashizu, T. (1984) *Furutovengurā*, Tokyo: Iwanami Shoten.

Yamaguchi, K. (1993) *Sakoku to Kaikoku,* Tokyo: Iwanami Shoten.

Yamamoto, A. (1986) *Sengo Fūzokushi*, Osaka: Osaka Shoseki.

Yasuhara, K. (1993) *"Amerika no Okama ni Narisagatta Nihonjin," Tosho Shinbun* (4 September): 3.

Yoshino, K. (1992) *Cultural Nationalism in Contemporary Japan: A Sociological Enquiry*, London: Routledge.

5 The singularities of international migration of women to Japan

Past, present and future

Mike Douglass

The social construction of gender and migration to Japan

Gender is a socially constructed concept. The roles that women and men play in society, the different values and rewards for their actions – even when these actions are the same – and the types of mobility each enjoys are products of cultural institutions and social divisions of power as well as the product of nature (Guest 1993). Gender differences in migration are also the outcomes of socio-cultural relations. Many countries have poor women, for example, but not all offer the option for these women to migrate from village to city or overseas where income prospects are perceived to be higher (Sassen 1994). To do so requires a number of other conditions, including at least some degree of cultural acceptance, recruitment networks and information channels, and, for international migration in contemporary times, often the involvement of the state as a key agent. As such, a genuine historical perspective on gender and international migration rests on the inclusion of localized socio-cultural and political factors – including the national and the local state – into the framework of analysis.

Conventional models of migration have, however, tended to look for universal patterns and general theories rather than reveal more localized processes and explanations that account for the great variations in migration patterns. While, for example, neoclassical economists assume that patterns of migration are principally reflections of rational individual economic responses to income differences over space, and Marxist political economists propose that structural conditions in the world economy determine flows of migration, both views fail to account for the very high variations in patterns of male and female migration from country to country and across national boundaries (Lycklama á Nijeholt 1992). Thus, in recognizing that migration streams are reflections of both structural conditions in the world economy and micro-economic decisions of would-be migrants, it is equally important to understand that migration is also a function of the ways in which different societies construct gender roles that divide movers from stayers and determine which occupations female and male migrants are most likely to enter.

In this regard, the recent worldwide trend toward increases in female migration represents not only an inclusion of women in a wider range of occupational categories but, in most cases, it is reversing traditional male-female relations, with women taking on the roles of international migrant and household breadwinner. In the specific case of Japan, however, both the emigration of Japanese women in the first half of this century and the immigration of Asian women to Japan in the latter half represent anomalies in international patterns of female migration. Unlike most other countries, women were the vanguard of Japan's imperialist expansion into Asia from the Meiji era to the Second World War and also comprised the majority of migrants from Asia to Japan in the period 1945 to the late 1980s.

Japan appears to be the only country in the world for which the vast majority of women have been legally and illegally recruited for a single purpose: sexual services. Even in the late 1980s as the structure of employment in Japan radically changed and "simple" (unskilled) labor began to exponentially increase in the migration streams to Japan, foreign women were not significantly included in the variety of occupations – domestic helpers, nurses, custodial and related service workers – common to migrants entering Europe, the US and other East and South-East Asian countries but, instead, continued to increase in numbers as hostesses, erotic dancers and prostitutes. In contrast, legal and illegal male immigrants soon equaled women in number and began to occupy a number of arduous jobs in domestic-market serving and export-manufacturing occupations.

The purpose of this chapter is to explore Japan's unique position with regard to international female migration. It presents the view that a number of specific characteristics of Japanese society and its economy have limited the scope of all migration to Japan, including the migration of women. From the late 1980s, these same characteristics continued to prevail for women and to a lesser extent men. In the future, however, a number of trends in Japan suggest that the immigration of women could both increase and diversify but much will depend upon the level of critical awareness and social mobilization to confront issues of gender, class and race in Japan.

The development of the international sex industry in Japan

The international trade in women for what has been too euphemistically called "entertainment" has been a feature of Japan's internationalization since the early Meiji period beginning in 1868.[1] By the time of Japan's industrial revolution in the 1880s, poor rural families, either knowingly or unwittingly, were already selling their daughters to agents who transported these "*karayuki-san*" to Japanese-run brothels throughout South-East and East Asia and even to the United States (Kaplan and Dubro 1987).[2]

The sending of prostitutes and the establishment of brothels in Asia were more than minor activities. They grew to involve tens of thousands of women and were explicitly linked to the success of Japanese imperialism.[3] Newspaper editorials around the turn of the century argued that Japan's two centuries of self-imposed isolation from the outside world had left it with little else to call on to establish an international commercial sphere for the country. In a para-doxical and convoluted manner, prostitution promoted Japan's emergence as a great world power. Implicitly, the greater the number of brothels that appeared, the higher the index of Japan's successful global expansion. Leading the way were the "adventurous" women of Kyūshū, who were reported to out-number other Japanese women sent to other parts of Asia as prostitutes. By the turn of the century:

Japan had become an important supplier of prostitutes to other areas of Asia, particularly Southeast Asia with Singapore as a focal point. Public brothels had not existed in Korea until the Japanese introduced them. The Japanese made Dairen a flourishing center for public brothels. One Japanese newspaper commented, 'The management of Manchuria starts with the establishment of dens of iniquity.' It is estimated that 30,000 prostitutes were brought into Manchuria by the Japanese. By the early twentieth century, Japanese brothels could be found in most areas of Asia including Siberia, Korea, China, Manchuria, Hong Kong, Singapore, Borneo, Cambodia, Vietnam, Thailand, Malaya, and the Philippines. Hawaii and California were also targeted.

(Hane 1982: 219)

The sending of women abroad for prostitution continued into the Second World War when as many as 200,000 "comfort women" from Korea, Indonesia, the Netherlands, China, Taiwan, Malaysia and the Philippines were forced into sexual slavery with Japanese government complicity to service the Japanese army as Japanese imperialism spread throughout East and South-East Asia.

In the early post-Second World War years, Japanese operators once again began to smuggle Japanese women abroad in large numbers for prostitution (Ohshima and Francis 1989). As Japanese women became less available for this activity abroad, another variation of the international trade in sexual services in Japan appeared during the 1960s in the form of organized sex tours for Japanese men to such destinations as the Philippines, Korea, Taiwan and Thailand. These were often paralleled by another uniquely Japanese practice that still continues: the establishment of exclusive hostess clubs in major cities in Asia that admit only Japanese men as customers. The economic success of these operations led to the active recruitment of Asian women to Japan. In recognition that this represented a reversal of past practices of sending Japanese *karayuki* to brothels abroad, the women coming to Japan were given the title of *Japayuki* (coming to Japan) to provide sexual services to Japanese men in Japan. Taking 1979 as "*Japayuki* Year Zero" (Komai 1995: 72), there were an estimated 100,000–300,000 foreign women engaged in the sex trade in all but one prefecture in Japan by the 1990s.[4]

The movement of Asian women to Japan has become highly structured and complex as agents, brokers, prostitution organizers and entertainment establishments in Japanese cities have created extensive networks of recruitment and distribution of foreign women in Japan. By the 1990s, a potential customer had only to call one of the scores of telephone numbers posted nightly in public telephones to be linked up with the estimated $5 billion profits annually made in the sex industry in Japan: an amount equal to the entire defense budget of the nation (Matsuda 1993: 2). The extent of the sex industry and its foreign linkages is reflected in data showing that, even today, no other female immigration stream in Japan has come close to matching it.

What is clear from a historical perspective is that Japan's experience in recruiting women into the sex industry did not suddenly appear in the 1970s with the arrival of Asian women but internationally stretches back more than a century and much longer as a purely domestic preoccupation (Seigle 1993, Hane 1982). Recognizing that this long history exists poses serious challenges to contemporary views in Japan that explain away the massive recruitment of Asian women into the sex industry as a "foreigner" problem largely generated by forces external to Japan. It suggests, rather, that the origins of this immigration lie much deeper in Japanese society and economy.

Explanations for Japan's (inter)national trade in women

All of the almost unbroken history of female migration for sex-related services from and to Japan raises the question of why Japan should occupy such an ignoble position in the world of female migration. Given the striking singularities, it is surprising that this question seems to be rarely raised in Japan. Perhaps this is because the industry itself is veiled as entertainment and is not considered,to be a subject for public discussion. Like the plight of the *Burakumin* and other minorities, it is also possible that many Japanese are simply kept unaware of the scale and the conditions in which many foreign women are kept in contemporary Japan (Lie ch. 4, Murphy-Shigematsu ch. 9).

Although the official classification of visas related to the sex industry work is entertainment, Matsuda (1993: 3) estimates that over 60 percent of foreign women in this category in Tokyo are forced into prostitution by establishment owners. Given the very large scale of this activity, these proportions suggests that the question of why the topic remains concealed is not sufficiently answered by its status as a taboo subject for polite discussion. The large numbers of women involved in the sex industry in Japan raises larger questions about the ways in which it is understood and explained away. A perusal of this subject reveals at least six types of perspectives that prevent a critical awareness of its exploitative nature in Japan:

- Economic explanations that suggest that poverty in the sending countries (historically from Japan as well) "causes" prostitution.
- Entering the sex industry is a matter of a woman's free choice, women enter the trade to earn enormous amounts of money.
- Cultural explanations that accept the selling of sexual services as a necessary part of Japanese society and its particular form of patriarchy.
- Class perspectives that see migrants in the sex industry as being inferior.
- Racism that places immigrants into the category of "other" people not worthy of attention or support.
- The *yakuza* who are portrayed as autonomously organizing the profession.

The obscure economics of international female migration

As with many aspects of the economic lives of women and "women's work," the movement of women across national borders is systematically disregarded in economic studies of migration. Typical explanations for this exclusion include the view that a high proportion of women who move internationally are refugees whose migration is not "economic" in its origins or cannot be explained by conventional "income-gap" formulations of migration (Salt 1993, Castles and Miller 1993). A variation of this is that female migration is "secondary," that is, following with spouse or family, and thus passively mirrors rather than leads migration (Fawcett *et al.* 1984).

Lycklama á Nijeholt (1992), pointing to the absence of studies on the international migration of women for domestic work, suggests that a more central reason is the obsessive emphasis given by economists and economic demographers to the manufacturing sector and, in the past, the "guest workers" phenomenon that filled European cities with migrants from former colonies and other low-income countries. Since the emergence of a new international division of labor in the late 1960s, the pattern of labor chasing capital to high-income industrialized countries has experienced virtual wholesale relocation to low-income countries. In other words, labor-intensive light manufacturing has chased women to developing countries. With women comprising 80 percent or more of employees in foreign-invested firms in such key industries as textiles and electronics in Asia, migration to countries such as Japan for such work is thus not thought to be a significant element of labor demand.

While generally accurate, this view fails to account for the continuing use of low-wage female labor in light assembly work in small- and medium-sized enterprises in Japan that, in the future, could become a source of female immigration as well. Whether such a possibility will be realized is, however, a separate question from why the ever-increasing numbers of women who migrate for service occupations are not considered worthy of economic study or, as many activists in Japan have indicated, policy concern. Some writers point directly toward patriarchy in Japan's academia as the reason why the international recruitment of women for all types of services are seen as "non-economic" or otherwise not of scholarly importance (Yamanaka 1993).

Another particular reason in the case of migration for sexual services to Japan is that visas for entertainers coming to Japan are given only for short-term stays. Conventional notions of migration used by economists look only at longer-term or permanent migration streams, even though temporary migration is being increasingly recognized by demographers as an emerging dominant form of international movement of people for work (Kritz and Zlotnik 1992).[5]

An equally likely explanation is that migration for sexual services puts mainstream economists' assumptions about migration and the buying and selling of labor power in an extremely awkward light. Neoclassical economic formulations of labor migration have as a central tenet the proposition that, in addition to differences in income earning potential between sending and receiving countries, international migration responds to gaps between domestic supply and demand for labor. But it looks closely at neither the specific ways in which the supply of women as sex workers is created nor at what social forces expand the demand for sexual services – even during Japan's economic recession in the 1990s when "consumption" has generally stagnated (Matsuda 1993). On the supply side, the implicit thesis of many studies that poverty causes prostitution cannot be sustained. Many societies with extreme poverty and deprivation do not show a high level of export of women for the sex trade. Moreover, even assuming unlimited supplies of poor women for this trade, close discussion of demand raises questions not only of patriarchy but also of culture, class and racism that have been largely ignored.[6]

Whatever the reason, the degree to which the migration of women to Japan is ignored in the international migration literature is striking.[7] The failure to confront issues associated with the international recruitment and subsequent exploitation of women has deeper implications than just for migration studies alone. First and foremost, to peel away the layers that mask this subject requires concrete historical analysis that includes not only economics but also the socio-cultural institutions and political structures that have served to sustain the bases for recruiting women for sexual services and, at the same time, obscure its connection to elements of Japanese society.

Human agency: struggles and choice

Another explanation of the large presence of foreign women in the sex industry – as well as the sending of Japanese women to brothels abroad in earlier times – that obviates the need, for some people, to look into society or culture for a cause, is that women enter into this occupation of their own free will and often earn extra-ordinary amounts of money. On one extreme, this view reverses the gender of victim, with men being the subject of the cunning of women rather than women being forced into offering sexual services by men. On the other hand, some argue that viewing women as essentially being helplessly victimized by a larger system dominated by men is fundamentally flawed in that it does not allow for any self-empowerment or exercise of women's own autonomy. In either case, though from fundamentally different points of view, the sex industry is portrayed as an activity that is intentionally entered into by women for their own economic gain.

Such a view was put forth in Japan as early as the Meiji period when Japanese-run brothels were being established abroad. Meiji newspaper reports stated that the women sent to South-East Asia were voluntary "stowaways" in search of easy money. A female reporter wrote in 1916 about the *karayuki-san* from Kyūshū that, "rather than eat yam and do hard physical work, they prefer this life because they can eat good food, wear soft kimonos, and make money while leading a sedate life" (Hane 1982: 208). She further claimed that, upon returning to Kyūshū, the women were treated with great respect by everyone.

A contemporary view presented by Watanabe (1995) puts forth a feminist-Marxist argument that the migration of foreign women to Japan, including those entering the sex industry, is tightly integrated into the struggle of Japanese women against the productive and reproductive roles assigned to them in Japan's capitalist society. Their refusal to bear children, which is leading to Japan's future negative popu-lation growth rate, is part of their own self-empowerment. Partly in response to this, but also as part of their own struggles in their own societies and economies, women migrate to Japan to fill niches left by Japanese women, which presumably includes the phenomenon of marrying Japanese farmers who cannot find Japanese women.

> The increased flow has been brought about by women's struggles on both sides, i.e., that of Japanese women's and that of migrant women's, even though there may exist factors mobilizing those women such as state policies to import/export female labor power and the expansion of organized crime syn-dicates all over Asia and the Pacific
>
> (Watanabe 1995: 1)

The possibility that women (and men) enter into the sex trade of their own free will cannot be dismissed. Nor can such arguments be dismissed concerning foreign workers coming into the dirty, dangerous and difficult occupations in Japan (Douglass and Roberts ch. 1). Nevertheless, there are two further considerations about the sex industry being a matter of choice. First, as Watanabe recognizes, the autonomy being exercised is occurring in particular structural and cultural settings that both open the avenues to work in the sex industry and limit routes to alternative occupations. In the case of Japan, the question still remains why, unlike almost any other society, foreign women have been brought to this society almost exclusively for this purpose and almost no other. The same question needs to be asked of the sending societies that specialize in this form of human trafficking.

There is also considerable evidence that significant numbers of women do not enter the sex trade voluntarily or, if they do, it is often under the belief that it will not turn out to be so dehumanizing. In Japan in the past parents were compelled to sell their daughters into sexual servitude. The "comfort women" serving the Japanese army in the Second World War were forced into sexual slavery. In recent years, many women from Asian countries have been brought into the sex industry in Japan under false pretenses and, once in Japan, are at least in some cases kept in slave-like conditions. A 1997 survey of Filipinas coming to Japan concludes that the alarming rate of increase in the trafficking of women is accomplished by luring women with offers of well paid non-sex related jobs and that:

> Once firmly trapped within an illegal migration environment in the receiving country, they are vulnerable to many forms of abuse ranging in the extreme to bonded labour and forced prostitution. . . In most cases, the recruiter or agent provides all necessary documents and cash outlay; consequently, the process of being trafficked to Japan appears to women to be free from obstacles, and most of them are unaware of the degree to which they might have to be involved in illicit activity.
>
> (IOM 1997: 1)

Of the women interviewed, only about one-tenth said that they had been told that they had to work as prostitutes, while four-fifths stated that they had been entrapped into doing so, and even the ones who had an idea that they would be involved in some form of sex-related activity "were unprepared for the total control that the employers would wield over their daily lives and activities" (IOM 1997: 1). A principal means of exerting total control is to confiscate passports which severely limits the movement of women within Japan. In the cases of Filipinas interviewed who were forced to engage in prostitution:

> Most of the women were provided with a room without windows, had no right to leave their accommodation unescorted and the employers kept at least 75 percent of their income. Almost half of the women complained of a lack of food and heating facilities. Nearly 50 percent were victims of physical and psychological abuse. . . . These oppressive working conditions forced many to attempt escape; a few succeed with the help of NGOs, friends and the Philippine Embassy.
>
> (IOM 1997: 1)

Of these Filipinas who had returned to the Philippines, one-third of those surveyed had done so because they had been dismissed from their jobs due to pregnancy. Three-quarters suffered from health problems, including sexually transmitted diseases. In addition, a new trend is emerging between Japan and the Philippines: due to such factors as the threat of HIV/AIDS, the demand for younger prostitutes is increasing and more and more girls are being abducted, bought, sold and trafficked across borders to serve as prostitutes.

What is clear from the evidence is that the demand for sexual services from women appears to be far greater than the supply of willing women. This has generated a vast industry of recruiters and enforcers and it is only in this context that any exercise of choice on the part of women can be considered. While struggles against oppression and poverty certainly play a role in constructing incentives for women to become sex workers, they are insufficient explanations why women come to Japan in so many numbers just for this purpose.

Japanese culture and patriarchy

Given the lack of understanding of gender relations, government policy on the entrance of workers in Japan seems to be unmistakably clear:

> The government's policies on the acceptance of foreign workers decided by the Cabinet in July 1992 [is that] it will not allow the entry of unskilled workers, in view of the wide-ranging long-term impact that would be caused by their entry, as well as the difficulty social systems will have in responding to their acceptance.
>
> (MOFA 1998: 1)

This statement is not only extraordinary in terms of all of the underlying attitudes about the socially undesirable nature of having large numbers of foreign workers residing in Japan, which is a subject taken up by several authors in this book (Lie, Murphy-Shigematsu, Pollack), but also because over the past hundred years Japan has itself sent millions of its people as workers to permanently settle in other societies. Equally revealing is the fact that more than 100,000 women are legally allowed to enter Japan as sex workers every year but are not seen as either being workers as such or a concern to the morals and ethics of Japanese culture. The fact that the great majority of women coming into Japan under entertainment visas are actually working as hostesses or prostitutes is well-known in Japan, and must certainly be well-known to the government as well. It thus appears that the term worker implies the entrance of unskilled male workers who presumably represent the source of a cultural and moral threat to Japanese society, while women entering Japan's sex industry from the same countries are somehow acceptable and non-threatening to the established order.

One reason for this different attitude toward women and men may lie in a reportedly prevalent attitude in Japan that the selling of women for sexual purposes is somehow part of human nature, or more specifically, the nature of men. Prominent educators in Japan at the turn of the century argued, for example, that it was necessary for prostitutes to accompany Japanese men in the early stages of Japanese expansion abroad in order to "console the men until Japanese settlements and communities could be established."[8] More recent interviews with Japanese women have found some saying that sex with partners outside of marriage is "a man's disease" that women must simply tolerate (Lebra 1985: 141).

Despite assertions about the universal nature of men, the scale and organization of the sex industry varies greatly among societies. In Japan, the magnitude of organized prostitution has led some Japanese writers to point toward the social pressures imposed upon Japanese marriages as its source of demand. A common theme is that the Japanese institution of marriage, based on social standing rather than affection, means that married couples prefer to remain together for social reasons even in the absence of romantic relations. Pressure to stay married leads wives to endure husbands having sexual liaisons outside of the marriage. This "inside marriage divorce" may not be the norm but is reported with sufficient frequency to suggest that, for some married couples, the practice is routine.

Others have focused attention directly on Japan's unique form of patriarchy as a root cause of the huge sex industry. Although patriarchy is a dominating force throughout the world, a substantial literature portrays Japan as a particularized version of Confucian values that has subordinated women to men in all spheres of gender relations (Lebra 1985, Hane 1982, Imamura 1987, Kodera 1993, Nakamura 1994). Along with Japan's very rapid pace of urbanization over the past four decades, patriarchy and gender inequality have, in many ways, been magnified in the urban setting as shared male and female struggles of peasant household existence have given way to the rise of the salaried company worker and an extreme separation of gender roles in the city. Thus, according to Lebra (1985), while men are given specialized roles that carry honor and prestige as breadwinner moving up clearly identified rungs in the corporate hierarchy, women are given generalized roles that carry an "invisible" workload – such as housekeeping – that is neither considered work nor given high status. This, in turn, "feeds into unequal social status that dictates women to be inferior, submissive, more constrained, and more backstage than men; that they be lower in status, power, autonomy and role visibility" (Lebra 1985: 100).

The extreme separation of expected roles of men and women, with women taking over almost total responsibility for the domestic sphere – and increasingly working as well – while men become wholly devoted to the company, is directly related to the organization and selling of sexual services, which "thrives thanks to sex segregation in the larger society." While husbands and wives are inhibited from sharing many aspects of their lives together, there is a "culturally institutionalized tolerance of or even support for male promiscuity in contrast to the sanction against female infidelity" (Lebra 1985: 138).[9]

Somewhat paradoxically, because of the specialized roles, it is often women who take charge of running a brothel or bar that caters exclusively to male clients. Prevented by men from holding occupations above the level of routine blue or white collar worker, and regarded as being generally inferior to men, women may enter these *mizushobai* occupations "reluctantly, or only because there are no other occupations available to them" (Lebra 1985: 303). At the same time, when confronted with philandering husbands, women are reluctant to divorce them for very basic reasons: loss of income and loss of social standing. The result can be that "peaceful, passion-free co-living is regarded by many as an ideal of a durable marital life" (ibid.: 256) and the sexual distance between a married couple in Japan is "structurally entrenched" (ibid.: 298) as a woman's sexual identity, "which predominates her earlier life stage, is overshadowed by her maternal preoccupation, from which she derives *ikigai* (worthiness in life)."

Confronting the connections between Japanese society at large and the specific practices of bringing women to Japan for sexual services is made all the more complex when you realize that cultural institutions are intertwined with two other issues: class and racism.

Class and gender

While patriarchy may go a long way to explain the ways in which the sex industry is justified and has become institutionally entrenched in Japanese society, it does not necessarily explain how women are brought into it. Many observers believe that social class is a key factor that makes sex workers out of women. Popular images promoted by the Japanese government and business portray Japan as a homogeneous, classless (or almost wholly middle-class) society. As Japanese writers have often noted, the reality is somewhat different. Income data is not comparable to that of other countries, and a great amount of wealth is hidden by the still large merchant class. In the corporate world, income is disguised as company assets that are, in practice, exclusively provided to top executives through extraordinary entertainment accounts, villas, cars and other benefits that are not attributed to income or personal assets. Over the past decade income inequalities have been widening. A recent adjustment to government income survey data by Ishizaki (1994), which included income from assets not fully declared, concluded that Japan, with a Gini Coefficient in 1991 of 0.43, had the highest level of income inequality among OECD countries. While such findings may be subject to further debate, the less controversial conclusion from many studies is that economic disparities in Japan are much wider than public data and images claim and that gender and class differences are intrinsic to Japan's "upstairs" corporate and "downstairs" sub-contracting labor system (Murakami *et al.* 1980, Nakagawa 1985, Ishizaki 1994).

Economic class and gender are intricately linked in the history of female participation in the Japanese economy. Historically, as explained by Tsurumi (1990), the women who provided the bulk of the super-exploited factory labor force, which in the late nineteenth and early twentieth century was concentrated in silk and textiles, were almost exclusively girls from the poorest peasant families.[10] This poverty was also the source of women sold to brothels throughout Asia during the same period. This extension of urban elites taking advantage of and exploiting poorer peasant families is described most poignantly by Hane:

> Among the most pitiful victims of agrarian as well as urban poverty in prewar Japan were the young farm girls who were sold to brothels. Their number increased markedly in years of crop failure and ensuing famine; but even in normal years a steady flow of young girls was being channeled into brothels at home and abroad. . . In all major cities there were sections given

over to houses of prostitution, where the women were on display as if in a slave market.

(Hane 1982: 207–8, 213)

Girls as young as ten years old were sold to brothels in Japan and abroad. The parents of many were paid for a six-year contract, which included "costs" to agents that were added to the overwhelming debt that faced each girl from the first day of her servitude. In order to repay an average debt of 600 yen, it was calculated that a girl would have to service 2,143 customers in the six years. According to Hane, the root cause of this system was not only rural poverty, but:

> To justify this practice, society played up the sacrifice of the daughters as an exemplary manifestation of filial piety. The ethos of the society conditioned the girls into believing that it was their duty as daughters to become prostitutes to aid their families.

(Hane 1982: 213)

Miyake (1994) describes how the advent of capitalism and private enterprise led to the rapid expansion of slums at the end of the nineteenth century in Tokyo. In these slums a wide array of petty commodity production, ranging from the making of matchboxes to soap and chemical makers, all turned to lower-class women as sources of labor. Prostitution was part of the scene, and the setting up of brothels in cities carried into the 1920s and beyond:

> Child abandonment was very high in the Meiji period, [but] the most common practice was that of selling daughters to brothels . . . The defenders of the brothel system argued that in major urban centers like Tokyo, where there was a concentration of single men who had come to work in industrial and commercial institutions, such facilities were a necessity . . . Since Japan had a long tradition of permitting public brothels as 'necessary' outlets for lustful men, the defenders of the system contended that, if public brothels were abolished, unlicensed prostitution would increase, and the wives and daughters of 'refined families' would be victimized by frustrated men.

(Hane 1994: 210)

By 1924 there were more than 50,000 women in Japan's public brothels. Although anti-brothel campaigns, often based on the bad reputation of Japan in the outside world rather than on the plight of the women, did occur, it was probably not until the 1970s that the view that prostitution was a choice for most women was challenged. The national and international exposure given to the *karayuki-san* in Yamazaki's (1972) novel and subsequent movie, *Sandakan Hachiban Shōkan* (Sandakan Brothel no. 8), highlighted the demeaning lives of prostitutes from Kyūshū, who were sent abroad and, contrary to the female reporter previously cited, who were treated with little respect upon returning to Japan. Patriarchy and its violence against women became an established theme taken up by others (Morisaki 1976, Mihapoulos 1994). But the critique concerned Japanese women and was directed toward Japan's modernization prior to the Second World War. The connection between Imperial Japan up to and during the Second World War and the internationalization of Japan in the post-war years was not explicitly made even though the parallels in the trade in women are obvious. One reason for not making the connection between Imperial history and contemporary practices may be that, by the 1970s, this international trade had turned to women from other Asian countries who were presumed to be inferior to Japanese and more willing to be sex workers.

Racism: non-Japanese as inferior others

The 1990 Immigration Law, which opened legal immigration to unskilled workers of Japanese descent abroad, most of whom were born in Latin America and speak little or no Japanese, strengthened sanctions against unskilled worker entry by all other racial groups. It also confirmed that the idea of a single Japanese race set apart from all other peoples remains deeply seated in Japanese society and politics. This sense of racial purity has mixed with patriarchy and class to further distance the plight of foreign women immigrants from social concern in Japan. While patriarchy still leaves women inferior to men, Japanese women have gained enough economic power to increasingly avoid sexual service occupations. Foreign women have been recruited to take their place as a new underclass along with foreign men in the bottom of the Japanese labor system:

> It would seem that the secondary sector of Japan's economy, largely peopled by migrant workers, principally consists of sweat shops and sex dens. Its employers have little regard for the same workers' rights that its own Japanese work force are militant about. This stance is racist and exploitative.
>
> (Tiglao-Torres 1993: 100)

This view is echoed by Yamanaka (1993: 82), who states that the lack of concern among policymakers for foreign women in the sex industry "suggests that both racism and sexism play a role in determining policy priorities." Other writers acknowledge this capacity to reduce foreign women to "others" not worthy of concern.[11] Ohshima and Francis (1989: 155) state that, while Japanese men "justify their own behavior by recognizing the existence of prostitutes as a necessary evil," Japanese women express "pride in their cool, rational approach to the matter" by joining the men in saying, "For those [foreign] women, it's just their way of life." Others add to this perspective by arguing the foreign workers in Japan are significantly under-represented in the service sector (outside of the sex industry) because, in Japan, jobs like housekeeping, street sweeping, and garbage collecting, which are heavily immigrant dominated in other high-income countries, are too visible, and that "many employers in the retail and service sectors do not want to use foreigners in highly visible jobs where they might offend their Japanese customers. They prefer, instead, to use them in invisible "back-of-the-house" jobs.

In addition, excluding foreigners from domestic service jobs is partly attributed to persistent male chauvinism and racism:

The Japanese woman is socialized to regard care of the family and the home as her main purpose in life, and delegating this expected social role to a foreign household servant would invite social ostracism as well as intense personal guilt feelings. The centuries-old concept of "purity/impurity" that is embedded in Japanese culture may also explain some of the hesitancy to accept foreign workers in the home.[12]

(Cornelius *et al.* 1994: 385)

Matsuda reaches similar conclusions by stating that the purchase of a woman's sexual favors is consistent with "the traditional Japanese patriarchal system" and that:

In the sex industry 'foreigners' are welcomed, for in this situation such relations are not considered to be on the same order of common human discourse within Japan, and therefore foreign women can be treated as common chattel for men . . . This means that a woman can be purchased by a man for instant gratification . . . without any sense of sin or shame. The wife pretends to have no interest in the husband's conduct in this regard as long as the family is not altered by it. Thus, Japanese women are not interested in knowing whether or not prostitution is being forced on foreign women, nor whether or not their human rights are being violated.

Matsuda (1993: 4)

Xenophobic images of Asian immigrants abound in Japan. Newspaper articles pander to the fear of foreigners through headlines declaring new foreigner crime waves and implying that more foreigners will undermine the unique racial and cultural fabric of Japan:

The mass media have projected a vision of waves of darker-skinned 'others' hitting the shores of Japan and threatening social cohesion and integrity. These views are ironic given that over 80 percent had entered Japan through the agency of Japanese recruiters and brokers, who had recruited them to work in jobs that most Japanese are unwilling to undertake.

(Lie 1992: 38)

The AIDS epidemic has only served to further construct foreigners – especially foreign women in the sex industry – as the problem that feeds into what Lie (Chapter Four of this volume) calls "grassroots racism." The xenophobic attitudes played up by the press are part of an entrenched notion of superiority to other Asians that allows discrimination in all aspects of a foreigner's daily life – work, residence, use of parks and public space, government assistance. This is mixed with the belief of Japanese as being wholly middle class, which allows Asian immigrants to be relegated to the lower class regardless of their levels of education or class status – which tend to be higher than their Japanese counterparts in any given occupation. Given the combination of patriarchy, class and racism, this same tendency is easily directed at foreign women in the sex industry who are given little regard by society as a whole.

The yakuza

One of the easiest means of diverting attention away from critically assessing the social basis of the sex industry in Japan is to simply declare that it is the sole creation of organized crime syndicates, the *yakuza* (Ohshima and Francis 1989, Matsuda 1993). The foreign press puts the matter more bluntly: "sexual slavery is a growing social menace in Japan, a trade that is controlled by the *yakuza*" (*Win News* 1995). In Tokyo alone, there are reported to be fifty *yakuza* organizations involved in organized prostitution, which includes traditional *okiya* brothels, soapland sex baths, bars and secret clubs for prostitution, telephone clubs and streetwalkers (Matsuda 1993).

While the functional role played the *yakuza* is a key element in Japan's sex industry, the explanation that the *yakuza* have autonomously created the massive systems of sexual services in Japan is insufficient. On the connection between criminal organizations and migration throughout the world, Pollack concluded that:

> The failure of the governments of industrialized nations to recognize and deal adequately with mass migrations of people around the globe has given organized crime everywhere one of its most fruitful social functions, and has enabled always-latent atavistic xenophobia to have conspicuous targets. Organized crime is, in this sense, not merely outlaw, in the banal sense of that which goes on outside the law, but its true complementary relationship to society lies in the vacated space between law and reality.
>
> (Pollack ch. 7, p. 166)

In the case of Japan, while law has declared much of the sex industry and its related immigration to be illegal, the demand for its services is so great that the *yakuza* are filling the gap and they are doing so in super-exploitative ways. This has also become the case for illegal migration of men to work in construction and other activities in Japan (Douglass and Roberts Chapter One of this volume).

Another important theme related to the *yakuza* is the extreme isolation of women under systems of recruitment controlled by gangsters, brokers and other professional organizers. Unlike many other receiving countries such as Hong Kong or Singapore, in which female migrants have formed their own extensive social networks, the *yakuza* and other recruiters have reportedly replaced and prevented these networks from forming in Japan (Tiglao-Torres 1993). This leaves many women exceptionally vulnerable. In the extreme cases in which women are essentially kept as slaves to be dispatched to "love hotels" from cramped suburban "dormitories," women may not even know where in Japan they are or how to do simple daily tasks in their neighborhood. In contrast, in Hong Kong where Filipinas are principally hired as domestic workers, the parks and bus terminals are filled on Sundays with thousands of Filipinas meeting, exchanging information, and selling and buying items to send back to the Philippines.[13] Because of the illegal nature of much of the sex industry and the professional recruitment of women by gangsters, the system of social support for Filipina or any other foreign women is limited. The result is a magnification of loneliness and vulnerability that allows for extreme exploitation of migrant women.

Female migration and the sending countries

Just as Japan has its singularities with regard to the recruitment of foreign women, sending countries also have theirs. Specifically, female migration for sexual services to Japan has come from a limited number of countries, particularly Korea, the Philippines, Taiwan and Thailand. Officially allowed entry of "entertainers" is dominated by the Philippines and, from the late 1980s, Thailand has also become a principal source of both legal and illegal migrants in the sex industry. The government of the Philippines is one of the most active governments in the world in encouraging its own citizens to emigrate. Through government-promoted contracts, more than 700,000 Filipinos, with women outnumbering men, are now living and working in 130 countries. Japan is the destination of slightly more than 10 percent of the official total, but is estimated to have many more people from the Philippines as illegal migrants. Until the late 1980s almost all legal and illegal migrants from the Philippines were women. Moreover, data from 1987 show that Japan accounted for 90 percent of all of the migrants from the Philippines who were deployed worldwide as "entertainers."[14] Japan, as far as Philippine women are concerned, is the only country to which the sex industry is the overwhelming organizer of international migration.[15]

As previously noted, while poverty may be the root cause leading women by one means or another into the sex trade in Japan, it cannot be seen as the sole reason why women enter this occupation. In this light, why women are recruited from certain countries for this trade in Japan also raises the question of why *only* these countries provide these women. Full investigation is beyond the scope of this discussion. However, the importance of the need to look at both receiving and sending countries can be illustrated by comparing patterns of population movement to Japan by gender and age. As shown in Figure 5.1, for example, the distribution of foreign entrants to Japan from the Philippines in 1996 reveals an overwhelming preponderance of women. Three-quarters of the 106,000 entrants from the Philippines were women, which represented both an absolute and relative increase to men over previous years. Some estimates are that as many as 90 percent of these women enter as entertainers or illegally work in the sex industry (Komai 1995). Unlike Filipina domestic workers moving to other Asian countries, who tend to have an extended age profile, those moving to Japan fall mostly within their twenties. Men, in contrast, have a more even distribution across all age groups.

By way of contrast, Figure 5.2 shows migration to Japan from Indonesia which, after China, is Japan's largest recipient of both direct foreign investment and foreign assistance in Asia. Not only are entrant levels much lower than those from the Philippines, but 70 percent of the total 37,000 are men and there are higher percentages of both male and female immigrants over age thirty compared with the Philippine profile. Available studies also show that the participation of Indonesian women in Japan's sex industry is rare.

Figure 5.3 displays the percentage male–female distribution of all entrants into Japan from Asia in 1996 by age group. The data shows that women account for two-thirds of all entrants in the 20–24 age group, whereas the relationship is inverted for older entrants. Throughout the 1990s the total share of male and female entrants has been almost equal, with men comprising 52 percent of all legal entrants in 1996. These data reflect the heavy concentration of women entering the sex trade at a young age and the greater tendency for men of differing ages to enter as workers and businessmen.

Given the open door policy toward immigrants of Japanese descent from abroad, it is revealing to compare Figures 5.1 to 5.3 with Figure 5.4, which shows profiles from Brazil, which is the source of the great majority of these immigrants. Although men outnumber women (55 percent of the 94,000 entrants), the age profiles for men and women are virtually the same. Few of these women are reported to be in the sex trade; most are reported to be either the accompanying spouses of workers or are gainfully employed in Japan in light manufacturing, assembly, and other service occupations (Yamanaka, Chapter Six of this volume).

The data for Brazil is typical of migration streams in most settings, with a peak in the 20–30 age group, normally consisting of the most able and better educated workers at a given income level and with a gradual declining slope thereafter. In contrast to Filipinas, two-thirds of the women are either over age 30 or under age 20. The *Nikkeijin* experience suggests that if the immigration of workers were legalized for other would-be migrants, it would be very likely to result in whole families, including more than one generation in the household, trying to settle in Japan. Such a pattern contrasts vividly with the Asian women who are now being recruited to work in Japan.

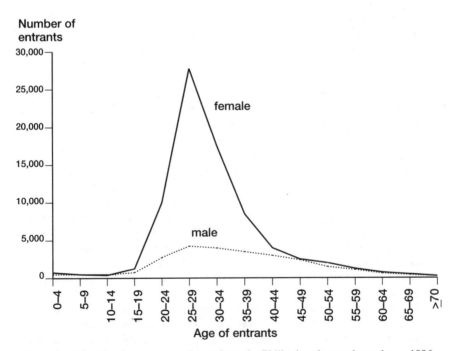

Figure 5.1 Number of entrants into Japan from the Philippines by gender and age, 1996
Source: Ministry of Justice, *Annual Report of Statistics on Legal Migrants 1997* (Tokyo), Section III, table 12.

Japanese and foreign women in Japan's labor system

The preponderance of women entering Japan to provide sexual services invites the question why, in contrast to most countries, so few women from other Asian countries are migrating to Japan for work commonly employing cheap female immigrant labor: light manufacturing, domestic and health services, janitorial work, waitressing and so on. The answer is directly linked to gender relations in the Japanese labor system and reveals a much more complex picture than the more popular one that Japanese women have advanced out of socially undesirable work and toward more equality with men. While some segments of the female population have advanced into higher levels of occupational status and income, the continuing exploitation of Japanese female labor is equally observable.

Three general trends are noteworthy in the transformations and continuities in the economic roles of Japanese women and their impact on the migration of foreign women to Japan. First, with the depletion of steady supplies of migrant men from rural areas by the late 1960s, women began to be increasingly brought into the labor force to become the labor reserve allowing employment to expand and shrink as business cycles and structural changes impacted on the demand for labor in Japan. It has not been uncommon in the recession of the 1990s, for

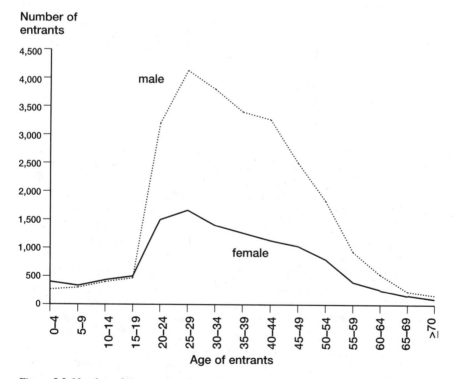

Figure 5.2 Number of entrants into Japan from Indonesia by gender and age, 1996
Source: Ministry of Justice, *Annual Report of Statistics on Legal Migrants 1997* (Tokyo), Section III, table 12.

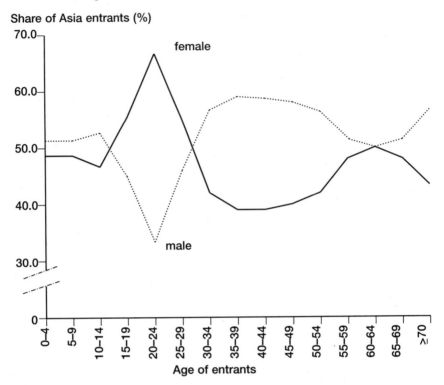

Figure 5.3 Share of female/male entrants from Asia by age group, 1996
Source: Ministry of Justice, *Annual Report of Statistics on Legal Migrants 1997* (Tokyo), Section III, table 12.

example, for large companies to officially announce that they will hire only men and no women from the national pool of recently graduated college students.

Second, much of the large-scale labor-intensive textile and electronics assembly-line production that brought women into the factory system from the late Meiji (Tsurumi 1990) to almost the end of the Showa Era in the late 1980s have been put off-shore in East and South-East Asia.[16] This has resulted in women increasingly being hired either by small- and medium-scale manufacturing firms or in the service sector.[17] Most of the female labor in the small-scale manufacturing sector consists of low-wage middle-age and elderly women. Thus while the "M-shape" curve of female employment – a sharp rise between ages 18–24, a steep fall until children are out of school and a more shallow rise among middle-age women – remains, more and more women are being brought back into the labor force in their forties and older to take on insecure, low-wage jobs. Almost all of these older women – part of an aging society with smaller families – are recruited as part-time employees paid an hourly wage with no other benefits and no career advancement opportunities. In terms of wages and benefits, this segment of the labor force overlaps with that potentially filled by immigrant labor, especially *Nikkei* women who are legally allowed to work in Japan (Yamanaka, ch. 6).

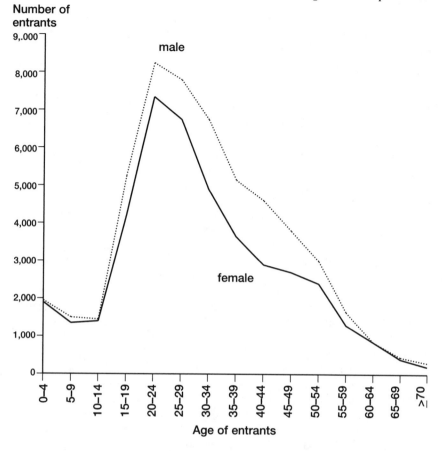

Number of entrants

Figure 5.4 Entrants from Brazil to Japan by gender and age, 1996
Source: JIA (1994).

Third, although there is a modest trend towards life-long employment of women, that is, not dropping out of the labor force during child-rearing age, women have not made significant gains in achieving managerial or executive positions (NIEVR 1988). The more prominent trend is one of increasing part-time work for women. In 1960, female part-time employees made up only 9 percent of total women employees but, by 1991, they accounted for almost one-third.[18] During the same period, the female labor force expanded at a higher rate than men as women became the cutting edge of an increasingly "flexible" labor system.

During the 1990s, younger women with college education have become as disposable as the older part-time female employees. As explained by Kodera (1993), the strategic use of part-time labor has changed dramatically over the decades. In the 1960s, it still consisted mostly of men migrating seasonally from rural areas and was principally used as a device to augment the work force during a period of high economic growth. Following the oil crisis in 1973, part-timers began to be used to substitute for regular workers. By the late 1980s, it had become an essential component of company strategies to deal with the tremendous growth of the service economy and the volatile changes in demand for labor under rapid technological innovation in office work and accelerated efforts at corporate down-sizing (Houseman and Abraham 1993).

Data from Japan's current recession underscores the use of women as a labor reserve by showing that the participation rate of women following the collapse of the bubble economy in the early 1990s dropped to its lowest point since the 1970s, while that for men stays almost constant (Friedland 1994).[19] The government reportedly no longer includes women who quit to get married or have a baby in its unemployment statistics, making women all the more invisible in the Japanese economy.

Throughout all of these phases, the glass ceiling in the advancement of women in corporate Japan has remained in place despite the passage of the Equal Employment Opportunity Law (1986) and the Childcare Leave Act (1992).[20] The labor force participation rate was 51 percent for women in 1991 but female managers were only 1 percent of all paid female employees compared to 7 percent of men. In that same year, women earned only 60 percent of an average man's gross monthly cash earnings (Kodera 1993). A United Nations (1991: 8) study of wages paid to women in relation to those paid to men for the years 1970–90 found that Japan was on a par with Korea and Cyprus in having the most unfavorable ratios for women among all countries of the world for which data were available.

The rules and practices of Japanese personnel management make a clear distinction between core employees, mostly composed of men in large enterprises who enjoy permanent employment, seniority-based wages, internal career development through job rotation and in-company training, and non-core employees overly represented by women in small firms who are completely excluded from these privileges. This division is rationalized as livelihood protection, namely, the position that male salaries should cover household living costs and, by extension, women should principally be housekeepers with earnings only as an auxiliary source of income (Nakamura 1994, Lo 1990, Roberts 1994). As such:

> Gender-based discrimination is built into the very concept of the Japanese style of management . . . As a result, female workers are stuck in positions offering low wages and less opportunity, and play marginal roles as peripheral workers who help maintain the flexibility of the employment system.[21]
> (Kodera 1993: 142)

The combined effect on female migration of each of the three trends summarized above is that the bulk of work offered to women has been filled by Japanese women who themselves continue to experience severe inequities in employment opportunities and benefits (Ozawa 1989).[22] Japanese women face both lateral (equal pay for equal job) and vertical (advancement) discrimination. In this sense, foreign women provide yet another layer of gendered inequality, working in the "floating world" of sex-related entertainment which Japanese women have apparently been able to earn higher incomes from, or to reject as an occupational option (NIEVR 1988, Yamanaka 1994). In 1991, there were 84,368 foreigners, almost all of whom were women, who entered Japan under visas as entertainers (JIA 1993). About 60 percent of this category came from the Philippines. Added to this are 7,000 identified illegal migrants who worked as hostesses or prostitutes. In 1996, the number of entertainers legally entering Japan had dropped to about 54,000. There was a drop to 40 percent from the Philippines, due to increases from Thailand and a new presence of 4,400 women in this category from Russia which, after the collapse of the Soviet Union, has become a new source of sex workers in East Asia.

There is also an undocumented number of women who come with false Japanese passports or who work in the sex industry under student or other visas. Unless a women actually overstays her visa or is directly apprehended by the authorities while working in the sex industry, the government has no way of tallying the number of women who are working in the sex industry in any given year. Numbers on foreign nationals working in Japan, prepared by foreign embassies such as the Philippines, are often twice or more than those given by the Japanese government. Therefore, using official data to conclude that between 100 and 200,000 are entering Japan either legally or illegally each year for sex-related work is a conservative estimate.

The future of female migration to Japan

A survey of world migration trends has highlighted that one of the major factors expected over next twenty years is the increased "feminization of migration," with women playing an expanding role in all regions and all types of migration that will lead to a reversal of previous male-dominated trends (Castles and Miller 1993: 8). As with many other aspects of migration to Japan, such global treatments reveal how Japan's experience is singularly different from the general case. As previously noted, up to the 1980s, women dominated entrants into Japan from Asia, and it has only been in the last ten years that the number of men from Asia and Latin America has surpassed that of women. These observations raise the question of whether a new wave of female migration as part of the global feminization of migration will come to Japan in the future.

The answer this, the prospects for employment to be made available to foreign women outside the sex industry need to be gauged. A strong case can be made that such employment opportunities will not materialize. The Japanese government's view is that immigration of low-wage workers is unnecessary to the Japanese economy; its policy is that it will not be allowed.

In contrast to government policy, business interests in Japan have pressured the government into allowing more immigrants to fill low-wage jobs. As with the US and Europe, the government has seemingly not been as strict in tracking down illegal migrants as it might otherwise have been. It has, for example, mostly ignored the thousands of workers, particularly from China, who pay brokers very large fees to enter Japan for language study in supposed language schools but are, in fact, working full-time in low-wage jobs. But even as these breaches in the immigration laws are gradually widened, the labor demand is still being met largely by men and, secondarily, *Nikkeijin* women. Labor-intensive light manufacturing that traditionally employs women continues to be put offshore by Japanese companies. In a country with extremely limited pension and social security systems for older citizens, the aging Japanese population, particularly the post-the Second World War population bulge, can simultaneously be expected to provide increasing numbers of older women for the most vulnerable, part-time jobs being specifically created for women. Finally, difficulties facing foreign workers of either gender in housing and integration into Japanese neighborhoods remain formidable and uninviting.

A closer look at elements of the Japanese economy that cannot be externalized suggests that, if the Japanese want to follow the government's campaign to become a "Superpower of Life" in the world's most rapidly aging society, there will be tremendous pent-up demand for the international migration of women to Japan to fill a wide variety of service jobs outside the entertainment sector. Data on illegal migrants (Figure 5.5 and Table 5.1) show that, despite government prohibitions, foreign women are already beginning to be find a number of service jobs such as porters, cooks, waitresses, bartenders, and dishwashers. The data also show an apparent decline in the share of illegal female migrants in the sex industry, with 56 percent in 1990 and 40 percent in 1996. Caution must be used in interpreting such data: the drop is in share, not in numbers – the 1996 figure was almost triple that of 1990. Given this caveat, there is none the less a measurable increase in the number of women illegally working in other sectors of the economy.

At least six reasons can be put forth to show that, contrary to government expectations, greater outward flows of investment by Japanese corporations setting up labor-intensive production abroad will be paralleled by equally great increases in inward flows of immigrants:

- Outward investment flows represent, in part, rising labor costs in Japan and an emerging chronic demand in Japan's massive sub-contracting system for cheap labor.
- Foreign investment strengthens migration networks to Japan through more information, job experiences in Japanese companies abroad, and exposure to learning the Japanese language. Advances in communications are also facilitating the ease of interaction and networking among migrants from country to country.
- Perhaps most important, the majority of jobs being taken on by migrants, most especially by female migrants, have almost nothing to do with Japan's export competitiveness but, instead, serve the economy in activities that simply cannot be exported.
- Japan will soon experience absolute population decline (Douglass and Roberts Chapter One of this volume), resulting in chronic demand for young low-wage workers for the more physically demanding service jobs, many of which serve the needs of the elderly.
- Income gaps between Japan and the rest of Asia continue to grow and no amount of direct foreign investment will dry up the pools of low-wage labor in most of these countries.
- Marriage between non-Japanese and Japanese citizens is rapidly increasing. In some rural villages in Japan, the major source of brides for farmers has become foreign women. In one rural district alone in Yamagata Prefecture there have been more than 1,000 marriages between Japanese men and foreign women since 1985 (Kubota 1996). Marriage and labor recruitment are

intermingled as foreign women are brought not only for their reproductive function of bearing children for rural households but are also taking on many agricultural duties as rural Japan continues to be depopulated of its prime-age labor force.

The propensity to migrate to Japan will remain high, networks of migration will become better established, and the desire among Japanese to join and stay in the middle class in an aging society can only mean that they and their economic enterprises will increase their demand for immigrant labor. None of these factors suggest that controlling migration to Japan is simply a matter of a strong government policy or that such a policy is sufficient to the task (Morita and Iyotani 1994).

Conclusions

Overt specialization in female immigration for sexual services and the limited alternative occupational opportunities available to immigrant women set Japan apart from other high-income societies. In part, these singularities reflect gender and patriarchal socio-cultural realities in Japan but they are linked to conditions in sending countries and they are a reflection of a long history of the sex trade in Japan that has relied on class stratification to provide poor women for the pleasure of middle and upper-class men. From the 1970s, these disparities have been exacerbated by the massive recruitment of foreign women from the 1970s that continues to be fuelled by ever-widening income gaps between Japan and the rest of Asia. Japanese beliefs in the homogeneity of their society and the distancing from foreigners based on race has further obscured the plight of immigrant women. Finally, patterns of female immigration are also outcomes of the use of Japanese women as low-wage disposable workers in Japan's labor system.

All of these factors illustrate that immigration of women comes about because of a host of socio-political factors including organized recruitment networks that disguise as much information as they reveal and regulated routes of access that involve governments and businesses in the sex trade. When looking at all the various explanations of the peculiarities of female migration to Japan, it also becomes obvious that the issues surrounding female immigration cannot be dealt as an immigration control problem, although that is what happens currently. This segment of migration, in fact, raises questions that reach into the heart of Japanese households, the gender differences in employment, and other social and economic roles.

Since the social construction of gender roles is a central feature of female migration to Japan, one strategy put forth by some writers calls for government and industry to revitalize the Japanese female workforce by fundamentally reorganizing gender divisions of labor so as to allow women to develop long-term careers in Japan's expanding higher order service and technology development sectors (Kodera 1993). Recognizing that education levels of women are still rising, families have fewer children, and technological advances have reduced the time required for domestic chores, this strategy proposes that Japan can more readily meet its labor challenges by giving women leading roles in all spheres of the economy.

What would be the outcome for female immigration if Japanese women were to win more equality with men and a better place in the labor system? The simple

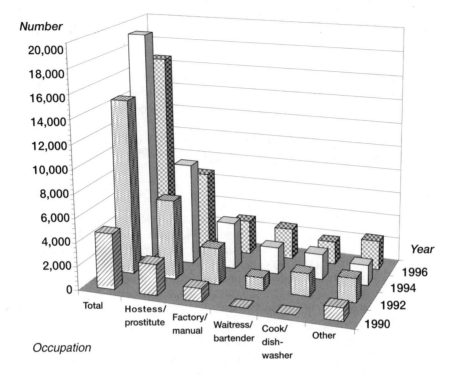

Figure 5.5 Occupation of apprehended illegal female entrants, 1990–6
Source: Japan Immigration Association (1997), *Summary of Statistics on Immigration Control 1996* (Tokyo, in Japanese).

Table 5.1 Occupational distribution of apprehended illegal female migrants,1990–6

Occupation	1990 (no.)	(%)	1992 (no.)	(%)	1994 (no.)	(%)	1996 (no.)	(%)
Host/hostess/prostitute	2,602	55.5	6,636	45.3	8,589	44.4	6,720	40.4
Production/manual	1,088	23.2	3,051	20.8	3,939	20.3	2,910	17.5
Waitress/bartender	—	—	1,062	7.3	2,242	11.6	2,631	15.8
Cook/dishwasher	—	—	1,900	13.0	2,156	11.1	1,925	11.6
Others	995	21.2	1,991	13.6	2,397	12.4	2,439	14.7
Total	4,685	100.0	14,640	100.0	19,323	100.0	16,625	100.0

Source: see Figure 5.5.

answer is that the demand for female immigrant labor would go up rather than down as Japanese women leave lower- for higher-status jobs. Put the other way around, it is extremely ironic that the continued vulnerability of Japanese women in the labor force is implicitly a mechanism for dampening the demand for foreign female labor. Although it may diversify the opportunities open to foreign women, a move toward greater gender equality among Japanese will not automatically translate into improved economic welfare for female immigrants. Efforts to gain such improvements for foreign women will have to be directed along lines of class and race as well as gender.

Gender inequality along with patriarchy, class divisions, racism and gangsterism exist in various forms in virtually every society. Just as it is reproduced through power structures, it is also being challenged not only by those who are marginalized by these forces, but also by citizen groups and human rights organizations that have dedicated themselves to the cause of social justice for women regardless of origin. The establishment of HELP and other support organizations for foreign women caught up in the sex industry in Japan is part of a growing recognition of the extreme vulnerability and loss of human dignity that such work entails even when women knowingly choose to enter it (Matsuda 1993, Ohshima and Francis 1989).

With levels of female immigration projected to increase in the coming decades (Kono 1994), the challenges are formidable. What is at issue is not just how Japanese people treat foreign women or men but also how Japanese society confronts its own construction of gender relations, deals with new forms of social inequality, adjusts to the employment implications of a rapidly aging population, and faces an increasingly multicultural society.

Notes

1 The term "sex industry" is used to cover activities ranging from hostesses who sit with customers, work in nude or semi-nude "snack" bars, provide sexual services in massage parlors and "soap lands," and work as call girls and other types of prostitutes. It does not imply that all women in this industry are prostitutes, although the preponderance of evidence suggests that a very large share of female migrants from such countries as Thailand and the Philippines are engaged in prostitution.

2 Although originally applied to both men and women, by the turn of the century the term "*karayuki-san*" was principally used only for women recruited to go abroad as prostitutes (Mihapoulos 1994).

3 From at least the 1890s the term *roshigun* was used as an alternative to *karayuki-san* to denote prostitutes sent abroad as female warriors in a critical first wave of Japanese overseas expansion. According to Mihapoulos (1994), *roshigun* is derived from the word *joshigun* (Amazonian troops) referring to a Chinese legend of the T'ang Dynasty when Princess Ping Yang organized an army of women. Celebrating fifty years of presence in Singapore in the early twentieth century, the Japanese newspaper *Nanyo Nichinichi* (South Seas Daily) editorialized that the Japanese commercial expansion in Singapore had gone through five distinct stages since the arrival of the first Japanese in the early Meiji period. The first of these stages was classified as the *roshigun* period, which laid the foundations for further modernization of Japan. Thus, "*karayuki-san* presence abroad became one of many encoded categories by which to measure and judge the progress of Japan used by journalists, academics and officials until end of World War I" (Mihapoulos 1994: 178).

4 *Win News* (1995), estimates that probably 100,000 foreign women work in Tokyo and

Osaka alone. For Filipinas alone, the Geneva-based International Organization for Migration gives a 1997 estimate of between 100 and 150,000 which if Thai, Korean and Taiwanese women were included along with other new streams such as that reportedly coming from Colombia the total would be 200–300,000.

5   Sassen (1994) also argues that the movement of women to and from Japan from the Meiji period to the present is not migration but rather forced labor.

6   Confirming the systematic neglect of female migration for this industry and other services, Yamanaka (1994: 412) points out that the migration of women for sexual services to Japan was not given attention until the late 1980s when the migration of men became a national issue in Japan.

7   A special issue of *International Migration* (1993) devoted to Japan does not have a single article that discusses international migration and the sex industry with more than a passing reference.

8   As argued by Fukuzawa Yukichi (1835–1901), a leading educator and social commentator, in *"Jinmin no iju to shofu no dekasegi"* (The Migration of Japanese Subjects and Prostitutes Working Away from Home), *Jiji Shimpo*, 18 January 1896 (cited in Mihapoulos 1994). Some foreign observers apply a similar sentiment to sex industry workers from Asia going to Japan. According to Tiglao-Torres (1993: 100), the immigration of Asian women for sexual services in Japan is "essential . . . for the leisure and entertainment of its overzealous workers and managers in the formal sector" in this country that "ritualizes female servitude to males."

9   Lebra (1985: 141) goes on to say that "a wife's patience with the husband's promiscuity is regarded as admirable."

10   This includes extremely low (or no) wages, inadequate diets of food, unhealthy living environments, long hours including double shifts, sexual harassment, and virtual absence of even the most basic personal freedoms such as going to the toilet. Nishinarita (1994: 7) observes that while the majority of female workers in early textile industry in Japan were under the age of twenty, more than 60 percent in England were over twenty and married. He concludes that "The unusually high proportion of unwed adolescent women in the workforce is one of the distinguishing features of Japan's early cotton industry." In Japan the recruited women were essentially bonded or indentured workers. Under this system, female mill operatives were forced to work a double shift extending far into the night, and for lower wages than their counterparts even in colonial India.

11   The othering of women engaged in prostitution was also used to disassociate Japanese society from the *karayuki-san*, who were thought to almost exclusively consist of Kyūshū women, especially those from the island of Amakusa, and who were described as being from a special sub-culture that, through extreme poverty and long-established practices of sending women away from their home village to earn income for their dowry, made women somehow willing to be sent abroad as prostitutes. In fact, by the late 1800s, all ports in Japan that were connected to outside trade had employment agencies helping to send women from many regions of Japan for employment overseas. Typically advertised as jobs for servants, waitresses or nannies, linkages with brothels at the destination were common (Mihapoulos 1994).

12   Everything external to the home is considered to be "impure" and should not be brought into the home. Foreign workers, in this sense, would be considered impure.

13   In 1992, there were almost 66,000 Filipina domestic workers in Hong Kong. Singapore had at least 50,000 foreign domestic workers, including 30,000 Filipina, 10,000 Sri Lankans and 5,000 Indonesians. Saudi Arabia had 750,000 foreign domestic workers in 1983 (Lycklama á Nijeholt 1992: 44).

14   Data compiled by the Philippine Embassy estimates that there were 142,000 Filipinos working in Japan in 1990, more than double the official estimate, indicating that as much as half of the Filipinos in Japan are there illegally. 87 percent were entertainers with trainees (4 percent) and domestic helpers (2.5 percent, most of whom work for foreign embassies) far behind. Almost two-thirds of all migrant entertainers in Japan

were from Philippines in 1991. Most were under the age of twenty-three and single. More recently, girls as young as eleven to fourteen are being recruited for Japan (Tiglao-Torres 1993: 93). Close to 90 percent of these entertainers are classified as dancers rather than singers, musicians or theatrical performers.

15 Japan attracts the younger age groups – in some cases barely teenagers – while Hong Kong and Singapore, the destination of domestic helpers, show significantly higher average ages. Philippine female migrants internationally thus have a much wider age band than do men, who are mostly within the 25–34 age group. Both men and women have relatively high levels of education, with only 10 percent of migrants not having finished elementary school and about one-quarter having finished at least high school (Tiglao-Torres 1993).

16 In the 1960s, the owners of textile factories in Japan had began to press for immigrant labor as Japan's previous labor surpluses began to turn to labor scarcities, but "the bureaucracy quietly clamped down on it" (Brimelow 1993: 58).

17 Manufacturing employment as a share of total employment of women decreased from 32 percent in 1970 to 24 percent by the early 1980s. Wholesale and retail trade (including restaurants and drinking establishments) increased from 25 to 35 percent, with the rapidly advancing finance, insurance and real estate sectors remaining almost constant at 32 percent (NIEVR 1988).

18 The share of female wage workers has increased at the expense of unpaid family workers, which has fallen sharply. 30 percent of working women were wage workers in 1955; in 1990 the proportion had grown to 72 percent. During the same period, family workers fell from 55 to 17 percent, and the self-employed fell from 15 to 11 percent.

19 The female participation rate reached a lowpoint of 46 percent in 1975 and subsequently showed steady increases to reach 50 percent in 1990 (JIWE 1991). In 1993, however, a Ministry of Labor survey of 1,000 firms reported that more than half were reducing the recruitment of new female employees so that they could continue hiring males in the usual numbers. One reason given was that males would stay with a firm far longer than women and would not request childcare leaves. Such reasons are not allowed under laws adopted after 1986 (Cornelius, Martin and Hollifield 1994).

20 Molony (1995) argues that these laws have helped to change attitudes toward women and create a more career-oriented image of women. The net effects were to encourage a division of the workplace into a "mommy" track and an elite track, to increase the enrolment of women in four-year colleges to get into the elite track, and a further decrease in the birth-rate.

21 Women officially hired to work less than 35 hours increased from 600,000 in 1960 to 5 million in 1991. However, part-time does not refer to hours worked but to job status. About one-third of part-timers actually work the same hours as full-time workers. Most women who left their jobs during child-bearing years can only find employment later in the "downstairs" labor market in small- and medium-size firms. Wages earned by full-time females aged 50–54 are only half those of males in the same age group. Educational attainment, unlike that for men, is "entirely irrelevant" for women's position and advancement (Kodera 1993).

22 For older women, wages are about 50–60 percent of those of men in the same age brackets. For younger women, wage differences are narrow and levels are estimated at about 80–90 percent at the "fresh(wo)man" level of employment. These ratios have not significantly changed over the past three decades (NIEVR 1988).

References

Brimelow, P. (1993) "Closed Door," *Forbes* 152, 2 (Aug. 30): 58–9.

Castles, S. and Miller, M. J. (1993) *The Age of Migration*, New York: Guilford Press.

Cornelius, W. A., Martin, P. L. and Hollifield, J. F. (1994) "Japan: the Illusion of

Immigration Control," in W. Cornelius, P. Martin and J. Hollifield (eds) *Controlling Immigration: a Global Perspective*, Stanford: Stanford University Press: 375–414.

Fawcett, J., Siew-Ean, K. and Smith, P. C. (eds) (1984) *Women in the Cities of Asia: Migration and Urban Adaptation*, Boulder: Westview Press.

Friedland, J. (1994) "Career Lady's Curse: Japanese Recession Is a Setback for Women," *Far Eastern Economic Review* 157, 4 (27 Jan.): 44–5.

Guest, P. (1993) "Gender and Migration in Southeast Asia," in J. Ariffin (ed.), *Proceedings from the International Colloquium "Migration, Development and Gender in the ASEAN Region"*. Kuala Lumpur: University of Malaysia: 1–24.

Hane, M. (1982) *Peasants, Rebels, and Outcasts: the Underside of Modern Japan*, New York: Pantheon.

Houseman, S. and Abraham, K. (1993) "Female Workers as a Buffer in the Japanese Economy," *American Economic Review* 83, 2 (May): 45–51.

Imamura, A. (1987) *Urban Japanese Housewives*, Honolulu: University of Hawaii Press.

International Migration (1993) "Special Issue on Japan and International Migration," 31, 2–3.

IOM (International Organization on Migration) (1997) "Filipino Women in Japan: Trapped in the Sex Business," *IOM News Release* No 792, (11 July).

Ishizaki, T. (1994) "*Shotoku Bumpai Byōdō no 'Shinwa' wa Kuzureta*" (The 'Myth' of Income Distribution Equality has Collapsed), *Sekai* 72, (March).

Japan Institute of Women's Employment (JIWE) (1991) *Japan's Working Women Today*, Tokyo.

JIA (Japan Immigration Association) (1997) *Statistics on Immigration Control 1996*, Tokyo.

Kaplan, D. and Dubro, A. (1987) *Yakuza*, Reading, Mass.: Addisan-Wesley.

Kodera, K. (1993) "The Reality of Equality for Japanese Female Workers: Women's Careers within the Japanese Style of Management," *Social Justice* 21, 2 (Summer): 136–54.

Komai, H. (1995) *Migrant Workers in Japan*, New York: Kegan Paul International.

Kono, S. (1994) "International Migration in Japan: A Demographic Sketch," in W. Gooneratne, P. Martin and H. Sazanami (eds) *Regional Development Impacts of Labour Migration in Asia*, Nagoya: UNCRD Research Report Series no. 2: 122–58

Kritz, M. M. and Zlotnik, H. (1992) "Global Interactions: Migration Systems, Processes and Policies," in M. M. Kritz, L. L. Lim and H. Zlitnik (eds), *International Migration Systems: a Global Approach*, Oxford: Clarendon Press: 1–18.

Kubota, M. (1996) "*Kaihatsu to Josei Mondai to Hito no Nagare*" (The Problem of Development and Women and Flow of People), *Kokusai Jinryū* (May): 26–7.

Lebra, T. S. (1985) *Japanese Women*, Honolulu: University of Hawaii Press.

Lie, J. (1992) "Foreign Workers in Japan," *Monthly Review* 44, 1 (May): 35–43.

Lo, J. (1990) *Office Ladies, Factory Women: Life and Work at a Japanese Company*, London: M. E. Sharpe.

Lycklama á Nijeholt, G. (1992) "The Changing International Division of Labour and Domestic Workers: A Macro Overview (Regional)," in N. Heyzeer, G. Lycklama á Nijeholt and N. Weekrakoon (eds) *The Trade in Domestic Workers: Causes, Mechanisms and Consequences of International Migration,* London: Zed Books: 3–29.

Matsuda, M. (1993) "Foreign Workers in Japan: Gender, Civil Rights and Community Responses," presented at the Seminar on Foreign Workers in Japan: Gender, Civil Rights and Community Response, Center for Japanese Studies, University of Hawaii, (1–3 Dec.).

Mihapoulos, B. (1994) "The Making of Prostitutes in Japan: the '*Karayuki-san*'," *Social Justice* 21, 2 (Summer): 161–84.

Miyake, A. (1994) "Female Workers of the Urban Lower Class," in M. Nakamura (ed.) *Technological Change and Female Labour in Japan*, Tokyo: United Nations University Press: 97–131.

MOFA (Ministry of Foreign Affairs) (1998) "Japanese Viewpoints: Foreign Workers," Tokyo: Worldwide Web site: http://www2.nttca.com:8010/infomofa/viewpoints/hp.html#topics.

MOJ (Ministry of Justice) (1997) *Annual Report of Statistics on Legal Migrants 1997*, Tokyo.

Molony, B. (1995) "Japan's 1986 Equal Employment Opportunity Law and the Changing Discourse on Gender," *Signs* 20, 2 (Winter): 268–92.

Morisaki, K. (1976) *Karayuki-san*, Tokyo: Asahi Shinbunsha.

Morita, K. and Iyotani, T. (1994) "Japan and the Problem of Foreign Workers," in W. Gooneratne, P. Martin and H. Sazanami (eds) *Regional Development Impacts of Labour Migration in Asia*, Nagoya: UNCRD Research Report Series No 2.

Murakami, Y., Kishimoto, S. and Tominaga, K. (1980) *The Reality of the New Middle Class*. Tokyo: Foreign Press Center.

Nakagawa, K. (1985) *Nihon no Toshi Kasō* (Urban Underclass in Japan), Tokyo: Keiso Shobo.

Nakamura, M. (1994) "Conclusions," in M. Nakamura (ed.) *Technological Change and Female Labour in Japan*, Tokyo: United Nations University Press: 193–212.

NIEVR (National Institute of Employment and Vocational Research) (1988) *Women Workers in Japan*, Tokyo.

Nishinarita, Y. (1994) "Introduction: Types of Female Labour and Changes in the Workforce, 1890–1945," in M. Nakamura (ed.) *Technological Change and Female Labour in Japan*, Tokyo: United Nations University Press: 1–24.

Ohshima, S. and Francis, C. (1989) *Japan through the Eyes of Women Migrant Workers*, Tokyo: Japan Woman's Christian Temperance Union.

Ozawa, M. (ed.) (1989) *Women's life cycle and economic insecurity*, New York: Greenwood Press.

Roberts, G. S. (1994) *Staying on the Line: Blue-Collar Women in Contemporary Japan*, Honolulu: University of Honolulu Press.

Salt, J. (1993) "the Future of International Labor Migration," *International Migration Review* xxvi: 4: 1077–111.

Sassen, S. (1994) "Economic Internationalization: The New Migration in Japan and the United States," *Social Justice* 21, 2 (Summer): 62–81.

Tiglao-Torres, A. (1993) "Features of the Migration of Men and Women in the Philippines," Proceedings from the International Colloquium "Migration, Development and Gender in the ASEAN Region", Kuala Lumpur: University of Malaysia: 67–114.

Tsurumi, E. P. (1990) *Factory Girls*, Princeton: Princeton University Press.

United Nations (1991) *The World's Women 1970–1990: Trends and Statistics*, New York.

Watanabe, S. (1995) "Women's Struggles and Female Migration into Japan in the 1980s–1990s," Austin: Department of Economics, University of Texas at Austin, Ph.D. proposal.

Win News (1995) "Sex Trade Flourishing in Japan," 21, 1: 42.

Yamanaka, K. (1993) "New Immigration Policy and Unskilled Foreign Workers in Japan," *Pacific Affairs* 66, 1: 72–90.

—— (1994) "Theory versus Reality in Japanese Immigration Policy," in W. A. Cornelius, P. L. Martin and J. F. Hollifield (eds) *Controlling Immigration: A Global Perspective*, Stanford: Stanford University Press: 411–14.

Yamazaki, T. (1972) *Sandakan Hachiban Shōkan – Teihan Joseishi Joshō* (Sandakan Brothel Number Eight – Introduction to the History of Women in the Lowest Part of Society), Tokyo: Chikuma Shobo.

Part II
Livelihood and living in Japanese workplaces and communities

6 "I will go home, but when?"

Labor migration and circular diaspora formation by Japanese Brazilians in Japan

Keiko Yamanaka

Introduction

"Oh, I'll go back home to Brazil sometime . . . but I don't know when."

These are words I heard repeatedly while interviewing Japanese Brazilians in 1994 in the Tokai region of Japan. In response to the question, "When do you plan to return to Brazil?" very few of the *Nikkeijin* interviewees had a definite answer. They thought of Brazil as their homeland and clearly stated that they would "definitely go home." These poignant words, revealing both strong desire and a bit of confusion, strike a sympathetic chord in me as I remember that their grandparents and parents, who had traveled to Brazil as temporary migrants between 1908 and 1940, wished to return home but were unable to do so. These words also illustrate an irony of history, as children and grandchildren now repeat the experiences their ancestors suffered in Brazil more than a half century ago.[1]

Since 1990, approximately 200,000 descendants of Japanese emigrants to Latin America, primarily Brazil, have returned to their ancestral homeland as unskilled laborers in response to an increased demand for labor in jobs shunned by Japanese. Encouraged by the 1990 Japanese immigration reform law which granted second (*nisei*) and third (*sansei*) generation *Nikkeijin* a renewable stay of up to three years with unlimited access to labor markets, they looked forward to finding well-paying jobs as sojourners (*dekasegi*) in Japan, and to being welcomed as compatriots. The enabling law was intended to attract *Nikkeijin* as culturally familiar substitutes for what was perceived to be an alarming influx of non-Japanese Asian labor migrants. But these expectations and intentions were ill-fated. The *Nikkeijin* found themselves regarded as aliens and treated as secondary citizens by the Japanese, while the Japanese found the *Nikkeijin* to be disturbingly Brazilian and therefore foreign.

Historical changes in the capitalist world-economic system in the last 130 years have transformed Japan from one of the least prosperous to one of the most prosperous nations. Second and third generation descendants of Japanese immigrants who dreamed of a better life in Brazil are currently seeking better lives in the country of their ancestry. As their migration continues, their conditions of life and work in Japan will necessarily improve. There are already many commercial services and cultural associations in place which form key components of the loosely connected *Nikkeijin* community in Japan. Recent immigration statistics, however, point to the popularity of short, repeated migration by those *Nikkeijin* who are most experienced in working in Japan. This suggests that the migration undertaken by the younger generation of *Nikkeijin*, is a modern type in which the level of mobility is extremely high as a consequence of new technologies in transportation, information and communication. Underlying the rapid development of Brazilian *Nikkeijin* migration is the global spread of the process of transnationalism, shaping a process that I call "circular diaspora formation." In this process, *Nikkeijin* migrants circulate between their ancestral and adopted countries, alternating their homelands as they do so: often with one or more generations of settled residence between migrations.

The massive inflow of *Nikkeijin* return migrants in the early 1990s was triggered by an acute labor shortage in Japan's lifeline industry manufacturing, the brunt of which was borne by small-scale employers especially subcontractors of large automobile makers who are a majority of employers in the industry. However, economic or demographic factors alone associated with economic restructuring cannot explain the rapid settlement of this select group from the opposite side of the globe in less than five years. Any explanation must also include historical, cultural and political forces.

This paper describes and analyzes historical-structural forces and processes within which *Nikkei* Brazilian migrations have been constructed and reconstructed in the two homelands – Brazil and Japan – between 1908 and 1995. To do this, I had to draw on theoretical and empirical literature on migration, accounts of the history of Japanese Brazilian migration in its political and economic context, as well as using survey, interview and ethnographic field research among Japanese Brazilians in both countries so as to discover the social, structural and cultural reasons for this transnational labor migration and re-migration. The initial results of these efforts are presented here under four major headings.

The first comprises a brief overview of my theoretical stance as it has emerged from world systems theory and migration systems theory. This is followed by a relatively detailed history of Japanese labor migration to and from Brazil. Third, there is a descriptive analysis of the demography and social structuring of the Japanese Brazilian population in Japan and in its trans-Pacific aspects. The fourth and final section comprises the results of my own research into the cultural social, political and economic processes, and personal experiences which have accompanied and characterized recent and current Brazilian *Nikkeijin* labor migration. I believe that it is only through such a multifaceted approach that the complex process of labor migration can begin to be adequately understood and its global implications assessed.

World systems and migration systems

I have used two theories to explain the historical and structural forces and processes: world systems theory, to define labor migration as an integral part of the global capitalistic system; and migration systems theory, to link historical-structural forces to individuals, who choose migration as a means of survival. First I will analyze the history of labor migration and then discuss findings from 100 household interviews conducted in both Japan and Brazil between 1994 and 1995. In applying these theories to *Nikkeijin* return migration to Japan, I also take account of social-psychological factors determining migrants' behavior at both individual and collective levels. Once a migration flow begins, migrants tend to employ a number of strategies of social adaptation in order to sustain the flow, so that migration continues independently of the economic forces that triggered it.

World systems theory views the modern world economy as a single unit of division of labor (between the center and the periphery) within which multiple polities and cultures are included (Wallerstein 1974, 1982). The configuration of this global unit may change over time as capitalist world economies constantly pursue markets where realization of maximum profit is the ultimate goal. International labor migration occurs as part of the internal dynamics of the world system as capitalists' drives for profit-maximization and surplus-accumulation incorporate outlying areas and populations into the mechanisms of trading capital, goods and labor at the transnational level (Portes 1978). The net result of this penetration of the periphery by the core is ever-growing articulation and interdependence between the two sectors not only in the economy but also in political and cultural institutions.

Portes (1978: 10) argues that the major problems facing a labor-importing country entail questions of how to find, mobilize, release, transport and utilize a disposable labor force in a labor-exporting country. Although labor-importing countries of the world share common levels of industrialization, demographic composition and social class systems, they differ in how these problems are approached and solved depending on historical events and cultural heritage (Portes and Böröcz 1989). Japan is often cited as an example in which labor importation is not among its government's list of viable options for solving an increasingly acute labor shortage. The maintenance of ethnic and class homogeneity is said to be the primary reason for the country to maintain a closed door to unskilled foreigners (Kritz and Zlotnik 1992: 11).

Although these issues pertain to conditions under which migration begins, they do not address questions of why and how migrants themselves choose migration over alternative options. Nor do they question the basis for migrants' assumption that others will be able to follow and that they themselves will be able to return and remigrate in circular fashion. Migration systems theory, however, provides a useful framework with which to understand how macro-structural forces are linked intricately to individual migrants (Kritz, Lim and Zlotnik 1992, Castles and Miller 1993). Operating at the micro-structural level, this theory pays major attention to participation of migrants in the process of constructing their own systems for sustaining the flow of migrants between the two countries over time. While driven by push-pull factors specific to a particular historical context, the migrants actively mobilize individual, family and community resources, all of which are under their control and beyond the reach of outside forces. A result is the rapid development of extensive social and informational networks linking migrants in the receiving country with one another and with their kinsmen in the sending country (Boyd 1989).

Once the migrants' networks are formed in the receiving country, they tend to grow into small-scale ethnic communities with their own institutions and enterprises, including commercial services, employment agencies, cultural associations, entertainment sites, etc. (Castles and Miller 1993: 25). Immigration policies, business cycles and public attitudes toward foreigners and ethnic minorities in the host society significantly influence the development of migrant populations and ethnic communities. However, these migrants' communities tend to remain resilient and flexible because family and community ties sustain the flow of immigrants, while the growing ethnic economy in the receiving country functions to absorb incoming immigrants and their families (Cornelius, Martin and Hollifield 1994, Massey *et al.* 1987).

Communities of immigrants thus created in receiving countries have a number of common characteristics; demographic, geographic, industrial and occupational concentrations are the most distinctive (Piore 1979, Bonacich and Cheng 1984). The primary constituents, at least during the early stages of immigration, are usually men of working age who have traveled alone. Communities, formed by these individuals and the families who have joined them, are characterized by distinctive values and ways of thinking. The fact that immigrants typically strongly believe that they will return to their homeland at some time is an example of such thinking. In reality, however, as the duration of their stay grows longer, the possibility that they will return diminishes. Nevertheless, by retaining this hope, they achieve psychological solace and are able to endure physical hardship in daily routines. This "myth of return" also serves to put the immigrant group in an extremely marginal position within the receiving society because the host population perceives its presence as being temporary and without substantial participation in social activities (Heisler 1986, Safran 1991).

Finally, migration systems theory focuses on the role played by the sending country in sustaining the migratory flow. Migration does not end with the settlement and cultural adaptation of migrants in the receiving country. A community which sends migrants constitutes an important network for migrants and becomes the source of subsequent chain migration (Alexander 1991). Returnees bring the latest information about the receiving country to the sending country, thus greatly assisting those who will migrate next (Morawska 1991). As they face a prolonged stay, immigrants often seek to reunite their families in the host country, as has been the case among Mexican migrants (Massey *et al.* 1987, Hondagneu-Sotelo 1994). Moreover, if the host government changes its policies and restricts immigration to families of resident immigrants, the latter promptly send for them. A case in point is that of Turkish "guest workers" in the former West Germany (Castles 1984, Wilpert 1992).

This kind of mutual exchange between the sending and receiving countries results, over time, in the diffusion of what has been called "socialization of migration" (Pellerin 1993: 249) or a "migration mentality" (Arnold 1992: 211) within migrant communities in both countries. Once migration and circulation are established as household survival strategies, migrants and families progressively develop a culture for coping with the social and psychological costs that long-term migration typically incurs. As a result, the migrants experience little guilt for having left, while their families attempt to counteract the effects of their absences by mobilizing extended family networks (Simmons and Guengant 1992). Those who adapt most successfully to long periods of sojourning, such as young people with few family responsibilities, tend to become caught up in the flow of circular migration and to migrate repeatedly (Massey *et al.* 1987: 174–90). On the other hand, those who are less adaptable, typically parents or children of the migrants, remain in the home community. They also experience the indirect socialization of migration through correspondence, return visits by migrants and, occasionally, by their own visits to the migrants. The impact on children is particularly great, leading them to continue the pattern of migration in the next generation. Socialization of migration consequently serves to supplement, and in some instances may replace, economic motives for international migration (Pellerin 1993).

In the next section, I will discuss the history of Japanese Brazilian migration, first from Japan to Brazil, and then from Brazil to Japan. My objective is to illustrate a complex set of socio-historic and politico-economic forces that have contributed to the process of circular migration for three generations of *Nikkei* Brazilians from 1908 to 1995.

The analysis begins with Japanese emigration to Hawaii as early as the mid-1880s, followed by emigration to Brazil two decades later when Japan was rapidly emerging as a semi-periphery of the capitalist world economy (Chirot 1977). The development of Japanese ethnic communities in both rural and urban areas of southern Brazil from the 1910s to the 1970s is then analysed, followed by a discussion of the contexts within which descendants of the emigrants returned from Brazil to Japan in the early 1990s, which is two decades after Japan's rapid ascendance to the center of the Asia-Pacific rim economy. Finally, this section will present a demographic analysis of the 200,000 *Nikkei* Brazilians in Japan during the late 1980s and early 1990s and the development of migration networks among them.

History of labor migration: Japan to Brazil and return

Japanese emigration to North and South America 1880–1908

Emigration from Japan was prohibited by the feudal Tokugawa government until its fall in 1868. By the late 1880s, twenty years of Meiji government reforms under the national slogan "Rich Country, Strong Military" had led to the brink of bankruptcy. The drastic deflationary policy of the government succeeded in controlling massive inflation but in lowering the price of rice, which severely hit farmers already burdened with heavy taxes. Failed farmers and landless tenants moved to cities where they could not be absorbed by newly-developing industrialization and latent capitalism. In South-western Japan, where land holdings per household were small and recruitment efforts were most concentrated, a significant portion of this displaced population chose emigration rather than joining the unemployed (Moriyama 1984: 258–62).[2]

In 1885, the first group of Japanese immigrants, mainly young unmarried males responding to recruitment by sugar plantation owners, went to Hawaii to work as contract laborers (Ichioka 1988, Moriyama 1984). These emigrants to Hawaii, and later to the west coast of the United States replaced the Chinese laborers who had been expelled by the 1882 Chinese Exclusion Act. Japanese immigration to Hawaii and the west coast of the United States continued until it was curtailed by the limitations imposed by the "Gentlemen's Agreement" of 1907–8 between the United States and Japan (see the first column of Table 6.1). This diverted the flow of Japanese to Latin America.[3] At the same time, Brazil was experiencing a labor shortage which had begun with the abolition of slavery in 1888 and was exacerbated by the expanding demand for coffee in Europe. Large coffee plantation owners (*fazendeiros*) responded at first by recruiting approximately two million contract workers (*colonos*, farm hands) from Italy, Portugal and Spain between 1880 and 1910.

The Japanese were relative late comers among the successive waves of immigrants into Brazil after 1880. The first ship carrying immigrants to Brazil, *Kasatomaru*, took 781 Japanese to the port of Santos in 1908. This marked the beginning of the nearly ninety-year history of Japanese immigration to Brazil. Unlike the Japanese who emigrated to North America, most of those arriving in Brazil were accompanied by their families. In an effort to secure the stability of their labor force, employers required in the contracts that a family unit comprise three to ten laborers aged between twelve and forty-five (Suzuki 1992: 141). Frequently unable to meet this requirement, the emigrants often created "paper families" (*kōsei kazoku*, "constituted families") of unrelated people. Typically, a married couple incorporated relatives, friends and neighbors into their family unit and traveled together. Upon their arrival, many paper families were dissolved and members reverted to their original relationships (Maeyama 1996: 43).

Based on changes in immigrants' plans, occupations and community leadership, Japanese immigration to Brazil may be divided into three periods: 1908 to 1924, short-term migrant workers; 1925 to 1941, long-term migrant workers; and 1945 to the present, permanent settlers (see the second column of Table 6.1).[4]

Japanese Brazilian migration, 1908 to the present

Brazil 1908 to 1924: short-term migrant workers

About 35,000 Japanese entered Brazil during the first period, 1908–24 (see Table 6.2). These immigrants worked as contract farm hands in large coffee plantations (*fazendas*) scattered in Southern Brazil, primarily in the state of São Paulo. They were farmers and their families, mostly from South-western Japan, who intended to work as laborers for a few years and then return home with substantial savings. However, employer-employee relations on the *fazendas* reflected the fact that slavery had only been abolished two decades before. Working conditions were brutal, wages extremely low and employers autocratic. The immigrants resisted, often refusing to work, and many employers responded with threats, and sometimes acts, of violence. As a result, immigrants' dreams of getting rich quickly and returning home were shattered.

Brazil 1925–1941: long-term migrant workers

In 1925 the Japanese government made it national policy to promote emigration to Brazil. As a result the decade from 1925 to 1934 witnessed the peak of Japanese immigration to Brazil with more than 120,000 immigrants, among whom women accounted for 41 percent (see Table 6.2). This large influx of non-European immigrants, however, inevitably led to the anti-immigration policy of Brazil's nationalist government (Skidmore 1990, Lesser 1995).[5] Passage of the 1934 Constitution drastically cut the admission of Japanese immigrants and Japan's subsequent participation in the Second World War completely halted emigration from Japan to Brazil.

During the period 1925 to 1941, most immigrants left the plantations upon the completion of their contracts and became independent farmers (*sitiantes*), first by leasing, then by purchasing, land in more remote and undeveloped areas. Cultivation of rice, coffee, cotton and other crops brought relative success and stability but the immigrants' plans to return home were indefinitely delayed because of slow returns on agricultural investment. Isolated from cities and "civilization," these immigrants lived in their own ethnic settlements (*colonias Japonesas*) where Japanese language and community ethos were maintained.

Brazil, 1945 to the present: permanent settlers

Japan's surrender in 1945 caused severe shock and much confusion among Japanese Brazilians, most of whom had been convinced that victory for Japan was inevitable. As they came to realize that the Japan to which they had hoped to return no longer existed, most immigrants made the decision to settle permanently in Brazil. After 1945 declining agriculture in Brazil pushed many immigrants to cities so that, by the end of the 1950s, almost half the Japanese immigrants lived in cities of Southern Brazil, mostly in the State of São Paulo.

During the same period, Japan re-entered the international community, giving rise in 1953 to a new flow of Japanese migrants to Brazil (see the third column of Table 6.1). Economic hardships resulting from the devastation of war led some to emigrate permanently. However, Japanese economic prosperity in the 1960s quickly eliminated the economic advantages of emigration until, in 1973, the Japanese government officially announced discontinuation of its emigration program.[6] A total of almost 60,000 Japanese had emigrated to Brazil during two decades (1953 to 1973), of which an estimated 30 to 40 percent were women (see Table 6.2).[7]

Brazil, social differentiation and labor migration

During the prosperous 1960s – the "economic miracle of Brazil" – the *Nikkeijin* population underwent rapid internal changes. Based on a census of Japanese Brazilians in 1958, Maeyama (1990: 213) reports that a sample of approximately 66,000 non-agricultural people aged ten and over (extracted from a total population of 430,000) revealed the formation of three social classes: "old middle class," "new middle class," and "working class." The old middle class, comprising primarily the self-employed engaged in family business, accounted for 63 percent of the sample. These were mostly *issei* (first generation) and older *nisei* (second generation) who lacked formal Brazilian education. As latecomers to urban commercial occupations, their entrepreneurship survived by relying heavily on unpaid labor provided by wives and children.

The new middle class, comprising primarily the children of members of the old middle class and made up of salaried employees in occupations requiring professional and technical skills, accounted for 20 percent of the sample. Japanese parents, while persevering in family businesses, sought a brighter future for their sons by sending them to universities for professional training. As a result of traditional gender roles, daughters received less education, most remaining at home to assist their parents until they married. Thus, members of the new middle class comprised younger Brazilian-born, Portuguese speaking *nisei* and *sansei* (third generation)

Table 6.1 Chronology of Japanese migration to Brazil and return to Japan, 1908–95

Year	Historical Events in Brazil, Japan and US	Pre-Second World War Japanese Immigrants in Brazil	Post-Second World War Japanese Immigrants in Brazil
1905			
1910	U.S. Gentlemen's Agreement (1908)	Period I "Short-term Migrant Workers" (1908–24) [First immigrants (*Issei*) arrive, 1908] *Colonos* (contract laborers) in coffee plantations	
1915	First World War (1914–18)		
1920			
1925	U.S. Immigration Act (1924)	Period II "Long-term Migrant Workers" (1925–41) [Arrival of the largest number of immigrants, 1925–34] *Sitiantes* (independent farmers) in Japanese colonies	
1930	Great Depression (1929) Brazil's *Estado Nôvo* (1930–45)		
1935	Japan's Occupation of Manchuria (1931–45) Brazil's New Constitution (1934)		
1940			
1945	Second World War (1941–45) Japan's Surrender (1945)	Period III "Permanent Settlers" Period (1945 to Present) [Coming of age of second generation (*Nisei*)]:	

Table 6.1 (continued)

	Urban migration and occupational differentiation		
1950			
1955	US–Japan Peace Treaty (1951)		First Post-War Immigrants (*Issei*) arrive, 1953: Permanent settlers in agriculture; Families of pre-Second World War immigrants
1960			
1965	Japan's Economic Miracle (1960–73)	Coming of age of third generation (*Sansei*)	Coming of age of second generation (*Nisei*)
1970	OPEC Oil Embargo (1973)		
1975	Brazil's Economic Crisis (1981–91)		
1980			
1985	G7 Plaza Agreement (1985)	Coming of age of fourth generation (*Yonsei*); Labor migration to Japan limited to those having Japanese citizenship (most of whom are *Nisei*)	Labor migration to Japan limited to those having Japanese citizenship (most of whom are *Issei*)
1990	The Bubble Economy (1988–91); Japan's Immigration Reform (1990)	Massive migration to Japan by *Nisei* and *Sansei* without Japanese citizenship	Migration to Japan by *Nisei* without Japanese citizenship
1995	Major Economic Recession (1992–present)	Alien Registration records 201,795 Brazilians as of December 1996	

men and their families. The working class, made up of wage laborers (including students holding such jobs), constituted the remaining 17 percent of the sample.[8]

The economic crises that hit Brazil in the 1970s and 1980s caused serious financial trouble for most Brazilians. Hyper-inflation and unemployment primarily threatened the urban employed class. By the mid-1980s, many Brazilians had come to view emigration as a route to economic survival (Goza 1994, Margolis 1994). A small but unknown number of Japanese Brazilians joined the exodus in the mid-1980s. Typically, these were men and women of middle age and older – *nisei* and postwar *issei* – who were engaged in agriculture and traditional small business, but spoke fluent Japanese and, more importantly, retained Japanese citizenship.

As Brazil's economic crisis continued to worsen into the late 1980s, stable middle-class *nisei* and *sansei* who held professional and managerial positions, mostly men, began to migrate to Japan. A legal barrier, however, confronted the majority of them because they did not hold Japanese citizenship. Japan follows the principle of *jus sanguinis* (law of blood) in determining Japanese citizenship and required that a child's birth be registered with Japanese authorities within fourteen days after birth for the child to be granted citizenship.[9] For immigrant parents living in remote areas of Brazil, this registration was a hardship so that many second generation Japanese children (*nisei*) were not registered as Japanese citizens and, therefore, under the Japanese Nationality Law were defined as foreigners despite their Japanese ancestry.

Japan's new immigration policy and the Nikkeijin *influx*

The rising tide of arrivals in Japan of *nisei* and *sansei* of Brazilian citizenship in the late 1980s brought to the surface a number of inconsistencies and inadequacies in Japanese immigration laws and policies (Yamanaka 1996a). Prior to their arrival, illegal employment of Asians in unskilled sectors had attracted national attention

Table 6.2 Number of Japanese emigrants from Brazil, 1908–89, and proportion of women, 1908–42

Year	Total (1)	Total (2)	Women	% women
1908–10	1,714	1,703	571	33.5
1911–20	26,947	26,914	10,421	38.7
1921–30	70,914	64,480	29,839	46.3
1931–42	89,411	87,780	34,414	39.2
1945–50	10	—	—	—
1951–60	44,655	—	—	—
1961–70	14,938	—	—	—
1971–80	8,333	—	—	—
1981–89	3,436	—	—	—
Total	260,358	180,877	75,245	41.6

Source: Watanabe 1994, CCEYH 1991.

Notes: Total (1) is derived from emigration records (Watanabe 1994: 126).

Total (2) is derived from immigrant lists by immigration companies (CCEYH 1991: 86).

The statistics on women are derived from Total (2).

(Morita and Sassen 1994, Yamawaki ch. 2). Faced with an increasing number of illegal workers, the Japanese government revised its 1951 Immigration Control and Refugee Recognition Law in 1989. The new law, which took effect on 1 June 1990, maintained the old principle of limiting imported labor to skilled occupations but implemented two important new measures. First, in order to eliminate illegal labor, it instituted criminal penalties for the recruitment and hiring of unskilled foreign workers.[10] Second, the law created a new "long-term" visa exclusively for descendants (up to the third generation) of Japanese emigrants. This visa, designed to attract cheap "Japanese" (*Nikkeijin*) labor, granted up to three years' residence without restriction on socio-economic activities (Yamanaka 1993, 1996a, Cornelius 1994).[11] Spouses and children of *Nikkeijin* immigrants would also be permitted to stay, usually for up to one year. Renewal of visas of this category would easily (and therefore frequently) be done, as a result of which the *Nikkeijin* and their families could remain even longer than initially permitted.

The interests of, and pressure from, small-scale employers were clearly reflected in these measures of the Revised Immigration Law. Most importantly, the legal admission of *Nikkeijin* was a political compromise on the part of the Japanese government taken, on the one hand, to accommodate labor-starved small-scale employers and, on the other, as an attempt to maintain racial, ethnic and social homogeneity in the face of progressive internationalization (Lie ch. 4). By constructing the new category of *Nikkeijin* immigrants, the incumbent government was able to avoid complaints and accusations by one of its most influential constituencies, small-scale factory owners.[12] Simultaneously, the government could maintain the core principle of the nationality and immigration laws, *jus sanguinis*, thus making the revision a technical rather than political one. The conservative agenda of maintaining ethnic and social homogeneity was therefore upheld without being subject to criticism as "racially" motivated. A precedent for this policy existed in the fact that special admission of descendants of former emigrants had been widely practiced in such European countries as Italy and Spain (*Immigration Newsmagazine* 1990). To summarize, the 1.28 million descendants of Japanese immigrants in Brazil came to be viewed in Japan as an expedient: a source of ethnically acceptable unskilled labor, highly motivated to come to Japan (Yamanaka 1996a).

Demography and social structure of the *Nikkei* Brazilian population in Japan

Population

Flow and stock

An influx of *Nikkeijin* followed immediately upon implementation of the Revised Immigration Law on 1 June 1990 (Table 6.3). Legitimized as residents and workers by the new policy, young *nisei* and *sansei* men and women and their families constituted an overwhelming majority of *Nikkeijin* immigrants. In 1991 the annual influx of Brazilian nationals, mostly persons of Japanese ancestry, reached a peak of 96,377. This was followed by a sharp drop of 15 percent in 1992 when the Japanese economy plunged into a serious recession (Table 6.3, first column). In the same year, during Japan's deepening recession, many *Nikkeijin* lost their jobs, and 26,500 exited whilst 81,500 entered (Table 6.3 columns 1 and 5). This contrasts with figures from 1991, when 20,200 exited and 96,400 entered. The number who re-entered doubled from 12,600 in 1991 to 23,900 in 1992, representing an increase in the proportion of re-entries among all entries from 13 percent in 1991 to 29 percent in 1992 (Table 6.3 columns 3 and 4). The Brazilian influx over the next two years (1993–94) dropped to 70,000, of which more than one third were re-entries. In these two years, the proportion of exits (an average of 35,000 per year) to entries also rose to 50 percent, revealing a high turnover among *Nikkei* Brazilian migrants. Admissions surged again in 1995 by 25 percent to 90,000 and increased in 1996 to 94,000: the highest since 1991. These exit and re-entry statistics clearly indicate that by 1996, six years after the immigration reform, the wave of new arrivals had subsided, giving way to repeat arrivals who circulate frequently between the two countries.

Despite its transient nature, the *Nikkei* Brazilian population in Japan has grown enormously since 1990 according to *Zairyū Gaikokujin Tōkei* (Statistics on Alien Residents), an annual publication by the Japan Immigration Association (1990–6). As shown in column 7 of table 6.3, the number of registered Brazilians staying longer than three months doubled from 56,000 in 1990 to 120,000 in 1991.[13] The population continued to grow and reached over 200,000 by 1996, making this ethnic group the third largest immigrant population behind 700,000 Koreans and 220,000 Chinese.[14] In Brazil, the Japanese Brazilian population was estimated at 1.28 million in 1988. The 200,000 *Nikkeijin* in Japan are 16 percent of the number of people of Japanese descent in Brazil. This proportion increases to 25 percent, if the calculation is limited to the working age population between 16 and 60 years of age (São Paulo *Jinbun Kagaku Kenkyujo* 1988: 29).[15] The impact of this exodus on Japanese Brazilian communities in Brazil is socially, economically and politically immeasurable.

Table 6.3 Flows and stock of Brazilian population in Japan, 1989–96

| Year | Flows (Entries and Exits) | | | | | | Stock |
	Total entries*	First-time entries**	Repeat entries***	Rate of repeat entries	Total exits	Rate of exits	Alien registration
	[1]	[2]	[3]	[4]	[5]	[6]	[7]
1989	29,241	27,819	1,422	4.9	14,831	50.7	14,528
1990	67,303	63,462	3,841	5.7	17,122	25.4	56,429
1991	96,377	83,785	12,592	13.1	20,185	20.9	119,333
1992	81,495	57,574	23,921	29.4	26,511	32.5	147,803
1993	70,719	44,804	25,915	36.6	35,674	50.4	154,650
1994	72,236	45,790	26,446	36.6	34,287	47.5	159,619
1995	90,322	57,020	33,302	36.9	33,346	36.9	176,440
1996	94,068	60,187	33,881	36.0	30.461	32.4	201,795

Source: Japan Immigration Association (1990–97, 1989–97).
Notes: * Total number of entries in the year
** Number of new entries in the year.
*** Number of multiple entries in the year
[3]=[1]-[2]; [4]=[3]/[1]x100; [6]=[5]/[1]x100; [7] = total number of foreigners who registered as alien residents to stay for more than three months.

Age structure and sex ratio

Following the legalization of *Nikkei* migration in 1990, the inflow of Brazilians has become increasingly younger and feminized. As Table 6.4 shows, the age structure and sex ratio of Brazilian arrivals changed significantly between 1988 and 1994, from a pattern of working age male predominance to one of a more balanced age and sex composition. In 1988, males from fifteen to forty-four years of age comprised two-thirds of all male arrivals and outnumbered female arrivals by 23 percent. This pattern changed as the sojourning boom intensified in 1990. Male arrivals increased in nearly all age categories, resulting in a sharp rise in sex ratio (from 134 to 159) accompanied by an equally sharp drop in the average age (from thirty-seven to thirty-two). By 1994, females had increased in all but two age categories, lowering the sex ratio to 132. Finally, the proportion of children aged under fourteen among the migrants increased from 4.5 to 6.8 percent between 1988 and 1994. Clearly, *Nikkei* Brazilian migration to Japan is family-oriented, involving a high proportion of women and children. This demographic characteristic bears crucial importance to understanding patterns and processes of *Nikkei* Brazilian migration, settlement and adaptation in Japan (Yamanaka 1997).

Residence and occupations

According to *Zairyū Gaikokujin Tōkei,* which provides geographic and occupational distributions of alien residents, *Nikkei* Brazilians are concentrated in non-metropolitan localities where manufacturing industries are heavily represented. In 1995, about half the registered Brazilians in Japan lived in five prefectures of the Tokai (central Pacific coast) and the Kanto (north-central) regions: Aichi, Shizuoka, Kanagawa, Saitama and Gunma (see Table 6.6). Among these, the prefectures with the highest proportions of Brazilians in the prefectural populations were Shizuoka, Gunma and Aichi. Within these non-metropolitan prefectures, *Nikkeijin* were concentrated primarily in cities and towns where manufacturing industries were clustered, for example Hamamatsu in Shizuoka Prefecture, and Ota and Oizumi in Gunma Prefecture.

In 1995, more than two-thirds of Brazilians men and half the Brazilian women, nationwide, were machine operators engaged in assembling automobile and electric appliance parts in factories (see table 6.6). Implied in these statistics is the unprecedented social change currently sweeping many non-metropolitan, working class localities, such as Hamamatsu and Ota, where residents rarely saw "foreigners" prior to the influx of *Nikkeijin*.

Structural linkage and migration networks

This analysis of Japanese Brazilian migration history from 1908 to 1995 reveals a number of socio-historic and politico-economic forces at work in shaping structures and processes of migration between the two countries. The most important of these occurred at the turn of the twentieth century when the Japanese economy rose to the status of a "semi-peripheral" economy (Chirot 1977). By the 1960s, Japan had become the center of the Asian-Pacific regional

Table 6.4 Age structure and sex ratio of Brazilian arrivals in Japan, 1988–94

Age	1988			1990			1992			1994*		
	Male %	Female %	Sex ratio	Male %	Female %	Sex ratio	Male %	Female %	Sex ratio	Male %	Female %	Sex ratio
0–14	4.1	5.1	109	4.3	6.9	98	5.9	8.6	100	6.2	7.6	108
15–24	14.5	21.7	89	29.0	30.2	153	26.3	29.0	132	26.3	28.6	121
25–34	25.3	27.7	122	30.5	28.7	169	29.5	28.0	153	29.0	28.3	135
35–44	25.7	18.4	187	18.5	15.1	195	19.8	14.9	193	10.3	8.3	163
45–54	17.0	13.3	170	12.1	12.8	150	13.0	12.9	147	16.8	14.0	158
55–64	8.9	9.8	122	4.3	5.1	135	4.0	5.1	114	8.2	9.4	116
65–70+	4.4	4.1	144	1.3	1.2	171	1.3	1.5	133	3.2	4.0	108
Total	100.0	100.0	134	100.0	100.0	159	100.0	100.0	145	100.0	100.0	132
Mean age	38.1	35.8	37.2	32.2	31.4	31.9	32.3	31.3	31.9	32.1	31.6	31.9
Number	9,603	7,186	—	41,316	25,987	—	48,247	33,248	—	41,054	31,182	—

Source: Japan Immigration Association (1989–97).
Note: *The age brackets for 1994 are classified differently from the previous years. They are: 0–14, 15–24, 25–34, 35–39, 40–49, 50–59 and 60+.

economy. During the same period, stagnation in agriculture and delayed large-scale industrialization had plummeted Brazil from one of the world's major labor importing countries to a large labor exporter (Margolis 1994). As a result of this reversal of fortunes, Japanese immigrants and their descendants in Brazil were forced to return from Brazil to Japan in the early 1990s in their search of better economic opportunities. Although global economic restructuring played the key role in mobilizing *Nikkeijin*, this historical analysis has also identified the powerful effect of political forces in breaking down legal barriers which had long excluded unskilled foreigners from Japan.

In addition to the politico-economic forces directly responsible for *Nikkeijin*'s return migration, close cultural links through family and kinship ties between the *Nikkeijin* community in Brazil and its ancestral homeland played a part. The large representation of women in the *Nikkeijin* immigrant population throughout its history in Brazil no doubt contributed to the maintenance of such transnational family networks across the Pacific (Yanagisako 1995). In the late 1980s and early 1990s, two patterns of migration emerged based on the extensive information networks among *Nikkeijin* migrants.

The first is "return migration" to Japan by older, Japanese speaking generations comprising both post-war *issei* immigrants and children (*nisei*) of pre-war immigrants. When the 1990 Revised Immigration Law was implemented, a second pattern emerged: "family chain migration," whereby children (*nisei*) of postwar *issei* and grand children (*sansei*) of pre-war immigrants followed in their parents' footsteps. Major changes in age structure and sex ratio among Brazilian arrivals accompanied this second pattern of migration (see table 6.4). Unlike former generations, these younger generations speak only Portuguese and have little first-hand experience with Japanese culture.

Nikkeijin as transnational and return migrants

In 1994 and 1995, I conducted research in both Japan and Brazil in order to understand the migration mechanisms through which *Nikkei* Brazilians circulate between the two countries over time. In March and November 1994, I carried out

Table 6.5 Residence of registered Brazilians in Japan: the top five prefectures, 1995

Prefecture	Number of Brazilians	% of total Brazilian population in Japan	% of total population in prefecture*
Aichi	29,787	16.9	0.44
Shizuoka	25,012	14.2	0.68
Kanagawa	13,958	7.9	0.17
Saitama	10,804	6.1	0.16
Gunnma	10,305	5.8	0.52
Total	89,866	50.9	0.33

Source: Japan Immigration Association (1990–7)
Note: * Population in March 1992 (*Asahi Shimbun* 1993: 272)

Table 6.6 Occupation of registered Brazilians in Japan, 1995

Occupation	Men	%	Women	%	Total	%
Machine operator	66,353	65.3	35,338	47.3	101,691	57.6
Clerical worker	7,201	7.1	4,510	6.0	11,711	6.6
Service worker	1,462	1.4	4,142	5.5	5,604	3.2
Sales worker	355	0.3	315	0.4	670	0.4
General worker	2,629	2.6	1,449	1.9	4,078	2.3
No occupation	21,993	21.6	28,229	37.8	50,222	28.5
Other	23,684	23.3	29,002	38.8	52,686	29.9
Total	101,684	100.0	74,756	100.0	176,440	100.0

Source: Japan Immigration Association (1990–7).

unstructured interviews with members of sixty-three *Nikkeijin* households in Hamamatsu (Shizuoka Prefecture) and Toyohashi (Aichi Prefecture) of the Tokai Region, Central Japan.[16] In July 1995, I conducted a similar study with members of thirty three households of *Nikkeijin* who had returned from Japan to three major cities in Southern Brazil: São Paulo, Londrina and Porto Alegre. These surveys yielded data (referred to below as *Nikkeijin* data) containing information on 171 individuals aged fifteen and over: eighty-one women and ninety men. In addition, a questionnaire in Portuguese was issued to 100 people of which fifty-three were returned.

These interviews with *Nikkeijin* in Japan and Brazil reveal that, while *nisei* and *sansei* generations of prime working age constitute the majority of the sample, there are also a small number (fourteen) of older *issei* and *nisei* as well as a substantial number (twenty-eight) of Brazilian spouses of *Nikkeijin* men and women.[17] Findings from the data suggest that the migrants came primarily from the middle-class strata of Brazilian society. Among young *nisei* and *sansei*, education beyond high school was the norm; half have a high school education and a third have some years at college or a bachelor's degree. Prior to coming to Japan, most had held white collar or professional occupations such as engineer, lawyer, dentist, student, secretary, sales clerk and teacher. Older *issei* and *nisei* were commonly engaged in traditional family farm and small-business activities, while a few reported less lucrative occupations such as vendors and tenant farmers (for statistical findings, see Yamanaka and Koga 1996).[18] Thus, for many *Nikkeijin* migrants, contract labor in Japanese factories is a form of downward social mobility, however profitable it may be from an economic point of view.

I will now examine the findings from the *Nikkeijin* data. These are presented under four headings: motivation for migration; work experience and social marginality; family and ethnic community; and circular migration between Japan and Brazil.

Motivation for migration

Labor migrants are generally thought to emigrate in search of economic opportunities which are better than those available to them in their home country. Although this view applies to most *Nikkeijin* migrants, the 171 individuals studied in this research reveal much more complicated sets of factors than simple economic drives. Gender, age, generation, class and ethnicity prove to be the major variables generating differential responses to calls for labor from *Nikkeijin*'s ancestral homeland. Subtle variations in motives for migration emerge in interviews with older *nisei* who grew up as Japanese (*Nihonjin*) in *colonias Japonesas*. Benefiting from two generations of investment, they are already financially secure, usually owning a house or condominium in Brazil. Asked about their primary motives for migration to Japan, these *Nikkeijin* in their sixties emphasized personal curiosity and a chance to travel rather than monetary goals. Historical and family ties to Japan come to the fore when they speak of their motives for the journey. Sixty-two year-old Yoko Ikeda elaborated her long cherished dream of going to Japan:

> I wanted to go to Japan all my life. It was the homeland where my parents were born and my relatives still live. In Brazil, before the war when the government prohibited teaching foreign languages, we learned to speak Japanese underground. More recently, my eldest daughter received a fellowship to study Japanese in Japan and went there as a student. I myself wished to go . . . it was a dream. But finally, when I decided to work in Japan, my second daughter did not like the idea. She must have felt embarrassed. I was disheartened. If I had given up my dream then, I would not have been able to do what I wanted to do. One should be given an opportunity to realize one's wish. Telling me not to go did not deter me when I wanted to go at any cost.

The cultural factor motivating this woman poses a sharp contrast with the economic motivations of the younger, well educated *nisei* and *sansei* generations. With three-quarters of them married, the majority with children of school age, they were often accompanied in their migration by their spouses and children, hoping to get rich quickly in Japan and return to Brazil to re-establish themselves: buy a house, apartment or land and start a family business with their savings. As their forebears' history demonstrates, the immigrants' desire to be their "own boss" is deeply rooted in Japanese Brazilian immigration history and must be understood as a manifestation of household strategies employed to climb the socio-economic ladder of Brazilian society. Faced with economic chaos, young *Nikkeijin* sought a solution by returning to the strategy of establishing a family business, rather than preparing for salaried employment through higher education.

Motivations for migration among the twenty-eight Brazilian spouses of *Nikkeijin* men and women differed profoundly from those of either the older or younger *Nikkeijin* generations. The Brazilians were in a unique legal and social position as non-*Nikkeijin* spouses did not want to be separated from their *Nikkeijin* partners. Prior to departure from Brazil, few of these spouses were personally interested in Japanese culture or spoke Japanese. However, owing to the prevailing division of labor by gender, men in the workplace and women at home, these non-*Nikkeijin* husbands and wives tend to show divergent responses to migration. Asked why they migrated to Japan, non-*Nikkeijin* wives consistently referred to their *Nikkeijin* husbands' interest in migrating, while non-*Nikkeijin* husbands stressed economic motives rather than familial reasons for accompanying their *Nikkeijin* wives.

Work experience and social marginality

Having arrived in Japan all men and women, regardless of their backgrounds, worked as temporary contract laborers, filling gaps in the labor supply created by variations in labor demand, reflecting fluctuations in the business cycle and demographic change.

In the cities of Hamamatsu and Toyohashi manufacturing, especially of automobile parts, is a major industry. In Hamamatsu over 6,000 small sub-contractors – 50 percent of whom have less than five employees, and over 90 percent of whom have less than thirty – supply parts to large automobile assemblers such as Suzuki, Honda, Yamaha, Toyota and Nissan (Hamamatsu Municipal Office 1992). According to Castles (1984: 12), the migrant or "guest worker" system embodies institutional discrimination which is "designed to recruit and control temporary migrant workers" of foreign origin. In *Nikkeijin*'s employment, this institutional discrimination is manifest in the hiring system by which they are employed on short-term contracts by job brokers or job dispatchers (*assen* or *haken gyōsha*) who, in turn, send them to their actual workplaces in sub-contractors' factories. Their work requires physical strength and on-the-job experience but no complex technical or communication skills. The *Nikkeijin* "guest worker" system is designed, therefore, to function as a shock absorber or adjustment valve between peaks and troughs of the economy, so that Japanese workers' jobs and their wages remain secure during recessions. In addition to this dispatching service, most *Nikkeijin* rely heavily on job brokers in every aspect of their lives in Japan, including securing housing, furniture, documentation and their children's education. Job brokers charge substantial fees for many of these services with the result that *Nikkeijin* are unable to save as much money as they had originally hoped.

In the Hamamatsu and Toyohashi area, wages of *Nikkeijin* workers decreased by approximately 20 percent in 1992 when the Japanese economy went into a deep recession. At the same time, hours of overtime substantially decreased. During the depth of the recession, hundreds of *Nikkeijin* were discharged and returned home. None the less, the average monthly earnings (before tax, rent and other fees were deducted) of full-time factory workers ranged from 1,100 to 1,450 yen (eleven to fourteen dollars fifty cents) per hour for men aged from eighteen to fifty-four and from 900 to 1,000 yen (nine to ten dollars) per hour for women of similar age (see Table 6.7). These rates per hour equate to incomes of $1,900 to $3,000 per month for working eight hours per day and twenty-six days a month. One exception is older *issei* and *nisei* women who work as convalescent attendants in hospitals and private homes in the Tokyo metropolitan area and who receive about 14,000 yen ($140) per day for their around-the-clock, emotionally-charged jobs taking care of the terminally ill and bed-stricken elderly (Yamanaka 1996b, 1997). Japanese employers deduct the employment fee, taxes, apartment rents, utilities and other expenses from these monthly earnings. These deductions are usually offset by overtime and weekend work as rates are 25 percent higher than straight time. Thus the worker's take home pay is probably not significantly different from the figures shown in Table 6.7.

The high levels of income earned in Japan far exceeded those which *Nikkeijin* brought home in Brazil while working as professionals, secretaries, sales clerks and self-employed prior to migration. The Brazilian Institute of Geography and

Statistics calculates Brazilian wage standards by minimum monthly living wages. In April 1990 it was the equivalent of $70 (JETRO São Paulo Center 1992). Results from my written survey conducted in Brazil in July 1995 suggest that *Nikkeijin* migrants had earned on the average three to five times this minimum wage in Brazil prior to their departure for Japan.[19] Between 1988 and 1991 at the height of the economic growth, an unskilled male factory worker in Japan earned more than $100 per day including a few hours overtime. Women, because of gender inequality, usually earned 20 percent less than men for comparable jobs (Brinton 1993). These daily wages were equivalent to what he or she might earn in a month in Brazil.

The monetary rewards of migration, however, scarcely matched the psychological pain and social isolation *Nikkeijin* men and women endured in Japan. In addition to their vulnerability to systematic exploitation by job brokers, *Nikkeijin* factory workers all experienced blatant prejudice and discrimination in the workplace. Because of *Nikkeijin*'s ancestry and appearance, Japanese managers and co-workers tended to expect them to behave and speak like Japanese. It did not take the Japanese long to realize that most *Nikkeijin* are not the Japanese they had expected but "foreigners" who neither spoke Japanese nor conformed to Japanese practices and customs. When expectations of their "Japaneseness" were overtly contradicted, the Japanese often verbally abused them, calling them stupid, secondary Japanese and uncivilized people from a backward country.[20] They were regarded as slow and lazy in their work, impolite and rude in personal interactions.

Individual experiences of discrimination based on ethnicity varied according to *Nikkeijin*'s language ability, cultural understanding and work environment. None the less, the widespread discrimination against *Nikkeijin* by the Japanese suggests that Japanese definitions of cultural righteousness and their notions of ethnic hierarchy deserve close examination in future studies. Individual reactions of *Nikkeijin* men and women to such demeaning experiences reflected their varying cultural resources and social structural situations. Speaking fluent Japanese and working individually, older *issei* and *nisei* readily recognized indications of discrimination and therefore experienced Japanese discriminatory practices as personal affronts and persecution. In contrast, younger *nisei* and *sansei*, not speaking functional Japanese and working in teams on assembly lines, experienced cultural clashes with Japanese, not as individual problems, but as shared conditions of *Nikkeijin* factory employment. Consequently they managed to largely escape feelings of personal persecution based on their foreignness.

In response to such insulting treatment by people they thought of as fellow Japanese, *Nikkeijin* were confused and deeply hurt. Having grown up as *Japonês* in Brazil, the unexpectedly chilly welcome in their ancestral homeland seriously challenged their self-perceived ethnic identity. As a result, *Nikkeijin* began to distance themselves psychologically from the Japanese and came to see themselves as foreign Brazilians rather than *Nikkeijin* who are descendants of the Japanese (Yamanaka 1997). At the same time, they adopted the attitude of the temporary resident, saying "I'll be going home soon," or "I've come just to work." By consciously shifting their collective identity from ethnicity to nationality and believing in the sojourners' myth of return, *Nikkeijin* immigrants found psychological support for their long-term stays as "foreigners" in the host community:

Table 6.7 Wages (in yen) earned by Japanese Brazilian workers in Japan by gender and age, 1990–5

Gender	Occupation	Age	Hourly wage	Monthly wage
Male	Factory	Less than 17, more than 55	750– 900	156,000–187,200
		18–54	1,100–1,450	228,800–301,600
	Service	All ages	1,000–1,125	208,000–234,000
Female	Factory	Less than 17, more than 45	650–850	135,200–176,800
		18–44	900–1,000	187,200–208,000
	Service	All ages	800–1,000	166,400–208,000
	Convalescent attendant	More than 45	14,000 (daily)	364,000

Source: Nikkeijin data.
Note: Monthly wage is calculated by multiplying daily wage by 8 hours/day and 26 days/month.

"outsiders" in their ancestral homeland. This sense of cultural alienation in Japan culminates in the loss of feelings of belonging to either Japan or Brazil. Many *Nikkeijin* poignantly remarked on their displacement: "In Brazil, we were called *Japonês*, but in Japan we became *gaijin* (foreigners) or *Burajiru-jin* (Brazilians). No matter where we go, we *Nikkeijin*, have no home."

Nikkeijin *family and ethnic community*

Among the *Nikkeijin* in Japan, a demographic shift from a male-dominant sojourning population to one comprising men and women accompanied by their families occurred in 1990 (see Table 6.4). Findings from interviews with migrants in both Japan and Brazil in 1994 and 1995 confirm this population change. Most interviewees went to Japan with their families, apart from a few older *issei* and *nisei* who spoke good Japanese and were familiar with society and culture. Even single *Nikkeijin,* and those who currently live alone, usually have a family member working in Japan. Here the term "family" includes not only spouses, children, parents and siblings but other relatives such as uncles, aunts and cousins. When *Nikkeijin* families which had been dispersed by emigration were reunited in Japan, those who came first helped to establish the personal lives of the latecomers in their unfamiliar environment. While the arrival of children and elderly parents increases living expenses, it decreases the anxieties that afflict dispersed families and the loneliness that comes with long-term solitary migration. However, all able-bodied members of the family usually engage either formally or informally in gainful activities, thus increasing the total family income while decreasing individual food and rent expenses. Older relatives stay at home to look after the children while the parents work. The family also serves as a unit of mutual support in other ways: advancing money for moving expenses, finding jobs and housing, pooling salaries and savings, and sharing social life, leisure and travel.

Outside this intimate family unit, there are distant relatives and close friends who broaden the circles of interaction and solidarity. At weekends *Nikkeijin* workers relax, shop, visit friends or relatives and enjoy soccer games. School-age children attend nearby public schools during the day, often bringing *Nikkeijin* households their only meaningful contact with Japanese society. In April 1994, out of tens of thousands of students there were 338 Brazilian and Peruvian children enrolled in public elementary and junior high schools in Hamamatsu. Younger children quickly learn Japanese through school and television and emulate the behavior of their Japanese classmates. While their parents are impressed with the children's rapid acclimatisation, they wish them to retain Portuguese, their mother tongue, as they expect to return to Brazil in the near future. For this reason, the Hamamatsu Educational Board and private language schools offer Portuguese classes for *Nikkeijin* children at weekends. When I visited one of these classes, the children were studying Portuguese and Brazilian educational materials but, during breaks, they chatted in Japanese.

Six years after the mass migration of *Nikkeijin*, Hamamatsu has witnessed the rapid growth of small ethnic businesses geared to the diverse needs of the migrants and their families from Brazil. These establishments, which are mostly run by *Nikkeijin* entrepreneurs, include retail stores selling import Brazilian food, drinks, snacks, clothes, cosmetics, books, magazines, newspapers, videos, tapes and compact disks. As the Brazilian population rapidly grows (from 3,500 in 1990 to 7,000 in 1995), Hamamatsu has also seen the arrival of other kinds of commercial and cultural establishments for Brazilians, including restaurants, discos, banks, travel agents, Japanese language schools, employment services, legal consultation, hobby and sports clubs, catering services, day-care services, etc. Moreover, several Portuguese-language newspapers are published weekly throughout Japan. From my observations, *Nikkei* Brazilians in Japan are living in a Brazilian cultural enclave complete with familiar goods and symbols. At both the workplace and in their private lives, they communicate among themselves in Portuguese, cook and eat Brazilian food at home and in restaurants, wear clothing imported from Brazil, watch videos of Brazilian television broadcasts and dramas and read the latest information in Portuguese-language newspapers and magazines.

No matter how peripheral *Nikkeijin* may be in Japanese society, most are able to satisfy their basic material and cultural needs within their own narrowly defined ethnic community. By ethnic community, I mean a community of people who share a common ethnic background and relate to one another through work, family and friendship. In Hamamatsu, *Nikkeijin* and their families live in apartments scattered throughout the city that have been assigned to them by their employers so that there are no large concentrations of people of distinct ethnic and cultural background in particular areas. In addition to the relatively satisfactory material and family life *Nikkeijin* enjoy in Japan, the low-crime living environment is an attractive feature to those Brazilians who had experienced rampant violence in the streets of Brazilian cities. *Nikkeijin* appreciate the peaceful and stable life they experience in Japan despite being socially marginalised.

Nikkeijin *circular migration between Japan and Brazil*

How are these *Nikkeijin* men and women faring when they resettle in Brazil after having returned from their sojourn in Japan? How have they readjusted to their own society and economy after having worked in Japan? Do they plan to re-migrate to Japan if they find Brazil unsatisfactory in providing economic opportunities equivalent or better than those available in Japan? This final section will be limited to discussion of interviews with twenty-four men and twenty-seven women who returned from Japan and resettled in their home environments in São Paulo, Londrina and Porto Alegre. I have also found profound differential experiences and responses, in this resettlement process, according to gender, age, generation, social class, ethnicity and timing of return.

Among the twenty-seven women, eighteen belong to younger generations, either *nisei* or *sansei*, while two are non-*Nikkeijin*. Both groups had returned to Brazil in the past year and were still in the midst of transition from the migrant's life in Japan to the resident's life in Brazil. Many of the married women, and their husbands, have already bought new houses or apartments with their savings. Their material satisfaction is indicated by their stylishly-furnished modern homes and new cars. The remaining seven women include four Brazilian-born *nisei* and three Japanese-born post-Second World War *issei*. These older groups went to Japan between 1989 and 1992 and returned between 1991 and 1994. They had, therefore, been back one to four years by the time of the interviews. Free from work and family responsibility, the four *nisei* women appear to have readjusted fully to Brazilian society, devoting much of their energy to taking care of family affairs and socializing with friends.

In contrast, the three post-Second World War *issei* women work in the family businesses in which they and their husbands have invested their savings from their Japanese employment. Their concerns centered on their economic future in Brazil, their adopted country, instead of their emotional ties with it. Yoshiko Akiyama, fifty-seven, who opened a flower shop but whose excitement quickly evaporated because of rising inflation, raised questions about Brazilian political institutions and pondered the wisdom of having returned from Japan to Brazil.

> I don't know what to think about this country. In Brazil no one can foresee what will happen next. Why don't people revolt? My shop may not last too long because the rent has become too steep. I have lived in this country since 1964, but the longer I live the more I'm lost. Why did I return here? Maybe, my family. Maybe there is something else I have not yet figured out what it is in Brazil that keeps me coming back.

The economic insecurity revealed in Yoshiko's statement is a disturbing but common response among the twenty-four male returnees, both *Nikkeijin* and non-*Nikkeijin,* whose ages range across the spectrum. In January 1995, newly-elected President Fernando Henrique Cardoso and his government launched a new economic plan to control inflation. By July 1995, this austere policy had brought about a staggering rise in prices and bankruptcies (Veja 1995). Although anxious to start new businesses, many *Nikkeijin* returnees are discouraged from investing their hard-won savings acquired in Japan, and chose instead to wait in the hope that the economy will improve.

This slow and uncertain process of resettling is apparent in the distribution of the principal activities of the twenty men of working age. Seven are still catching up with their families, friends and communities, while collecting information about job opportunities and business climate. Six who had already started their own businesses, have chosen video production, architectural design, delicatessen, flower shop and a chain of meat shops. Three men had returned to the previous jobs they had before migration, or had taken over their parents' businesses, and another four had returned to school to further their education. Among twenty women of working age: nine are primarily housewives, raising children and participating in family affairs; four are operating new family businesses with their husbands or parents; two have returned to their former jobs or family businesses; four are preparing new family businesses; one has found a new salaried job.

Such profound economic insecurity has pushed many *Nikkeijin* to re-migrate to Japan. In my interviews of July 1995, I repeatedly heard stories of *Nikkeijin* returning to Japan after having failed in newly-established businesses. Although none of my forty interviewees of working age explicitly said that they planned to return to Japan for employment in the near future, they did not rule it out because of the unpromising economy in Brazil. If the business they started were to fail, or if one they had planned seemed unlikely to succeed, they indicated that they would be likely to return to Japan. The option of returning to Japan thus serves as a back-up to their decision to persevere in Brazil under the rapidly-deteriorating economic climate. For those who decide to return to Japan, the second migration is easier than the first because they have already experienced life and employment there. In addition, family members may be working in the area and will provide them with assistance upon arrival.

Because of this frequent traffic between Brazil and Japan, many *Nikkeijin* families in Brazil experience a near empty household and the community at large suffers from the absence of members. In the communities of *Nikkeijin* I interviewed, it was rare to find a household in which no one had migrated. A seventy-one-year-old post-Second World War immigrant man described *Nikkeijin* society in Londrina, with its many absences, as being "just like during the war (in Japan), when all the houses were empty." All this man's family, including his wife, daughter and her family, had gone to Japan, and he was left to look after the house on his own. In Londrina (a city of half a million), the *Nikkeijin* community has traditionally been active in organizing its members into a variety of cultural and social activities. Baseball, for example, is the most popular sports activity enjoyed by boys, girls and young men. However, the migration boom has created serious problems in recruiting the requisite athletes and coaches because so many have gone to Japan. Commenting on the impact of migration on *Nikkeijin* society, Antonio Ueno, a long-term Federal Congressman from the State of Parana, considered the boom to be the second biggest event in the postwar period – second to the violent post-wartime dispute between those *Nikkeijin* who believed Japan would be victorious in the Second World War and those who did not, which left a deep and abiding scar in the *Nikkeijin* community (Maeyama 1982b).[21]

Conclusion

This study has emphasized the importance of historical and cultural, as well as economic, factors in analyzing the mechanisms by which 200,000 descendants of Japanese immigrants have returned from Brazil to Japan in the early 1990s and begun to circulate between the two countries. According to Wallerstein (1982), the capitalistic principle of profit maximization requires constant long-term adjustment in the world economic order so that members of nation states constituting the global economic center constantly change. A case in point is Japan's rapid socio-economic transformation over 130 years that has reversed the direction of labor force flows between Japan and Brazil. This historic change has occurred in the context of cultural, political and economic interdependence between Japan and Brazil based on century-old ties of family, kinship and community. Historical analysis of emigration, immigration and return migration reveals a complex set of socio-historic and politico-economic forces operating to mobilize, release, transport and utilize a surplus labor force in Brazil (Portes 1978). Such large structural forces are also found at work in the rapid development of migration networks, the speedy process of settlement and the growing emergence of ethnic communities in Japan.

The process of circular diaspora formation in Japan by second and third generation Japanese Brazilians grows out of cultural and historical circumstances within which supply-push and demand-pull factors are embedded. The legalization of immigration in 1990 catalyzed massive, increasingly younger and feminized, flows of *Nikkeijin* migrants into Japan from Brazil. Although business interests were directly responsible for the recruitment of migrants, the migration process generated its own momentum as the migrants brought family- and community-based resources into play. Meanwhile, their cultural and material needs were met in the host society through extensive social networks and emerging ethnic entrepreneurship. An exploitative labor contract system, saddled with pervasive prejudice, reduced *Nikkeijin* to the status of temporary foreign workers living on the periphery of Japanese economy and society. Although discouraged and disoriented by the humiliation they encountered in Japan, many *Nikkeijin* none the less saw labor migration as the only means to maintain their middle-class life styles in Brazil under its worsening economy. Circulation between the two homelands, Brazil and Japan, thus became a way to secure a reliable source of income which was difficult to obtain in Brazil.

These findings suggest two major areas for future research that may shed light on long-term trends of immigration and ethnic minority relations in Japan. First is the transnational family strategies as *Nikkeijin* men and women accommodate to long-term migration between Brazil and Japan. The history of international migration is full of strategies which migrants have adopted for maintaining family and household cohesion under the pressures caused by geographic separation. Early Chinese immigrants in the United States, for example, maintained family continuity by splitting the household by gender between China and the United States (Glenn 1983). Some pre-Second World War Japanese immigrants sent their American-born children back to Japan for education in order to preserve their cultural identity (those who underwent this experience are called *kibei*) (Leighton 1946: 79–80). *Nikkeijin* migrant families are not exceptional and are in the process of rapidly developing their own family strategies as they adjust to long-term migration. Future studies must pay close attention to such emerging family and household adaptive patterns as they are shaped by *Nikkeijin* migrants at both ends of their transnational communities.

Second is the rapid development of *Nikkeijin* ethnic communities in non-metropolitan, primarily working-class cities. The increased and sustained presence of women and families in them is expected to contribute significantly to the enhancement of social and cultural interaction between immigrants and Japanese. *Nikkeijin* children's assimilation bridges the two communities which, though separated by history and language, share ethnic roots. However, given the exclusivity of Japanese society and culture with regard to foreigners it is unrealistic to expect rapid change in Japanese responses to *Nikkeijin* and their families. None the less, close interaction with the *Nikkeijin* in the workplace, schools and neighborhoods may well bring individual Japanese to multi-cultural and multi-linguistic awareness, tolerance and even respect in this age of transnational migration. If acceptance of ethnic diversity increases at the grass roots level, this may in turn increase Japan's ability to handle the increasingly pervasive political and social problems associated with such diversity in its domestic and international affairs. Future studies must not overlook the implications of the social and cultural ties *Nikkeijin* families and communities are establishing, largely unnoticed, with Japanese citizens in such localities as Hamamatsu and Toyohashi, where Portuguese conversations are now commonly heard on public transport and in shopping arcades.

Notes

The research was funded by the Abe Fellowship program sponsored by the Center for Global Partnership and the Social Science Research Council. Many individuals helped me in this research: Celia Nakamura, João Mashiko, Michio Matsuyama and Masuzo Ishikawa during field research, Eunice Koga in interviews with Portuguese speakers and Gerald Berreman and Ruth Hamilton in providing useful comments on the paper. I thank them all for their contributions.

1 In this chapter, *Nikkeijin* will refer exclusively to Japanese who immigrated into Latin America – Mexico, Peru, Brazil, Argentina, Bolivia and Paraguay – between the 1890s and 1970s and to their descendants, including holders of Japanese nationality or dual citizenship. *Nikkeijin* from other nations do not constitute a large, unskilled immigrant group in contemporary Japan and are not included.
2 The four emigrant prefectures in South-western Japan include Hiroshima, Yamaguchi, Fukuoka and Kumamoto. According to Moriyama (1984: 260–1), Hiroshima prefecture had the smallest amount of land per household and per individual. Yamaguchi and Fukuoka Prefectures had landholdings of approximately the national average. Recruiters from Hawaii had close political connections with the Japanese government and trading companies and were instructed by the Japanese to place their emphasis on recruitment in the prefectures of Yamaguchi, Hiroshima and Kumamoto. At that time, emigrants were called *kimin* (abandoned people) because they were pushed out of the country as a result of poverty.
3 The first Japanese immigrants to Latin America went to Mexico and Peru in the 1890s. More than 10,000 Japanese had emigrated to Mexico by 1910, while only a few hundred did so after then. Between 1898 and 1945, 27,000 Japanese emigrated to Peru (*Immigration Newsmagazine* 1990b: 22–3). For further information on Japanese emigration to Mexico, see Ueno (1994) and to Peru, see Morimoto (1992). Like Japanese

Brazilians, descendants of Japanese immigrants to Peru and Mexico also migrated to Japan for wage labor in the early 1900s.

4 Information for the summary history in this and the following sections is derived from a variety of sources, including Suzuki (1965), Fujimura (1970), Sims (1972), Saito (1976), Maeyama (1982a,1982b, 1984, 1986), Takahashi (1990), the Committee for Compiling Eighty-Year History of Japanese Immigration to Brazil (CCEYH 1991), and Suzuki (1992).

5 The growing presence of Japanese, and their marked success in agriculture, fueled anti-Japanese sentiments among the predominantly European-descended population. Brazil had long experienced racial problems between whites on the one hand and blacks and indigenous people on the other. Japanese came to be viewed as a problem because of their "alleged failure" to assimilate into Brazilian society (Skidmore 1990: 25). The new constitution limited immigration for any nationality to 2 percent of the total number of persons of a given nationality residing in Brazil during the preceding fifty years. This restriction, aimed at the Japanese, succeeded in sharply reducing immigration from Japan.

6 In the same period (1953–73), Japanese also emigrated to Argentina (4,600), Paraguay (7,500) and Bolivia (5,200). Emigrants to these countries and their descendants also returned to Japan to work in the late 1980s and the early 1990s.

7 According to Oshimoto's Chart 11 (1967: 13), the proportion of women among the emigrants was 30 to 40 percent between 1946 and 1960. Because numbers are not presented in the bar chart, it is impossible to measure the proportion precisely.

8 The working class will almost certainly diminish in the near future as its elderly immigrant members die off and the young Brazilian-born student members graduate into the new middle class.

9 The rule requiring parents to register the birth of a child at the Japanese authority within fourteen days was intended to prevent dual citizenship in the case of Japanese born in countries where the principle of *jus soli* (law of place) prevailed, as in Brazil and the United States (Yamada and Tsuchiya 1984: 68–71). This period was lengthened from fourteen days to three months under the revised 1985 Nationality Law.

10 Employers of illegal workers became liable to two years imprisonment or a maximum of two million yen ($20,000). Japanese policy-makers were influenced in this by their American counterparts who instituted the regulatory employer sanction policy in the United States with passage of the Immigration Reform and Control Act in 1986.

11 For legal definitions of *nisei* and *sansei*, see Ministry of Justice Decree No 132 of 24 May 1990.

12 Berrier (1985) discusses a similar compromise made by the French government in the 1970s. To win the political support of small-scale factory owners, the government permitted the importation of foreign workers in the textile industry, rather than encouraging that industry to modernize the production process, thereby reducing the need for labor.

13 Foreigners staying in Japan for more than three months are required by the Alien Registration Law to register their residence within ninety days of their arrival. The total given here does not include new arrivals who had not yet reported their residence.

14 Descendants of Korean and Chinese immigrants are accorded special permanent visas that allow them and their families to live in Japan with no restrictions on their activities (Yamada and Kuroki 1990: 108–12). As non-Japanese citizens, they are not granted political rights at either national or local levels.

15 The *Nikkeijin* population between 16 and 60 in Brazil was reported to be 736,000 in 1988. The estimated *Nikkeijin* population in this age category in Japan was 180,000 in 1995. The proportion of *Nikkeijin* in Japan in 1995, to those in Brazil in 1988, is therefore 24.5 percent.

16 These interviews were conducted in either Portuguese or Japanese and questions were answered in an open conversational style.

17 Interracial marriage between *Nikkeijin* and non-*Nikkeijin* in Brazil accounted for 45.9

percent of total marriages among the *Nikkeijin* population according to the *Nikkeijin* census of 1988 (São Paulo Jinbun Kagaku Kenkyujo 1988: 104). Inter-racial marriage rates vary considerably by region in Brazil, ranging from 69.2 percent in Central West to 23.3 in South. This seems to reflect differences in the size of Japanese population by region which is a result of different histories of Japanese community settlement: the South being the oldest and largest settlement region, compared to the Central West and North which are more recent and therefore constitute smaller settlement regions (São Paulo *Jinbun Kagaku Kenkyujo* 1988: 104–5). The relatively high rate of inter-racial marriage has resulted in the substantial number of non-*Nikkeijin* Brazilian men and women included in recent migration to Japan.

18 Findings from published accounts of *Nikkeijin* in Japan, such as a nation-wide study (N=1,027) by the Japan International Cooperation Agency (1992) and a survey (N=429) in Hamamatsu by the Hamamatsu Municipal Office (1993), generally support the demographic profiles of the *Nikkeijin* found in my study. These studies and mine differ in their methods and scales but they report similar trends in the demographic distribution and social class backgrounds among the *Nikkeijin* samples. My survey is different because I used personal interviews rather than structured questionnaires and focused on families rather than individuals.

19 The Brazilian statistics on income are expressed in multiples of the minimum wage. Because of the rapid change in inflation rates, the minimum wage is adjusted every four months.

20 Many informants were surprised and angry at the ignorance about Brazil exhibited by Japanese co-workers. Many Japanese believed Brazil to be backward, its people living like Indians in the Amazon rain forest.

21 Personal interview, 27 July 1995, Londrina.

References

Alexander, J. G. (1991) "Moving into and out of Pittsburgh: Ongoing Chain Migration," in R. J. Vecoli and S. M. Sinke (eds) *A Century of European Migrations, 1830–1930,* Urbana, Ill.: University of Illinois Press.

Arnold, F. (1992) "The Contribution of Remittances to Economic and Social Development," in M. Kritz, L. L. Lim and H. Zlotnik (eds) *International Migration: A Global Approach,* Oxford: Clarendon Press.

Asahi Shimbun (1994) *Japan Almanac 1994,* Tokyo: Asahi Shimbun.

Berrier, R. J. (1985) "The French Textile Industry: A Segmented Labor Market," in R. Rogers (ed.) *Guests Come to Stay: The Effects of European Labor Migration on Sending and Receiving Countries,* Boulder: Westview Press.

Bonacich, E. and Cheng, L. (1984) "Introduction: A Theoretical Orientation to International Labor Migration," in L. Cheng and E. Bonacich (eds) *Labor Migration under Capitalism: Asian Workers in the United States before World War II,* Berkeley: University of California Press.

Boyd, M. (1989) "Family and Personal Networks in International Migration: Recent Developments and New Agenda," *International Migration Review* 23, 3: 638–80.

Brinton, M. C. (1993) *Women and the Economic Miracle: Gender and Work in Postwar Japan,* Berkeley: University of California Press.

Castles, S. (1984) *Here for Good: Western Europe's New Ethnic Minorities,* London: Pluto Press.

Castles, S. and Miller, M. J. (1993) *The Age of Migration: International Population Movements in the Modern World,* New York: Guilford Press.

Committee for Compiling Eighty-Year History of Japanese Immigration to Brazil (CCEYH) (1991) *Burajiru Nihon Imin Hachijūnenshi* (Eighty Years History of Japanese

Immigrants to Brazil), São Paulo: Burajiru Nihon Bunka Kyōkai.

Chirot, D. (1977) *Social Change in the Twentieth Century,* New York: Harcourt Brace Jovanovich.

Cornelius, W. A. (1994) "Japan: The Illusion of Immigration Control," in W. A. Cornelius, P. L. Martin, and J. F. Hollifield (eds) *Controlling Immigration: A Global Perspective,* Stanford, Calif.: Stanford University Press.

Cornelius, W. A., Martin, P. L., and Hollifield, J. F. (eds) (1994) *Controlling Immigration: A Global Perspective,* Stanford, Calif.: Stanford University Press.

Fujimura, J. (1970) *"Burajiru ni Okeru Nikkei Shakai no Kōzō to sono Tenkai Katei – Nikkei Nōmin no Seikatsu wo Chūshin to Shite"* (Structure of the Japanese Brazilian Community in Brazil and Process of its Development – Life Patterns of Japanese Farmers), *Iju Kenkyū* 6 (September): 37–51.

Glenn, E. N. (1983) "Split Household, Small Producer and Dual Wage Earners: An Analysis of Chinese-American Family Strategies," *Journal of Marriage and the Family* 45, 1: 35–46.

Goza, F. (1994) "Brazilian Immigration to North America," *International Migration Review* 28, 1: 136–52.

Hamamatsu Municipal Office (1992) *Hamamatsu-shi Tōkeisho* (Statistics on Hamamatsu City), Hamamatsu City, Japan

—— (1993) *Hamamatsu-shi ni Okeru Gaikokujin no Seikatsu Jittai, Ishiki Chōsa–Nikkei Burajiru, Perūjin wo Chūshin ni* (Fact Finding Survey Report on Life and Attitudes of Foreign Residents in Hamamatsu City – *Nikkei* Brazilians and Peruvians), Hamamatsu City, Japan.

Heisler, B. S. (1986) "Immigrant Settlement and the Structure of Emergent Immigrant Communities in Western Europe," *Annals of the American Academy of Political and Social Science* 485 (May): 76–86.

Hondagnue-Sotelo, P. (1994) *Gendered Transitions: Mexican Experiences of Immigration,* Berkeley: University of California Press.

Ichioka, Y. (1988) *The Issei: The World of the First Generation Japanese Immigrants, 1885–1924,* New York: Free Press.

Immigration Newsmagazine (*Kokusai Jinryu*) (1990a) *"Intabyū: Gaimushō, Rōdōshō, Hōmusho Nikkeijin no U-tān Genshō wo kō Miru"* (Interviews with Ministries of Foreign Affairs, Labor and Justice 'Our View on the Return Migration of *Nikkeijin*'), *Immigration Newsmagazine* 38 (July): 11–6.

—— (1990b) *"Tōkei ni miru Nihonjin no Kaigai Ijū"* (Japanese Emigration According to Statistics), *Immigration Newsmagazine* 38 (July): 20–8.

Japan Immigration Association (1989–97) *Shutsunyū Kanri Kankei Tōkei Gaiyō* (Statistics on Immigration Control), Tokyo.

—— (1990–4) *Zairyū Gaikokujin Tōkei* (Statistics on Alien Residents), Tokyo, Japan.

Japan International Cooperation Agency (JICA) (1992) *Nikkeijin Honpō Shurō Jittai Chōsa Hōkokusho* (*Nikkeijin* Employment Fact Finding Survey Report), Tokyo.

JETRO São Paulo Center (1992) *Burajiru Kiso Jōhōshū* (Basic Information about Brazil), São Paulo: JETRO Center.

Kritz, M. M. and Zlotnik, H. (1992) "Global Interactions: Migration Systems, Processes, and Policies," in M. M. Kritz, L. L. Lim and H. Zlotnik (eds) *International Migration: A Global Approach,* Oxford: Clarendon Press.

Kritz, M. M., Lim L. L. and Zlotnik, H. (eds) (1992) *International Migration: A Global Approach,* Oxford: Clarendon Press.

Leighton, A. H. (1946) T*he Governing of Men: General Principles and Recommend-ations Based on Experience at a Japanese Relocation Camp,* Princeton: Princeton University Press.

Lesser, J. (1995) *Welcoming the Undesirables: Brazil and the Jewish Question*, Berkeley: University of California Press.

Maeyama, T. (1982a) *"Burajiru no Nikkeijin ni Okeru Aidentitii no Hensen – Tokuni* Sutoratejii tono Kanren ni Oite" (Transformation in Identities among Japanese in Brazil – With an Emphasis on its Relationship with Strategy), *Latin American Studies* 4: 181–217.

—— (1982b) *Imin no Nihon Kaiki Undō* (Return Movement of Immigrants), Tokyo: NHK.

—— (1984) *"Burajiru Nikkeijin ni Okeru Esunishitii to Aidentitii–Ninshikiteki, Seijiteki Genshō Toshite"* (Ethnicity and Identity of Japanese-Brazilians – As a Cognitive, Political Phenomenon), *Minzokugaku Kenkyū* 48, 4: 444–58.

—— (1986) *"Burajiru Nikkeijin ni Okeru Bunretsu to Tōgō – Esunishitii to Aidentitii no Mondai"* (Disintegration and Integration among Japanese Brazilians – Issues on Ethnicity and Identity), in K. Shigematsu (ed.) *Gendai Ajia Imin–Sono Kyōsei no Genri wo Motomete* (Contemporary Asian Immigrants – In Search of Principles of Co-existence), Nagoya: Nagoya Daigaku Shuppankai.

—— (1990) *"Nikkeijin (Burajiru)–Chūkan Mainoritii no Mondai"* (Japanese Brazilians – Problems as Middleman Minority), *Bunka Jinruigaku* 7: 208–21.

—— (1996) *Dona Marugarida Watanabe: Imin, Rōjin Fukushi no 53 Nen* (Dona Marugarida Watanabe: 53 Years of Social Welfare for Immigrants and Older People), Tokyo: Ochanomizu Shobō.

Margolis, M. (1994) *Little Brazil: An Ethnography of Brazilian Immigrants in New York City,* Princeton: Princeton University Press.

Massey, D. *et al.* (1987) *Return to Aztlan: The Social Process of International Migration from Western Mexico*, Berkeley: University of California Press.

Morawska, E. (1991) "Return Migrations: Theoretical and Research Agenda," in R. J. Vecoli and S. M. Sinke (eds) *A Century of European Migrations, 1830–1930*, Urbana, Ill.: University of Illinois Press.

Morimoto, A. (1992) *Perū no Nihonjin Imin* (Japanese Immigrants in Peru), Tokyo: Hyōronsha.

Morita, K. and Sassen, S. (1994) "The New Illegal Immigration in Japan, 1980–1992," *International Migration Review* 28, 1: 153–63.

Moriyama, A. (1984) "The Causes of Emigration: The Background of Japanese Emigration to Hawaii, 1885–1894," in L. Cheng and E. Bonacich (eds) *Labor Immigration Under Capitalism: Asian Workers in the United States before World War II,* Berkeley: University of California Press.

Oshimoto, N. (1967) *"Tōkei Kara Mita Sengo Kaigai Ijūno Keikō"* (Trends in Patterns of post-Second World War Immigration, Using Statistics), *Ijū Kenkū* 1 (October): 9–17.

Pellerin, H. (1993) "Global Restructuring in the World Economy and Migration: The Globalization of Migration Dynamics," *International Journal* 48, 2: 240–55.

Piore, M. J. (1979) *Birds of Passage: Migrant Labor and Industrial Societies,* Cambridge: Cambridge University Press.

Portes, A. (1978) "Migration and Underdevelopment," *Politics and Society* 8, 1: 1–48.

Portes, A. and Böröcz, J. (1989) "Contemporary Immigration: Theoretical Perspectives on its Determinants and Modes of Incorporation," *International Migration Review* 23 (Fall): 606–30.

Safran, W. (1991) "Diaspora in Modern Societies: Myths of Homeland and Return," *Diaspora* 1, 1: 83–99.

Saito, H. (1976) "The Integration and Participation of the Japanese and their Descendants in Brazilian Society," *International Migration* 14, 3: 183–199.

São Paulo Jinbun Kagaku Kenkyūjo (1988) *Burajiru ni Okeru Nikkei Jinkō Chōsa Hōkokusho – 1987, 1988* (Research Report on Japanese Population in Brazil – 1987,

1988), São Paulo, Brazil.

Simmons, A. B. and Guengant, J. P. (1992) "Caribbean Exodus and the World System," in M. Kritz, L. L. Lim and H. Zlotnik (eds) *International Migration: A Global Approach,* Oxford: Clarendon Press.

Sims, H. D. (1972) "Japanese Postwar Migration to Brazil: An Analysis of Data Presently Available," *International Migration Review* 6, 3: 246–65.

Skidmore, T. E. (1990) "Racial Ideas and Social Policy in Brazil, 1870–1940," in T. E. Skidmore, A. Helg and A. Knight (eds) *The Idea of Race in Latin America, 1870–1940,* Austin: University of Texas Press.

Suzuki, J. (1992) *Nihonjin Dekasegi Imin* (Japanese Oversea Sojourners), *Heibonsha Sensho* 145, Tokyo: Heibonsha.

Suzuki, T. (1965) "Japanese Immigrants in Brazil," *Population Index* 31, 2: 1177–1238.

Takahashi, Y. (1990) *Sobo no Daichi* (The Earth of People), Tokyo: Kodansha.

Ueno, H. (1994) *Mekishiko Enomoto Shokumin – Enomoto Buyō no Risō to Genjitsu* (Enomoto Immigrants in Mexico – Ideals and Reality of Enomoto Buyō), *Chūkō Shinsho* 1180, Tokyo: Chūō Kōronsha.

Veja (1995) "*Os preços Muito Loucos da Era do Real,*" (Crazy Prices in the Era of Real), *Veja* (19 July): 18–24, Brazil.

Wallerstein, I. (1974) *The Modern World-System, Capitalist Agriculture and the Origins of the European World-Economy in the Sixteenth Century,* New York: Academic Press.

—— (1982) "The Rise and Future Demise of the World Capitalist System: Concepts for Comparative Analysis," in H. Alavi and T. Shanin (eds) *Introduction to the Sociology of "Developing Societies,"* New York: Monthly Review Press.

Watanabe, S. (1994) "The Lewisian Turning Point and International Migration: The Case of Japan," *Asian and Pacific Migration Journal* 3, 1: 119–48.

Wilpert, C. (1992) "The Use of Social Networks in Turkish Migration to Germany," in M. Kritz, L. L. Lim and H. Zlotnik (eds) *International Migration: A Global Approach,* Oxford: Clarendon Press.

Yamada, R. and Fumiaki, T. (1984) *Wakariyasui Shinkokusekihō* (Easy New Nationality Law), *Yuhikaku Livret* no. 7, Tokyo: Yuhikaku.

Yamada, R. and Kuroki (1990) *Wakariyasui Nyūkanhō* (Easy Immigration Law), *Yuhikaku Livret* no. 26, Tokyo: Yuhikaku.

Yamanaka, K. (1993) "New Immigration Policy and Unskilled Foreign Workers in Japan," *Pacific Affairs* 66, 1: 72–90.

—— (1996a) "Return Migration of Japanese-Brazilians in Japan: *Nikkeijin* as Ethnic Minority and Political Construct," *Diaspora* 5, 1: 65–97.

—— (1996b) "Factory Workers and Convalescent Attendants: Japanese–Brazilian Migrant Women and their Families in Japan," in *International Female Migration and Japan: Networking, Settlement and Human Rights,* International Peace Institute, Meiji Gakuin University, Tokyo.

—— (1997) "Return Migration of Japanese Brazilian women: Household Strategies and Search for the 'Homeland,'" in R. Krulfeld and D. Baxter (eds) *Beyond Boundaries,* Washington D.C.: American Anthropological Association.

Yamanaka, K. and Koga, E. A. I. (1996) "*Nikkei Burajirujin no Nihon Taizai Chōkika to Esunikku Komyunitii no Keisei*" (The Prolonged Stay and Development of Ethnic Community of Japanese-Brazilians in Japan), *Ijū Kenkyū* 33 (April): 55–72.

Yanagisako, S. (1995) "Transforming Orientalism: Gender, Nationality, and Class in Asian American Studies," in S. Yanagisako and C. Delany (eds) *Naturalizing Power: Essays in Feminist Cultural Analysis,* London: Routledge.

7 Aliens, gangsters and myth in Kon Satoshi's *World Apartment Horror*

David Pollack

World Apartment Horror (Japanese title: "*Waarudo Apaatomento Horaa*") by Kon Satoshi, with Otomo Katsuhiro and Nobumoto Keiko, is a work of fiction that raises important issues and problems of nationalism, immigration, identity and gender in Japan today. It concerns Japan's recent experiences with illegal immigration: the Chinese, Filipinos, South-east Asians, Indians, Pakistanis and others who, attracted by the promise of a better quality standard of living in Japan, arrive only to find themselves in the clutches of *yakuza* (gangsters) who are organized to prey on them. This experience has proved so traumatic and unthinkable that *Horror's* detailed examination of it seems unique in literature, art or film. Its treatment of the important subjects of war, memory, history, myth, and gender, offers an equally unique glimpse into questions of how other nationalities are treated in Japan today, questions that have scarcely even begun to be asked, let alone responded to.

The genre

Horror is in the *manga* genre, which spans a broad spectrum from children's comics and four-frame funnies published in the daily newspapers or in weekly and monthly magazines to books such as the one we are concerned with here, sophisticated illustrated fiction aimed at adult audiences.[1] *Manga* are so popular in Japan that entire sections and even whole floors of large bookstores have been devoted to it. Though *manga* readership ranges from very young children and teens to middle-aged adults, each age-group has its own specialized market niche although the *manga* sections of bookstores are largely patronized by young teenagers.

The genre of illustrated fiction is less familiar and accepted in the US than in Japan, and so requires some preliminary discussion here. Apart from a very few "serious" works like Art Spiegelman's *Maus*, equivalent genres in the US are regarded at best as too childish and frivolous to be truly "serious" literature and, at worst, as a form of evil degeneracy unsuitable even for decent adults, let alone for children. Ever since the appearance of the new cartoon styles in the 1960s pioneered by writers like Robert Crumb, the adult comic genre has accumulated ever more unsavory underground counter-culture associations. This has undoubtedly contributed to the gradual decline of the unrelated and very popular Super-hero and Archie-and-Jughead varieties of comics. Consequently, the techno-fantasy, violence, pornography and sadomasochism of today's more extreme (and popular) comic-book styles have been almost entirely excluded from "proper" bookstores and relegated to scruffier shops where the Japanese techno-fantasy and sci-fi *animé manga* sub-genres are also well-represented and have large cult followings. *Horror* has never been easy to find even in Japan and Kodansha International seems to have no intention of publishing such works for the English-language market.[2]

Horror is actually something of a throwback. It resembles the styles and themes of late-1960s and early-1970s modes of social realism more than anything. Today's *manga* are usually in one or another simple cartoon style or they adhere to the uniformly androgynous and wide-eyed characters, unmarked either by race or by gender, that Japanese writers have turned into something of an international style. In keeping with its nature as a narrative of social turmoil told through a relatively mimetically realistic style, *Horror* conveys its themes through a technique most closely resembling modern cinematic techniques of narration and explanation of facts. (Figure 7.1).

The narrative

The work's protagonist is a rather dim-witted *yakuza* hoodlum and gang member of the Black Dragon Society (*Kokuryū-kai*) in Tokyo named Itta. Itta runs of one of the gang's shady Tokyo enterprises, an Asian callgirl operation called Paradise Asia

Figure 7.1

dealing in Filipinas, South-East Asians and other women carefully specified as non-Japanese and non-Western ("Sorry, sir," is the agency's telephone refrain, "No western women!"). The story opens with the gang's boss, Kokubu, dispatching Itta to South Seas Apartments (Figure 7.1), a rundown tenement building it owns, to find out what has become of Hidé, another gang member who was sent there a while ago and has not been seen since. Itta discovers Hidé in a distraught psychological condition: when Itta knocks at his door, Hidé nearly kills him with gunfire (Figure 7.2) and mumbles that he will come back to the gang soon (Figure 7.3).

Itta returns to his callgirl agency and the pleasant attentions of his cheery Filipina girl-friend Annie (Figure 7.4). In response to an emergency call from headquarters, Itta rushes off to discover that Hidé has torn the place apart. The gang's boss, a pudgy middle-aged man named Kokubu with a permanent cold, orders Itta to clean out the illegal aliens who occupy the tenement where Hidé has been holed up (Figure 7.5). The English-language resumé for the film provides essential information which the story leaves unclear but which is immediately understood by any Japanese:

Figure 7.2

Figure 7.3

This run-down apartment occupies a strategic position on a plot of land marked for redevelopment. The land is worthless unless the apartment house's inhabitants are forced out and the structure demolished. The *yakuza* group Kokuryū-kai is entrusted with this task.

It is a story familiar enough one to anyone who reads the Japanese newspapers. Tokyo land prices have reached astronomical levels and Japan has such strong tenants' rights laws that developers frequently resort to *yakuza* muscle to "encourage" recalcitrant tenants to leave. A Japanese acquaintance once gave me what seemed a perfectly plausible explanation for the relative dearth of lawyers in Japan: "In America you have lawyers; in Japan we have *yakuza*."

The rundown tenement is filled with Pakistanis, Filipinos, Chinese and other

Figure 7.4

Figure 7.5

"undocumented" Asian immigrants (to heighten the social-realism style of drawing, the Chinese speak real Chinese which is written in the simplified mainland characters generally incomprehensible to Japanese and so translated into Japanese in tiny print at the bottom of the page) (Figure 7.6). Itta's demands that the Asians leave fall on uncomprehending ears (Itta, who thinks he's speaking English and therefore being "international": "*Wan uiiku inai ni getto autto!*" (Get out within one week!) (Figure 7.7). The Pakistani, who understands little Japanese or English: "No spea' Japanee." Itta, screaming in Japanese: "Who the hell's speaking Japanese!" The only one of the Asians who can communicate fluently with Itta in Japanese is the Taiwanese college student Zhang Guanghui ("Bright Zhang") (Figure 7.8), whose UCLA sweatshirt (seen later in Figure 7.15) symbolizes his aspirations. Zhang's extensive Chinese vocabulary is as exasperating to Itta as fancy Latin rhetoric would be to an American thug: "Stop using so many damned characters when you talk!" Itta screams at him (Figure 7.9).

Having had no success at intimidating the Asians into leaving, Itta tries blasting them out with his earsplitting renditions of karaoke songs (Figure 7.10); but the Asians, deciding that he is having a party, manage to commandeer the karaoke set for themselves (Figure 7.11). Settling into the tenement for what looks like a long haul (also Hidé's mistake), Itta is visited by Annie (Figure 7.12), who informs him as they make love that she is pregnant with his child. The horrified Itta offers her a doctor's services, by which he means an abortion, and is even more horrified when he realizes that she thinks he is only concerned for their future child's health. "It's alright," she coos soothingly at the agitated Itta: "It will be such a cute baby!" (Figure 7.13)

Itta soon discovers that the Asians believe the tenement is haunted. He dismisses these fears, calling them merely silly Asian superstitions ("If you're trying to fool Japanese with ghost stories, you're fifty years too late!"). Having

Figure 7.6

Figure 7.7

Figure 7.8

decided that the weird sounds he hears coming from the walls are just rats, and seeing his chance to get rid of the Asians whom he deliberately associates with these vermin, Itta sets off several pest-extermination smoke bombs and yells "Fire!" This ploy also fails however and Itta panics when he finds himself beset by swarms of fleeing rats and he goes after the Asians with a chain-saw (Figure 7.14). "Why are you doing this to us?" they cry; "We're all fellow Asians!" "Japanese aren't Asians!" declares the frustrated Itta to the astonished throng – "We're *whites*!" The Asians react with stunned incomprehension (Figure 7.15). Later, relieving himself in the communal bathroom, Itta is further infuriated to hear the Asians sneering that "The only thing big about him is his attitude!" Oddly enough, the next time he tries to make love to Annie, Itta suddenly turns violently paranoid and accuses her of trying to kill him just like all the other

Figure 7.9

Figure 7.10

Figure 7.11

Asians (Figure 7.16). It begins to dawn on the reader why Hidé has gone berserk.

Several days pass with no progress. Boss Kokubu sends word that if Itta can't evict the Asians, he will come and get the job done personally. Itta decides it is time to take his task more seriously, and actually sets the building on fire. As it burns, a bizarre demon-mask mural painted on the bathroom wall comes to life, and the evil spirit it contains possesses him (Figure 7.17).

Meanwhile Annie has convinced the understandably reluctant Asians to help Itta and Mohammed brings home his fellow day-laborer Shandra, an African who claims to be able to exorcise demons. After smoking and inhaling various substances (and demanding his fee up front) (Figure 7.18), Shandra puts the violent Itta into a deep trance.

The scenes that follow are narrated from inside Itta's demented brain. He is wading through a bizarre Asian landscape drenched with blood and filled with mangled

Figure 7.12

bodies. A much younger Kokubu, dressed in a Second World War Japanese army officer's uniform, brandishes a machine-gun standing on a huge pile of Asian corpses. He threatens Itta that if Itta will not kill the Asian enemy he will shoot him as a deserter (Figure 7.19). The tenement comes floating by with its Asian occupants calling out to Itta that he should get on board. Suddenly the enormous fanged monster rises up behind Kokubu and swallows him, Itta, and the burning building (Figure 7.20).

The monster is transformed into a design painted on the belly of an enormous woman crouching over Tokyo and the tenement, along with its multitude of characters, plummets from her belly to earth. Shandra has succeeded in exorcising the

Figure 7.13

Figure 7.14

Figure 7.15

Figure 7.16

Figure 7.17

Figure 7.18

demon that has possessed Itta and the story returns to its original exterior frame of narration.

The demon turns out to be the spirit of a mask brought to Tokyo by Carla, one of the Filipinos. During the Second World War Japanese soldiers had slaughtered many of the people in Carla's village and, more recently, his younger sister had arrived in Japan seeking work only to be forced like Annie into prostitution by gangsters like Itta. Humiliated and mortified, Carla's sister had hanged herself in the toilet of this particular tenement. In response to these tragedies, Carla brought

Figure 7.20

Figure 7.19

the demon mask to Tokyo to avenge his people and his sister. When he accuses Annie of sleeping with the enemy, however, she comes fiercely to Itta's defense with the retort that "not all Japanese are evil!" The other Asians also turn on Carla. They complain that, instead of this profitless obsession with revenge, he should be working as hard as them to send money home. Carla breaks down and concedes that they are right (Figure 7.21).

However, as Itta emerges from his trance, Hidé reappears decked out in a bizarre outfit that combines the appearance of the traditional Japanese ghost (*yūrei*) with the imagined dress of the ancient Yamato race (Figure 7.22). Brandishing the replica of an ancient barbarian-routing sword that he has stolen from a museum, Hidé challenges Itta in the vocabulary of the extremist right-wing nationalist ideologue to "draw your sword and purify our sacred Japan." At that moment Kokubu arrives, gunzels in tow, to tear the tenement down, and a fight between Hidé and Kokubu ensues. The two combatants use the distinctive languages of religion (Hidé) and fascism (Kokubu) (Figure 7.23):

Hidé: What would a damned heretic like you know about expelling barbar-
          ians (*jōi*)?
Kokubu: And what would a damned fool like you know about honor (*jingi*)?

As the two prepare to fight to the death, the monster returns to pull down the tenement. When the dust has finally settled, everyone is found to be safe: except for Hidé and Kokubu, who have both disappeared in the rubble. Annie tells the startled Itta how pleased she is that the two of them are safe, or rather, patting her belly, the three, or maybe the six of them (Figure 7.24). In the final frame, the good-natured Shandra complains to the now-homeless Asians who have moved in with him that they are a worse curse than any demon (Figure 7.25).

Figure 7.22

Figure 7.21

Analysis: nationalism and identity

Unlike the flatter characters Hidé and Kokubu, who will be discussed later, the two main protagonists Itta and Annie are at once simple stereotypes and complex figures whose ambiguities are central to both the narrative's successes and problems. Itta's Japanese identity is established in both positive and negative terms but always in relation to other Asians, a term now expanded to include Pakistanis and Africans. Thus, Itta does not merely run the gang's Asian prostitute ring. He is shown to be entirely sympathetic to his women, one of whom is his loyal and loving girlfriend. The reason Itta has been chosen to remove the Asian men from the gang's apartment, Kokubu cunningly tells him, is that he has "that international

Figure 7.23

sense" (*intanashanaru na kankaku*); Kokubu ironically sees in this same quality the source of Itta's knack for exploiting Asian prostitutes.

In this contradiction lies the crucial problem of Itta's ambiguous identity *vis-à-vis* the Asians. The construction of his positive Japanese identity appears to depend on a construction of the others' identity as negative. The invidious reallocation of good and evil conceals the fact that the relationship between the two is really one of one-sided brutal exploitation. Itta's agreeable relationship with Annie, while perhaps conceivable, is scarcely consonant with the wretchedness of the many Asian women lured to Japan each year by the promise of work. They come to be entertainers, bar-hostesses, waitresses and mail-order brides, only to find themselves virtually enslaved and prostituted by gangsters who steal their passports and threaten them with death or deportation if they make trouble. This exploitation is the more recent and less notorious domestic side of the Japanese sex-tourism industry in South-east Asia and has become increasingly dominated by Chinese gangs.

This is a problem that no one can feel smug about. Recent attention paid to the problems of the uses and abuses of "undocumented aliens" in the US and Europe suggests that the problem is, in fact, common in all first-world/third-world relations and not restricted to Japan. It is, however, a problem both complicated and exacerbated in Japan's case by a conveniently ambiguous claim to be simultaneously both a first and a third-world nation which is eternally victimized by the unchanging

Figure 7.24

Figure 7.25

hegemonist and racist attitudes of Euro-Americans even though the country has overtaken these peoples in many of the accepted categories of social and economic well-being. If Japan is still considered a third-world nation, it is only in the rather strained sense of its forced opening to the West in the nineteenth century, its history of condescending and belligerent treatment by Western powers over the past hundred years, its traumatic ordeal of wartime defeat and 'still-questionable nuclear bombing, and the cynical terms of its occupation and of the security arrangements dictated to it by the US during the Cold War. It is against this background that the novelist Ōe Kenzaburō's (1988) somewhat startling recent reiteration of Japan's historically problematic claim to be the natural leader of an emergent third-world Asia out of an unspecified oppression must be read (an argument which has never sat very well with the rest of Asia). Although Ōe certainly never intended to imply a Japanese racial superiority over the rest of Asia, Itta's remarkable statement that "Japanese aren't Asian – we're white" reveals the danger lurking just beyond the good intentions. Japan needs to decide if it is part of Asia. Itta's statement illustrates that, currently, there is little or no solidarity with the rest of Asia.

The failure of the governments of industrialized nations to recognize and deal adequately with mass migrations of people around the globe has given organized crime everywhere one of its most fruitful social functions and has enabled always-latent atavistic xenophobia to have conspicuous targets. Organized crime is, in this sense, not merely outlaw, in the banal sense of that which goes on outside the law, but its true complementary relationship to society lies in the vacated space between law and reality. In Freudian terms, what we fail to deal with consciously we must inevitably deal with unconsciously. Repression and memory failure only guarantee the overdetermined return of that which has been repressed and forgotten. *World Apartment Horror* is clearly about the recent return of memories of violence which Japan has kept harshly repressed or forgotten. The longer and more ruthless the history of that repression, the more violent the inevitable return.

The construction of Itta's positive Japanese male position is made possible only by concomitant relegation of other Asians to that marginal and negative space that has come under his control. It is the gang's perception of Itta's "international sense," a quantity ironically acquired through the exploitation of Asian women, which qualifies him for the job of persecuting Asian men. This exploitation and persecution turns out to be merely the logical extension of the official invocation in Japan over the past decade and more of an increased *kokusaika* or internationalization. Officially described as an increased knowledge about and sensitivity toward foreigners, in actual practice *kokusaika* has taken on a more sinister and instrumental connotation. Its cultivation amounts to a set of martial arts techniques for isolating and controlling an alien enemy and, crucial to this task, is timely and accurate knowledge about the other. More than most, Japan has come to make a fetish of the acquisition of information: no longer merely the older neutral *jōhō*, but the newer, more instrumental and sinister foreign quantity called *infomeeshon* that is appropriate to the new arena of the *intanashonaru*, an arena scarcely built on neutral ground.

Multinational corporations collect and manipulate all types of information as a kind of international competition that allows whoever controls its technologies to take advantage of the tiniest discrepancies in the distribution of information to achieve and maintain worldwide dominance over others. In the wake of Edward Said's revered orientalism, first-world and third-world relations are now largely understood by most theorists as involving precisely such a systematic disadvantaging of others as the inevitable complement of advantaging oneself. This is not necessarily something that has been worked out consciously. Indeed it is often hidden away from consciousness and public view because it is unsuited to the delicate sympathies of decent people. However, invidious geopolitical arrangements are no less onerous in their effect than formal articles of slavery.

The insignificant likes of Itta are always in danger of getting lost in the grander visions of post-colonial theory. At his modest level, these sorts of intellectual thoughts are reduced to the lowest common denominator of human ignorance. What makes Itta appealingly human is his swaggering, good-natured, and all-too-human, stupidity. The portrait of a simple man who is not really so very evil, which is surely how even the worst of us see ourselves, he serves admirably as a kind of Everyman. Compassionate to his exploited women (whose victimization is surely not his fault), pathetically loyal to his exploitative boss and sinister friends, he is really just another inadequate sad sack male whose world is limited entirely to his group affiliations and loyalties. He is not all that different from the world of the average salaryman worker with his total and constricted sense of identification with his own cramped corporate identity.

Except for the crucial corporate identity part, Itta is a little like the low-class nice-guy loner created in popular culture in the role of the good-hearted, itinerant peddler Tora-san, hero of the amazingly durable film series *Otoko wa Tsurai yo* (It's tough to be a man!"), which generated two films a year for approximately twenty years. People forget that even the beloved Tora-san was a member of the large *tekiya*, a shrine-fair peddler sub-group of Japan's extensive and highly organized *yakuza* world (Raz 1992).

When Itta tries to swagger he only trips, and when he tries to bully no one takes him seriously. In his comic attempts to rout the Asians from the tenement, he ends up appearing almost endearingly ineffectual, a sort of anti-Superman: less powerful than a Pakistani, less intelligent than a Taiwanese, less compassionate than a Filipino, less spiritually potent than an African. Indeed, he is rather less industrious and imaginative than any of them and amounts to little more than a punk hood with a bantam strut. His only apparent potency, as he insists on demonstrating publicly on the embarrassed Annie to the Asians, is sexual. Even so, the Asian men have a good laugh over the size of his penis (a frequent stereotyped source of anxiety on the part of the dominant race about others in both Japan and the US).[3]

Itta's identity *vis-à-vis* the Asians begins by telling them his very definition of Japanese: Japanese aren't Asians at all, he shouts at the height of his frustration; you're Asians; we're whites. If one old Western stereotype maintains that the Chinese, a literate, close-knit, diasporized and mercantile people, are the Jews of Asia, then the Japanese apparently want to think themselves as Asia's privileged (might one say anti-Sinitic?) WASPs! In the end, however, these despised Asians prove responsible not only for determining Itta's Japaneseness but also for whatever humanity he also possesses, and even for his life. It is the need to come to terms with these different people who have had to come to terms with an indifferent or hostile Japan, that finally gives Itta his most human dimension.

The classic depiction of Itta's sort of character is director Louis Malle's study in the film *Lacombe, Lucien* (1974) of how the right-wing fascist goon mentality springs up in ordinary small-town life. Lucien is an emotionally troubled youth whose personal problems are shown to be rooted almost exclusively in those of his social class, the economically traumatized small-town petit-bourgeoisie. In this social-realist analysis of the development of fascism in Europe evil, far from being a consequence of any flaw in character, is understood entirely in terms of abstract forces.[4]

In much the same way, there is little truly unambiguous and concrete evil in *World Apartment Horror.* Whatever palpable sense of evil there is seems by the *manga's* end to have been projected onto the pathetic Carla. Initially drawn as a thoroughly unpleasant character skulking about with a mean look on his face, Carla with his demon-mask and witchcraft is finally left responsible for the whole terrible affair. The reality, of course, is that it is only the crisis that Carla instigates that permits the entire subject of Japan's long-repressed memories of its wartime actions to surface in the first place. The improbable demon-mask makes possible, even as its very outlandishness conceals, the otherwise unspeakable Japanese social taboo against remembering its actions in Asia during the Second World War. Even the gang boss Kokubu, given his portly figure and chronic colds, cuts a pretty pathetic figure as an antagonist. The truly insidious nature of his sort of banal evil emerges only from his role in Itta's delirious trans-generational memories in which he becomes the living avatar of the brutal Japanese officer in Asia during the Second World War ordering his troops to massacre and rape the inferior and therefore inhuman non-Japanese Asian enemy. While there has been no dearth of those in Japan willing to call the world's attention to the horrors of its nuclear holocaust in 1945, only a few novelists such as Endō Shūsaku (in his *Sea and Poison and Scandal*) have had the strength to surface, in the face of society's resistance, the deeply-repressed memories of incomprehensible evil that Japan has so diligently worked to dismiss from its modern consciousness. But Endō really had little choice. One of Japan's tiny population of not merely Christian but Catholic intellectuals, he simply found it impossible to ignore the fundamental problem of the presence of evil and its meaning for religious belief, a concern that has little place in modern Japanese Buddhist or Shinto practice or theory. Unlike Germany, Japan has made an all-out official effort to forget its wartime past, even though the rest of Asia keeps offering to help Japan remember it.[5]

The xenophobic vision of the military officer motivates Kokubu who, both gangster and soldier, says that he will shoot Itta as a traitor if he fails to carry out his orders to eliminate "the enemy" with unquestioning obedience. In both these roles, Kokubu mobilizes the still-attractive right-wing myth of the samurai, who alone embodies the powerful ideological glue that holds together the Japanese way of life. Without absolute feudal obedience to a strong central authority, it seems to be a way of life which is always in danger of falling into a repetition of the sixteenth-century's long experience of civil disorder during times of social unrest. This myth constructs an image of a pyramid with an imaginary emperor at its apex who is in an unbroken succession from the gods, and who therefore transcends history and its problems. At its base is a single and homogeneous race, equally exempt from history, for whom anything foreign can only represent a contamination requiring disinfecting. Between these two imaginary social formations is a class of *samurai* which also springs from the soil but is bound by feudal loyalties to the social order represented by the emperor.

The critic Karatani Kōjin has described this vision as simultaneously modern and anti-modern, and therefore untenable. He traces its contemporary origins in the early decades of this century to the project of Yanagida Kunio, the noted anthropologist and folklorist who, Karatani (1991: 206) writes, "located the ancient origins of the imperial ceremonies in village ceremonies." Prior to this time, the idea of the emperor had, for centuries, exercised almost no real significance in the popular imagination but it was resuscitated by a small elite for ideological purposes only during the Meiji Restoration of 1868 in the guise of a German-style sovereign monarch around whom a modern state could be created. Yanagida's project, as Karatani and others such as the anthropologist Marilyn Ivy have observed, involved linking the village masses and the emperor in a new form of community (*kyōdōtai*). And as Karatani notes, it is significant that Yanagida was a bureaucrat deeply involved in the 1910 annexation of Korea. Japanese folklore, Karatani comments, thus "itself came into existence with the colonization of Korea" (Karatani 1991: 205–6). Yanagida cannot of course be held responsible for this phenomenon, but his life's work is an important nexus of intellectual currents, political ideology and social practices that have persisted into the present.[6]

Hidé, Itta's "elder brother" (*aniki*) in the gang, serves to embody the other contemporary alternative fascist solution to the problem of other Asians. Literally deranged by the impossibility of coping with this unthinkable new alien presence right in the heart of Japan itself, Hidé has retreated into the religious-right mythical memories of an original, sacred, and undefiled Japan created by the nationalist philosophers of the Edo period (1603–1868). Hidé re-enacts, so literally as to amount to a comic parody, the ancient myth of the founding deity Yamato Takeru. Having stolen a replica of Yamato Takeru's magical sword Kusanagi or Weed-mower from a museum, he undertakes to "expel the barbarians" (*jōi*) from Japan, with his battle-cry "The life of the Japanese nation is at stake!" (*Nippon no ichidaiji da*). The phrase "expel the barbarians" automatically conjures up here its absent but regular counterpart *sonnō*, "revere the emperor." Hidé's target in this holy mission, however, includes not merely the aliens but also Kokubu, who could not care less about such arcane nuttiness. It does not concern the pragmatic gang boss that there are "barbarians" in Japan, since his very livelihood depends on the presence and systematic exploitation of these illegal immigrants (he even sends his "recruiters" through Asia to bring them to Japan). But Hidé, who objects on ideological grounds to their very presence, has mobilized this other set of mythological terms to his own cause. In their combat at the end of the story, Hidé brands Kokubu a heretic (*gedō*, a word straight from Shinto creed), while Kokubu denounces Hidé as someone who "knows nothing of honor" (*jingi mo wakimaenee*, a phrase from the world of the Tokyo gangster). These two positions of archaic and essentially anti-modern social mythologies collide with and annihilate one another.

Japan's need for foreign immigrants to perform work no one else cares to do perfectly matches the pressing need of impoverished Asians for gainful employment of any sort. Like the US, Germany and Britain, Japan is having difficulty acknowledging the presence of these people whom the French poet François Villon, more than 500 years ago, had given the evocatively dehumanizing name of *la poussière humaine,* "human dust". As in these countries, the process in Japan threatens to unleash powerfully xenophobic reactions at home. One of the tenets of the post-colonial critique is the careful attention to deliberately blurring details of difference for ideological purposes into the illusion of a unitary whole. It is to Kon Satoshi's credit that he has distinguished and even set these two distinctly different elements, *yakuza* and *samurai*, in opposition into a simple and unitary fascist ideology.

Beyond mythical solutions

Given the work's happy ending, it may seem somehow like Japan-bashing to insist on continuing to examine the problems entailed by this heart-warming and even perceptive little narrative of social reality. There are, in fact, several more intractable problems than such a simple solution is willing or able to accommodate. In the end, we are still left with all the pragmatic sorts of problems myth entails.

We notice that Asians are shown to believe in, and act with, masks and witch-doctors, while the Japanese deploy the more modern sorts of beliefs and technologies of a highly industrialized nation (although, for all his karaoke sets, chainsaws, and extermination bombs, Itta still remains remarkably ineffectual, and only for that reason problematically human). If the story sets primitive alien religious practice on the side of the aliens and pits it against modern Japanese memory, it is precisely the failure of that modern memory that has called into being the terrible effects of powerful alien superstition. The story suggests that if the Japanese had only allowed themselves to remember and make amends for the evil they perpetrated in the Second World War, this vengeful alien presence would never have come to haunt them.

The problem of this alien intrusion is present in a variety of contexts in Japan, including the need, reflected in the story, for relatively inexpensive Asian labor to fill another need created by its very disappearance in modern Japan. At a deeper level, there are echoes of the fact that South-East Asian rice will sooner or later replace the Japanese rice which priced itself out of any reasonable market long ago, and has had to be maintained at great expense. It is seen as something too close to the national soul to be abandoned (a myth encouraged by a corrupt ruling party to ensure the continued support of its backbone rural constituency).[7]

There is also a problem with the portrayal of Itta as a generally well-meaning sort of guy who is perhaps a bit dim and no doubt a nasty bully, but funny, loyal to his friends, solicitous of the prostitutes who work for him, and affectionate and loyal to his girlfriend. Given to an easy violence and definitely on the wrong side of the law, Itta could almost be mistaken for the sort of iconoclastic culture-hero played, until his untimely death in 1989, by the brilliant young actor Matsuda Yūsaku in films like *The Family Game* (he also played the wild punk in Ridley Scott's *Black Rain*, a film widely deplored in Japan). Matsuda's wild and lawless characters, mirroring the unruly mythical figure of *Susano-o*, caricature and demolish old worn-out social myths and create new and empowering ones in their place.

For Itta, however, there is little that is new and empowering. There can be only a return to the same old life of pimping and exploiting foreign prostitutes as it is all he knows and, all that permits him to make a decent living, even if he reduces others' lives to indecency in the process. Nor does he seem much like Matsuda's wonderfully hedonistic punk gangster in *Tanpopo*, who is blissfully engrossed in Rabelaisian food-sex with his girlfriend. Itta is not mythical but a parody, and he possesses neither imagination nor style. For Itta, rabble and Asian are synonymous.

Another acute problem is the boundless faith the story places in the idea of the "native" woman as forgiving and healing mother-nature. The story sustains the notion that the good heart and natural fecundity of the Asian female has a capacity to nurture and socialize needy Japanese males like Itta, and thereby solve the problems of a national superstructure of male identity badly in need of shoring-up. Annie, of course, has little choice but to yield to Itta's assumption of natural superiority. To the discomfort of males, Japanese women have recently begun to find it much more problematic. Now that Japanese women are showing signs of asserting themselves, Japanese men, in a maneuver familiar in the West since the end of the Second World War, are also taking increasing recourse in the idea of the more submissive "Asian" woman to fill traditional sexual and maternal roles (even if she does have to be forced into recognizing and fulfilling her essential nature). The good-hearted Annie, of course, does not even have to be forced because she has come to Japan precisely to fulfill that role and seems all too happy to do it.[8]

Another aspect of this same problem of gender identity and political domination is that the Asian men are also depicted as acceptable only so long as they remain poor, needy, subservient and unlikely to make trouble. This can be ensured so long as they remain illegal. In other words, Itta establishes his masculinity not merely by his exploitation of women, but also by effectively reducing the Asian men to the status of females. In fact, his ability to humiliate other men is all that he can feel manly about, and this includes sexual possession of their women. The latter is an issue raised most poignantly by Carla, who is especially outraged by Annie's sleeping with a Japanese precisely because she is a Filipina. The homeless men gathered in Shandra's apartment at the end of the story will have no other recourse. They must return to their labor, living wretched and exploited lives so they can earn the money they came to Japan for in the first place and continue sending money back home to their hungry families. Like the women, the men are also replacements, in their case for the dwindling supply of presumably Japanese men who occupied the major urban slums of San'ya in Tokyo and Kamagasaki in Osaka and whom the *yakuza* organizations traditionally exploited to supply cheap labor.

As long as Asian immigrants of either sex remain intentionally unrecognized by the Japanese government, and thus inevitably allowed to fall under the alternative domination of organized crime, they can conveniently be controlled, marginalized and kept easily disposable. Kokubu understands that there is about as much likelihood of the Asians complaining to the police as there would have been of a foreign nanny complaining to the US police that her social security taxes had not been paid.

The exotic business of the demon-mask that Carla brings to Japan for revenge on the Japanese is a useful plot device in so far as it provides an imaginary site for the confrontation, otherwise difficult to effect, of myth and memory, self and other. By its very nature as mythology, it also obscures the important fact that these "aliens" have already begun to exact a kind of revenge. They are the distressing symptoms of repressed memory, ready to erupt into national consciousness (thus the significance of the name of Hidé's stolen sword, Weed-mower, whose name appears in Japan's earliest myths), and the power the mask possesses is the power of raw memory itself to possess and haunt Japan. It will take more than the childish sexual bullying of Itta and the fecund and maternal bullied sexuality of Annie to effect any real solution to these problems.

Finally, there remains the problem that *World Apartment Horror*'s deployment of this colorful and exotic new breed of "aliens" effectively conceals, even entirely erases: the presence in Japan of a much older group of marginalized others. These include people of Korean ancestry, Okinawans, and *Ainus*, as well as the group known through history by the increasingly euphemistic titles of "filth" (*eta*), "non-humans" (*hinin*), "hamlet people" (*burakumin*), and "new citizens" (*shinkokumin*) - a group was often referred to only by the gesture of raising the little finger (the same gesture used to indicate women), and now most often not even referred to at all, since discrimination against them, though widely practiced, has been forbidden by law (it is not easy even to find such words in most dictionaries).

The novelist Õe Kenzaburõ is well-known for the way he has identified with and worked to highlight the plight of such "invisible" peoples, whose social marginalization has been so important in maintaining the identity of the dominant group. *World Apartment Horror*'s focus on this newer and more exotic group of Asians is achieved at the expense of concealing others whose own long-denied recognition has thus been effectively usurped. One is reminded of the way in which much earlier African-American and Latin-American populations in cities like Los Angeles and New York have been displaced on the economic and social ladder by the relatively more recent immigrant populations of Koreans and South-East Asians, and the ensuing resentment over the way that the former continue to be pushed ever further into the background and their problems ever more forcefully ignored. This is not only true of minorities: recent newspaper surveys have suggested that Asians as a group (and this idea of Asians as comprising a single group has increasingly become unacceptably problematic in the US) (Lowe 1991) are substantially better educated and earn more in family income than whites.

If this problem of displacement seems entirely outside the frame of this story, we might consider the irony that, 'in the popular imagination', Japanese of Korean ancestry living in Japan are generally thought of as gangsters who run the *pachinko* (pinball) industry. Doi Takako, the woman who as leader of the Japan Socialist Party for many years was one of Japan's few visible female political figures, was brought down by a coalition of good old boys in the ruling Liberal Democratic Party (LDP). The smear campaign they orchestrated accused her both of a monstrous lack of motherhood and of receiving donations from *Zenyūren*, an organization of *pachinko* parlor groups labeled in the public mind as not only Korean but as North Korean and therefore doubly insidious. When these same LDP members were themselves subsequently found to have been far more heavily subsidized by *yakuza* and other similar groups, there was little reaction since it was assumed that they were entirely Japanese gangsters – our sort of people – and therefore represented no problem.

The sorts of suitable fragmentary solutions reflect the continuing postmodern fragmentation of an earlier modern order. They challenge both that order's reassuring faith in closed systems of binary oppositions and the cultural myths of their ready mediation within a presumption of cultural consensus (e.g. *wa*). Nationalism, in the rubble of the Cold War, seems less a solution than a resurgent danger. Yet the sort of stability implied in the old idea of nationhood remains the great hope of those convinced that only associations of true nations (whatever that may mean) can transcend the terrible instabilities of tribal hostilities. Given the world's fractious animosities, it is not hard to support the hope of the post-colonial theorist Homi Bhabha in what he has termed the "revolutionary credo" expressed by Frantz Fanon in *The Wretched of the Earth*: "National consciousness, *which is not nationalism*," Fanon writes, "is the only thing that will give us an international dimension" (Bhabha 1990). Given the painfully tribal nature of human social consciousness, however, which in this story is based in and reinforced by shared painful memories of social trauma, it seems all too likely that national consciousness will continue to materialize in the form of exclusive nationalisms until that improbable time – indeed that millennium – when there is no longer need for the repression of dangerous memories and therefore no longer a return of what has been repressed. We should not hold our breath.

World Apartment Horror brings many of these destabilizing issues admirably into the foreground. However, solutions to the problems it raises, and which continue to remain deeply buried within it, are nowhere near as simple, or as amenable to simple human desire, as the *manga* suggests. Thus it is not difficult to juxtapose to the credo of Fanon cited by Bhabha with another, cited by Karatani Kōjin from the social philosopher Takeuchi Yoshimi's study *Nationalism and Social Revolution*:

> If nationalism is desired at all costs, what is to be done? Since it is impossible to evade the peril of ultra-nationalism and maintain only nationalism, our sole path lies, rather, in drawing out a genuine nationalism from within ultra-nationalism. That is, to draw out revolution from within counter-revolution.
>
> (Karatani 1991: 198)

Takeuchi could be explaining Germany's and Japan's rapid drift toward fascism prior to the Second World War, or even their postwar successes in belatedly moving closer to something resembling their respective wartime goals of hegemony over Europe and Asia. In any case, Karatani notes, Takeuchi's call to action mobilizes the same "near-religious logic" of that which it is ostensibly trying to overcome, a logic which holds, in Karatani's paraphrase, that "it is only by passing through evil that salvation is possible." The extreme polarization and elimination of the middle ground implied by the invocation of evil and salvation in the same breath should make us think, as Karatani undoubtedly intends us to. For such rhetoric has historically been the overture to the orchestration of human suffering on a truly grand scale. By putting nationalist ideas like these into the mouths of the brutal Kokubu and the demented Hidé, Kon Satoshi mocks them and makes us laugh. However, in spite of the theatrical example of Mishima Yukio in 1970, such words are more likely to be uttered today by sober, well-spoken young academics dressed in business suits than by deranged ultra-nationalists decked out in paramilitary uniforms.

Notes

1 *World Apartment Horror* was originally serialized in *Young Magazine* (1991) issues 14–18. The version under discussion is a paperback book of the same title, published together with three other stories by Kōdansha in 1991. The story was made into a low-budget film the following year, directed by one of the co-authors, Ōtomo Katsuhiro, whose famous *animé manga* series and 1988 feature film *Akira* have made him undoubtedly Japan's best known *manga* artist abroad. In the book the drawing is credited to Kon Satoshi and the story to Ōtomo and Nobumoto Keiko; the film credits Kon with the conception and Ōtomo and Nobumoto with the screenplay.

2 Though it is still listed in the standard reference work *Manga Shuppan Mokuroku* (*Manga* in Print), I was able to find *Horror* only at Aoyama Book Center in Tokyo, an establishment specializing in newer and more experimental *manga* as well as in the graphic arts in general. Kodansha's disinterest in the genre in general was indicated to me in response to a suggestion that they consider publishing an English translation of the work.

3 A recent brochure for the official English-teaching JET program sponsored by the Japanese Ministry of Education informs foreign male applicants that they are likely to be asked, among other things, "how big they are down there." Newsletters and journals catering to foreigners in Japan regularly contain advertisements for "the larger size condoms unavailable in Japan."

4 The film thus demonstrates the influence of Hannah Arendt's famous thesis concerning "the banality of evil" in her work *Eichmann in Jerusalem* (1964), whose subtitle contains the now commonplace phrase.

5 See Ian Buruma, *The Wages of Guilt: Memories of War in Germany and Japan* (1994). Norma Field (1991) considers the difficult position of three of the relatively few Japanese who have found it necessary to oppose their country's powerful social taboos: an Okinawan who burned a Japanese flag in protest against Japan's actions there in the Second World War; a Christian woman who objected to the customary deification of her dead soldier husband by the military as a Shinto god; and the mayor of Nagasaki, shot by a "patriotic" *yakuza* for suggesting that Emperor Hirohito ought to have assumed greater responsibility for Japan's actions in Asia during the Second World War.

6 In this regard it is interesting to note the importance that has been almost universally attached in Japan to the social provenance of Hosokawa Morihiro, the head of the Japan New Party who became Prime Minister after the fall of the LDP government in July 1993 in an atmosphere of scandal and corruption. Hosokawa's ancient samurai roots in a part of Japan long considered a locus of activist opposition to the establishment signaled him as someone with both impeccable credentials as a reformer as well as the necessary legitimacy to re-establish dangerously sundered ties between an increasingly vague notion of the role of the emperor and the increasingly volatile and confused situation of the common people. With this political capital to work with, he was swift in calling for an unprecedented examination of Japan's wartime activities. He did not last long.

7 American trade negotiators seem unaware of the fact that it is South-East Asia and not California and Louisiana that will benefit from liberalized Japanese rice markets.

8 This situation is reminiscent of many organizations and publications that specialize in catering to the similar desire of American men for "submissive" Asian wives (these advertisements are often found in magazines like *Soldier of Fortune,* thus supporting the notion that one of the historic attractions of war has been the opportunity to rape and enslave foreign women, those at home being of course sacred and ineligible for such attentions). It is not a coincidence that the painful issue of so-called Korean and other "comfort women" (*jūgunianfu*) enslaved during the Pacific War to provide sexual services for Japanese soldiers broke into the news only recently, though the media almost managed to lose sight of it in the silly scandal of a short-lived Prime

Minister's follies with his *geisha* mistress. Since some of the most urgent issues of post-colonial identity fall within the well-tended social realm of problems such as sexual identity, it seems no coincidence that the controversial British film *The Crying Game*, with its confusing displacements of race and gender, surfaced as America's best-kept secret just as Bill Clinton was suggesting to American soldiers that they would soon be showering with homosexuals.

References

Arendt, H. (1964) *Eichmann in Jerusalem: A Report on the Banality of Evil*, New York: Viking.

Bhabha, H. (ed.) (1990) *Nation and Narration*, New York and London: Routledge.

Buruma, I. (1994) *The Wages of Guilt: Memories of War in Germany and Japan*, New York: Farrar, Strauss and Giroux.

Field, N. (1991) *In the Realm of a Dying Emperor: Japan at Century's End*, New York: Vintage.

Karatani, K. (1991) "The Discursive Space of Modern Japan," *Boundary* 2 18, 3 (Fall).

Kon, S., Ōtomo, K., and Nobumoto, K. (1991) *World Apartment Horror*, Tokyo: Kōdansha.

Lowe, L. (1991) "Heterogeneity, Hybridity, Multiplicity: Marking Asian American Differences," *Diaspora* 1, 1 (Spring): 24–44.

Ōe, K. (1988) *World Literature Today* 62, 3: 359–69.

Raz, J. (1992) "Self-Presentation and Performance in the *Yakuza* Way of Life," in R. Goodman and K. Refsing (eds) *Ideology and Practice in Modern Japan,* London and New York: Routledge.

8 Local settlement patterns of foreign workers in Greater Tokyo

Growing diversity and its consequences

Takashi Machimura

The aim of this chapter is to elaborate on the recent settlement of foreign workers in local communities in Japan. Due to the sudden influx of foreign migrant workers since the mid-1980s, Japanese society has experienced an unexpected change in the ethnic composition of its population. Internationalization (*kokusaika*) soon became one of the most frequently quoted words in documents published by local governments. Yet there is still little consistency in the policy agenda for foreign migrants at a national level, and almost no institutional arrangements have been established for the coming multi-ethnic situation.

Since the economic bubble burst in the early 1990s, foreign labor in-migration has slowed down and public agitation over the migrant worker issue also seems to be less serious than during periods of economic growth. However, in localities where foreign workers are concentrated, the impact is still considerable. Thus, local communities are now becoming the frontier of Japan's internationalization and, especially important, the arena for political debate on the reception of foreign migrants. Some local governments eagerly try to adopt more substantial policies to ease the transformation to multi-ethnic communities, while the majority continue to ignore or underestimate the significance of the foreign population in spite of the huge contribution they make to the local economy. The ethnic factor should be more systematically incorporated into policy formation at the local government level in order to assure equal opportunity for all residents.

Integrating foreign workers into local communities also requires wider and more systematic recognition of the diversity of local settlement. This chapter focuses on several cases in the Greater Tokyo area that illuminate the different forms of both exclusion and inclusion of foreign workers in local communities. First, the general position of foreign residents, especially as revealed in recent demographic trends of Greater Tokyo, are summarized. The next section discusses the characteristics of four major types of foreign migrant workers. Each case reflects various social and economic factors, both structural and temporal, which have resulted in recent increases in foreign migrant workers in Tokyo. Third, three types of local settlement patterns are discussed in detail in terms of the invisible concentration of undocumented workers in traditional industrial areas, the compartmentalized incorporation of Nikkei families through local institutions and the search for more self-sufficient ethnic communities in inner Tokyo.

Foreign migrants in an emerging world city

Since the 1980's, advanced industrial countries, including Japan, have experienced the globalization of their national economies including the influx of foreign migrant workers. The resulting impacts on core cities are often described as urban restructuring or world city formation (Friedmann 1986, Sassen 1988). The essence of the urban restructuring hypothesis can be summarized as: an increase in both higher-wage and lower-wage workers in a growing urban service economy; a decline of middle-income, unionized, skilled workers in less competitive manufacturing industries; and an influx of foreign workers into expanding lower-income sectors, establishing a cheap and flexible labor force and a new urban underclass in inner-city areas. This hypothesis also gives us an effective starting point for the analysis of Japanese cities (Machimura 1992).

When applied to Tokyo's case, however, the hypothesis must be re-formulated on the basis of the Japanese context and experience. In short, world city formation in Tokyo, at least in its initial phase, has depended not only upon expanding financial and service industries but also upon competitive manufacturing industries. During the period of the bubble economy in the late 1980s, the function of Tokyo as a money-supplying world city was expanded tremendously by huge amounts of capital coming from the domestic land and stock markets (Kamo 1993). This process was further accelerated by capital accumulated by some booming industries such as automobile, electric and electronics manufacturing (Machimura 1994). Under these economic conditions, labor shortages became highly acute in both service and manufacturing industries. As a result, a larger number of foreign workers have been selectively brought into both growing and declining industrial sectors. Although their occupational positions tended to be more diverse than before, most of them were placed at the bottom of a hierarchical labor system as a flexible low-paid segment of the labor force in Greater Tokyo.

Before the start of the huge foreign worker influx in the 1980s, the Tokyo Metropolis was already the second largest prefecture in terms of the number of registered foreign residents. Only Osaka, which has contained the largest Korean community since the pre-Second World War days, was larger. In 1980, 114,000 registered foreigners lived in the Tokyo Metropolis and 82,000 lived in the outer parts of Greater Tokyo, which includes six prefectures surrounding the Tokyo Metropolis: Kanagawa, Saitama, Chiba, Ibaraki, Tochigi, and Gunma.[1] Because of the accelerated concentration of newcomer migrants in the 1980s, the Tokyo Metropolis soon surpassed Osaka in the size of the foreign population. By the end of 1997, the population of registered foreign residents in the Tokyo Metropolis had more than doubled the 1980 level at 256,000, and had increased by about four times to 324,000 in the rest of the Greater Tokyo region. As a result, Greater Tokyo's share of the total registered foreign population in Japan rose significantly, from 25 percent in 1980 to 39.1 percent in 1997, and the Tokyo Metropolis share also rose from 14.6 percent in 1980 to 20.9 percent in 1988. Although its share decreased slightly to 17.3 percent of the national total in 1997 (Table 8.1), the share of registered foreigners in the population of the Tokyo Metropolis went up to 2.17 percent by the end of 1997 (Hōmūsho Nyūkoku Kanri Kyoku 1998).

The geographical distribution of undocumented workers also confirms the

Table 8.1 Population of registered foreign residents in Greater Tokyo, 1980–97 (end of the year, in thousands)

Prefecture	1980	1982	1984	1986	1988	1990	1992	1994	1996	1997
Greater Tokyo	196	208	237	258	320	393	497	529	553	580
Tokyo	114	122	139	155	196	213	247	250	251	256
Kanagawa	42	43	47	49	55	77	97	100	104	109
Saitama	14	15	18	19	25	37	53	60	64	67
Chiba	14	15	18	19	24	32	43	53	56	61
Gunma	4	4	4	5	6	12	21	23	27	31
Tochigi	3	3	4	4	5	10	17	19	22	24
Ibaraki	5	6	7	7	9	12	19	24	29	32
Japan	783	802	842	867	941	1,075	1,282	1,354	1,415	1,483
Tokyo Metro as % Japan	14.6	15.2	16.5	17.9	20.9	19.8	19.3	18.5	17.7	17.3
Greater Tokyo as % Japan	25.0	25.9	27.8	29.7	34.0	36.6	38.8	39.1	39.1	39.1

Source: Hōmudaijin Kanbō Shihō Hōsei Chōsa Bu (annual reports).

recent concentration of foreigners in the Greater Tokyo area. According to a Ministry of Justice estimate, the total number of unauthorized visa-overstayers in Japan amounted to 297,000 in November 1993. The number then slightly decreased mainly due to the economic recession and tight control of immigration, but began to increase again towards the end of the decade (see Douglass and Roberts ChapterOne of this volume). The geographical distribution of foreign workers is not included in the original statistics but a rough estimation is possible by using other related information.

In 1984, among the annual total of apprehended undocumented foreign workers in Japan, 16.6 percent took jobs in the Tokyo Metropolis and 29.5 percent took jobs in its surrounding four prefectures (Kanagawa, Saitama, Chiba, and Ibaraki) (Table 8.2). Reflecting their continuous concentration in these areas, the percentages rose to 29.5 percent and 38 percent respectively in 1993. Despite the recent slight decrease in the total number of foreign workers in Japan, the share in Tokyo Metropolis continued to rise to 33.4 percent (15,980) in 1996 (Homusho Nyūkoku Kanri Kyoku 1997). If such a distribution were applied to the total number of illegal foreigners the estimated population would be 94,500 in Tokyo Metropolis and 96,000 elsewhere in the greater Tokyo Region in 1996. Consequently, it can be estimated that approximately 345,000 legal and illegal foreign entrants lived in Tokyo Metropolis and more than 376,000 lived in its surrounding area in 1996.

When compared with other major global cities such as New York or London, the size of the foreign population in Tokyo is still extremely small, even if the considerable number of undocumented workers is counted. In spite of its relatively small size, a sudden influx of foreign residents has caused an impact significant enough to transform Tokyo's urban structure. This population is now broadly incorporated into the changing labor market in Greater Tokyo. At the same time, as shown in Figure 8.1 in the case of Korean and non-Korean labor, the social composition of foreign residents in Greater Tokyo varies considerably among different parts of the area. (See also Figures 8.2 and 8.3.) Metropolitan Tokyo is characterized mainly by having the most diversified occupational structure of foreigners among all areas of the region. While professional and clerical workers comprise the major share, undocumented workers employed in various industries are also concentrated in the metropolis. Moreover, a huge number of officially out of the labor force residents are actually employed part-time or full-time in service industries in the urban core.

By contrast, in the northern three prefectures of Ibaraki, Tochigi and Gunma which have recently experienced rapid growth of manufacturing industries, both registered and undocumented manual workers are the overwhelming majority. Three prefectures in Outer Tokyo (Kanagawa, Saitama, Chiba) are in-between in terms of social composition. Such a geographical variation certainly reflects both recent changes in industrial locations and an emerging ethnic division of labor.

The living conditions of migrant workers have also become more and more diversified depending upon nationality and legal status, position in the local labor market, the support and resources available through ethnic ties and the availability of social services for foreign migrants. There has recently emerged a more clear-cut differentiation in working conditions among foreign migrants (Mori

Table 8.2 Apprehended undocumented foreign workers by place of work, 1984–96

Place of work	Number of apprehended undocumented workers								
(Prefecture)	1984	1988	1989	1990	1991	1992	1993	1994	1996
Greater Tokyo	2,205	9,261	11,022	14,643	21,184	40,600	43,419	39,396	32,149
Tokyo	792	3,916	4,986	6,339	9,273	17,870	18,998	19,297	15,980
Kanagawa	316	890	1,503	2,164	3,488	6,582	7,087	5,025	4,027
Saitama	254	1,468	1,698	2,232	3,043	6,763	6,635	5,800	5,172
Chiba	386	2,316	2,189	2,750	3,526	5,726	6,159	5,133	4,231
Ibaraki	457	671	646	1,158	1,854	3,659	4,540	4,141	2,739
Japan	4,783	14,314	16,608	29,884	32,908	62,161	64,341	59,352	47,785
Tokyo as % Japan	16.6	27.4	30.0	21.2	28.2	28.7	29.5	32.5	33.4
Greater Tokyo as % Japan	46.1	64.7	66.4	49.0	64.4	65.3	67.5	66.4	67.3

Source: Kokusai Jinryū (issued monthly)
Note: Japan total in 1990 includes the number of those of whom working places are not identified.

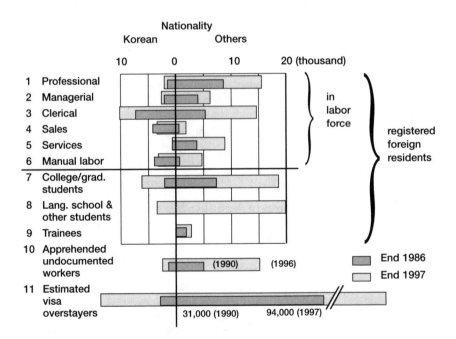

Figure 8.1 Occupational distribution of Korean and other foreign residents in the Tokyo Metropolis

Sources: Nyūkan Kyōkai, *Zairyū Gaikokujin Tōkei* (Annual Statistics of Registered Foreign Residents); *Honpō ni Okeru Fuhō Zanryūsha Su* (Number of Illegal Overstayers in Japan), *Kokusai Jinryū* (issued monthly).

Note: Number of visa overstayers in each area is estimated by the author from statistics of visa overstayers and apprehended undocumented workers compiled by the Ministry of Justice.

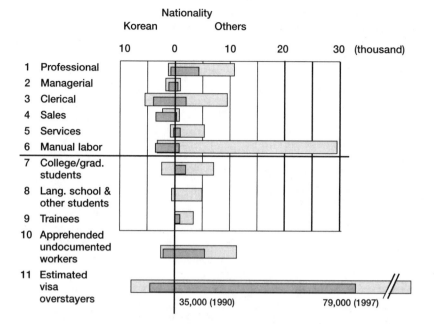

Figure 8.2 Occupational distribution of Korean and other foreign residents in Kanagawa, Saitama and Chiba prefectures

Sources and notes: see Figure 8.1

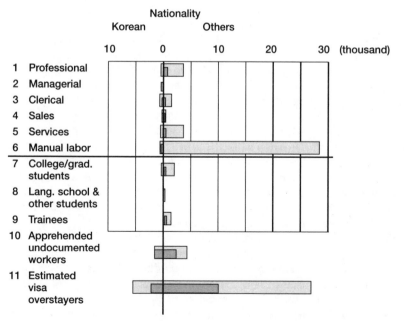

Figure 8.3 Occupational distribution of Korean and other foreign residents in Ibaraki, Gunma and Tochigi prefectures

Sources and notes: see Figure 8.1

1994). Social discrimination against ethnic minority groups is often perceived as a local problem but its seriousness varies considerably among communities. Some migrant groups create their own business, media and churches by mobilizing ethnic resources but others often lack even basic channels for communication. Therefore, a single picture cannot represent these divergent forms of employment of migrant workers and their local settlement patterns.

Four types of migrant workers

Recently the types of foreign migrant workers have been becoming more divergent in Greater Tokyo. Among foreign workers at least four types can be taken as comprising the major groups: service workers in the cities; Latin Americans of Japanese descent in company towns; undocumented workers in small factories and construction sites; female workers in nightclubs and entertainment industries. Such diversity partly reflects the changing labor demand in the urban economy, and is partly based on differences in legal, economic and social conditions among various foreign workers.

The first group is mostly composed of young workers who enter into various types of service jobs that are especially concentrated in the urban Tokyo. While some of them are professional or technical workers, the majority take full-time and part-time low-wage and unstable jobs, in restaurants, various consumer goods factories and growing producer services such as building cleaners. Furthermore a recent decrease in the number of Japanese residents in central Tokyo especially in the youth population, has in effect expanded job opportunities for foreign residents. From 1985 to 1997, the twenty-three central wards (*ku*) area lost 370,000 existing residents but gained at least 97,000 foreign residents. Labor market replacement demand (Cross and Waldinger 1992) created by the Japanese exodus from the inner-city areas has accelerated the shift in ethnic composition. A more multi-ethnic community is now slowly but surely taking shape in the city of Tokyo.

Most of these workers in the central areas came from mainland China and other parts of Asia. Many of them have been student workers permitted to work only on a part-time basis, although they have sometimes been employed full-time. Thus, their legal status as a worker is usually very unstable. In spite of this, or rather because of it, they were soon incorporated into various urban industry sectors as low-paid workers, often working under unfavorable conditions. Today, Tokyo's more service-oriented economy can no longer function without a cheap and flexible labor force, such as is provided by foreign workers, part-time Japanese female workers, working students and elderly people.

While the type of foreign workers discussed above has been mainly incorporated into the service industries, the next two groups are mostly incorporated into various manufacturing sectors. During the period of the bubble economy, a huge number of Latin Americans of Japanese origin were recruited to Japan and hired as manual workers mostly by sub-contractors of the booming automobile and electronics industries. In 1990, Japan's immigration law, which imposed sanctions on employers who hired illegal workers, was amended to relax restrictions and expand opportunities exclusively for descendants of overseas Japanese immigrants to work legally in Japan. These *Nikkei* workers soon became one of the major foreign groups in Japan. Due to their ethnic origin, they were regarded as Japanese by the government which, until 1990, had officially rejected any manual workers coming from foreign countries. This decision reflects the remaining influence of the single nation ideology deeply rooted in Japanese society (Tanaka 1995). In reality, they are expected to be and, in most cases, are treated only as "legal" manual workers from a foreign country rather than as Japanese *per se*. By the end of 1997, the total population of ethnic Japanese migrants throughout Japan from Brazil and Peru was 273,000. They tended to be concentrated in factory towns surrounding big cities such as Tokyo or Nagoya and thus showed a quite different pattern of geographical distribution from other foreign groups.

The third group is comprised of the large population of undocumented workers attracted to even smaller-size factories and construction sites. These workers come primarily from Malaysia, Iran, Bangladesh, Pakistan, other developing countries in Asia and Africa. The small-size firms employing this group of workers are characteristically scattered throughout the congested, run-down inner-city areas or in the urban sprawl surrounding them and have faced an acute structural shortage of laborers. Such workplaces are typically avoided by younger Japanese workers because of their unfavorable working conditions and less attractive image, summed up in the "three Ks": *kitanai* (dirty), *kiken* (dangerous), and *kitsui* (laborious). Employers in these industries use the newcomer foreign workers as a substitute for the shrinking Japanese workforce.

Fourth, bars, nightclubs, entertainment industries and some sex industries have been major workplaces for young female workers from the Philippines, Thailand, South Korea and other countries (see Douglass Chapter Five of this volume). Such industries, which are often ignored by official labor statistics and government labor policies, constitute a large part of the economic activity in commercial areas and represented one of the most rapidly expanding service sectors in the period of the bubble economy. In some "amusement" areas within Greater Tokyo, the female workforce is often made up of a single foreign ethnic group (Ballescas 1992).

Although these female workers are often regarded as marginal, they are deeply enmeshed within the Japanese corporate economy and in the ethnic and gender division of labor. The industries employing these women are substantially supported by the huge entertainment expense accounts (*settaihi*) set up by companies to entertain workers and clients at away from work as a means of strengthening business relationships (Allison 1994: 9). This custom partly reflects traditional gendered relationships emphasizing male-dominance in both the workplace and family in Japan. Because of their unstable legal status and limited job opportunities, female workers in these occupations are often also compelled to depend upon criminal organizations (*bōryokudan*), which are usually deeply involved in the entertainment and "sex" business. As a result, female workers employed in the entertainment industries are directly and indirectly exploited by criminal organizations.

Growing diversity in local settlement patterns

An increased number of foreign migrants are currently living among local Japanese communities for longer periods of time. Although many of them do not consider themselves permanently settled, they are firmly incorporated into both the local labor market and local social settings. However, great diversity in settlement patterns remains among different groups.

There are many factors that contribute to differences in the local settlement patterns of foreign workers but two major ones are especially relevant in determining the degree of social exclusion and inclusion foreign workers will face. First, the legal status of the foreign worker is the most crucial factor affecting the possible range of actions and reactions taken by both the migrants themselves and the local Japanese community. In closed societies, such as Japan, legitimate legal status alone does not provide sufficient protection or support for foreigners to improve their quality of life. In present day Japan, legally documented newcomer workers, and even *Zainichi* Koreans, are still not free from discrimination in the workplace and local community. Given their legal status as workers, the official opportunity to receive basic social services is, more or less, open to them. In contrast, undocumented workers are basically excluded from the realm of public policy, no matter how they contribute to the local economy and society.

Second, the local presence of industries that hire foreign workers determines whether any institutional arrangement can be established to assist foreigners in securing housing, settling into a community and accessing services. Employers in locally-influential industries can connect their economic interests more effectively to local political processes (through both collective actions and individual connections with local élite) than those without access to political influence. The larger and more visible the public presence of those industries within the local community, the more effective will be the institutional response to accommodate the needs of the migrant labor force.

The combination of these two factors produces four possible types of local settlement pattern of foreign migrants and three of these exist in Japan. These are illustrated in Table 8.3. Documented workers hired by locally-prominent industries have a better chance to openly seek settlement arrangements through existing public institutions. Employers are also involved in policy-making to facilitate the local incorporation of foreign residents, usually with a view to reducing labor costs (Type I). In contrast, when industries are less influential and/or less visible fewer institutional arrangements are established for foreign residents. Regardless of the status of the hiring firms, migrants with stable legal status can build their own community and social support system based on ethnic ties. Therefore, they tend to depend more heavily on the ethnic community network to enhance their life (Type II). Migrants who do not have legal work status are usually totally ignored, except when concern is expressed about immigration and crime control. Illegal migrant workers employed in industries that have little influence in the local political and social scene are totally hidden and forced to be invisible in the local community (Type IV).

Although each pattern is an idealized type, such a classification can provide a helpful framework for a more systematic investigation of Japanese cases. Roughly speaking, the case of Nikkei residents in company towns is most similar to Type I: social incorporation through local institutions. At the opposite

Table 8.3 Local settlement patterns of foreign migrant workers in Japan

Public presence of industry hiring foreign workers	*Legal status of foreign workers*	
	documented	*undocumented*
Large	I (compartmentalized) incorporation through local institutions	III —
Small	II more self-sufficient community with ethnic ties	IV invisible concentration isolated from local community

extreme, most undocumented workers in manufacturing industries seem to belong to Type IV, the invisible concentration isolated from the local community.

The other two groups, service workers in Tokyo Metropolis and female workers in commercial areas take different positions in labor market segmentation. However, both groups share some common features that allow them to be classified together. First, they are both employed in urban service industries, often located among very marginal sectors in which very small-scale companies and self-employed entrepreneurs compete against each other. Second, though they are legally documented workers, their legal status is often the subject of suspicion. Third, most of them live in inner-city areas around the city center and thus often share a similar pattern of local settlement. Because these groups are typically employed in industries with little political influence they rely instead on ethnic ties for support. This pattern therefore seems to equate to Type II, self-sufficient communities established along ethnic lines, though each of these two groups actually contains various sub-groups.

While recognizing that there are many exceptions and borderline cases the following discussion focuses on the characteristic of the above three patterns of local settlement so as to make the analysis less complex.

Invisible concentration of undocumented workers in industrial areas

In the history of modern Tokyo, the inner-city has been characterized by mixed land uses, including manufacturing industries which have traditionally been the most dependent on the labor of migrant workers. These areas attracted large numbers of both domestic and foreign unstable, unskilled or semi-skilled workers, providing them with opportunities for low-wage jobs and low-cost accommodation. In the period prior to 1941, Korean workers who immigrated to Japan from their colonialized homeland were also forced to develop small communities in the inner-city because of severe discrimination in both labor and housing markets elsewhere in Tokyo and other regions of Japan. Today, the inner-city area and surrounding area continue to be one of the major destinations for temporary migrant workers. However the worker population is now comprised of a variety of groups from other Asian countries such as the Philippines, Malaysia, Pakistan, Bangladesh and Iran.

In addition to historical factors, contemporary processes of economic change have contributed to the concentration of numerous unskilled foreign migrant workers in the inner city. A four-year economic boom, beginning in 1986, accel- erated the demand for manual workers in both manufacturing and construction industries. Unlike metropolitan regions in many other advanced economies, man- ufacturing industries remain one of the most important sectors in Tokyo's economy. Since the 1980s, the development of production systems based on flex- ible specialization, which has been credited with making possible Japan's more recent economic growth (Fujita 1991), has created an important role for small firms in production networks, especially as suppliers of various components for both mass production and R&D. Nevertheless, the business environment is not necessarily favorable to small-scale and medium-scale manufacturers. Under highly competitive conditions, small firms, which depend upon sub-contracting from larger firms, are under constant pressure from contractors to cut production costs. Because these firms are usually located at the bottom of the pyramid in the sub-contracting system, there are few options other than accepting an urgent request by parent or patron companies to lower the price of products. Thus, they cannot afford to pay salaries large enough to attract Japanese workers who also generally dislike the type of work they offer.

The dependence on low-paid foreign workers is quite significant among rela- tively smaller firms. According to research on the Japanese firms in which Bangladeshi workers were employed, in those firms employing ten workers or less, foreign workers comprised more than 40 percent of the total labor force (Mahmood 1993: 76). Such studies show that employing foreign workers has become an easy way to reduce labor costs in competitive as well as declining sec- tors of urban industry.

Nevertheless, the presence of foreign workers is often not well-perceived or is simply ignored by Japanese residents, even though the contribution of these workers to the local economy has expanded. One obvious reason for this is that the relatively small population of foreign workers is swallowed up among the large number of Japanese residents. Another reason may be that many migrant workers, cautious of their questionable legal status, tend to keep themselves iso- lated from the local Japanese community. They usually live together in small wooden apartment houses and work together in small factories or at construction sites. There are few opportunities for making social contacts with the mainstream Japanese world. Moreover, as the regional economy has generally been deindus- trialized, the economic role of small manufacturers has become less visible and less significant than previously. This trend is even stronger in suburban areas and beyond where factories are more thinly dispersed.

In short, foreign migrant workers are still invisible residents in the local community. Ordinary Japanese citizens have little exposure to them and thus little opportunity to develop a positive image of them. The widespread stereotype that migrant workers may be illegal has enhanced negative attitudes. In such an unfavorable social climate, even basic public services such as medical treatment or compensation for industrial accidents are not usually made available to foreign migrant workers.

Even worse, the appearance of foreigners has often brought about a conservative or defensive attitude among local Japanese residents. For instance, local communities, which have long been integrated by a well-established social order, have experienced a steady influx of newcomers from rural areas, which has resulted in the breakdown of traditional social community relations. In such an unstable situation, newly-arrived foreigners are often blamed for the deterioration of the old community. These negative feelings spread among ordinary Japanese residents and are sometimes displayed in negative psychological reactions and collective anti-foreigner behavior. As a result, foreign workers are often exposed to harsh discrimination not only in the workplace but also in the local community. Discrimination can also give rise to ugly and unfounded rumors about foreigners' criminal tendencies.[2]

One of the typical reactions of Japanese society to the foreign workers has been to exclude them from public places. A recent example in Greater Tokyo concerning a Sunday market for Iranian workers provides one of the most blatant examples.[3] In the fall of 1990, a gathering of Iranian migrants was first observed in Yoyogi Park, a famous public park located in central Tokyo. The park subsequently attracted more and more Iranians every Sunday, serving as a small bazaar for them. By late 1992, more than thirty temporary streetshops were selling such items as food, rugs, shoes, Iranian videos, cassettes, CDs and newspapers to thousands of Iranians who gathered there from all over Greater Tokyo. In April 1993, a couple of months before the Royal wedding, the area used by the Iranians for their bazaar was suddenly closed and renovated by the metropolitan government for the sake of "beautifying the city." After the renovation, the Iranians no longer had an appropriate place to congregate in the park. As a result, they were kept out of this "public" place. Those who could formerly congregate in a public place were once again hidden from ordinary Japanese.

However, in such an inhospitable environment, foreign workers have developed various ways of improving their working and living conditions by mobilizing their own ethnic networks and by developing cooperative ties with outside organizations. Migrants of a common nationality often create their own meeting space and establish their own channels for distributing ethnic goods and sharing information. Available resources and strategies vary considerably. For instance, Filipinos often utilize such existing institutions as Catholic churches to establish their own social networks. Workers from Muslim countries such as Iran, Pakistan and Malaysia have recently built four small Islamic mosques in the Greater Tokyo area. These are all located in industrial areas, mostly near small-scale factories where both documented and undocumented foreign workers are concentrated (AERA 1996).

Some labor unions and other supporting groups are very active in improving conditions for foreign manual workers trapped at the social margin. According to recent research on major labor unions that organize foreign manual workers, union members are geographically concentrated in the Outer Tokyo area as well as within Metropolitan Tokyo and most of them are working in manufacturing and construction industries. These organizations have been very effective, especially at helping undocumented workers who have met various troubles at the workplace (for example Gaikokujin Rōdōsha Kenri Hakusho Henshū Iinkai 1995).

Compartmentalized incorporation of *Nikkei* families in booming company towns

In the early 1990s, a lot of small communities of Latin American *Nikkei* workers and their families suddenly appeared on the outskirts of Greater Tokyo. The population of registered Brazilian *Nikkei* residents in Greater Tokyo drastically increased from 1,000 in 1987 to 71,000 in 1997. A similar change was found in the case of those from Peru, whose numbers rose from 200 in 1987 to 22,000 in 1997. Eight out of ten of both nationalities live outside the Tokyo Metropolis.

Such drastic changes are mainly attributed to Japan's economic boom which was at its height between 1986 and 1990. In localities where the major automobile, electric and electronics industries ran their huge factories, the demand for low-wage manual workers was huge. As previously mentioned, labor shortages were particularly severe among the numerous small-size and medium-size manufacturers, which mostly produced various parts and components exclusively for large parent firms.

Nikkei workers from Latin America are generally compartmentalized in relatively isolated groups in both local labor and housing markets. As a low-wage labor force, they are typically relegated to the bottom of local class structure (Nishizawa 1995). However, when compared with other migrant workers in Japan, the Latin Americans have several unique characteristics (Kitagawa 1993, Komai 1995). First, they are *Nikkei* Latin Americans. This means that, unlike many other temporary workers, most of them have working visas which permit them to be legally employed in any kind of job.

Second, at least in the first stage of migration, *Nikkei* workers were heavily concentrated in several company towns in the suburbs of Tokyo and Nagoya. Since housing facilities were usually collectively provided by the labor recruiters or hiring companies themselves, small, highly concentrated communities of *Nikkei*, often separated from neighboring Japanese residents, suddenly appeared in the midst of traditional neighborhoods and local public housing (Tsuzuki 1995).

Third, thanks to their legal status, *Nikkei* have been able to bring their families. This soon created an urgent need for daycare, education, welfare and other public services. Consequently, *Nikkei* Latin Americans were more institutionally incorporated into local society than other groups. A wider range of policies, though still insufficient, was adopted for the *Nikkei* residents by several local governments (Sōmuchō Gyōsei Kansatsu Kyoku 1992, Ishii and Inaba 1996). Portuguese-speaking assistants in public schools, language services in public facilities, publicly-supported festivals for *Nikkei* Latin Americans, job information services, public housing and other services have been provided.

The relative advantages available to *Nikkei* Latin Americans in Japan can be primarily explained by their legal status. In general, only *Nikkei* Latin Americans are perceived as officially permitted foreign workers authorized to take employment in any job. Such an advantage has allowed them greater visibility in contrast with other foreign migrants. Additionally, *Nikkei* Latin Americans are sometimes regarded by ordinary Japanese people as Japanese from abroad, in other words, their Japanese origins and appearance has encouraged relatively positive public feeling toward them.

The perceived economic dependency of the local society upon those leading industries that have hired *Nikkei* workers has sometimes also paved the road to acceptance of these migrants. These workers are rarely employed directly by the top companies in the local industrial hierarchy but, generally got jobs through recruiters from various small sub-contracting firms. When the interests of employers are effectively represented by local politicians, broad policies to assist migrants to settle in the area are established more quickly. A good example of this is Oizumi in Gunma Prefecture which has quickly emerged as one of the principal concentrations of *Nikkei* workers. From an economic point of view, such political willingness to assist is usually a means of reducing labor costs by supporting foreign labor recruitment and has sometimes also reduced the social costs involved in the settlement of foreign residents.

The local incorporation of *Nikkei* Latin Americans has also been advanced by their own numerous ethnic-related institutions (Higuchi and Takahashi 1997). *Nikkei* neighborhoods have established ethnic restaurants, ethnic shopping malls, small shops for ethnic goods, travel agencies and other miscellaneous social institutions such as soccer teams. Two weekly Portuguese newspapers were started by *Nikkei* residents in 1991. The larger of the two, published by a returned *Nikkei* first-generation (*issei*) immigrant in the suburban city of Atsugi in Greater Tokyo, had a circulation of over 38,000 in 1993.[4] In 1996, the owner of this paper started broadcasting TV programs for Brazilians in Japan via satellite links.

In terms of the availability of ethnic-based resources, *Nikkei* Latin Americans have enjoyed several advantages not available to other foreigners. First, demographic factors such as the relatively large numbers and high density of the *Nikkei* population have facilitated the rapid formation of a substantial market to support ethnic businesses. Second, *Nikkei* Latin Americans are able to utilize various channels of support, not only from the inside of their own community, but also from mainstream Japanese society (Hirota 1994). Third, the first-generation (*Issei*) immigrants of *Nikkei* Latin Americans, who often speak both Japanese and Portuguese/Spanish, can serve as mediators between two different social worlds and, in some cases, as entrepreneurs of ethnic businesses. Consequently, although the main in-migration of *Nikkei*, which began in 1990, started relatively later than other ethnic groups, their ethnic-related institutions developed more extensively than those of any other ethnic group except the Koreans and Chinese.

However, almost a decade after their initial influx, *Nikkei* Latin Americans are now showing more diversified forms of local settlement. Thus, a simple image cannot cover the total picture of recent *Nikkei* communities. First, since the economic boom ended, the working conditions of *Nikkei* workers have generally become very unstable. *Nikkei* are geographically more dispersed now than in the initial stage. This is caused partly by the development of ethnic ties which have tended to accelerate mobility. Additionally, settlement patterns have begun to be differentiated among various *Nikkei* ethnic groups, such as Brazilians, Peruvians, and Bolivians. For instance, Peruvian groups tend to concentrate in limited areas for the sake of their ethnic network while Brazilian groups are often more widely dispersed (Tajima 1995).

Second, different pathways of upward mobility are now being pioneered among some *Nikkei* communities. Expanded ethnic markets are creating greater opportunities for starting new businesses, mostly those oriented to *Nikkei* Latin Americans' growing and more diversified demands for goods and services. Within local companies some *Nikkei* workers are taking positions as 'middlemen' between Japanese managers and other *Nikkei* workers (Nishizawa 1995). Thus, the second stage of settlement is now taking place among more differentiated *Nikkei* communities.

The search for more self-sufficient ethnic communities within inner Tokyo

Before the huge influx started in the middle of the 1980s, large commercial and amusement centers in Tokyo such as Shinju-ku and Ikebukuro had already provided numerous opportunities for housing and jobs to many foreign workers. In 1987, about 14,000 registered foreign residents lived in Shinjuku Ward (*ku*) and about 10,000 lived in Toshima Ward (*ku*), which includes Ikebukuro. By the end of 1991, this number had gone up to 18,165 and 15,431 respectively.

However, the point to be emphasized here is not just the increase in the foreign population in general, but an emergence of more self-sufficient ethnic communities among specific nationalities. For example, as a result of a huge influx of Chinese workers and students, the registered Chinese population increased from 5,394 in 1987 to 8,321 in 1991 in Toshima ward. In addition, the total Chinese population within the surrounding six wards (Shinjuku, Nakano, Suginami, Itabashi, Nerima, and Kita) also increased from 14,283 to 26,721 in the same period. This means that a Chinese community of at least 35,000 appeared in the midst of central Tokyo.

A similar change, though less apparent, is also found in the Korean population. Until recently, the majority of Koreans in inner Tokyo, as in all areas in Japan, belonged to a *Zainichi* (staying in Japan) group, whose population had been relatively stable.[5] In 1987 there were 5,763 registered Koreans living in Shinju-ku Ward. The subsequent influx from South Korea increased the Korean population here to 8,584 by 1998. In the surrounding five wards (Toshima, Nakano, Suginami, Itabashi and Nerima) the total Korean population increased from 12,314 in 1987 to 16,111 in 1991. Although it had slightly decreased to 15,648 by 1998, the current population is still significantly greater than it was before the economic boom of the late 1980s.

Emerging ethnic communities do not have a focal point similar to Koreatown in Los Angeles or the many Chinatowns in North America. Many foreign workers in Japan found accommodation in small units within wooden apartment houses which were usually very old and had only poor facilities. They then looked for work in nearby restaurants, bars, and other miscellaneous service and manufacturing industries (Okuda and Tajima 1993, 1995). When examined more closely, such areas clearly began to take on the trappings of an ethnic community.

A lot of ethnic restaurants, small markets for ethnic foods and goods, video rental shops, ethnic churches and other activities have now become more visible in Japanese neighborhoods. Local Tokyo-based free papers printed in Korean or Chinese language are filled with numerous advertisements for immigrant-related institutions including legal services, travel agents, real estate agents, churches and grocery stores. These institutions are often owned and managed not by Korean or Chinese but by Japanese. Yet, in many cases, those who can speak their mother tongue are hired to serve their co-ethnic customers.

An ethnic enclave in a strict sense does not yet exist in Tokyo (Portes and Rumbaut 1990: 21–2). A broad array of economic and social activities along ethnic lines are gradually being created and are cumulatively increasing. In this context, the term ethnic community can possibly be used in Japan. Often, these communities are further divided into several sub-ethnic groups, such as Taiwanese, Shanghainese and Fujianese in the Chinese case (Okuda and Tajima 1995). Such communities are more complicated than others in their ethnic ties and institutional arrangements.

In spite of the drastic transformation over the past decade, local governments are usually reluctant or fragmented in their response to the settlement of foreigners within their jurisdiction. Some governments have put up bilingual signs in public places and publish newsletters on public and local affairs in several languages. The basic attitude of local governments toward a more ethnically diversified community, however, still seems awkward or, at least, very vague.

Such reluctance is partly because groups of Korean or Chinese residents would like to have their own more self-sufficient and exclusively integrated communities. Another reason is the inconsistency of local governments toward future forms of urban community. They are often very eager to provide various opportunities for a better life to foreigners so long as they are temporary guests in the Japanese community. Once foreigners try to settle locally on a longer-term basis and to establish their own self-sufficient communities, local governments usually simply ignore their presence and refuse to adapt to the reality of the changing situations. It is therefore very difficult for migrants to find out about public policies on how they can settle into an area and be part of it. Furthermore, there are hardly any local political channels for representing foreigners' needs. This is partly due to foreign workers' own indifference, their unstable legal status, and, sometimes, to the low political effectiveness of their employers. Consequently even well-established local ethnic communities find it difficult to positively visualize a future multi-ethnic community.

Conclusion

The examples I have given demonstrate that, although newcomer foreign workers often share common problems such as discrimination, helplessness and isolation, their actual life styles and working conditions are increasingly becoming more diverse. A more varied and elaborate approach is therefore required to solving the problems that different groups of foreign workers are now facing. Isolated foreign workers in industrial districts who do not enjoy legal work status usually lack even the chance to receive basic public services because of the weakness of their visa status. Therefore the first major problem that they have to overcome is not merely social distress but the trouble caused by their illegal status and the economic instability accompanying it. Even if such situations persist, community-based support is also needed if foreign workers are to improve their position in such unfavorable conditions. Not least of their difficulties in everyday life comes from the absence of communication and the resultant mutual misunderstanding within the local populace. In this sense, the contribution of those workers to the local economy should be more generally recognized by Japanese as well as foreign residents.

The case of *Nikkei* Latin Americans might give a more positive impression. Their advantages in legal status and availability of ethnic resources has contributed to the swift establishment of more firmly-integrated ethnic neighborhoods. However, as long as their employment depends upon economic conditions, *Nikkei* neighborhoods cannot be free from cyclical or structural fluctuations in the regional economy and the social instability that accompanies it. As revealed in the late 1990s, the long economic recession has brought various problems among *Nikkei* workers, including unemployment, discrimination and homelessness (AERA 1998). Thus, it is difficult to generalize from the previous patterns of economic and social incorporation of foreign workers and simply project them uncritically into the future. From a long-term perspective, the more possible scenario for the future migration of the *Nikkei* Latin American population will be frequent mobility, not only inside Japan but also between Japan and the home countries in Latin America. The development of ethnic neighborhoods and institutions in Japan will depend, in part, upon whether various groups of foreigners can continue to effectively provide ethnic goods and services to an increasingly divergent ethnic and sub-ethnic mix of foreign workers that can be expected the emerge in the coming years.

The different patterns of settlement, work and access to public facilities can be found among Asian ethnic communities in the central Tokyo. As their latent social networks take a more obvious shape in supporting ethnic-based economic activities, the existing local communities will be subject to gradual fragmentation along vaguely emergent ethnic lines. Such trends will possibly lead to the formation of a more multi-ethnic Tokyo. In common with other cities throughout the world where cultural diversity has taken place Tokyo will need a policy agenda that specifically focuses on issues of ethnic diversity so as to integrate an increasingly ethnically-fragmented metropolitan region.

Some progressive local governments are currently trying to establish a more substantial basis for incorporating foreigners politically and socially into the community and public area. Kawasaki, which is a major industrial city located adjacent to Tokyo, has traditionally contained a large *Zainichi* Korean community, and, recently, it has been attracting various groups of foreigners including *Nikkei* Latin American workers and Filipinas. A policy package to counter discrimination against foreigners was formulated through collaboration with *Zainichi* Korean organizations. It contained provisions aimed at more equal receipt of social and public services and established a community center for ethnic culture. Other attempts have been developed into more institutionalized forms, e.g. a foreign residents' representative assembly (Kawasaki-shi Shimin-kyoku 1993). This is obviously one of the most advanced cases but gradual progress can also be found among other local governments e.g. the Tokyo Metropolitan Government (Tokyo-to 1994; Tegtmeyer Pak, Chapter Eleven of this volume).

Whatever laws are passed to improve the current situation, better solutions to the various problems within the community context should be rooted in a more accurate understanding of current settlement processes. There is no generic or general foreign worker living in the local community. The problems encountered by a *Nikkei* Brazilian factory worker and an undocumented construction worker from Iran are substantially different. The economic and social routes followed by a female entertainer from the Philippines and a male ethnic entrepreneur from South Korea are also characteristically different. In other words, opportunities among foreign workers are differentiated by ethnicity, class, gender and legal status.

Foreign migrants are often subject to discrimination as a result of structural economic conditions and processes that restrict their opportunities. However, they are not mere victims who are only exploited by their employers or recruiters. As new residents in Tokyo, they are becoming more independent and actively involved in the formation and the reformation of Japan's urban society. From this broader understanding of the processes through which foreign workers integrate into urban communities, initial steps should be taken to broaden and elaborate the varied possibilities for dynamic and creative relationships among Japanese and various foreign residents in an increasingly multi-ethnic Tokyo.

Notes

1 In this chapter, the numbers of registered foreign residents are based on the data compiled by the author from prefectural reports on registered foreign residents (*Gaikokujin Tōroku Kokuseki Betsu Jin-in Chōsa Hyō*) and Hōmushō (Ministry of Justice's reports) (Hōmudaijin Kanbō Shihō Hōsei Chōsa Bu each year, *Hōmushō Nyūkoku Kanri Kyoku* 1985, 1988, 1991, 1993a, 1995, 1997, 1998).

2 According to newspapers and TV programs, such rumors were spread in Saitama, Tokyo, Tochigi, Gunma and elsewhere (*Asahi Shimbun* 20 November 1990; NHK's TV program *Tokuhō Shutoken '91: Uwasa wa Naze Hirogattaka, Gaikokujin Hanzai Dema Sōdō*, 26 January 1991).

3 This description is based on the author's series of observation in Yoyogi Park from November 1990 to May 1993.

4 Interviews with the papers' publishers were conducted in April and June 1992.

5 When the Second World War ended in 1945, more than two million Korean residents, who had been legally treated as Japanese citizens under a colonial system, lived in Japan. After Japan's defeat and the liberation of Korea, many workers, who had often been conscripted into mines, factories and construction sites, returned to Korea, but more than 500,000 people stayed in Japan and emerged as "*Zai-Nichi*" ("staying in Japan") Koreans. Until the recent influx of foreign population Korean nationals had been the overwhelming majority of foreigners living in Greater Tokyo. In 1984, Koreans occupied 59.5 percent of total registered residents in Tokyo Metropolis and 69.1 percent of those in its surrounding area (six prefectures). In 1994, the Koreans were still the most populous but the proportion had decreased significantly: to 37.6 percent and 27.8 percent respectively.

References

AERA (1996) "*Tōbu Isezaki Sen no Ekimae Mosuku,*" *AERA*, 9–25: 42–5.

—— (1998) "*Sogaikan Tuyomeru Burajiru Jin,*" *AERA*, 11–40: 25–7.

Allison, A. (1994) *Nightwork: Sexuality, Pleasure, and Corporate Masculinity in a Tokyo Hostess Club*, Chicago: University of Chicago Press.

Ballescas, R. P. (1992) *Filipino Entertainers in Japan: An Introduction,* Quezon City, Philippines: The Foundation for Nationalist Studies.

Cross, M. and Waldinger, R. (1992) "Migrants, Minorities, and the Ethnic Division of Labour" in S. Fainstein, I. Gordon, and M. Harloe (eds) *Divided Cities: New York and London in the Contemporary World,* Oxford: Blackwell: 151–74.

Friedmann, J. (1986) "The World City Hypothesis," *Development and Change* 17: 69–83.

Fujita, K. (1991) "A World City and Flexible Specialization: Restructuring the Tokyo Metropolis," *International Journal of Urban and Regional Research* 15: 269–84.

Gaikokujin Rōdōsha Kenri Hakusho Henshū Iinkai (ed.) (1995) *Gaikokujin Rōdōsha Kenri Hakusho: Hataraku Nakama, Gaikokujin Rōdōsha,* Tokyo: Gaikokujin Rōdōsha Kenri Hakusho Henshū Iinakai.

Higuchi, N. and Takahashi, S. (1997) "*Zainichi Brazil Jin no Esunikku Bijinesu: Kigyōka Kyōkyū Sisutemu no Hatten to Shijō no Hirogari wo Chūshin ni,*" paper presented at theAnnual Meeting of the Japanese Sociological Association, Chiba University.

Hirota, Y. (1994) "*Nikkeijin Kazoku no Ikikata,*" in M. Okuda, Y. Hirota and J. Tajima (eds) *Gaikokujin Kyojūsha to Nihon no Chiikishakai,* Tokyo: Akashi Shoten.

Hōmudaijin Kanbō Shihō Hōsei Chōsa Bu (ed.) (annually) *Shutsunyūkoku Kanri Tōkei Nenpō,* Tokyo: Ōkurashō Insatsu Kyoku.

Hōmushō Nyūkoku Kanri Kyoku (ed.) (1985) *Shōwa 60 Nenban Zairyū Gaikokujin Tōkei,* Tokyo: Okurasho Insatsu Kyoku.

—— (1988) *Shōwa 62 Nenban Zairyū Gaikokujin Tōkei,* Tokyo: Ōkurashō Insatsu Kyoku.

—— (1991) *Heisei 3 Nenban Zairyū Gaikokujin Tōkei,* Tokyo: Nyūkan Kyōkai.

—— (1993a) *Heisei 5 Nenban Zairyū Gaikokujin Tōkei,* Tokyo: Nyūkan Kyōkai.

—— (1993b) *Heisei 4 Nenban Shutsunyū-koku Kanri,* Tokyo: Ōkurashō Insatsu Kyoku.

—— (1995) *Heisei 7 Nenban Zairyū Gaikokujin Tōkei,* Tokyo: Nyūkan Kyōkai.

—— (1997) *Heisei 9 Nenban Zairyū Gaikokujin Tōkei,* Tokyo: Nyūkan Kyōkai.

—— (1998) *Heisei 10 Nenban Zairyū Gaikokujin Tōkei,* Tokyo: Nyūkan Kyōkai.

Ishii, Y. and Inaba, N. (1996) "*Jūtaku Mondai: Kyojū no Chōkika no Nakade,*" in T. Miyajima and T. Kajita (eds) *Gaikokujinn Rōdōsha kara Shimin he,* Tokyo: Yuhikaku: 41–64.

Kamo, T. (1993) "*Sōgo Izon teki Ristorakuchuaringu to Nichibei Kankei: Sekai Toshi to Sangyō Chiiki,*" in G. Shigemori and H. Enshu (eds) *Toshi Saisei no Seijikeizaigaku,* Tokyo: Keizai Shipōsha.

Kawasaki-shi, Shiminkyoku (1993) *Zai-nichi Gaikokujin wo Rikai suru tame no Handbook,* Kawasaki: Kawasaki-shi.

Kitagawa, T. (ed.) (1993) *Hamamatsu-shi ni Okeru Gaikokujin no Seikatsu Jittai Ishiki Chōsa,* Hamamatsu: Hamamatsu-shi, Kikakubu, Kokusai Kōryū Shitsu.

Komai, H. (ed.) (1995) *Teijūka suru Gaikokujin 'Kōza Gaikokujin Teijū Mondai 2',* Tokyo: Akashi Shoten.

Machimura, T. (1992) "The Urban Restructuring Process in Tokyo in the 1980s: Transforming Tokyo into a World City," *International Journal of Urban and Regional Research* 16: 114–28.

—— (1994) *Sekai Toshi Tokyo no Kozo Tenkan,* Tokyo: University of Tokyo Press.

Mahmood, R. A. (1993) *A Survey: Experiences of Bangladeshi Workers in Japan,* Tokyo:

National Institute for Research Advancement.

Mori, H. (1994) "Migrant Workers and Labor Market Segmentation In Japan," *Asian and Pacific Migration Journal* 3–4: 619–38.

Nishizawa, A. (1995) *Inpei sareta Gaibu*, Tokyo: Sairyūsha.

Okuda, M. and Tajima, J. (eds) (1993) *Shinjuku no Asia-kei Gaikokujin*, Tokyo: Mekon.

—— (1995) *Shipan Ikebukuro no Asia-kei Gaikokujin*, Tokyo: Akashi Shoten.

Portes, A. and Rumbaut, R. G. (1990) *Immigrant America: A Portrait*, Berkeley: University of California Press.

Sassen, S. (1988) *The Mobility of Labor and Capital*, Cambridge: Cambridge University Press.

Somucho Gyosei Kansatsu Kyoku (ed.) (1992) *Gaikokujin wo Meguru Gyōsei no Genjō to Kadai*, Tokyo: Okurasho Insatsu Kyoku.

Tajima, H. (1995) "Latin America *Nikkeijin no Teijūka: Shusshinkoku Betsu noKōsatsu*," *Komai*: 163–98.

Tanaka, H. (1995) *Zainichi Gaikokujin, Shinban*. Tokyo: Iwanami Shoten.

Tokyo-to (1994) *Tokyo Metropolitan Government Guidelines for the Promotion of International Policies: A New Approach to the International Policies for the 21st Century*, Tokyo: Tokyo-to.

Tsuzuki, K. (1995) "Chihō Toshi to Ethnicity," in Y. Matsumoto (ed.) *Zōshoku suru Network (21 Seiki no Toshi Shakaigaku)*, Tokyo: Keisō Shobo: 235–81.

9 Identities of multiethnic people in Japan

Stephen Murphy-Shigematsu

From ancient times migrants to Japan have mixed with the local inhabitants and produced offspring. While much ethnic mixing has occurred in the distant past, many contemporary persons trace their immediate ancestry to more than one ethnic source. Since 1988, I have been studying multiethnic individuals in Japan through interviews, psychological counseling and ethnographic fieldwork in Okinawa and Tokyo. In this chapter I will give examples of these lives and explain how their identities are influenced by a wide range of political, legal, ideological social and psychological forces and constraints. Although some of the conditions are favorable, I will focus on the problems that have become evident in my study.

First, I want to look briefly at the general ethnology of Japan. Anthropological theory of the peopling of the Japan describes a migration from South-East Asia, the Pacific and, later, East Asia probably over land bridges that once existed. The early settlers in the Jomon era (10,000 to 3,000 BC) included the ancestors of what are today called the *Ainu* and *Ryukyuan* (Okinawan) peoples and they were biologically closely related to Micronesians, Polynesians and South-east Asians. A later migration during the Yayoi era (300 BC – AD 300) occurred from continental Asia through the Korean peninsula into North Kyūshū, from which expansion was eastward and northward. These later immigrants were of a different genetic stock than the indigenous peoples with whom they mixed (Hanihara 1993, Hanihara and Omoto 1991).

The inhabitants of the Ryukyu islands had their own distinctive language and culture and strong ties with China before their independent kingdom was gradually, but forcibly, incorporated into the expanding Japanese empire. People who may have been the forerunners of the *Ainu* maintained their ethnic characteristics by moving north but the groups that arrived during the Yayoi era either exterminated, genetically absorbed or assimilated most but not all of the Jomon groups with whom they came into contact. These new groups, consisting of both Yayoi and Jomon elements, eventually consolideated into the clans known as *Yamato*, which formed the first Japanese state in the fifth century.

The diverse roots of present day Japanese spring from later large migrations of Chinese and Koreans and the smaller incursions of other races. Migration from China and Korea continued until the ninth century, by which time nearly one-third of the aristocratic clans in the Chinese-style Heian capital (present-day Kyoto), were of Korean or Chinese origin (Sansom 1952, Wetherall 1992). Many colonial subjects of the late nineteenth and twentieth century from Korea and Taiwan who settled in Japan or were pressed into pre-war or wartime labor there remained. After the Second World War the Allied Occupation and subsequent US military presence also brought a large, mostly transient, population of American men.

From the 1980s, laborers, businessmen, athletes, entertainers, students, English teachers and brides of Japanese men have come to Japan from all corners of the world in search of opportunity. Among the migrants are the descendants of former Japanese nationals who left Japan to seek their fortune elsewhere. Some of these newcomers have chosen to stay in Japan permanently or for extended periods.

Japanese society includes the more indigenous populations of *Ainu* and Okinawans and others of various non-mainstream, ethnic backgrounds who hold Japanese citizenship, particularly Koreans and Chinese. The resident foreign population is also composed of a diverse group of nationals, the largest group of whom are South Korean. Many of these persons have mixed with the majority Japanese population and created the variety of multiethnic people who exist today in Japan.

Despite the history of heterogeneity and diversity, there is a widely-shared racialistic myth of the Japanese in contemporary Japan. The people of Japan are commonly depicted as forming a single ethnic group. This myth of homogeneity implies that mixture of diverse original constituents has become complete and irrelevant. The existence of non-mainstream Japanese, such as persons of multiple ethnic ancestries, is either denied or relegated to the status of outsider. Children fathered and abandoned by American servicemen have attracted some public attention as a social problem but the existence of far greater numbers, such as those of Korean and Japanese ancestry, has been largely unnoticed.

Following their emergence in various fields however, there has been some positive public recognition in recent years of ethnically or racially mixed persons. In many societies, mixed people assume a major role in influencing the process and content of categories and meanings of race and ethnicity (Omi and Winant 1986). The situation in Japan reflects that in certain other societies such as the US and the UK where multiethnic individuals are becoming visible by challenging the strict divisions that have been constructed between racial groups (Root 1996, Tizard and Phoenix 1993). The emerging multiracial movement in the United States can be observed at community level, in nationwide networks and at the academic level in specialized courses and student clubs.

Ethnic and racial politics in the US and UK exert pressure on individuals to identify with only one group. The celebrated claim of golf sensation Tiger Woods to be a Cablinasian (Caucasian-Black-Indian-Asian), a self definition that asserts all the diverse aspects of his ethnic and racial background, not long ago would have been the subject of ridicule. It still rings alarms when Woods rejects the label of African-American but the kind of assertion that he makes is hardly unique to him and is now the subject of an intense and profound debate on ethnicity and race at the national level in the US (*Ebony* 1997). The question of whether to continue the racialistic "one-drop-rule" of classification by the US census is being challenged by those who believe that a new multiracial category is appropriate and by those who believe the system should be completely abolished (Nash 1997, Wright 1994).

A brief discussion of terminology is necessary. The people of Japan include Japanese and non-Japanese. In this chapter Japanese means pre-1945 subjects and post 1946 citizens of Japan, including multinationals. Japanese include both mainstream or majority persons, as well as non-mainstream or minority persons who are genetically, phenotypically, racially, culturally or linguistically differentiated. Non-Japanese include foreign nationals and stateless people. There is a non-racial, non-ethnic legal distinction between Japanese and non-Japanese. All other differentiations are personal or social and may or may not be considered discriminatory.

The Japanese word *jinshu* refers to conventional categories of race and is not used to describe Japanese groups but is reserved for blacks and whites, or to contrast "Japanese" and whites. It is used especially in labeling racial problems of other countries, as in *jinshu mondai*. The word *minzoku* is a confusion of race, nation, peoples and ethnic group and, while *jinshu* is clearly based on inherited physical characteristics, *minzoku* includes psychological, social, cultural or linguistic factors. Its usage has been marked by overtones of communal solidarity and ideology, or a set of beliefs that make one "Japanese" or a member of another ethnic group (Morris-Suzuki 1996). The *Yamato* or *Nihon minzoku* is assumed to share a common ancestry, history and culture in the same way as other *minzoku* (Weiner 1995). Today, *minzoku* refers to ethnicity (*minzokusei*), food (*minzoku ryori*) or music (*minzoku ongaku*). It continues to describe not only culture or nation but also biology or blood as evident in the popular confusion of *kokumin kokka* (citizens' state) with *minzoku kokka* (nation (ethnic) state) (Dower 1986, Weiner 1997).

In English, biracial, multiracial, and racially mixed are some of the more popular terms used for mixed ancestry. These terms imply biological differences and refer to mixes such as black and white or yellow and black. However, most of the individuals referred to in this chapter are mixtures of what would usually described as different *minzoku*, rather than different *jinshu*. Since ethnic is the closest English equivalent to *minzoku*, the term multiethnic is used rather than multiracial.

However, the term multiethnic begs the question of what makes a person ethnic? For example, is a fourth generation resident or citizen of a country still accurately described as having ethnic characteristics that distinguish him or her from the majority population? Is there a point at which these characteristics are so diluted as to become inconsequential as an identifying factor for the individual? Is one multiethnic simply by virtue of being born to a "mixed" couple? Some of the examples used would be labeled as ethnic because of visible traits but many of those biologically or genetically-mixed would not be grouped in any particular way other than "Japanese" because they "look Japanese".

In reality, there is likely to be a great deal of variation from family to family and from individual to individual. If one parent is passingas majority Japanese, or if the whole family is passing, the children might be well into their teens before they even discover that they are other than "Japanese" or "Korean". Grouping all persons who are ethnically mixed denies individual difference as well as choice. The construction of such an artificial category also ignores the heterogeneous origins of majority Japanese and therefore indirectly reinforces the myth of their racial purity. Regional variations in Japan that could make the child of a couple from Kanto and Kansai a cultural, if not racial, mixture are also ignored. Class differences are not considered but the children of a couple in which one partner was a *Burakumin* (a quasi-ethnic group) or the children of the emperor who is married to a commoner might also be described as from a mixed background. Therefore, the word multiethnic is simply a term of convenience, used to limit and define the scope of the discussion. It is a term that is more appropriate for some persons of mixed ancestry than others.

I will introduce several case studies and then discuss some of the main factors that influence the identities and experiences of these individuals in Japanese society. As in many other countries, those of mixed ancestry are the products of colonialism, imperialism and occupation (Gist and Dworkin 1972). They are being born into a social environment that bears the legacy of former military ventures and they themselves become living remnants of the past and symbols of resident foreign armies. They are also influenced by the transforming ideologies of the nation and conceptions of nationalism which are based in legal and social definitions of ethnicity and citizenship.

Acceptance of the existence and identities of multiethnic persons is viewed as part of the development of society in becoming more multicultural; a society in which diversity of origin is respected as a personal matter but overlooked as a basis of personal judgment (Wetherall 1992, Hollinger 1995, Glazer 1997). Case studies will be used to illustrate how individuals are not simply passive victims, but influence social structures through their attempts at empowerment. All case studies come from interviews conducted in Japan between 1988 and 1996 by the author.

The legacy of colonialism and militarism

Kim Young Sook is a twenty-two-year-old student at an American college in Tokyo. Her mother is Japanese; her father is Korean. At first she went to a public school where she was often teased by boys on her way home from school and forced to eat her lunch alone having been isolated by the other girls. Eventually they gave her a chance and she felt so well adjusted that she one day gave her father a playful dig by saying, "When I grow up I will marry a Japanese boy." The next day he enrolled her at a private Korean elementary school.

Young Sook's paternal grandparents came to Japan from South Korea in 1930 in search of a better life. They had been forcibly made Japanese nationals and required to use Japanese names and speak Japanese. After the Second World War they decided to remain in Japan but were stripped of their Japanese nationality in 1952 by the San Francisco Peace Treaty.

Young Sook considers herself Korean and that is the nationality she bears. She considers herself to be so despite being born, raised and living her whole life in Japan, speaking Japanese better than Korean, and knowing Japanese culture and society better than Korean culture and society. Young Sook, like most other Koreans in Japan, could become Japanese through naturalization but says that she does not "because I can't, I'm Korean."

However, Young Sook now finds herself in the same position as her mother many years ago, entering into a secret love affair. She has become seriously involved with a Japanese worker at her parents' Korean restaurant and is planning to marry him. She expects to be disowned by her father when she announces her plans.

In Japan the forced nationalization of the *Ainu* of Hokkaido, Northern and Southern Kurils and Southern Sakhalin and the people of Ogasawara, the *Ryukyus*, Korea and Taiwan led to their mixing with mainstream Japanese and the birth of multiethnic offspring. However, the policies of territorial expansion and forced assimilation have left bitter memories, as has the postwar disowning of many people who either considered themselves Japanese or who chose to remain in Japan as Japanese nationals. These failed policies of the past of aggression and neglect have left a legacy that still complicates life for many multiethnic persons. I will briefly examine the situation of persons of mixed Korean-Japanese ancestry.

Marriage between Japanese and Koreans occurred throughout the colonial period and has become increasingly common. Many of the Koreans who were in Japan at the end of the Second World War chose to remain and have intermarried. Young Korean residents are now much more likely to marry a Japanese than a Korean. With an ever increasing intermarriage rate of approximately 80 percent, the number of mixed ancestry Korean-Japanese is likely to be at least half a million (Harajiri 1995). The combined number of naturalized former Koreans and mixed Korean-Japanese is therefore now about the same as the total number of Korean residents, signifying a major change in the situation of Korean ancestry people in Japan.

People of mixed Korean Japanese ancestry are brought into the historical and political confusion affecting all those of Korean ancestry in Japan. They feel pressure from Koreans to identify as Korean and pressure from Japanese to at least appear to be part of the majority. In either case, because of the animosity between the two sides, the coercion to deny one part of their ancestry is strongly felt.

Although they may be called *konketsuji* (mixed blood children), their physical appearance is usually indistinguishable from majority Japanese or Koreans. Their invisibility encourages many to attempt to pass as majority members with only one ethnic background. For some, this pressure is intensely felt like a secret waiting to be discovered and revealed to others. For others, it may not figure in their consciousness during their youth, but appear as a significant concern later in life, at times of employment or marriage.

Marriage with Japanese and naturalization often go together, especially when Korean women marry Japanese men (the more common type of intermarriage) and are considered to be selling out by some Koreans who view such actions as directly threatening the existence of Korean ethnicity (Wagatsuma 1981). Those who consider marriage with a fellow Korean unnecessary or distinguish between ethnicity and nationality may be viewed as disloyal by those Koreans who insist on maintaining boundaries between themselves and the Japanese as a necessary condition for ethnic survival. They also might not be accepted as Japanese by majority Japanese who know of their Korean ancestry.

Mixed Japanese-Koreans born today become Japanese citizens through registration of their birth to a Japanese father or mother. Those adolescents and adults who do not have Japanese citizenship can acquire it by naturalization. Those who do are part of a major movement toward naturalization that, in 1993, exceeded 10,000 for the first time, 80 percent of whom were Koreans (Homu Nenkan 1995). In 1994 the number of Koreans who were naturalized exceeded 10,000 and nearly 200,000 persons formerly of South Korean nationality have naturalized in total (Homu Nenkan 1996).

Others of mixed ancestry resist naturalization and remain permanent residents. They do so partly because of the way the government seems to equate nationality with ethnicity and also because of their own insistence on the inseparability of their Korean ancestry and nationality. Some of the descendants of those who remained in Japan after the war are now third and fourth generation Koreans of mixed ancestry who still say that the reason they do not want to become Japanese is because of the history of brutal rule and forced assimilation in names and language. Some claim that maintaining symbolic ties with Korea is necessary for the fight against assimilation into Japanese society and discrimination that still exists (Ryang 1997).

Some mixed youth claim ambiguously that they cannot become Japanese since they are Korean, thereby asserting the equation of nationality and ethnicity. There are young people who are unaware that there was a period when they could have become Japanese through simple registration. Some lack knowledge of the opportunity of naturalization and others are aware but are ignorant of the ease of the application process, the high probability of success and the possibility of maintaining part, if not all, of one's name. This lack of awareness is a product of stereotype and myth in the mind of the would-be naturalizer as well as a creation of image in the mass media.

The children of Korean-Japanese couples may become multiethnic individuals whose identity is heavily influenced by the history of animosity between Koreans and Japanese. As they become more politically aware, they often feel that they are faced with a decision of either identifying with the oppressor or with the oppressed (Freire 1970). Neither choice allows them the freedom of identifying with both parts of their ancestry and the assertion of a Korean and Japanese identity may be an elusive dream for many.

The pressures are greatest for those who are affiliated with North Korea because of the political tension that exists between the two countries and the image among the Japanese of North Korea as a menacing pariah. Most public incidents of overt discrimination in Japan against those of Korean ancestry in recent years have been directed at those who can be readily identified as affiliated with North Korea, namely the children who wear the distinctive uniforms of the *Chōsen gakko* (North Korean supported schools). Many of those who would not consider the possibility of naturalizing sympathise politically with North Korea (Ryang 1997). Integrating an identity composed of Japanese and North Korean ties is therefore an especially challenging task that most individuals probably avoid by choosing to identify only with one part of their ancestry and attempting to reduce the other part to an almost unessential detail of family background.

Similar pressures may also exist for some other multiethnic individuals such as those of partial *Ainu*, Okinawan, or Taiwanese descent. Like Koreans, all these groups were subjected to cultural destruction and forced assimilation. Although the social distance of each of these groups from majority Japanese varies, the heritage of many multiethnic individuals includes both sides of oppression. These historical circumstances still influence them to value or devalue their minority ancestry. They are also on their own in integrating and asserting a multiethnic identity that remains unrecognized by others.

Uehara Shigeo is a thirty-nine year old worker in a large tourist hotel in Okinawa. His mother and stepfather are Okinawan Japanese; his biological father African-American. His father left when his mother was eight months pregnant, saying that he was being sent to Vietnam. He sent a few letters and a little money in the first year but nothing since, then disappeared. His mother's attempts at tracing him were thwarted by the her lack of knowledge of his background, language limitations and by a policy of non-cooperation by the US military authorities. His mother remarried and he grew up with his stepfather and half-siblings. When the family visited the grandparents he was told to wait at the gate and given a lollipop to suck on. While he was growing up, dodging rocks and fighting on the way home from school were daily activities. As a teenager he learned of Malcolm X and Martin Luther King and began to develop a greater feeling of pride in his African-American ancestry. He now loves Michael Jordan but jokes that he can't get a buzz cut because he has too many scars on his head from the rocks that hit him as a child.

Shigeo remembers when the demonstrations against the B52 bombers swept Okinawa and, along with his classmates, he participated in one rally. He felt however that all eyes were on him, as though somehow he was to blame. He feels lucky to have a good job. A girl he briefly dated in high school broke off the relationship without explanation but he is sure that her parents forced her to end it. Now he is serious about another young woman and hoping to marry soon.

People of mixed ancestry have existed in various parts of Japan where American military troops have been stationed since the postwar Occupation. In recent years, they have become concentrated in Okinawa where their lives have gained attention as a social problem linked with the military bases and local struggles for self determination (Murphy-Shigematsu 1993, Asahi 1998). There one finds a special poignancy in the way that lives are connected with political and social movements.

During the Occupation period of recovery, reform and rebuilding, American men and Japanese women met in a wide variety of circumstances and formed relationships. At first these relationships were marred by social and legal barriers. The refusal of the military to take any role in encouraging responsibility in relationships, birth control or fathering, and the opposition to American-Japanese marriages by the US government contributed to massive child abandonment (Shade 1984).

By the early fifties, legal barriers had been lifted and marriages flourished. Legally and socially, American-Japanese children born in wedlock were considered to belong to the father's family and therefore regarded as American. Nationality law, based on the patriarchal family system, and racial attitudes, based on the myth of ethnic purity of Japanese people, labeled them as non-Japanese. In fact, many have accompanied their parents to the United States (Thornton 1992). Children were only officially recognized as Japanese if their American father did not acknowledge paternity and, during the early periods of the Occupation, when the US Embassy did not recognize marriages between Japanese and Americans. However, the legal status of these Japanese nationals was in contrast to prevalent social attitudes that regarded them as foreign and made them targets of prejudice and discrimination.

The most conspicuous group who remained in Japan were abandoned orphans who became a cause for Sawada Miki and, later, novelist Pearl S. Buck. Policies for these children included isolating them and sending them abroad either through adoption by Americans or as a group to a friendly environment like Brazil (Hemphill 1980). Others who favored their integration into Japanese society believed that the best solution was to eliminate their foreignness through inter-marriage with majority Japanese.

The stationing of American troops in Japan has led to the maintenance of service industries for them and continued births of children fathered by Americans both in and out of marriage. They became concentrated in large cities, in employment in fashion and entertainment industries or on military bases. They were strongly stereotyped in the mass media as living fast and loose lives, due to the confusion created by the mixture of their genes (De Vos *et al.* 1983). In fact, they became over represented in single parent families and school dropouts. Identity issues for many were complicated by racial and class prejudice, stereotyping and abandonment (Wagatsuma 1976, Murphy-Shigematsu 1993).

The majority of American-Japanese have visible traits that make them physically identifiable and therefore easy targets of daily social discrimination. The phenomenon of passing as majority Japanese. which is widely practiced among Japanese minorities, including those of mixed ancestry, is possible for only a small number of American-Japanese. They are usually labeled as foreigners although many speak no other language than Japanese and have spent their whole lives in Japan. However, admiration of all things Western also distinguishes many American-Japanese from multiethnic people originating from Japan's colonial empire. The acceptance of white standards of beauty by the majority of Japanese contributes to images of some American-Japanese as having ideal physical attributes and their popularity in the entertainment world.

Most American-Japanese who live outside the bases have no connection with the military. They have American fathers who are businessmen or English teachers or they may have American mothers. They attend public schools but, those who can afford them and live near enough, attend private international schools where mixed kids are numerous and prejudice on that basis is both mild and reserved for those with darker skin color. Although old associations and stereotypes of the military, poverty, and illegitimacy are fading, American-Japanese with military fathers may feel pressured into denying their background and claim instead that their fathers are businessmen, thereby making them appear to be real international people in the eyes of the majority of Japanese (Williams 1992). American-Japanese also show an increasing tendency to identify themselves as Japanese as Japan's international prestige has grown and the authority of the United States has waned. As individuals make their marks in various fields, they challenge social barriers and the racially-exclusive image of who is Japanese.

Apart from a few local areas where bases continue to exist, it is mostly in Okinawa that the lives of American-Japanese are still influenced by the presence of tens of thousands of US military forces. Although it is often said that the environment for American-Japanese in Okinawa has been less harsh than on the mainland, they have been targets of prejudice aggravated by military defeat, extended occupation and the prolonged presence of the bases. Stereotyping and discrimination against American-Japanese has been a common occurrence as Okinawan Japanese struggle with the American and Japanese governments for the right of self-determination. In most parts of Japan, the American military has become just a memory or a minor inconvenience but, in Okinawa, they continue to exercise control over large areas of land and this creates tensions that are always potentially dangerous for making multiethnic Japanese scapegoats (Murphy-Shigematsu 1993). The brutal rape of a schoolgirl by US servicemen in the fall of 1995 became an international incident and ignited local furor against the military bases. This is the kind of situation in which American-Japanese children become the easiest targets of hostility (Asahi 1998).

Legal and extra-legal pressures

Hamamatsu Yoshiko is a thirty-one year old office worker. Like Young Sook, her mother is Japanese and her father is South Korean. Unlike Young Sook, Yoshiko is a Japanese citizen. Her twenty-nine year old brother who was born from the same parents, and goes through life under the legal alias of Hamamatsu Taro, is also legally known as Haku Sung Char and is a Korean citizen. The reason for different nationalities is that Yoshiko's parents were not married when she was born but were at the time of her brother's birth. Under the nationality laws in effect at the time of their births, Yoshiko became a Japanese while her brother became a Korean.

Sanchez Yoko is a thirty-two year old born in Japan but taken to the US following her mother's remarriage. She was raised there but, following divorce, returned with her mother to Japan. Yoko enrolled in public school but found difficulties in language and culture and moved to a Christian English school. As an adult, she has become a bilingual radio and television star but, despite her popularity, she says that she feels much more at home in the US and hopes to return to live there. Her nationality is Japanese.

Her twenty-nine year old brother was born in the US but raised in Japan. He attended public schools and continued there until graduation. He now only speaks Japanese and says that he feels Japanese but, unlike his sister who is Japanese, he is an American citizen. He says that he wants to be Japanese but has never tried to naturalize. He did not take advantage of the government's offer of automatic citizenship without naturalization that was part of the revised law granting nationality to all those with Japanese mothers. He says that he heard about it from a friend but his mother did not tell him anything. Although he expects to continue to live in Japan, he still has not pursued naturalization because he "won't be accepted as Japanese anyway" since he "doesn't look Japanese".

Nationality law is of special concern to couples in which partners hold different nationalities, not only for the rights of the foreign partner but also for their children. Problems with nationality laws were most prominent among some stateless individuals of American and Japanese ancestry up to 1985. However, other problematic concerns have existed for mixed individuals of various combinations.

The offspring of Japanese women and certain categories of foreign men were banished from the country in the seventeenth century and then forbidden to leave in the eighteenth century. By the middle of the nineteenth century, the patrilineal view that was standard in continental Europe was adopted (Wetherall 1992). From their inception in 1899 until 1985, nationality laws were based on the principle of *jus sanguinis,* or specifically, patrilineal descent. Anyone with a Japanese father was eligible for Japanese nationality but those with a Japanese mother and a non-Japanese father were not eligible for Japanese nationality unless their father was unknown or stateless.

Immediately after the Second World War, children born to Japanese women and American men outside marriage became Japanese citizens. Later, however, children born to married couples became American citizens. Many persons of mixed ancestry therefore started life as foreigners in Japan and some remained foreigners following their parents' divorce.

In Japan, nationality is not conferred by the principle of *jus soli,* therefore individuals are not able to receive Japanese nationality through birth on Japanese soil. Koreans and Taiwanese, like other former Japanese nationals, and those born in Japan to parents who non-Japanese nationals and any other foreigners, can only become citizens through individual application for naturalization. Those who have chosen not to be naturalized and their descendants therefore do not hold Japanese nationality.

Nationalities within mixed families were often complicated prior to the revision of the nationality law in 1985. In some cases, siblings held different nationalities and family names. To the extent that one's nationality and name become part of one's identity, brothers and sisters were torn in different directions by the nationality law. The difference in nationality laws of the United States and Japan also led to some American-Japanese being born stateless, unable to acquire either the Japanese nationality of their mother or the American nationality of their father (Honda 1982). By Japanese laws the children of non-Japanese fathers could not acquire nationality and, by American law, the children of men who had not resided in the United States for at least five years after the age of fourteen could not acquire nationality. This problem was especially acute in Okinawa (Murphy-Shigematsu 1993).

Pressure to end sexual discrimination against women regarding the ineligibility of their children to receive Japanese nationality led to revisions in the law in 1985. The preceding years were marked by several publicized legal cases that challenged the state's right to deny Japanese citizenship to children born to Japanese women and foreign men (Tanaka 1995). As a result, nearly all people of multiethnic ancestry no longer encounter legal barriers to equality. Those who choose to live as foreign nationals will still face certain limitations on their lives and unequal treatment in certain laws but these restrictions are dwindling in number and importance.

The revised law has helped many multiethnic individuals to live in Japan as Japanese citizens. The law was retroactive to cover all minors and many multi-ethnic individuals acquired Japanese nationality then without going through naturalization procedures. They usually adopted their mother's family name in the process and their new name and nationality enabled some to feel more Japanese.

However, some parents neglected to inform their children of this right or refused to allow them to become Japanese. The revised law raises problems for parents who do not want their children to become Japanese as it requires the birth of all children born to either a Japanese father or mother in Japan to be registered at a local city or ward office. The child can only be registered in the family register of the Japanese parent, as the non-Japanese parent does not have a family register in Japan and is not included in the register of the Japanese partner. This means that the child is registered as Japanese, a procedure that is objectionable to those who desire to choose only the nationality of the non-Japanese parent.

The child must also be registered in the family name of the family register and therefore under the name of the Japanese parent. Unless the Japanese partner has acquired the family name of his or her spouse, the family register name is therefore one's original Japanese name. The child will, therefore, be registered as a Japanese citizen with the name of the Japanese parent. Those who see names as an extension of the equation that nationality equals ethnicity regard this situation as intolerable (Ota *et al.* 1995).

However, such parents are not powerless to have the child acquire the nationality of the non-Japanese parent. After registering at the city or ward office, they can go to their embassy and register their child as a citizen of their own country. They can then renounce Japanese nationality for the child and register the child as an alien. It is mainly Koreans who object to this procedure and attack it as a form of forced assimilation. As South Korea is also one of the few countries that has the family reg-istration system, the original Japanese nationality and its renunciation is recorded in the Korean family register. Those who cannot distinguish between ethnicity and nationality regard the record of Japanese nationality, albeit surrendered, like a stain on the family honour (Ota *et al.* 1995).

Another problem has arisen for people with a Japanese father and a non-Japanese mother. Everyone with a Japanese mother can receive Japanese nationality but, only those whose Japanese fathers are married and acknowledge paternity are permitted to acquire Japanese nationality. In principle the acknowledgment must be made before the birth although exceptions have been made in cases where the father was unaware of his paternity until afterwards. Statelessness for abandoned children fathered by Japanese men and born to non-Japanese women has become a new legal problem in Japan and other Asian countries, especially the Philippines. Recent court cases have challenged the limits of the nationality law, most notably in a publicized case brought by the adoptive parents of an abandoned boy believed to be the child of a Japanese father and Filipino mother who had been denied Japanese nationality.

For those of mixed ancestry who, for various reasons, did not acquire Japanese nationality, naturalization is fairly simple. Naturalization requirements are less stringent for those with family connections with Japanese, making it easier for multi-ethnic individuals with recent Japanese ancestry to acquire Japanese nationality (Yamada 1986). Although minors are permitted to hold more than one nationality, they are instructed to make a decision about their nationality at the age of twenty, as the new law was also instituted to eliminate dual nationality in adults. Japan's nationality laws are thus widely regarded as limiting choices for many binational persons and therefore preventing the ideal of allowing legal recognition of one's connection to each nation of ancestry (Kokusai Kekkon o Kangaeru Kai 1991).

The nationality law is based on an assumption that a person can properly be a cit-izen of only one state and that a state can protect only citizens who are duty-bound to it and no other. While it attempts to resolve the legal conflicts that an adult with multiple nationalities is expected to have, it does not prevent an individual from maintaining or even acquiring dual nationality. The law does require naturalized cit-izens to relinquish other nationalities as a prerequisite for acquiring Japanese nationality but, in practice, a confirmation of intent to renounce is all that is requested. An individual holding dual or multiple nationalities is informed of the rule (*ruuru*) to choose one but confirmation of intent to keep Japanese nationality is all that is required to maintain it. The law does not provide for loss of citizenship should a dual national both confirm his or her nationality and continue to maintain another one.

Nevertheless, it is widely believed that the law limits choices of nationality. This myth is perpetuated by the Ministry of Justice to reduce the number of individuals who are dual nationals. Would-be applicants for naturalization are informed that they must renounce their present nationality as a prerequisite for naturalization. Parents of dual nationals are also instructed that their children must choose one of their nationalities upon becoming an adult. The media also perpetuates this myth by reporting that a choice of nationalities is required by law. One result is that appli-cants for naturalization are limited and another is that many uninformed dual nationals unwillingly relinquish one of their nationalities in the belief that they have no choice.

Ueno Reiko is the daughter of a Korean father and Japanese mother. She is about to enter into the job market and is plagued by doubts about her strategy. Should she attempt to disguise her Korean ancestry and risk being discovered later? Should she state at the beginning that she is of part Korean ancestry and risk discrimination? She sees more Koreans emerging in public in various positions and wonders if it is true that she would not be hired just because of her ethnic background. She wonders if she should avoid humiliation and disappointment by limiting her job search to Korean-owned companies. Her brother used her father's connections and now works for a Korean company but her older sister decided not to reveal her background and now is employed by a Japanese company.

Nakayama Taro used to be Lee Sung Char. After considerable thought, he decided to give up the South Korean nationality which he had received through his father and to become a naturalized Japanese citizen. He reasoned that it was natural to acquire the nationality of the country in which he had been born and raised and the only country in which he had ever lived. He rationalized that his ethnic background would never be lost no matter what legal steps he took. He found the process fairly straightforward and the requirements reasonable.

After gathering the necessary documents, he submitted them to the Ministry of Justice. However, in his interview, it was suggested that he adopt a new name which would be more commonly recognized as Japanese. His mother's maiden name of Nakayama was recommended. He responded that this was not required by the law but the official told him that it was strongly recommended that he comply with the request as a gesture of his sincerity in becoming Japanese. When Lee failed to budge, the official told him to think about his children. "Why make life hard for them?" he was told. Lee felt quite sure that failure to go along with the official's demands would result in rejection of his application, so he grudgingly wrote the name Nakayama on the form. His application was approved and he is now a Japanese citizen.

The *koseki* or family register system, that functions as a principal means of social control, assumes importance in the lives of many persons of mixed ancestry. For those who attempt to pass in society as mainstream Japanese, it is often only through an examination of the family register that their multiethnic ancestry can be identified. The lack of a supposedly pure Yamato background, like other deviations from the norm such as illegitimate birth, adoption or ancestry that traces back to a *Burakumin* status in the distant past, all have a stigma. Although legal restrictions are now placed on the formerly routine practice of requiring family registers for employment, violations through purchase of specially-prepared name and address books, computer listings and the work of private investigators still occur. Discovery of a supposed impurity can lead to lost employment opportunities and broken marriage plans. On the other hand, discovery of having lied can result in nullification of employment agreements.

Only Japanese are recorded in *koseki* and, at least until 1985, the system did not accommodate non-Japanese who married Japanese and had children. By the time the family registration system also became a state instrument to register nationality, the Alien Registration Law was drafted to serve the same purpose for aliens (Marui

1989). Like the nationality laws of most countries, Japan assumed that the woman who married a non-Japanese would identify with her husband's nationality and that her nationality would also change. However, the law did accommodate foreign husbands who wanted to acquire Japanese nationality. Normally a husband and wife are both listed in the register but, when one was a non-Japanese, only the Japanese partner was listed. Next to each child's name the names of the father and mother are recorded but, when one was a non-Japanese, the corresponding box was left blank.

Such legal practices are disturbing to some persons of mixed ancestry who regard the treatment of the non-Japanese parent as discriminatory. When the father is non-Japanese, he is usually not regarded as the head of household and, although required to pay taxes, is not entitled to a certificate of residence. This is because he is not registered with the rest of the family in the residency registration (*juminhyo*) but separately in his or her own alien registration certificate. The non-Japanese father married to a Japanese is also unable to have his children registered as Japanese citizens in his family name. The children of such couples must be registered in the mother's family name and can only receive the father's name if the mother has changed her marital name to her husband's.

In addition to the legal limitations placed on individuals, multiethnics who attempt to naturalize may be affected by the extra-legal harassment of bureaucratic officials who circumvent the law by their actions (Sato 1993). Names have been a particular focus of attention. Legal restrictions limit them to two parts, a family name followed by a personal name. Another requirement disallows names in scripts other than a limited number of *kanji, katakana and hiragana*. Otherwise, neither the Nationality Law nor the Family Registration Law places any ethnic restrictions on the names of either naturalized or natural citizens.

Although the Ministry of Justice claims that applicants are free to choose their naturalized name, individuals have complained for some time that there is extra-legal pressure to renounce their name when becoming Japanese. Until recently, naturalization procedures specified that one should try "as much as possible to choose a Japanese-like name", and provided an example showing Kim becoming Kaneda. However, local bureaucrats have been known to harass and refuse applicants not conforming to this suggestion, leading many multiethnic persons and others to reject naturalization as a process because it forces them to surrender their ethnic identity to become Japanese. These people therefore regard naturalization as a state ritual whose purpose is to ethnically transform the successful applicant and permit him or her to engage in the fiction of being part of the Japanese ethnic group.

In a recent edition of the naturalization handbook printed in 1995, the recommendation to choose a Japanese-like name has been eliminated (Kika Tebiki 1995), and, at least in some interviews with officials at the Ministry of Justice, applicants have been informed that they are free to choose any name. However, the examples provided in the handbook still show Kim becoming Sekiguchi, which is shown to be the "passing name" of the husband.

Both examples make sense to the extent that most applicants may be presumed to be "passing" already or are Korean women who have married a Japanese man and intend to adopt his family name. However, the present naturalization handbook continues to make the usual assumptions about name passing and assimilation and still fails to show examples of applicants who may not be using passing names, have used passing names but now wish to use their Korean names or of Korean women who marry Japanese men and wish to keep their Korean names. In other words, they imply that it is appropriate to shed one's ethnicity in the process of becoming Japanese. The government's claim that there is no extra-legal pressure is widely questioned and there is certainly no official encouragement of maintaining ethnic emblems for those acquiring Japanese nationality (Asahi 1997). Many names of Chinese and Koreans are actually not on the list of approved *kanji*.

Extra-legal pressures also appear to have been applied arbitrarily. While some Asians claim to have been forced to relinquish their names, non-Asians generally appear to have not faced this pressure. The reason for this distinction is never made explicit but appears to be based on ideological factors described in the following section. According to this interpretation, while Asian naturalizers could participate in the fiction of being Japanese, non-Asians could not so there is no reason to force them to adopt a Japanese name. One might also say that this disparity of treatment is a reflection of condescending attitudes toward Asians and deferential attitudes toward white non-Asians.

One requirement that has been eliminated is the demand for fingerprints at the time of naturalization. While their purpose may have been simply to screen out criminals, this procedure also may have functioned as an intimidatory tactic or a ritual to impress naturalizers that they were honorary Japanese. In 1991, after being taken to court by three individuals, the government announced that they had ceased demanding fingerprints and later agreed to destroy the fingerprints of more than 220,000 naturalized citizens that they had held (*Japan Times* 1993).

Individuals who have surrendered their names in the naturalization process have sought the return of their names through the courts. Members of the *Minzokumei o Torimodosu Kai* (Association to Reclaim Ethnic Names), many of whom are of mixed ancestry, were successful following the passage of the revised Nationality Law and National Registration Laws and the approval of "non-Japanese names" for Japanese nationals. However, even before their efforts, the family courts had awarded decisions to plaintiffs allowing them to recover their original name (Wetherall 1983, Tanaka 1995).

However, most persons wanting to maintain their name and ethnicity simply reject naturalization as a process because it attempts to strip them of their ethnic emblem as a requirement for becoming Japanese. Although the extra-legal practices of intimidation and forced assimilation appear to have abated in recent years, they have influenced many multiethnic people into believing that acceptance in Japan is based on obedience to the state and constitutes ethnic suicide. Many multiethnic individuals are among those who reject the naturalization procedure for these reasons and remain foreigners in their own land.

Ideological and psychological constraints

Williams Kaori is a student in a public junior high school. She has a Japanese mother and American father. She has lots of friends and her parents and teachers describe her as well-adjusted. She considers herself a typical Japanese girl but acknowledges that some of her experiences may be unique. Occasionally someone says something unexpected like "it's strange to hear someone with your face speak perfect

Japanese!" Or she hears snide remarks like "you are just copying the manners of a Japanese!" When she does anything to distinguish herself from the group, she might hear someone say "see, she's a foreigner after all." Her accomplishments in English and basketball were dismissed by some students as natural, "since you're a *gaijin* (foreigner)." She talks of becoming a singer, but also says that she may want to go to college in the US.

The racialistic myth of the Japanese, that is widely shared by Japanese and others, exerts a powerful influence on those of mixed ancestry. Popular images of homogeneity create a narrowly defined group of (insiders) *uchi* and a marginalized group of (outsiders) *soto* (Creighton 1997). Among thoze marginalized are multiethnic persons. Many individuals will admit that other ethnic groups have been integrated into the gene pool of the *Nihon minzoku* but insist that it happened so long ago as to be insignificant today. The *Ainu*, the only minority that is officially recognized as existing, are a group that is commonly dismissed as inter-married, assimilated and depleted to the point that they are more of a quaint cultural remnant rather than a vibrant ethnic group.

The myth of the monoethnic state can be viewed as a modern state ideology brought about by the loss of the colonies following the Second World War but contradicted by the remains of the colonial period and other more indigenous and immigrant minorities. It is a postwar transformation of pre-war ideology that emphasized the superiority of the state and the Yamato people but now appears in a more acceptable form of emphasis on difference and uniqueness (Dale 1986). Its persistence among the majority of Japanese may lie in its power for community-building and cleansing the sins of past imperialism through its denial of the physical remnants of former colonial subjects of Korean and Taiwanese ancestry who live among them (Wetherall 1992).

This myth also leads to the view that Japanese who do not fit with this narrow image must be foreigners so that the existence of those who are different is either glossed over or relegated to the status of outsiders. Some of these individuals perceived to be outsiders or invisible Japanese are those of multiethnic ancestry. The monoethnic myth affects them by creating an idealized standard of society as homogeneous. Descriptions of the homogeneous society are colored with a sense of pride in the pureness of Japanese society in contrast to the troubles of multi-ethnic societies. In the mid to late 1980s, it was remarks like this that attracted controversy to high-ranking Japanese government officials most notably former Prime Minister Nakasone.

Such claims of the value of the homogeneous society leave multi-ethnics in a difficult position. Prevailing conceptions of nationalism demand a single national identity and therefore the multiple identities of multiethnic individuals that include foreign elements may be viewed as a threat to the state (Yoshino 1992). The ethnic nationalism of minority groups also views multiethnic individuals as traitors unless they prove their allegiance. Multiethnic individuals are pressured from both sides to deny part of their backgrounds as the price of becoming group members.

Despite the clearly non-racialistic legal definition of Japanese nationality, the expression of modern Japanese nationalism is a social attitude that what makes a person Japanese is "blood". "Japanese blood" is a popular expression of the concept of the *Nihon minzoku* and the related belief that Japanese society and culture have unique patterns of behavior and communication that one has to be born Japanese to understand (Dale 1986). Cultural knowledge is intimately connected to "Japanese blood" and certain art forms, tastes and the language itself are all thought to be the exclusive possession of "Japanese people" (Wetherall 1981, Yoshino 1992).

As the concept of Japanese blood assumes that Japanese have been blessed with breeding in isolation, it calls into question the inclusion of those of mixed ancestry. Those visibly different may be called *haafu* (from the English, half) or even *kuoota* (from the English, quarter). From the designation of *kuoota* as someone of three-fourths Japanese ancestry, it can be seen that this classification system is based on identifying the amount of foreign or impure blood, similar to that which existed in the United States for those called mulatto, quadroon and so on. Being Japanese in this social sense is based rigidly on a biological standard of purity and pollution in the same sense as racial boundaries.

Strong feelings about the *Nihon minzoku* feed into the prejudice and discrimination experienced by multiethnic people who may find it difficult to identify as Japanese since they are aware that they are likely to be regarded as non-Japanese if their full ancestry were known. They may be required to prove that they possess the required cultural knowledge. Certain behaviors will be understood as proof of the existence of Japanese blood, while deviations will be judged as verification of the influence of foreign genes.

The appearance of more individuals who do not fit in with these images is potentially leading to new attitudes; e.g. persons who "don't look Japanese" but who speak Japanese and possess cultural knowledge such as some American-Japanese. Those who "look Japanese" but do not possess cultural knowledge, such as some returnee youth and *Nikkei* from other countries, are another significant group who may challenge ethnic boundaries.

Identity resolutions and assertions vary among different persons and are also depend upon individual circumstances. Those seeking to avoid prejudice and discrimination may attempt to pass themselves off as majority Japanese by changing names and denying their ethnic roots. Those who cannot, or choose not to deny their ethnic origins, risk being labeled as foreigners and becoming victimized by discrimination. Those with identifiable "non-Yamato blood" find themselves considered foreigners and, while some struggle with this perceived rejection, others attempt to utilize it to their advantage. Skillfully manipulating one's identity to fit the situation, by being Japanese when it is advantageous and being foreign when it will bring some benefit, becomes a strategy of some multiethnic people with bilingual and bicultural abilities (Murphy-Shigematsu 1994). For those who desire it, greater experience and confidence in one's abilities and knowledge of one's cultural background leads to a wider possibility of complex and multiple identities and feelings of affiliation and belonging. While few individuals may actually serve as cultural bridges or even identify as multiethnic, many want the power to at least not reject or deny any part of their background (Murphy-Shigematsu 1997).

Keiko was born to a Japanese mother and a Korean father. From childhood she attended public schools under the name of Suzuki Keiko, a typical Japanese name. Most persons were unaware of her background and she herself only was told when she was a teenager and had to register for her Alien Registration Certificate. When the nationality law changed in 1985 her parents informed her that she would acquire

Japanese nationality. Although she makes no attempt to hide her Korean ancestry, it is unknown to all but her closest friends. She used to be more open about it but found that people tended to treat her differently, as though she was not Japanese.

In high school she was approached by some students who were part of a community youth group for Korean ethnic awareness. When she told them that she was not interested, they accused her of being ashamed of being Korean and a disgrace to her ethnic group. Keiko insists that she is not ashamed of being Korean but simply feels that it is of little significance in her life, as she was raised as a Japanese and was never close to the Korean side of her family, including her father. However, she also concedes that she does not really consider herself to be Japanese either. As she explains, if people know her background they do not think she is Japanese. She feels more comfortable with an identity that focuses on other aspects besides ethnicity.

In the latter half of the twentieth century, the terminology used to describe multiethnic persons has included various labels, some pejorative some adulatory. These evolving terms reflect changing social conditions and attitudes as well as the identities of multiethnic persons. During the postwar period, mixed children were commonly referred to as *ainoko*. The word literally indicates a child of two things brought together. It is used for animals as well as humans to denote mixture. As in many other societies, this coming together was viewed as problematic because it created a racially impure being of questionable belonging (Gist and Dworkin 1972). Cultural confusion was also thought to be associated with the marginal qualities of such persons.

The word *ainoko* is considered derogatory and evokes images of poverty, illegitimacy, racial impurity, prejudice and discrimination. As the Occupation era ended and memories of the war began to fade, it was gradually replaced in public usage by the more neutral term *konketsuji*, literally "the mixed-blood child." However, *konketsuji* also came to be a term associated with the social problems caused by the US military. Some mixed-race Americans emerged in the media in the sixties, creating a *konketsuji* boom of sudden popularity of American-Japanese entertainers. Sexual fascination was attached to erotic and exotic images and feelings of fascination and admiration for *konketsuji* models and singers was mixed with repulsion of those of mixed ancestry (De Vos *et al.* 1983, Strong 1978). In either case *konketsuji* were identified and set apart from the majority.

The term *haafu* became popular in the 1970s and remains the most common label and favorite term of self-definition. Today *haafu* signifies a bright image of a fashionable foreign-looking Japanese who speaks fluent English. Much of this image is still based on physical appearance as the white *haafu* image is perhaps the ideal physical type of the Japanese majority: long legs and white features but still Japanese enough to be familiar and comfortable.

While the *konketsuji* image was basically related to an attractive body and physical skills such as in sports (some of Japan's most famous professional athletes are of multiethnic ancestry), the *haafu* image also includes associations of mental attributes. Sexy idols who not only model and act but also appear as English instructors or announcers on television programs were promoted as not only beautiful but also intelligent. The popular sound of radio disc jockeys and television announcers and celebrities, with their smooth blend of native Japanese and English, also represents the new *haafu* image as bilingual, bi-cultural and international. That this image is an idealized one that does not always match reality is symbolized by the members of the singing group that helped to popularize the term, the *Golden Haafu*. Although they were promoted as a bilingual group, only one of the members actually spoke native English while the others spoke English at the level of an ordinary Japanese (Williams 1992).

In recent years, the increased appearance of American-Japanese raised bilingually and biculturally in the media has added these fashionable images to the popular stereotypes of so-called *haafu*. Whether denigrating or worshipping, the person labeled as "*haafu*" is vulnerable to depiction as different, making it difficult for them to be treated as individuals or as ordinary Japanese. In a society in which being different can be a sin punishable by ostracism, the visible distinction of many *haafu* can be the cause of bullying and rejection.

Despite the positive trends, the *haafu* image does not generally include anyone who is regarded as black. Those considered white may still encounter ambivalent and hostile attitudes but relatively less prejudice and discrimination. In contrast, those regarded as black are generally considered to have undesirable physical features and have encountered much more negative and derogatory social attitudes and stereotyping. They have suffered from prejudices toward blacks that regard them as culturally inferior outside the narrow areas of music, dancing and sport. The *haafu* image also does not include those who are physically indistinguishable from majority Japanese.

The *haafu* image is increasingly associated with children of families of high socio-economic status. These youths have lived and traveled abroad and live in areas and attend schools in Japan where they are relatively sheltered from prejudice and discrimination by the status of their families. They enjoy the less hostile environment of international schools or schools on the military bases (Murphy- Shigematsu 1994). These children have access to acquiring language and cultural skills that both earn them respect in Japanese society and increase their opportunities in other countries. In contrast, few of those raised in poor socio-economic conditions by single mothers have had access to international schools and bilingual and bicultural family environments.

The attempt to redefine the multiethnic person from negative to positive by emphasizing the international quality of their parentage and their cultural background led to the term *kokusaiji*, meaning international child (Oshiro 1984). This term describes new social conditions that include a wide range of marriages (now called international marriages) with nationals of many countries. In this age of so-called internationalization and globalism, these marriages usually do not involve military personnel and include all social classes. International marriages involve Japanese men three times as much as women, although Japanese-American marriages remain the exception, as they still mostly involve Japanese women and American men (Homu Nenkan 1995).

As in the United States, new terms have also appeared in opposition to those that emphasize blood or percentage of ancestry. Terms such as mixed-blood or half-breed are offensive and alienating to many multiethnic people. Some English-speaking parents and their children resent the derogatory English origin of the word *haafu* and prefer terms in English like bicultural or binational.

The term most commonly advocated today is also a blood term and is therefore problematic. The term *daburu* (from the English double) is promoted as correcting the deficiencies of the term *haafu*. It emphasizes that those of mixed ancestry are not half but are, instead, endowed with the ethnicity of both sides of their parentage. It is considered a positive statement and a term of empowerment. Though it is used as a explanatory concept by some who say that they consider themselves to be double more than half, it is rarely used as a self-identifying label. The use of the term ironically expresses the need for some multiethnics who feel discriminated against or unaccepted as Japanese to positively assert themselves in a way that emphasizes their superiority over others.

Daburu also denies personal choice about the meaning of ethnicity by implying that people of mixed ancestries are supposed to value and express their ethnicities, when many prefer to find their identity in other ways. Some who resist using the term feel that it solves nothing as it continues to identify them by a special term when they would prefer a term that indicates their actual ancestry, such as *Amerikakei Nihonjin* (American-Japanese). They say that *haafu* is used without any sense of its original English meaning and claim that self-definition has paradoxically taken place by embracing and redefining the inherently racist and negative term.

Conclusion

In Japan, the experiences and identities of persons of multiethnic ancestry are influenced by a number of historical, political, economic, legal, ideological and psychological forces. The history of colonization and occupation, nationality and family registration laws, extra-legal bureaucratic pressure and ideologies and attitudes about race and ethnicity all powerfully impact on their identity.

Perhaps more than any other minorities in Japan, multiethnic individuals may challenge notions of cultural nationalism if they choose to act out cultural differences. They cannot be easily dismissed simply as foreigners, for many are also Japanese citizens and of Japanese ancestry. They are both insiders and outsiders. Recognition of their existence may help to foster an acceptance of the fiction of Japanese uniqueness that erects seemingly insurmountable barriers between Japanese and others in the minds of many individuals.

The themes presented in this paper not only affect multiethnic individuals but represent some of Japan's current pressing political and legal problems. On a broader level, the need to come to grips with and accept the horrors of Japan's military past is seen by many as a necessary prerequisite to improved relations with Asian neighbors. Dealing with the often-ugly consequences of stationing foreign troops in Japan and the broader issues of self-defense and militarization have become more urgent with developments in Okinawa and outside Japan.

Issues of nationality that impact on multiethnic people are not only confined to them but also impact on the wider question of citizenship and rights in society. These issues emphasize the necessity of achieving more congruence between national laws that are the product of open legislative debate and democratic approval and bureaucratic guidelines of self-serving bodies that exercise arbitrary powers.

The myths and ideologies of the homogeneity of the nation that affect multiethnic people also pose a barrier to the acceptance of other minorities. Like other societies around the world, Japan is being challenged to become more civilized by moving from policies of forced assimilation to respect for diversity and personal choice. Mythologies of racialism and nationalism that insist on homogeneity as an ideal are being demolished and recognition is being given to the existence and contributions of the variety of individuals who comprise society.

Multiethnic individuals exist today within a Japan that is increasingly acknowledged to be a nation composed of people of various origins and which therefore must distinguish between nationality and ethnicity. Regardless of the interests of the state, individuals of mixed ancestries will continue to try and identify with all aspects of their heritage in which they discover personal meaning and some will attempt to creatively challenge the limits of cultural constraints on the kinds of identities that are deemed acceptable.

References

Asahi Shinbun (1997) *"Tensei Jingo"*, 1 October; 23 October.
—— (1998) *"Okinawa no Nijukokuseki Amerajian"* (Okinawa's Dual National Amerasians), 6 June.
Creighton, M. (1997) *"Sōtō Others and Uchi Others: Imaging Social Diversity, Imagining Homogeneous Japan"*, in M. Weiner (ed.) *Japan's Minorities: The Illusion of Homogeneity*, London: Routledge.
Dale, P. (1986) *The Myth of Japanese Uniqueness*, Oxford: University of Oxford and Nissan Institute for Japanese Studies.
De Vos, G., Wetherall, W. and Stearman, K. (1983) *Japan's Minorities (Burakumin, Koreans, Ainu, and Okinawans)*, London: Minority Rights Group.
Dower, J. W. (1986) *War Without Mercy*, New York: Pantheon.
Ebony (1997) "Black America and Tiger's Dilemma," 28–30 July: 138.
Freire, P. (1970) *Pedagogy of the Oppressed*, New York: Seabury.
Gist, N. P. and Dworkin, A. G. (1972) *The Blending of Races: Marginality and Identity in World Perspective*, New York: Wiley-Interscience.
Glazer, N. (1997) *We Are All Multiculturalists Now*, Cambridge: Harvard.
Hanihara, K. (1993) "The Origins of the Japanese People," Keynote Speech to the Pacific Science Inter-Congress, Okinawa, Japan, 23 June 1993.
Hanihara, K. and Omoto, K. (1991) *Karada de Sagasu Nihonjin no Gen* (Searching for the Roots of the Japanese People Through the Body,) 4th edn, Tokyo: Fukutake.
Harajiri, H. (1995) *Ibunkakan Kyoiku no Riso: Zainichi Chosenjin* (The Ideal of Inter-cultural Education in Japan: From the Perspective of the Study of Korean Residents in Japan), Tokyo, Intercultural/Transcultural Education.
Hemphill, E. A. (1980) *The Least of These: Miki Sawada and Her Children*, New York: Weatherhill.
Hollinger, D. A. (1995) *Postethnic America: Beyond Multiculturalism*, New York: Basic Books.
Homu Nenkan (Ministry of Justice Yearly Report) (1995) Tokyo: Homusho (Ministry of Justice).
—— (1996) Tokyo: Homusho (Ministry of Justice).
Honda, H. (1982) *Sonzai sinai Kodomotachi* (Children Who Don't Exist), Tokyo: Sekibunsha.
Japan Times (1993) "One More Step on Fingerprinting," 4 July 1993.
Kika Tebiki (Naturalization Handbook) (1995) Tokyo: Homusho (Ministry of Justice).
Kokusai Kekkon o Kangaeru Kai (Association of Multicultural Families) (1991) *Nijukokuseki* (Dual Nationality), Tokyo: Jiji Tsushinsha.
Marui, E. (1989) "Japan's Experience with Public Health Reform in the Early Occupation

Days," in M. R. Reich and E. Marui (eds) *International Cooperation for Health*, Dover, Mass.: Auburn House Publishing.

Morris-Suzuki, T. (1996) "A Descent into the Past: The Frontier in the Construction of Japanese Identity," in D. Denoon *et al.* (eds) *Multicultural Japan: Palaeolithic to Postmodern*, Cambridge: Cambridge University Press.

Murphy-Shigematsu, S. (1993) "Multiethnic Japan and the Monoethnic Myth," *MELUS, Journal of the Society for the Study of the Multiethnic Literature of the United States* 18, 4: 63–80.

—— (1994) *"Okinawa ni Okeru Nichibei Haafu no Sutereotaipu"* (Stereotypes of American-Japanese Haafu in Okinawa), in Okinawa Psychological Association (ed.) *Okinawa no Hito to Kokoro* (The People and Spirit of Okinawa), Kyūshū: University of Kyûshû Press: 53–7.

—— (1997) "Representations of Amerasians in Japan," *Japanese Society* vol. 1: 61–76.

Nash, P. T. (1997) "Will the Census Go Multiracial?" *Amerasia Journal* 23, 1: 18–25.

Omi, M. and Winant, H. (1986) *Racial Formation in the United States from the 1960s to the 1980s*, New York: Routledge and Kegan Paul.

Oshiro, Y. (1984) *"Kokusaiji no Kakaeru Mondai"*, in Y. Sasaki (ed.) *Okinawa no Bunka to Seishin Eisei*, Tokyo: Kobundu.

Ota, T., Taniai, K. and Youfu, T. (1995) *Koseki – Kokuseki to Kodomo no Jinken* (Family Registration, Nationality and Childrens' Rights), Tokyo: Akaishi Shoten.

Root, M. P. P. (ed.) (1996) *The Multiracial Experience,* Newbury Park, Calif: Sage.

Ryang, S. (1997) *North Koreans in Japan,* Boulder: Westview.

Sansom, G. B. (1952) *Japan: A Short Cultural History,* Stanford: Stanford University.

Sato, B. (1993) *Zainichi Gaikokujin no Dokuhon* (Reader on Foreigners in Japan), Tokyo: Midori Kaze Shuppan.

Shade, J. (1984) *America's Forgotten Children: The Amerasians,* Perkasie, Pa.: Pearl S. Buck Foundation.

Strong, N. (1978) *Patterns of Social Interactioon and Psychological Accommodations among Japan's Kanketsuji population*, Unpublished doctoral dissertation, University of California, Berkeley.

Tanaka, H. (1995) *Zainichi Gaikokujin* (Foreign Residents), Tokyo: Iwanami.

Thornton, M. C. (1992) "The Quiet Immigration: Foreign Spouses of U.S. Citizens, 1945–1985," in M. P. P. Root (ed.) *Racially Mixed People in America*, Newbury Park, Calif.: Sage.

Tizard, B. and Phoenix A. (1993) *Black, White or Mixed Race?* London: Routledge.

Wagatsuma, H. (1976) "Mixed-blood Children in Japan: An Exploratory Study," *Journal of Asian Affairs* vol. 2: 9–16.

—— (1981) "Some Problems of Koreans in Japan," in C. Lee and G. De Vos (eds) *Koreans in Japan*, Berkeley: University of California Press.

Weiner, M. (1995) "Discourses of Race, Nation and Empire in pre-1945 Japan," *Racial and Ethnic Studies* 18, 3, (July).

—— (1997) "'Self' and 'Other' in pre-war Japan," in M. Weiner (ed.) *Japan's Minorities: The Illusion of Homogeneity,* London: Routledge.

Wetherall, W. (1981) "Public Figures in Popular Culture: Identity Problems of Minority Heroes," in C. Lee and G. De Vos (eds) *Koreans in Japan*, Berkeley: University of California Press.

—— (1983) "If Ito can be American, why can't Pak be Japanese?" *Japan Times,* 3 July: 10.

—— (1992) "Nationality and Civilization of Japan", Yosha Research Institute, online at: http://www2.gol.com/users/yosha/ (13 January 1998).

Williams, T. K. (1992) "Prism Lives: Identity of Binational Amerasians," in M. P. P. Root (ed.) *Racially Mixed People in America,* Newbury Park, Calif.: Sage.

Wright, L. (1994) "One Drop of Blood," *New Yorker,* 25 July: 46–55.

Yamada, K. (1986) *An Easy Guide to the New Nationality Law*, Tokyo: Japan Times.

Yoshino, K. (1992) *Cultural Nationalism in Contemporary Japan,* London: Routledge.

Part III

Government policies and community responses

10 Labor law, civil law, immigration law and the reality of migrants and their children

Katsuko Terasawa

Introduction

From 1987, facing a growing shortage of labor, Japanese financial circles such as the *Keizaidōyūkai* (Japan Committee for Economic Development), the *Keizaidantai Rengōkai* (*Keidanren*) and the *Nihon Shokokaigisho* (Japan Chamber of Commerce) requested the Japanese government to accept foreigners as trainees. The response was two-fold and oblique: first, to accept foreigners as trainees, and second, to accept foreigners with Japanese ancestry. As a result, in 1996, approximately 284,500 illegal foreign workers were residing in Japan.

The background of this migration policy can be found in labor policies which the government had followed since 1985, encouraging life-time employment for a small number of core employees and increasingly using temporary and part-time workers with limited-term contracts. In 1996, the number of these employees without job stability was approximately ten million or 19.8 percent of all employees (Ministry of Labor 1996: 164, 438). Furthermore, the government approved policies deregulating labor laws and labor administration. From the beginning foreign workers were assigned as temporary workers with limited employment terms.

The cornerstone of government migration policy was and remains that of limiting the stay of the migrants and assuring their return to their home countries after two or three years. In 1990, the government approved the allocation of trainee visas as these are, clearly, short-term. Trainees are not workers, however, and are not able to receive the protection of labor laws. Foreigners with Japanese ancestry were accepted as "long-term residents" after 1990. By June 1995, their number had increased to approximately 195,000. They are permitted to stay between six months and one year, after which they must apply for a visa extension.

For the past fifteen years, I have played an active part in improving the working conditions of Japanese temporary and part-time workers and, for eight years I have dealt with foreign workers' cases in Japan. In this chapter, I will analyze the problems of Japanese migration policy, the legal framework and the actual situation of documented and undocumented foreigners.

Although Japan does not issue residential status visas for unskilled foreign workers, many still come to Japan. They are in miserable conditions. Even foreign workers who legally stay and work in Japan suffer discrimination because of the unstable conditions of their residential status. The Ministry of Labor has issued a circular stating, "Labor Laws are applicable to workers regardless of their nationality or residential status, whether or not they are working legally" (*Kyūshū Bengoshikai Rengōkai* November 1991: 376). This was one step toward improving foreign workers' working conditions. However, when labor trouble actually occurs, the labor laws are more honored in the breach than in the observance. Moreover, many foreign workers have recently been employed under the guise of trainees and trainees-in-practice. As trainees, they are not able to receive the protections of labor laws.

Before 1993, immigration policy was a much-debated topic and many books were published on how Japan could solve its labor shortage. The Japanese government allowed Japanese Brazilians and Peruvians to become long-term residents and planned to accept many trainees in order to solve the labor shortage. Because of the current recession, however, foreigners' problems have shifted to center on human rights issues.

In the first section of this chapter, I will explain the real conditions of the foreign workers and trainees and explain the laws as they stand before offering my solutions on how to protect their human rights. Some activists and groups in Japan act to support the rights of foreign workers. Most trade unions, however, are not in the least interested in foreign workers' conditions. This is ultimately self-defeating, as the poor working conditions foreigners face will also eventually lower the standards for Japanese workers as well.

The second section discusses the increasing number of family cases and I shall detail some cases which illustrate the problems of foreign women and children before putting forward my proposal for revisions of the Immigration Law. The aim of the proposals is not to address the long-term immigration policy of the Japanese government but to fulfill the immediate need to protect foreigners' human rights in Japan.

The reality of foreign workers in Japan: problems and solutions

Labor laws

The entry and residence of all foreigners in Japan is regulated by the Immigration-Control and Refugee-Recognition law, hereinafter referred to as the Immigration Law. The Immigration Law has twenty-seven categories of status of residence. Of these, those under which a foreigner can engage in professional or occupational activities are listed in Table 10.1.

Non-skilled manual labor is not included in this category. Thus, these workers, if employed, become classified as illegal workers. Foreigners who are spouses of Japanese or have Japanese ancestry such as Japanese Brazilian or Japanese Peruvian can choose jobs without restriction under the Immigration Law.

Labor relations laws such as the Labor Standards Law and the Employment Security Law do not discriminate between foreigners and Japanese workers and can be applied to foreigners regardless of whether their status is legal or illegal. In other words, these laws can be utilized by foreigners who have overstayed their visas and/or who are working without proper documents.[1]

The period of stay for foreign workers is regulated by the visa. Except for

Table 10.1 Authorized activities and period of stay by status of residence

Status of residence	Activities authorized under residence status	Period of stay
Professor	Activities for research, direction of research or education at colleges, equivalent educational institutions or technical high schools.	3 years, 1 year or 6 months
Artist	Activities for the arts that provide income, including music, the fine arts, literature, etc.	3 years, 1 year or 6 months
Investor/ business manager	Activities to commence the operation of international trade or other business, to invest in international trade or other business, and to operate or manage that business, or to operate or manage international trade or other business on behalf of foreign nationals (including foreign corporations); hereinafter in this section "foreign nationals" is to include foreign corporations, who have begun such an operation or have invested in such a business (excluding the activities to engage in the operation or management in business which are not allowed without the legal qualifications described in "Legal/accounting services").	3 years, 1 year or 6 months
Legal/ accounting services	Activities to engage in legal or accounting business, which is required to be carried out by attorneys recognized as foreign law specialists under the foreign lawyer's law (*Gaikokuhō Jimubengoshi*), certified public accoutants recognized as accountants practicing foreign accounting under the Accountant Law (*Gaikoku Kōninkaikeishi*), or those with other legal qualifications.	3 years, 1 year or 6 months
Medical services	Activities concerning medical treatment service that are required to be undertaken by physicians, dentists or those with other legal qualifications.	1 year or 6 months
Researcher	Activities to engage in research on the basis of a contract with public or private organizations in Japan.	1 year or 6 months
Instructor	Activities to engage in language instruction and other education at elementary schools, junior high schools, high schools, schools for the blind, handicapped children's schools, advanced vocational schools (*Sen-shugakko*), vocational schools (*Kakushūgakko*), or other educational institutions equivalent to vocational schools in facilities and curriculum.	1 year or 6 months
Engineer	Activities to engage in service, which requires technology and/or knowledge pertinent to physical science, engineering or other natural science fields, on the basis of a contract with public or private organizations in Japan.	1 year or 6 months
Specialist in humanities/ international services	Activities to engage in service which requires knowledge pertinent to jurisprudence, economics, sociology or other human science fields, or to engage in services which require specific ways of thought or sensitivity based on experience with foreign culture, based on a contract with public or private organizations in Japan.	1 year or 6 months

Table 10.1 (continued)

Status of residence	Activities authorized under residence status	Period of stay
Intra-company transferee	Activities on the part of personnel who are transferred to business offices in Japan for a limited period of time from business offices that are located in foreign countries by public or private organizations that have head offices, branch offices or other business offices in Japan, and who engage in these business offices in the activities described in the "Engineer" or "Specialist in humanities/ international services" column of this table.	1 year or 6 months
Entertainer	Activities to engage in theatrical performances, musical performances, sports or any other show business (excluding the activities described in the "Investor/business manager" column of this table).	1 year or 3 months
Skilled Labor	Activities to engage in services which require industrial techniques or skills belonging to fields on the basis of a contract with public or private organizations in Japan.	1 year or 6 months
Designated activities	Activities which are specifically designated by the Minister of Justice for foreign individuals.	

Source: Osaka Bar Association, *Human Rights Handbook for Foreigners in Japan in 18 Languages,* Osaka: Osaka Bar Association.

permanent residents, the period is up to three years. However, the Immigration authorities are reluctant to grant visas for three years. In many cases, the visa is granted for only six months or one year. As a result, 75 percent of foreign workers have six month or one year contracts. Even foreign spouses of Japanese citizens with spousal visas are generally granted limited-term employment contracts of six months to one year.

According to case law, the employer cannot dismiss his employee without clear justification. After the Supreme Court judgment of 22 July 1974, if a worker on a limited contract has it extended or renewed more than two or three times consecutively, the employer cannot terminate the employment contract without clear justification. This judgment held that after two or more extensions of the contract, a limited-term contract should be regarded in the same light as an open-ended contract. Hence the employer could not terminate the contract for the sole reason of expiration of the contract term. The employment contract will be renewed automatically. As a result of many years of labor movement activities and litigation, part-time workers on successive limited-term contracts have also been extended this protection and employers cannot terminate their contracts without justification.

For foreign workers, however, the term of the employment contract is linked with the period of their residence permit. If an employer wishes to terminate a foreigner's contract, he need only justify it by noting that the visa would have expired by the end of the contract term. During the recession of the past two years, many Japanese Brazilians, Peruvians and other foreign workers, have had their contracts terminated under this justification. Not only were their contracts not renewed, but it was usual practice for employers to deduct approximately ¥500,000

(US$5,000) from their wages for travel and miscellaneous expenses. This proves disastrous for the workers, as they make the investment to come to Japan with the intention to work at least two or three years. Otherwise, the transactions costs as well as the living costs are prohibitively expensive.

In order to obtain a visa extension from the Immigration Office, the foreign worker must have a renewed contract in his or her hand; or the residency request will not be granted. Hence, foreign workers do not enjoy equal protection with Japanese citizens under case law. For example on 31 March 1995, an Australian English teacher who had extended his one-year contract four times was denied a contract extension for a fifth year. He sued at Osaka District Court but lost his case, on 23 August 1995, because of limits on his residency. From surveying recent cases brought by English teachers, it has become increasingly apparent that they do not enjoy equal protection with Japanese people under case law.

This situation offers a marked contrast to that of four or five years ago when Japan had serious problems of labor shortage. Many employers tried to hire foreign workers and wanted to keep them employed for as long as possible. This led to legal violations as illustrated in the two cases described below.

In the first case, a Japanese Brazilian came to Japan with his family but he became ill after two months and wanted to return home. His employer told him that he could not leave before repaying the ¥560,000 (US$5,600) which the employer had advanced to bring with him to Japan. If he himself could not work, the employer told him that his wife could work on his behalf in lieu of the payment in cash. His wife, however, had no contract with this employer and therefore was under no obligation either to repay him or to work for him. Furthermore, according to the Labor Standards Law (hereinafter LSL) Article 24, an employer must pay full wages on a specific date each month, directly and in cash. According to LSL Article 17, it is also illegal for an employer to offset advanced payments against the employee's wages.

Other employers, wishing to prevent their foreign workers from changing jobs, withhold part of their wage and pay them in a lump sum when they leave Japan. This violates LSL Article 18, which prohibits employers from coercing workers into making savings.

In June 1994, unemployment in Japan rose to a seven-year high. When times were good, many employers tried to ensure they look after labor force and violated the Labor Law in doing so. When times became bad, foreign workers conditions suffered in comparison with those of Japanese workers because of the limits on residency as stipulated in their visas.

As has been noted above, foreign workers who wish to continue to stay and work in Japan need their employers' help (by way of contract renewal) to extend their visas. The employer's leverage often keeps the employee from requesting improvement in working conditions in case the employer fails to renew the contract. Workers, whether Japanese nationals or not, are entitled under the Labor Union Law to organize and form labor unions to negotiate for the improvement of working conditions. If an employer violates the LSL or other regulations, the worker may file a complaint against the employer at the Labor Standards Inspection Office (LISO). However, most foreign workers hesitate to organize and form labor unions and do not go to the LISO because of their unstable status of residence. The following case illustrates the instability of working conditions for foreign workers.

In 1991, an employer in the food industry made contracts with nineteen foreign workers who had visas as skilled workers (chefs). In the contract, their wages were stipulated as ¥290,000 per month. Once on the job, however, the workers found they were paid only ¥180,000 per month. Through the auspices of an attorney, these foreign workers negotiated with their employer, who reimbursed them ¥110,000 per month. At the end of one year, however, the employer told the foreign workers they must sign a new contract if they wished to continue working. The new contract clearly stipulated the wage as ¥180,000 per month. They had little recourse but to sign if they wished to renew their visas. Six of them refused to sign and were dismissed. After negotiation, however, they did renew their contracts and extended their visas. After further negotiation, the employer reinstated the ¥290,000 monthly wage. However, all the workers were dismissed and left Japan in 1993.

Illegal and legal foreign workers in Japan

According to a survey by the Ministry of Justice, on 1 May 1994 there were 293,800 illegal foreign residents in Japan a decrease of 4,800, or 1.6 percent, on 1 May 1993 (*Hōsō Jiho* 1995: 188, 223). Most of them were from other parts of Asia. Meanwhile, the number of foreigners deported for allegedly violating the Immigration law during the first half of 1994 amounted to 35,408, up about 100 over the same period last year and the largest number to date (*Hōsō Jiho* 1995: 188, 223).

Foreign workers often suffer from wage exploitation, either in the form of non-payment of wages, or, as in the case above, reneging on the contracted wage in lieu of a lower wage. Although by law (LSL Article 13), employers are bound to inform their workers in writing of working conditions, including wages, this is often ignored. Many employers hire foreigners on verbal promise and, if challenged, will not admit to the existence of employment contracts.[2] There are also cases where the foreign employee herself does not even know the employer's name, the name of the company or the business address.[3] Recruiters, agents, middlemen brokers and, sometimes, Japanese *yakuza* organize the employment. Given such arbitrariness in employment conditions, there are often cases where there is no evidence for the claim of unpaid wages.

Foreign workers' average wages range from 30 percent to 70 percent of those of their Japanese counterparts. Most foreign workers are employed on an hourly or daily basis. 79 percent of foreign workers received less than ¥1,000,000 (US$10,000) annually (Ministry of Labor 1988: 25). Although the Minimum Wage Law (MWL) Article 5, applies to manual foreign labor, many illegal foreign workers are in no position to bargain for a fair wage.

One case in point was discovered by a routine investigation by the Fukuyama City Labor Standards Inspection Office. The company found in violation had hired four Japanese-Filipinos who worked twenty-three days per month, and sixty-eight hours overtime per month in 1992. They received ¥56,580 in monthly wages with an additional ¥3,250 per month for overtime. This amounted to less than 60 percent of the minimum wage for the city of Fukuyama. LSIO accused the employer of breaching the LSL and the MWL. The amount of overtime hours performed by these workers was not atypical. Foreign workers' weekly hours in 1990 are in Table 10.2 (Ministry of Labour, 24 January 1991).

Foreign workers are often obliged to perform unhealthy and dangerous work without adequate protection. They are open to more risk of suffering injuries and accidents in the course of their work due to inadequate training and lack of safety features (see Roberts Chapter Twelve in this volume). Under the Workers' Accident Compensation Insurance Law, accident compensation is available to all workers, including foreigners regardless of their status of residence. The benefits of the Workers' Accidents Compensation Insurance are as follows:

*   Actual expenses incurred during treatment.
*   Compensation for lost income (80 percent of average wages).
*   Disability benefits (with fourteen levels of disability).
*   Funeral expenses (in case of death occurring at work).
*   Death benefits.
*   Injury and sickness compensation benefits.

Employers are required by law to pay premiums into the insurance program for each employee. Workers are entitled to the insurance even if the employer is remiss in paying into the workers' accident compensation system. However, some employers, fearing that their insurance rates will rise if they reveal the facts regarding workers' accidents, refuse to comply with the procedures necessary for claiming the insurance. In addition, after the Immigration Law was revised in 1990, employers also became subject to punishment for providing assistance to illegal workers. Hence many employers hide the facts from the authorities. Many foreigners are working illegally and have not been able to apply to claim insurance at the Labor Standards Inspection Office.

From the undocumented worker's viewpoint, there are also disincentives of making insurance claims. According to Immigration Law Article 62-2, all public officials should report any case found to be in violation of the Immigration Law to the Immigration Office. The 1988 Circular of the Ministry of Labor, noted above, spells out the same obligation. Thus, the LSIO is obliged to notify the Immigration Office if it receives an application for compensation insurance by an illegal foreign worker. Fearing deportation, many foreign workers refrain from applying. As one worker told me, "If I lost one finger, I would rather work than apply for compensation insurance. If I were injured more seriously, however, I would go to the LSIO." As long as an injured foreign worker is in the hospital, the deportation order is not enforced.

Table 10.2 Hours worked by foreigners

Hours per week	Percentage of workers
< 40	16.8
40–48	33.3
48–56	30.5
56–64	12.6
64–72	4.3
>72	2.5
Total	100.0

In August 1988, the Human Rights Bureau of the Ministry of Justice exempted those public officials who engage in consultation services for foreigners from the obligation to report overstayers.[4] Under pressure from protest movements, in 1989 the Ministry of Labor also issued a Circular (*Kikan Hatsu* no. 41, 31 October 1989) granting this exemption in principle to its public officials when they advise or receive claims from foreigners (Sōmucho Gyōsei Kansatsukyoku 1989: 25).

Although the law provides that worker's accident compensation insurance be available to foreign workers with Japanese ancestry, many of these workers are in fact forced (by brokers and employers) to purchase overseas travel injury insurance instead. When injured in an industrial accident, they are then compelled to use the private insurance. The worker is not only saddled with the cost of coverage but the extent of benefits is also inferior to national insurance.

When an employee is injured because of another worker's carelessness (Civil Law no. 715; Vicarious Liability), or the employer neglected his duty to provide safe working conditions, the employer is liable for damages. If the benefits from the worker's accident compensation insurance do not cover the damages, all workers, including undocumented foreigners, can require compensation for their damages from their employer. There are fourteen levels of disability, ranging from the highest level at 100 percent to level fourteen at 5 percent.

There has been some controversy, however, over the basis for the rate of compensation for foreigners. Some court justices are of the opinion that the base for foreigners should not necessarily be the same as that for Japanese. On 19 October 1991, at a meeting of attorneys from three Tokyo Bar Associations and the Tokyo District Court personnel, Mr Nagakubo Morio, a judge of the twenty-seventh Tokyo District Court, which deals with all traffic accident and industrial accident cases in Tokyo, expressed the following view about the standard for compensation:

> For foreigners, it is reasonable to decide the amount of compensation for disability based on the victims' status of residence. If they are permanent residents of Japan, they should be treated equally with Japanese. If they have working visas, compensation should be decided based on their wages in Japan during the period of residence. When the period of residence has expired, they have to leave Japan, so the amount of compensation should be based on the wage rates of workers of the same age as the victim in the victim's home country. When it comes to disability compensation for foreign workers who have overstayed their work visas, it should be decided based on their wages in Japan for one or two years and the rest then based on the average wage rates of their own country. If the foreigner has entered Japan illegally, compensation should be decided based on the average wage rates of workers in the same age bracket as the victim in his home country.
>
> (*Tokyo San Bengoshikai Kōtsūjikoshōri Iinkai* 1992: 114–16)[5]

One might wonder whether this District Court magistrate's opinion would carry legal weight throughout the system. In fact, the opinion of the Tokyo District court is highly influential.[6] Prior to Mr Nagakubo's statement, the Takamatsu High Court ruled:

All persons are equal before the law and are entitled without any discrimination to the equal protection of the law (Constitution Article 14). Disability compensation should be based on the same standard as that of Japanese, and should not be based on the real wages of China. In China, economic and social situations are different from those of Japan.

(Takamatsu High Court 25 June 1991)

Obviously Mr Nagakubo's opinion was contrary to that of the High Court. In traffic accident cases and industrial accident cases, there is a tendency for courts to determine the amount of compensation for disability on the same standard as that of Tokyo District Court.

The GNP of Pakistan is approximately one-fortieth of Japan's and that of Bangladesh is one-eightieth. If compensation for disability were determined on the basis of wage rates in home countries such as these, the amount of compensation would not even cover the transportation expenses for the worker's journey home.

According to a 1992 survey by the All Japan Labor Safety and Hygiene Center Liaison Conference (1992: 20), 60 percent of foreign victims had industrial accidents within three months of starting work. The rate is astonishingly high because the workers begin without any on-the-job training and work without adequate protection, in violation of the Labor Safety Law. When confronted by the Labor Standards Inspection Office, some employers tried to cover themselves by saying that they had told their foreign workers to put on helmets and protective garments but they had refused, so the resulting accident was their own fault. If this deception is accepted as an adequate excuse by the LSIO and employers are relieved of their responsibility to compensate an accident victim, labor conditions for foreign workers will become far worse.

Trainees and trainees in practice

A trainee is an individual accepted by a public or private organization in Japan, including private corporations, to enter a training program to learn industrial techniques or skills under curricula which satisfy the standards of such training programs as established by the Ministry of Justice.

The Japanese government planned to accept trainees for the purpose of promoting cooperation with developing countries. In reality, however, many foreign workers have been employed under the guise of trainees in order to compensate for the labor shortage. In spite of the standards established by the Ministry of Justice under Immigration Law Article 7-1-2 (Ministry of Justice Regulations no. 16, 24 May 1990), many companies force trainees to work as unskilled laborers under the pretext of being in training. In one case it was found that so-called trainees were forced to weed the gardens. In another case, trainees were forced to be lavatory attendants.

According to the official standards, actual on-the-job training is not to exceed two-thirds of the total training hours. A survey by the Ministry of Justice in 1989 found that 57.7 percent of companies required trainees to perform actual work for 100 percent of their training period i.e. there was no educational component (*Kanto Bengoshikai Rengōkai* 1990: 32–3). Furthermore, 70 percent of companies required trainees to do overtime training, which means overtime work. Some companies forced trainees to work ten hours a day, and some also made trainees work on holidays.

As they are not classified as workers they are not eligible for wages nor are they protected by the labor standards laws. Trainees are eligible to receive a training allowance of up to ¥100,000 (US$1,000) per month. Before 1992, the amount was ¥60,000 to ¥80,000. Employers seem to interpret this as a maximum compensation rather than a guideline for fair remuneration. According to the 1989 Ministry of Justice Survey, almost all trainees received ¥40,000 to ¥50,000 even if they worked overtime. The survey reported one case where trainees received ¥50,000 per month while Japanese workers performing the same jobs for the same number of hours received ¥280,000, more than five times the trainees' wage.

According to a 1992 Prime Minister's Office survey, trainees received from ¥30,000 to ¥180,000 per month (Sōmucho Gyōsei Kansatsukyoku 1992: 103, 118). The Immigration Office investigated the case, decided that these trainees were workers and refused to extend their visas. Some of them were deported, having been forced to work without acquiring any of the much-vaunted industrial techniques.

If a foreigner's status of residence is trainee, but the Labor Ministry deems his actual status as that of worker, then he is able to receive the protection of the labor laws. This became possible in March 1990, when the Labor Ministry decided that such cases should be entitled to protection. Hence there have been cases where trainees suffered industrial accidents and made use of the Workers Accident Compensation Insurance Law.

According to the fifth provision of the ministerial ordinance of the Immigration Law (regulation no. 16), the company or other organizations must provide the trainee with accommodations. Trainees are expected to live in the accommodation provided by their companies and to be trained at factories close by. In fact, however, some companies use the trainee system as a cover to access cheap unskilled labor, require trainees to work an eight hour day plus overtime and provide no educational training. The monthly wage paid to these trainees by companies found to engage in such practices ranged from a mere ¥30,000 to ¥50,000, perhaps one-sixth of the normal wage. The companies have designed various schemes to conceal this and have prevented the trainees from contacting the outer world. In extreme cases, the employers confined the trainees within company grounds. Such trainees have been unable to obtain necessary information or express their opinions. Japanese volunteers have had difficulty making contact with trainees confined in this way.

Because trainees are not only workers but also students, their identity is ambiguous. There is neither an authority established to supervise and investigate the practices of trainee schemes nor is there a mechanism through which the opinions of trainees can be directly heard. From April 1991 to March 1992, the Osaka Regional Immigration Bureau granted 90 percent of the 3,000 trainee applications received. However, according to the officials of the bureau, they suspect that roughly two-thirds of these 3,000 entered Japan with the intent to work. Yet with only three officials in charge of trainees, it is difficult to investigate their real conditions. One case in particular illustrates the exploitative conditions under which some trainees work.

In 1990, twenty-seven Filipinos came to Osaka as trainees. They were forced to work as key punchers for twelve hours per day without holidays. They were not trained in any industrial skill, and received only ¥63,000 per month. Dissatisfied with these conditions, twenty-four of them contacted a local trade union and had the union negotiate with their employer to pay them overtime payments for overtime worked. This action was successful, but after they left Japan in 1991, they were threatened by labor brokers who told them that, because they had organized a trade union, they would keep them from ever being employed in the Philippines.

The trainee-in-practice system was introduced in April of 1993 to run in tandem with the trainee system. Under this system, the trainee first spends at least six months in training, which includes language and study outside the factory. After this, the employer can offer an employment contract to the trainee for eighteen months. The trainees can work as trainees-in-practice and receive wages. The trainee-in-practice is able to receive the protection of the labor laws for the eighteen months of employment. In the area controlled by the Osaka Regional Immigration Bureau, however, only twenty trainees-in-practice were admitted up to December of 1993. There is no data about new trainees in the practice system.

A particular case illustrates the problems with this new trainee-in-practice program. In March 1993, eleven Filipina nurses entered Japan as language students. They had been recruited by a Japanese doctor who aimed to introduce foreign-registered nurses into Japan to compensate for the nursing shortage. The agreement between the doctor and the nurses stipulated that:

- The nurses were to study the Japanese language for no more than a year, whereupon they were to test for the second level of the nursing license.
- They were to take the entrance examination for a nursing school which grants the associate nursing degree, study for two years there and pass the associate nurse examination.
- With license in hand, they were then to work in the doctor's clinic for at least three or up to four years, as associate-nurse trainees.
- During the trainee period, the nurses would be housed in boarding facilities provided by the doctor.
- If the nurses transferred to another employer without the permission of the original sponsor, or if they were to quit for any reason other than illness, the sponsor retained the right to claim damages against the nurse in order to recover the expenses he had advanced.

In November 1993, a doctor told the eleven Filipina nurses that if they failed to pass the second level in the Japanese licensing examination to be held on 5 December, they would be required to repay three million yen, the expenses already advanced, to their guarantor doctors. The same doctor also sent letters to this effect to the fathers of these nurses. The nurses, seeking to know their legal position, contacted me as they had heard about me through consultation. The nurses said they had been putting a lot of effort into studying Japanese and would try their best to pass the examination, but they feared it would be too difficult. They were afraid that if they failed to pass the examination they and their fathers would have to pay the three million in compensation. Moreover, if they passed the language exam but failed to pass the associate-nurse qualifying exam two years later, they would then be required to repay at least nine million yen.

Another problem centered on the credentials of these nurses prior to entering Japan. They had received credentials as registered nurses in the Philippines, having successfully completed a five-year training program. This is actually a more rigorous and sophisticated technical training program than is required for the Associate Nurse's degree in Japan but these nurses were not informed of this. What the brokers had told them was that, after spending a year learning the Japanese language, they would be allowed to work as nurses in Japan from March 1993 to the end of March 1994 (Article 7–1–2 of the Immigration Law). Upon arriving at their Japanese training sites, however, they found they had been duped. Some were ordered to perform menial chores such as cleaning and mopping-up at the hospital or even the private home of their guarantor doctor. Others were told to provide medical treatment to patients, which was illegal. Furthermore, they were bound by an agreement for seven years, despite the illegality of this practice (LSL Article 14 states that it is illegal to bind a person by an agreement to work for more than one year). The nurses' case was resolved when an attorney contacted the doctors involved and pointed out the legal violations. The doctors renounced their claims to compensation and the nurses returned to the Philippines. Four of them eventually returned to Japan, but left again after the Hanshin earthquake in January 1995.[7]

Solutions

As mentioned above, many trainees were forced to work without wages for over ten or twelve hours a day but they were not protected by the labor laws. Trainees should not be treated as alternatives to foreign workers to resolve the labor shortage. Formally, of course, the government position is the same. Trainees should be accepted only when the trainee would benefit from learning specific industrial skills and techniques in Japan. When a Japanese citizen is employed, he receives on-the-job training, over the course of which he is paid wages and is protected by the labor laws. Why should a foreign trainee be treated any differently?

In January 1992, a Prime Minister's Office survey recommended that trainees' conditions be improved (Sōmuchō Gyōsei Kansatsukyoku 1992: 105). After April 1993, the trainee-in-practice system was introduced and the Immigration Office was supposed to become strict in dispensing trainee visas. The trainee-in-practice system was to eventually replace the trainee system. Even in the trainee-in-practice system, trainees are not considered as workers and are discriminated against in treatment. Neither trainees nor trainees-in-practice should be treated as alternatives to unskilled foreign workers. The Labor Ministry should supervise both of them.

Documented foreigners working legitimately on limited-term contracts are faced with the problem of termination of contract by the employer, and subsequent refusal of visa extension by the Immigration Office. This is also a common problem among Japanese part-time workers and temporary workers, most of whom have contracts with term limits. Employers commonly renew these contracts in succession but, in times of economic downturn, they terminate the contract suddenly without justification. In 1989, fifteen Japanese part-timer workers filed suit in Osaka District Court against the Sanyo Electric Company, who had terminated their contracts citing economic slowdown as the excuse. They won the case in 1991 and were reinstated in 1992. Their victory greatly encouraged part-timers. In April 1993, eleven part-timer workers, who were told that their factory would be closed and their contracts would be terminated, organized a trade union and succeeded in convincing their employer to withdraw this proposal without bringing suit. Hence from now on, Japanese part-timers can settle their dismissal cases, even though the employer's ostensible justification is economic downturn.

If foreign workers also brought suit against such practices, the developing case law would eventually allow them to extend their contracts and improve their working conditions. If they bring suit and their cases are pending in court, the Immigration Office would be obliged to extend their visas, as they have done in divorce cases (see pages 233 to 238). Article 25 of the International Convention on the Protection of the Rights of All Migrant Workers and their Families, adopted by the UN General Assembly in 1990, hereinafter called the Convention of Migrant Workers and their Families, states:

- All migrant workers shall enjoy treatment not less favorable than that which applies to nationals receiving State in respect of remuneration.
- Other conditions of work, that is to say, overtime, hours of work, weekly rest, holidays with pay, safety, health, termination of the employment relationship and any other conditions of work which, according to national laws or practice are covered by this term.

Documented foreign workers should be treated equally at the termination of the employment contract. However, although labor protection laws are applicable to foreigners regardless of the legality of their resident or working status, there are obviously problems in implementing these protections: non-payment of wages, low wages, overtime work and industrial accidents.

First, many foreigners have no information about protective labor laws and do not realize that they are covered by them. Neither are they aware of the location of the Labor Standard Inspection Office. In 1991 to address this problem, the Osaka Bar Association published the *Human Rights Handbook for Foreigners in Japan* and translated it into eighteen languages. In addition, the Tokyo Bar, the Daiichi Tokyo Bar, the Tokyo Daini Bar and the Osaka Bar Associations have all established legal advice centers. Consulting services for foreigners are also available through the Ministry of Justice's Human Rights Bureau, and through local government offices and volunteer groups. These, however, are merely stop-gap measures.

The Ministry of Labor should require employers who employ foreign workers to be aware of relevant labor laws and require them to explain the details of fundamental labor laws to foreign workers in their native languages through leaflets or other specific methods, such as classes. Article 12 of the ILO Convention no. 143 Concerning Migrant Workers (Supplementary Provisions), 1975, and Article 33 of the Convention of Migrant Workers and their Families, regulate the obligations of the member states to provide information to migrant workers about their rights. Fifteen years ago, part-timers had similar problems of not knowing that the labor laws were applicable to them, and not knowing their rights. After women's groups became actively involved in this issue, the Ministry of Labor enacted the *Pāto Taimu Rōdōsha no Koyōkanri ni Kansuru Hōritsu* (Essential Measures for Part-time Workers) in 1984, and the *Tanjikan Rōdōsha no Koyōkanri to no Kaizen ni Kansuru Hōritsu* (Law for the Improvement of Labor Management and Working Conditions of Part-time Workers) in 1993. Under these regulations, employers had to inform part-timer workers of their working conditions in writing. Working conditions for part-timers have improved gradually after these came into effect.

In 1989, the Employment Security Bureau allocated officials to educate employers of foreign workers. In the same year, the Labor Standard Inspection Bureau also provided an advisory service for foreign workers in major LSIOs. The number of such officials was small, however, and the consultation service was only provided in English. Neither measure was effective. In 1993, The Ministry of Labor enacted guidelines entitled "Guidelines on Employment and Working Conditions of Foreign Workers " but they did not apply to undocumented foreign workers.

Second, if foreign workers are informed of the labor laws, those who are undocumented still refrain from applying for protection because they fear deportation. The requirement that public officials should report undocumented foreigners to the immigration authorities should be rescinded. In 1988, the Human Rights Bureau of the Ministry of Justice exempted those of their public officials who engage in consultation services or receive claims from foreigners from this obligation and in 1989, the Ministry of Labor followed suit. Yet this is not sufficient. The requirement should be revised so that only the police are obliged to report undocumented foreigners. The government should inform foreigners of this exemption.

Third, prior to deporting an illegal foreign worker, the Immigration Bureau should be required to inform the Labor Standards Inspection Office and the Public Employment Security Office if the Japanese employer has committed violations of the labor laws.

Fourth, the minimum status of illegal foreign workers should be secured so that they cannot be deported until after their rights have been recognized. When illegal foreign workers have been subject to forced expulsion and have not been given adequate legal aid or other assistance, the enforcement of the deportation order should be delayed.

Fifth, to protect foreign workers from callous employers and agents, a proper criminal justice system should be established to deal with the unlawful activities of these employers and middle-men brokers.

Sixth, according to the revised Immigration Law of 1990, employers should be indicted for hiring undocumented foreigners. This has not curbed the practice of hiring undocumented workers but it has been pushed underground. To protect themselves, employers hire now by verbal promise only. Thus, undocumented foreigners do not enjoy labor law protection. In February 1992, in order to strictly control undocumented foreigners, the chiefs of relevant bureaux from the Ministries of Justice and Labor and the Police Department held a meeting entitled *Fuhō Shūrō Gaikokujin Taisaku to Kankei Kyokucho Kaigi* (Meeting of the Bureau Chiefs related to Measures toward Illegal Foreign Workers). This subsequently developed into a series of meetings on the same topic. These aimed at capturing and deporting undocumented foreigners. Such practices merely force the undocumented to go underground, to the further detriment of their human rights. The Japanese government should legalize the status of foreigners who have been in Japan for more than five years.

Seventh, due to the economic recession, unemployment has been an increasing problem in Japan since 1992. Foreign workers, who generally work for the most marginal and economically vulnerable firms, have been confronted with dismissal, unemployment, disease and death, refusal of visa extension and deportation. This is attributable more to insufficient protection of their human rights than lack of migration policy. The Japanese government should ratify and implement the relevant ILO Conventions which are Convention no. 97 Concerning Migration for Employment, Revised 1949; Convention no. 143 Concerning Migrant Workers, Supplementary Provisions, 1975; and the International Convention on the Protection of the Rights of All Migrant Workers and their Families.

Civil law and immigration law in family cases

In this section I shall examine problems related to settlement, especially the creation or dissolution of legal relationships through marriage or childbirth and the accompanying question of residential status of the non-Japanese national spouse.

Extension of spouse visas and divorce

Immigration Law contains a category called "residential status, spouses of Japanese nationals". Spousal visas are issued for periods of stay as follows: three months, six months, one year or three years. Up to 30 July 1996, a foreigner who had divorced a Japanese spouse was not allowed to remain in Japan because the foreigner had lost his or her residence status, even if the foreigner was the parent of a Japanese child. Generally, the foreigner was the wife and, for the remainder of the chapter, I will assume that the wife is the non-Japanese. Many divorced foreign wives and their children suffered from their treatment by the Immigration Office. After strong lobbying and negotiation efforts by NGOs and other concerned citizens, the Ministry of Justice issued a Circular on 30 July 1996, stating that foreign parents with custody of children, including illegitimate children legally acknowledged to be Japanese by their respective Japanese parents, are permitted to change their residence status to that of long-term resident.

However, divorce is not the only reason for authorities to refuse the extension of a spousal visa. Increasing opportunities for foreigners to get jobs in Japan in the early 1990s has led to an increase in sham marriages. In 1991 and 1992, the Osaka Immigration Bureau prosecuted four hundred such marriages.[8] Owing to this sudden increase in sham marriages, the Immigration Bureau became reluctant to permit extension of the spouse visa unless the husband signs the paperwork and comes into the bureau personally. When the wife and husband are living apart, unless the bureau receives evidence of valid cause for these living arrangements from an employer or police detention center, they are reluctant to grant an extension. When the Immigration Office receives an application for the extension of the spousal visa, the officials often visit the foreigner's home in order to ascertain whether or not they are living with their Japanese spouse, as they claim. If the foreigner is found to be living separately from their spouse, the Immigration Bureau often refuses to extend the spouse visa. At a February 1993 meeting between the Osaka Immigration Bureau and the Osaka Bar Association, Immigration officials said that, according to the revised Immigration Law of 1990, residential status is given to a foreigner on the basis of his or her activities.

> If a foreign wife does not live with her husband, in our regard she is not fulfilling her duty in acting as a wife. Therefore, except for special cases, such as that of a wife whose husband is in prison, preventing them from cohabitation, the Immigration Office does not permit visa extension (when the foreigner lives apart from her spouse). This is also the official position of the Ministry of Justice.
>
> (Osaka Immigration Bureau, February 1993)

Before sham marriages became a problem, the usual procedure was that the Immigration Bureau would give a six-month spousal visa, a one-year extension, a three-year extension and, finally, after five years' residence in Japan as the spouse of a Japanese, many foreigners obtained permanent resident status. Foreigners must now go through several extensions of the initial six-month visa before receiving the one-year visa. Each time an application for renewal is made, the foreigner needs the cooperation of his/her spouse. Their private married life is therefore under the control and, to an extent, surveillance of the Immigration Office. Recently, it has also become very difficult for foreigners to obtain permanent residency status. Additionally because the Immigration Office is short-staffed, and because they now carry out time-consuming home investigations, it takes over five months to get permission for visa extension. Many foreign wives have to apply for an extension one month after receiving the current extension or, in some cases, even before obtaining permission for previous applications.

Although marriages where the spouses are living separately may appear to be sham, there are many legitimate reasons behind separate residence. Typically, the foreign spouse has been abandoned by her husband who has gone to live with a lover. However, the Immigration Office does not regard this as a legitimate excuse for living apart. There have been cases where foreign wives with children from their marriage but living apart from their Japanese spouse, were not granted visa extensions despite the legitimacy of their marriage.

If a foreign spouse receives an official letter from the Immigration Office denying her the extension of her spouse visa, she can sue the government. In the meantime, however, the Immigration Office will begin deportation procedures. Furthermore, in such cases, they pursue such deportations aggressively. After trying several times to negotiate, the foreign spouse usually gives up and returns home, even in the case of legitimate marriages.

Sometimes, the foreign spouse receives a postcard from the Immigration Office informing her that she cannot extend the spouse visa but, if she wishes, she will be granted a temporary three-month visa. Most people notified in this way do wish to stay in Japan so they agree to make the change from spouse to temporary visa, without realizing that a temporary visa cannot be extended. When they have been refused an extension of the temporary visa, the foreign spouses contact attorneys who then negotiate with the Immigration Office to change the visa back to a spouse visa. In some cases where the foreign spouse was not seeking divorce and where there were children involved, we succeeded. If the foreign spouse is seeking divorce, we apply for an extension of the three-month temporary visa and, in the meantime, negotiate the division of property or compensation and /or child support with their Japanese spouses. If there are children involved, attorneys have been successful in obtaining injunction orders to stop the deportation process.

In yet another kind of case, the foreign spouse receives a postcard from the Immigration Office informing her that permission will not given to extend the spouse visa. In these cases, we negotiate to extend the spouse visa and provide evidence that the marriage is *bona fide* even though the husband wants to live separately. We file a suit against the husband and submit the court document to the Immigration Office indicating that her case is pending. During this time, a visa extension is usually granted. If not, she might be allowed to change to a temporary visa or, failing that, we can sue the Japanese government. However, if the foreign spouse agrees to change her visa to a temporary one without consulting an attorney, it is more difficult to win her case. Judges tend to believe that it is not unreasonable to refuse to extend temporary visas because that is the principle behind that category of visa in the Immigration Law. We need to alert foreigners to this situation so that they do not simply agree to change their spouse visas to temporary ones.

On 22 March 1993, the Tokyo District Court ruled that a decision which refused the extension of the temporary visa should be overturned while the divorce case is pending, even though the couple continue to live separately (*Hanrei Jiho* 1993: 37–41). On 26 May 1994, the Tokyo High Court supported this judgment and, on 7 August 1996, the Supreme Court supported the Tokyo High Court Judgment (*Saibansho Jiho* 1996: 1, 2). The reason given, however, was "the refusal of extension of the temporary visa deprived (the party) of the chance to apply for a change from temporary visa to spouse visa." On 28 April 1994, the Tokyo District court ruled in a similar fashion (*Hanrei Jiho* 1994: 90–6). However, on 11 October 1995, the Tokyo District Court ruled that:

> the residential status of spouse is given to a foreigner in her role as a wife. If her marriage is not completely broken down, and she has the capability to act as a wife, the decision which refused the extension of the spouse visa should be overturned.
>
> (*Hanrei Taimusu* 1996: 62–8).

In contrast, on 18 December 1996, the Osaka District Court ruled that "the residential status of spouse is given to a foreigner in her role as a wife, and (when) her marriage is completely broken down, the decision to refuse the extension of the spousal visa is lawful."[9]

It is difficult for foreigners to obtain injunction orders to stop deportation. Only if a foreign wife has children and may be able to qualify for a resident (*teijū*) visa, can she obtain the injunction. So far, there have there been no cases of sham marriages between Japanese and foreigners from Europe and North America.

The Immigration Office uses extraordinarily stringent measures in the spouse visa extension process. This is motivated not only by the increase in sham marriages but also by racism on the part of officials who are prejudiced against Japanese marrying non-Caucasian women. The implementation of immigration policy – in this case, the decision to grant spousal visas of certain durations – rests totally in the hands of the immigration authorities.[10]

What can we learn from this? Recent trends in immigration control strongly affect not only the residential status but also the human rights of foreign spouses. In particular, I have detected discriminatory treatment against women from other parts of Asia. Since separate residence has become sufficient reason to refuse spousal visa extension, even a woman in an abusive marriage must put up with her husband's cruelty if she wishes to remain in Japan. Furthermore, because of the income differentials between Japan and their home countries, these women have much more to lose if they leave Japan than do their counterparts from highly industrialized nations. Many of them support their relatives back home through their wages from working in Japan. A few cases illustrate the desperation of these women.

A twenty year old Korean woman married a Japanese. He forced her to work as a bar hostess and put her on a highly restrictive diet because he reasoned that her earning potential would be hampered if she were to gain weight. She eventually became infected with tuberculosis, and on the advice of a public health nurse, received medical treatment. After a spell in hospital, she returned to her husband's home but he continued to restrict her diet. She began drinking to alleviate her hunger. Her husband began beating her in retaliation and she fled to the hospital. She contacted me to assist her in extending the spouse visa so as to maintain her national health insurance coverage. When she recovered, she decided to leave Japan and divorced her husband.

A Filipino woman married to a Japanese had two children, aged six and twenty months respectively. She had worked hard to support her husband's household up until her first pregnancy but could not continue once the babies were born. Her husband was lazy and did not work. They lived with her husband's father, surviving only on his pension. One day, she tried to persuade her husband to get a job and contribute to the household income. This enraged him and he threw boiling water at her. He missed and the children, who were nearby, were badly scalded. However, the woman hesitated to leave her husband, as she could see no way to work and raise the children if she returned to the Philippines. Although she wants to live apart from him, they have stayed together, mainly because her father-in-law has agreed to look after the grandchildren so that she can go back to work. Her husband remains unemployed.

Some women, unable to bear the violence, run away from their husbands. In these cases, the husbands may try to follow them or they may refuse to return their passports. Some also deliberately inform the Immigration Office that their wife has left them, and they try to prevent their wives from extending their visas without their cooperation. In this way, they try to force the woman to return. In these ways, foreign wives are under control of both their husbands and the Immigration Office. There are many battered foreign wives but they are forced by circumstances, and by deliberate policy, to bear their husbands' violence.

One might conclude that foreign spouses are handicapped under the Japanese legal code. This, however, is not the case. According to Japanese Civil Law, every person has the equal right to marry and divorce. Japanese law provides for divorce by mutual agreement, by conciliation, by adjustment (in family court) and by judicial decree (in district court). In addition, the International Covenant on Civil and Political Rights (ICCPR), which Japan ratified in 1979, states:

> Parties to the present Covenant shall take appropriate steps to ensure equality of rights and responsibilities of spouses as to marriage, during marriage and at its dissolution. In the case of dissolution, provision shall be made for the necessary protection of any children.
> (International Covenant on Civil and Political Rights Article 23(4)).

Article 26 states, "All persons are equal before the law and are entitled without any discrimination to the equal protection of the law."

What about asset distribution in divorce cases? In Japan, spouses can claim consolation money and/or the division of matrimonial assets. However, foreign wives from Asian countries do not enjoy equality. Foreign wives, because their visa extensions are not granted, end up leaving Japan without having had the requisite time to negotiate with their spouses or settle their cases in the courts. Most of them waive their right to the division of matrimonial assets and consolation money. Thus, the Immigration Office's refusal to grant a visa extension to women who are going through divorce proceedings prevents them from exercising their rights under Japanese law and under Articles 23(4) and 26 of the ICCPR.

However, there are ways round this predicament. A foreigner who has been refused an extension of her spousal visa can apply for permission to change her residency status, for example to that of a foreign English teacher. This is only possible for those foreigners who possess a recognized skill so that foreign wives from Asia are seldom able to change their status as most would be categorized as unskilled manual laborers. They could apply for status as temporary visitors which would allow them to extend their stay for three months, during which time they would have to settle their divorce proceedings. If a lawyer negotiates with the Immigration Office on a client's behalf or sends the office certification that a foreigner's divorce case is pending in court, the office can extend the temporary visa beyond three months or delay making a decision until the case is settled. There have been cases where foreign wives with children were initially denied extension of the spousal visa because they were living apart from the husbands but, after negotiation by their attorney, were re-issued with a spouse visa after first changing to the temporary status visa. However, this happens rarely as most foreign wives do not know of this process.

While the Immigration Office seeks to strictly control sham marriages, they turn a blind eye on false divorces. There have been cases where notification of divorce is filed without the agreement of the foreign wife. The husband forges his wife's signature or has his wife sign both marriage registration paper and divorce registration paper at the time of marriage. If the wife is illiterate in Japanese, she does not know what she is signing. Then, when he wishes, he files the divorce papers. In such cases, it is more difficult for the foreign spouse and her attorney to negotiate with the Immigration Office to delay making their decision or to issue a temporary visa until the case is settled. Although there are undeniably many sham marriages, the spouse visa should be given to the person to acknowledge the status of spouse and the Immigration Office should take other measures to prosecute sham marriages. For example, stricter procedures for marriage registration could be implemented to prevent sham marriages.

Sometimes, Japanese men deliberately delay registering their marriage to a foreigner. Sometimes, they decide not to marry this partner after all and either decide not to marry or to marry someone else (Japanese or foreign). By this time, the first partner may be pregnant or may have given birth to their child.

Although both the Immigration and Civil Registration Bureaux are under the Ministry of Justice, the public servants who work in them do not communicate with each other on how each handles problems concerning marriage. They should be in contact.

Marriage registration for Korean residents of Japan does not require any authentication. It is therefore difficult to check up. The Immigration Office can investigate the authenticity of the marriage before issuing the first spouse visa.

When *yakuza* groups arranged sham marriages, foreign "wives" are forced into prostitution without knowing their "husbands" at all. In other cases, brokers have arranged sham marriages between Chinese women and Japanese men with disabilities. The men, wanting to marry but unable to find a partner in Japan paid ¥1,500,000 (US$15,000) to get a bride from the Chinese mainland and entered the women on their household registers. On meeting their grooms at the Itami Airport in Osaka, however, the women refused to live with them and disappeared. Many Chinese have tried to smuggle themselves into Japan by ship but were caught as the ship neared land. Compared with this method of illegal entry, sham marriage seems the safer and more reliable way to enter Japan.

In my opinion, the Immigration Office and the Civil Registration Office should cooperate to strictly check marriage registrations and the first permission for spouse visas. The Japanese government should also cooperate with foreign governments and exchange information about problems. If the Immigration Office checks the first permission thoroughly but still fails to uncover some sham marriages, this would be an inevitable margin of error on its part. It should not be used as a reason to hassle the majority of foreign spouses. The spouse visa should be given to persons married to Japanese, regardless of whether or not they live together.

Marriage between Japanese and foreigners who have overstayed their visas

When a person violates the immigration laws by engaging in activities outside the limitation of visa status or by overstaying their visas, he or she will be ordered to leave Japan and will not be granted a spouse visa even if he or she marries a Japanese national after the violation. Many such cases currently occur in Japan. Out of fear of deportation, these people do not register their marriages, nor do they register their children. If deported, the foreign partner and unregistered children would not be able to legally return to Japan for a year after deportation (Immigration Law Article 5 (1) 9), and are not guaranteed re-entry. Although they may then apply for spouse visas, there is no time-limit for approval. As a result there are a number of stateless children not registered at birth. These children do not have access to any of the administrative services for infants such as medical check-ups or immunizations. They cannot even gain access to public education.

This violates ICCPR which states:

> No one shall be subject to arbitrary or unlawful interference with his privacy, family, home or correspondence, nor to unlawful attacks on his honor and reputation. Everyone has the right to the protection of the law against such interference or attacks.
>
> (ICCPR Article 17)

The Ministry of Justice changed its internal standards in the fall of 1992 following actions of some pressure groups.[11] If a couple's marriage is recognized as legal and *bona fide* and if the couple live together and the Minister of Justice acknowledges it, spouses of Japanese are permitted to reside in Japan by the discretion of the Minister of Justice, regardless of their visa status. Although formerly it was more difficult to gain permission for residence in such cases in the Kansai than the Kanto, it became easily obtained in the Kansai as well, after the Ministry of Justice issued a Circular on 30 July 1996, as mentioned previously. Therefore, legislation should be introduced either by reforming the current law or by administering it differently, to allow a spouse to stay legally in Japan even if the immigration law has been violated and he or she should be treated as in the process of applying for the spouse visa.

Stateless children

According to the Japanese Nationality Law:

> A child shall be a Japanese national when, at the time of its birth, the father or the mother is a Japanese national; when the father who died prior to the birth of the child was a Japanese at the time of his death; when both parents are unknown or have no nationality in the case where the child is born in Japan.
>
> (Japanese Nationality Law Article 2)

Article 3 states, "A child who is younger than twenty years old shall be a Japanese national when the parents marry after acknowledgment."

Let consider how these statements are interpreted by the Ministry of Justice. In Article 2, the phrase "at the time of its birth, the father or the mother is a Japanese national" is interpreted as "a father who legally married the mother before the birth of the baby or a father who legally acknowledged the baby before his or her birth." Merely being the biological father is not enough. However, if the mother is Japanese this is sufficient. If the father waits until after the child's birth to acknowledge paternity, the child cannot obtain Japanese citizenship.

The case of a child named Daisuke, a Japanese-Filipino boy, illustrates this problem. Daisuke's father is Japanese and acknowledges his son. Daisuke was not granted Japanese nationality, however, because city officials rejected his father's paternity claim on the grounds that his mother's documents were incomplete before his birth. Both parents filed to obtain Japanese nationality for their "illegitimate" child. They settled their case out of court in November 1996, Daisuke obtained Japanese nationality and his mother was permitted to reside in Japan.[12]

On 29 November 1995, in the case of a Korean, the Tokyo High Court overturned the Tokyo District Court's decision and ruled that if there was a special reason, for example because it was imposible to acknowledge paternity before childbirth, the child could obtain Japanese nationality (*Hanrei Jiho* 1996 (no. 1564): 139). On 17 October 1997, the Supreme Court admitted this decision (*Hanrei Jiho* (no. 1620):52").

In a book edited by the Ministry of Justice (1985: 11) Kiyoshi Hosokawa, the Chief of the 2nd Division of the Civil Bureau of the Ministry of Justice states : "As an illegitimate child is a child who is born under an unusual relationship, this child should be given different treatment from the legitimate child." Needless to say, this leads to discrimination against illegitimate children. There is no rational ground for basing the eligibility for Japanese nationality on acknowledgment of the *in utero* fetus. As the law stands, if a Japanese father attempts to make a paternity claim before his child's birth the claim is rejected, it is impossible to get acknowledgment before the baby is born.

The opacity of this law has also brought us such cases as baby Andrew, a stateless child. Andrew was abandoned by his foreign mother at birth. After giving birth, his mother left the hospital and disappeared. The hospital staff thought she was a Filipina but the Philippine Embassy refused Andrew's registration as his nationality could not legally be certified unless he was accompanied by his parent. Andrew was subsequently adopted by an American missionary couple who brought civil action against the Japanese government to certify his Japanese nationality. On 26 February 1993, the Tokyo District Court ruled that Andrew should be granted Japanese nationality as his parents are unknown. However, this judgment was overturned by the Tokyo High Court, on 26 January 1994. On 27 January 1995 the Supreme Court overthrew the High Court decision and ordered the government to grant Andrew Japanese citizenship.

There were seventy-four documented cases of stateless children in 1990 and 138 in 1992. Most are born to unmarried Japanese fathers and overstaying or visa-less migrant Asian mothers working in Japan. There are undoubtedly many more unregistered and stateless children who have yet to come to public attention. If the Immigration authorities followed the ICCPR, there would be no problem. ICCPR Article 24 states:

- Every child shall have, without any discrimination as to race, color, sex, language, national or social origin, property or birth, the right to such measures of protection as are required by his status as a minor, on the part of his family, society and the State.
- Every child shall be registered immediately after birth and shall have a name.
- Every child has the right to acquire a nationality.

Article 7 of The Convention on the Rights of the Child, which Japan ratified in 1994, states:

- The child shall be registered immediately after birth and have the rights from birth to a name, the rights to acquire a nationality, and, as far as possible, the right to know and be cared for by his or her parents.
- Parties shall ensure the implementation of these rights in accordance with their

national law and their obligations under the relevant international instruments in this field, in particular where the child otherwise be stateless.

In the cases I mention above, the Japanese government would be found in violation of both the ICCPR Article 24 and the Convention on the Rights of the Child, Article 7.

In my opinion, a child should be granted Japanese nationality if the parents' whereabouts have never been known, and any child of a foreign mother acknowledged by a Japanese father should be able to acquire Japanese citizenship.

On the recommendation of the UN Human Rights Committee, the government decided to revise the Civil Code to ensure equal rights to inheritance for illegitimate children. Before 1947, the Nationality Law granted Japanese citizenship to illegitimate children who had been acknowledged by their fathers. I think the Nationality Law will probably be revised some time in the future. The Ministry of Justice, however, has wide powers of discretion, and does not want to substantially change it. It will be rather difficult to revise. What we have to do now is to make it easier for people to change their visas to long-term resident status.

Recommendations

Recent trends in immigration control affect the human rights of foreign spouses by forcing them to stay in abusive marriages. The spouse visa should be given to those who have spousal status. It is sham marriages that should be prosecuted. The Immigration Office could do this by strictly checking all initial spouse visas. The Civil Registration Office should also take appropriate measures to avoid registration of sham marriages by cooperating with their foreign counterparts and exchanging information with the Immigration Office.

In the case of baby Andrew, the Supreme Court ordered the government to grant Japanese nationality to children whose parents' nationality is unknown. There are many cases, however, where undocumented foreign mothers cannot register their children (who have Japanese paternity) because they fear deportation. The Japanese Nationality Law should be reformed or the government's interpretation should be changed, to ensure that the child of a foreign mother who is acknowledged by a Japanese father is able to acquire Japanese nationality. Before 1947, the Japanese Nationality Law granted Japanese nationality to a child of a foreign mother acknowledged by a Japanese father. The Immigration Law should also be revised to enable a foreign mother whose child has been acknowledged by a Japanese father to acquire resident status as parent of a Japanese.

Undocumented foreigners who marry Japanese nationals do not register marriages or births out of fear of deportation. After September 1992, if a couple's marriage is recognized as legal and if the couple live together, spouses of Japanese are permitted to reside in Japan as long term residents at the discretion of the Ministry of Justice. Recently special discretionary permission was granted to foreigners who lived for more than fifteen years in Japan and are married to Japanese spouses. This discretionary permission benefits only a few. Legislation should be introduced either by reform of the current law or by establishing regulations so that the spouse visa would be sufficient to establish permanent residence.

Under the revised Immigration Law of 1990, regulations were put in place regarding the entry of foreigners into Japan. There are no regulations, however, concerning gaining permission for residence, extension of visa or change of visa status. The Immigration Bureau has criteria which are not disclosed to the public and which are sometimes changed. The Ministry of Justice has extensive discretion. The arbitrary refusal of the extension of spouse visa and other types of visa causes many serious problems. Regulations should be established to permit a foreigner to remain in Japan while extending a visa or changing its status.

On 4 October 1978, the Supreme Court granted the Minister of Justice extensive discretion of permission for visa extension. It is difficult to obtain an injunction order to stop deportation. It is important to establish clear regulations for the permission of residence, visa extension and change of visa status.

Notes

1　The Ministry of Labor Circular of 26 January 1988 reads as follows: "Labor relations laws, such as the Labor Standards Law, the Employment Security Law, and the Labor Dispatch Law, are applicable to workers in Japan regardless of their nationality, or whether they are working legally or not" (*Kyushu Bengoshikai Rengōkai* November 1991: 376).

2　Some employers hire on verbal promise to protect themselves from accusations of hiring a foreign worker. With others, it is common practice with foreigners and Japanese part-timers.

3　Most of them are undocumented foreign workers.

4　The Ministry of Justice has established branch offices of the Human Rights Bureau in each prefecture. The first, in Tokyo, was opened in 1988; an Osaka branch opened in 1989, followed by offices in Nagoya and other prefectures.

5　This Committee holds a yearly meeting with judges who belong to the Twenty-Seventh Tokyo District Court and, based on this meeting, each year the Committee publishes a new edition of the Standards. Lawyers all over the country are thus influenced by the Twenty-Seventh District Court in settling such cases.

6　Japanese attorneys, upon hearing Mr Nagakubo's views, felt he was not necessarily giving his own opinion but from that of the entire Tokyo District Court and, probably also, from the Supreme Court. Judges are of course independent but the Supreme Court influences the lower court by administrative measures. In principle, judges express their opinions only through judgements but, in this case, the judge expressed his opinion outside the courtroom.

7　Even if foreigners do pass the Japanese qualifying exams for nurses, however, this does not necessarily result in their gaining regular employment. In 1994, a Chinese woman who had come to Japan as a student passed both the associate-nurse qualifying exam and the nurse qualifying exam. Osaka city offered her employment as a nurse. Upon applying for a change in visa status at the Immigration Office, however, she was informed she could not obtain a nurse visa. The immigration official instead persuaded her to change to a trainee visa. Thus, she had to decline the employment offer from Osaka City and, instead, found employment with a private hospital as a trainee.

8　The Immigration Bureau did not investigate sham marriages before 1991 so we do not have comparative data for the previous years.

9　This decision has not yet been published.

10　A foreigner could sue for harassment and racial discrimination if she could prove that she was being treated differently from another foreign applicant solely on the basis of her race.

11　Criteria are not officially disclosed to the public. The Immigration Office has criteria but even after citizens campaigned to have them disclosed in court, they refused.

12　In a similar incident, a Japanese-Filipina couple filed the papers acknowledging their daughter Yoshika's Japanese parentage after rather than before her birth. The daughter was denied Japanese nationality. When her sister Sanami was born, however, they filed before her birth and obtained Japanese nationality. Yoshika and her mother filed in Osaka District Court to try to reverse the denial of Yoshika's nationality. On 28 June 1996, the Osaka District Court, and on 25 September 1998 the Osaka High Court, ruled that Yoshika should not be granted Japanese nationality because Article Two of the Japanese Nationality Law does not discriminate in favour of illegitimate children (*Hanrei Jiho* 1996 (no. 1604): 123). Her case is now pending in the Supreme Court.

References

All Japan Safety and Hygiene Center Liaison Conference (eds) (1992) *Foreign Workers Industrial Accidents White Paper 1992*, Tokyo: Kaifu Shobo.
Hanrei Jiho (1993) No 1467, Tokyo: Hanreijiho Co.: 37–41.
—— (1994) no. 1501, Tokyo: Hanreijiho Co.: 90–6.
—— (1996) no. 1564, Tokyo: Hanreijiho Co.: 139.
—— (1997) no. 1604, Tokyo: Hanreijiho Co.: 123.
Hanrei Taimusu (1996) no. 896, Tokyo: Hanrei Taimusu sha.: 62–8.
Hōmusho Minjikyoku nai Hōmukenkyūkai (ed.) (1985) (Ministry of Justice Research Group of Law Practice in the Civil Bureau of the Ministry of Justice) *Kaisei Kokusekihou Kokusekiho no Kaisetsu* (Explanatory Remarks on the Revised Nationality Law/the Civil Registration Law), Tokyo: Kinyu Zaiseijijo Kenkyukai.
Hōsō Jiho (August 1995) "*Heisei 6 Nen ni Okeru Shutunyūkoku Kanri no Gaiyō*" (An Outline of Immigration Control in Japan in 1994), 47, 8: 188, 223.
Kanto Bengoshikai Rengokai (ed.) (1990) "*Kenshū Jisshi Kigyō ni Kansuru Jittai Chōsa Kekka*" (Results of the Survey of the Actual Conditions of Trainees in Private Enterprises), in *Gaikokujin no Shuro to Jinken* (Foreigners' Working Conditions and Human Rights), Tokyo: Kanto Bengoshikai Rengōkai: 32–3.
Kyushu Bengoshikai Rengōkai (eds) (November 1991) "*Gaikokujin ni Taisuru Jinken Hoshō no Genjo wo Saguru*" (Research on the Real Situation of Protection of Foreigners' Human Rights) citing Ministry of Labor (26 January 1988) *Kihatsu no. 50, Shokuhatsu no. 31*, Kyushu: Kyushu Bengoshikai Rengōkai: 376.
Ministry of Justice (24 May 1990) Regulations no. 16, "The Criteria Provided for by the Ministry of Justice Ordinance under Article 7, paragraph 1, Item 2 of the Immigration Control Act", Tokyo: Ministry of Justice.
Ministry of Labor (26 December 1988) "*Gaikokujin Rōdōsha no Shūrojittai ni Tsuite*" (The Actual Working Conditions of Foreign Workers), in Nihon Rōdō Bengodan (1989) *Kikan Rōdōsha no Kenri* no. 178: 6.
—— (31 October 1989) "*Gaikokujin wo Meguru Gyōsei no Genjo to Kadai*" (The Present Condition and Problems of Administrative Measures concerning Foreigners), *Kikan-Hatsu* no. 41, Tokyo: Ministry of Labor: 25.
—— (ed.) White Paper on Labor in 1996, Tokyo: Japan Labor Research Center.
Saibansho Jiho (1996) *Saibansho Jiho* no. 1175, Tokyo: Saikōsaibansho Jimusōkyoku.
Sōmuchō Gyōsei Kansatsukyoku (ed.) (1992 [1989]) "*Gaikokujin wo Meguru Gyōsei no Genjo to Kadai*" (The Present Condition and Problems of Administrative Measures on Foreigners), Tokyo: Ōkurashō Insatsukyoku Hakkō.
Tokyo San Bengoshikai Kōotsūjikoshori Iinkai (ed.) (1992) "*Minji Kōtsūjiko Songaibaishō Soshō Songaibaishō gaku Santei Kijun*" (Standards to estimate the amount of compensation for traffic accidents in law suits), Tokyo: Tokyo San Bengoshikai Kōtsujikoshori Iinkai.

11 Foreigners are local citizens too

Local governments respond to international migration in Japan

Katherine Tegtmeyer Pak

Since about 1988 or 1989, lots of foreign workers have come to Kawasaki. At that point, the city decided that foreigners living in Kawasaki are local citizens, and that consequently, the same as Japanese local citizens, we had to ensure their access to city services.

(Interview with the Chief Counselor, Kawasaki City International Office, November 1995)

Introduction

Studies on the politics of immigration typically focus on the process of national policy-making and especially the role played by various interest groups and political parties. In the past few years, however, scholars have begun to observe that "in order to gain a complete understanding of the political aspects of immigration, one has to examine local-level developments" (Ireland 1994: 19). Because international migration unevenly affects particular cities and regions, politicization of immigration is frequently driven by people motivated by local conditions and needs. The framing of immigration-related political issues therefore should be understood as taking place between the center and periphery, between the institutions of national and local governance (Miller 1994, Body-Gendrot and Schain 1992).

Japanese experiences with international migration over the past decade illustrate the need to broaden our focus to include the local level. Responses at the national level to the dramatic emergence of Japan as a new destination for international labor migration have sought to reinforce the tight controls which keep most foreigners out of Japan, even though conflict amongst national ministries has generated some policies that tacitly encourage increased entries. Official rhetoric continues to deny the possibility of homogeneous Japan becoming a country of immigration. In sharp contradiction to the national policy attempts to reinforce this aspect of Japanese insularity, local governments in the regions most affected by the new immigration are filling the gap left by the national government's unwillingness to consider what is to be done with foreign migrants living in Japan. The series of local policy measures addressing pragmatic problems – how to prevent conflict between foreign and Japanese residents, how to fit non-citizens into the Japanese social welfare systems – have consequences for the understanding of community membership. Local governments, ascertaining the desirability for cooperation between citizens and non-citizens, intend their policies on foreign migrants to guide the construction of a new community in symbiosis with foreigners (*gaikokujin to no kyōsei shakai*). Some local governments have gone even further towards circumventing the national policy by committing themselves to treating foreigners as local citizens. Local government policies thus signal the potential for reconsideration of the dominant national identity and its implication in defining immigration as a political issue in Japan.

I will examine four cities' attempts to deal with international migration and demonstrate that local governments in Japan are acting autonomously in their creation of programs which incorporate foreigners into the community. Previous scholarly accounts of creative policy-making by Japan's local governments have stressed the importance of party politics, especially control of the elected office of chief executive, as the primary source of innovation. This study demonstrates that, even in the absence of local electoral demand for and executive commitment to a particular program of innovation, local governments engage in independent policy making through the activities of their officials.

Why are municipal governments developing programs which reach out to resident foreigners when the national government has deemed this unnecessary? Three forces in Japan have contributed to the advent of local policies incorporating foreigners. First, as with many other issues which have become the target of autonomous policy innovations by local governments, local officials encounter immigration in a different way from national officials. The key difference regarding immigration is in the proximity of foreign migrants. While officials at the national level only come into direct contact with migrants during the formal, depersonalizing process of entry and exit control, local officials meet them when they establish their individual presence in a specific community through registration, and subsequently, through requests for the social benefits which accompany residency. Any complaints about migrants from Japanese citizens are generally made to local authorities. This difference in encountering increased international migration creates a distinctive chain of defining and establishing what types of policy are desirable.

Second, the effect of the history of progressive local policy-making in Japan during the 1960s and 1970s, when local government was more responsive than the national government to demands for policy change on environmental and social welfare issues, was to make the pursuit of independent policy-making at the local level the norm across the spectrum of partisan allegiance. Local governments are now widely understood by the general public, scholars, and officials themselves to be legitimate policy innovators. Consequently, when an issue is not being addressed on the national political agenda, individuals and interest groups pursue the matter further with local governments whom they see as a potentially sympathetic target for their efforts. As far as immigration-related issues are concerned, groups impatient with the national government's denial of civil rights to long-term Korean residents and intellectuals seeking to prevent social conflict between recent migrants and Japanese and to protect the basic human rights of migrants have cooperated with particular local governments through local consultative councils.

The third force behind the innovation of local policies is the redefinition of the national government project for local internationalization to an alternative agenda which includes outreach to foreign residents. City bureaucrats have taken the local internationalization project as an opportunity for policy innovation. The specific catalysts for this process differ from city to city but, overall, the redefinition of local internationalization to include incorporation programs allows the bureaucrats-in-charge to expand the scope and importance of their programs.

The following discussion is divided into two parts. The first details the innovative incorporation programs being pursued by local governments. It also explains the development of local governments' distinctive approach to immigration-related issues. The second part elaborates the argument about the political sources of the policy programs. The evidence for my argument comes from the cities of Kawasaki, Hamamatsu, Kawaguchi and Shinjuku, which were selected to obtain difference in conditions likely to influence the policy environment.[1]

Japanese cities respond to the new international migration

Framing the issue

Popular perceptions notwithstanding, Japan has previously experienced significant immigration (see Chapter Two of this volume). Consequently, it might be assumed that Japanese cities have previous experience of policy making for their non-Japanese residents. With several notable exceptions, however, particularly Kawasaki, cities have followed the national government's lead in ignoring the oldcomer foreigners as well as enforcing registration controls (Komai 1997). For most local governments, attending to the foreigners in their communities through specific policies is a recent issue which has been prompted by the new international migration flows that began in the 1980s.

Between 1984 and 1994, the number of legally-resident foreigners in Japan increased by over 60 percent. Reflecting the general tendency for international migration to affect unevenly particular cities and regions (Miller 1994), the increase in registered foreign residents was even more dramatic in the four cities under discussion. As shown in Table 11.1, there was an 80 percent increase in Kawasaki and a 360 percent increase in Hamamatsu. Despite the rapid change and even though the percentages of non-Japanese residents are the highest in the postwar era, no dramatic disruptions to the social fabric have occurred which would necessarily demand the local officials' attention.

As Table 11.2 shows, registered foreign residents still comprise a fairly small percentage (an average of 3 percent) of the total population of the case cities. Although it should be noted that within particular neighborhoods in each city, the percentage of legally-resident foreigners is as high as 20 percent (Okuda and Tajima 1993). By comparison, cities in Western Europe or North America have foreign populations of 20 percent or higher. One does not have to subscribe to the threshold of tolerance theory to expect that there will be more noticeable social consequences of immigration when foreign migrants comprise a higher percentage of a community's population.[2]

Competition between foreign migrants and citizens over access to employment, housing, education, and health care has led to political conflict in many

Table 11.1 Registered foreign population: number of individuals (% change from previous year)

	Kawaguchi		Shinjuku		Kawasaki		Hamamatsu	
1985	2,600	+9.01%	9,535	+17.77%	—	—	—	—
1986	2,705	+4.04%	10,834	+13.62%	10,841	—	—	—
1987	2,976	+10.02%	12,439	+14.81%	11,207	+3.38%	2,557	—
1988	3,364	+13.04%	14,301	+14.97%	11,516	+2.76%	2,737	+7.04%
1989	4,427	+31.60%	16,961	+18.60%	12,831	+11.41%	3,088	+12.82%
1990	4,982	+12.54%	16,703	-1.52%	13,989	+9.03%	4,748	+53.76%
1991	5,616	+12.73%	16,782	+0.47%	16,397	+17.21%	8,023	+68.98%
1992	7,233	+28.79%	18,165	+8.24%	18,765	+14.44%	11,456	+42.79%
1993	8,106	+12.07%	18,761	+3.28%	19,720	+5.09%	11,700	+2.13%
1994	8,502	+4.89%	19,213	+2.41%	19,104	-3.12%	10,861	-7.17%
1995	8,645	+1.68%	18,815	-2.07%	19,496	+2.05%	11,775	+8.42%
total % change over entire time period charted								
		+232.5%		+97.3%		+79.8%		+360.5%

Sources: 1995 versions of city statistics from all the cities.
Notes: For Kawaguchi, Shinjuku, and Kawasaki they are current as of January 1 of each year.
For Hamamatsu the numbers are current for March 31 of each year.

Table 11.2 Registered foreign population as percentage of total population

Year	Kawaguchi	Shinjuku	Kawasaki	Hamamatsu
1987	0.72	3.75	1.02	0.49
1990	1.14	5.35	1.40	0.89
1992	1.62	6.09	1.65	2.06
1995	1.90	6.59	1.62	2.09

Sources: 1995 versions of city statistics from all the cities.
Notes: The numbers are calculated from statistics listing Japanese and foreign nationals registered with the municipal government.
For Kawaguchi, Shinjuku, and Kawasaki they are current as of January 1 of each year, for Hamamatsu the numbers are current for March 31 of each year.

European cities. Perceptions of competition have mixed with outright racism to give rise to anti-immigrant movements and even violence at the local level (Miller 1994, Layton-Henry 1992, Body-Gendrot and Schain 1992). In response, other local actors have mobilized to combat racism and to provide migrants with increased opportunities for economic and social advancement (Ireland 1994, Grillo 1985). The framing of immigration as a local political issue has alternatively reflected and shaped these circumstances.

In Japan today such obvious conflicts are noticeable by their absence.[3] Consequently, local politicians and local interest groups have been largely uninvolved in framing their communities' responses to foreign migrants. How then have immigration-related issues been introduced to urban agendas? The sheer drama of the rapid increase in foreign residents captured the attention of local bureaucrats. Enforcement of the Foreigners' Registration Act is the duty of local governments which, therefore, collect data – visa status, nationality, age, occupation, address, household composition, photographs and fingerprints – about each foreigner legally residing in their community for over three months. The registration requirement brings local bureaucrats into direct contact with foreigners so that media reports on the rapid increase in immigration are substantiated by migrants' appearance in city offices. Experience with foreign residents has created what the Japanese refer to as a problem consciousness (*mondai ishiki*). As the national government is not mediating relations between foreigners and Japanese, local bureaucrats have concluded that a new policy response is required at the city level in order to avoid the problems experienced in European cities.

This awareness of potential problems involving foreign migrants is shared by many city government departments with mandated duties that involve providing services to the non-citizens within their jurisdictions. Labor and Economic Affairs departments, health and welfare departments and boards of education all administer policies which are affected by the increase of foreign residents. Current problems affect the migrants themselves more than the Japanese residents. There is therefore some discussion on responding to the needs of migrants from the perspective of local commitment to protecting all residents' human rights. Some issues, such as unpaid medical expenses by migrants without insurance and the enrollment of children unable to speak Japanese in local schools, are already directly affecting local policy administration. Mindful of the European experiences, officials and outside observers are concerned that the migrants' problems that are left unresolved could lead to tension and outright conflict between foreigners and Japanese. They want to prevent the kind of social disruption which has been associated with international migration in other countries.

The infamous vertical administration (*tatewari gyōsei*) of Japanese bureaucracy discourages officials assigned to one section from considering issues that extend beyond their immediate jurisdiction. Managing the consequences of immigration in anything more than an issue-by-issue fashion is beyond the institutional capacity of these departments and the interests of most of the officials working within them.[4] There are typically three generalist departments within Japanese city government structures: planning, community services and general affairs. They are tied less tightly to the provision of centrally mandated services which leaves the officials assigned to them relatively free from the chain of command linking other departments to the central government.[5] General affairs departments, in addition to managing personnel issues, tend to be of a generalist nature and, as such, they are less prestigious to the bureaucrats working in the system than sections with clearer institutional assignments. Planning and community services, which deal with issues of direct interest to the general public, have more *cachet*.

The local bureaucrats who are the most involved in drawing-up incorporation programs are found in the various "International Offices" located within one of these three generalist departments.[6] The precise location of an International Office is an indication of the respect given it by an administration. The *de facto* designation of International Offices as the most likely base for programs to accommodate foreign residents is due to a coincidence of timing – growing foreign populations following hard on the heels of central government endorsement of local level internationalization in 1986 – and the influence of creative local policy making by local administrations like Kawasaki, Kanagawa and Tokyo which have taken advantage of the lack of a predetermined role for the International Offices to carve out a new policy category.

Creating incorporation programs as a facet of local internationalization

Local internationalization efforts provide the unifying framework for incorporation programs. These programs are classified as *uchi naru kokusaika* (inward internationalization). The term is used to distinguish the programs from the outward overseas focus of international exchange and cooperation activities in which local governments also engage. Usage of this term has important ideological connotations.[7]

Internationalization is a highly contested concept within Japanese politics. In its most general sense, it refers to the popular belief that Japanese society is being fundamentally changed through increasing interaction with the rest of the world through trade, tourism, communications, and most recently, immigration. However, in the progressive conceptualization, internationalization is not a passively experienced trend but an active process of increasing the openness of Japanese politics, assuming greater responsibilities towards the global community and ending discrimination at home (Mouer and Sugimoto 1983, Takahashi 1992).[8] This contrasts with the nationalistic conceptualization which seeks to expand Japanese influence overseas (Befu 1993). Local governments are thought to be appropriate promoters of inward internationalization since they are closer to grass-roots democracy and thus able to avoid the negative associations of the nation-state (Komai 1997, Takahashi 1992).

The four cities provide varying combinations of services to resident foreigners. However, the provision of these services to foreigners in and of itself does not necessarily support my claim that local governments are creating independent incorporation programs because the scope of eligibility for them is determined by the central government.[9] When local governments actively work to introduce social services to foreign residents and consider how best to meet the challenge of a changing local population, they are exercising their autonomy. Scattered attempts by one department or another to ease foreign residents into locally-managed policies become incorporation programs once they are understood to be related and therefore approached as a single issue by the city government.

Two caveats must be made about referring to the international migration-related policies of Japanese local governments as incorporation programs. First, the Japanese terminology for these policies varies widely from city to city. Kawasaki practices *gaikokujin jūmin seisaku* (foreign local citizens policy); Hamamatsu pursues *kokusaika shisaku* (internationalization policy measures); Kawaguchi has *zaijū gaikokujin ni taisuru shisaku* (policy measures related to resident foreigners); and Shinjuku has *kokusaika/kokusai kōryū jigyō* (internationalization and international exchange activities). I chose to use "incorporation program" to stand for all of these because it captures the mission of creating a local society where Japanese and non-Japanese peacefully co-exist: a *gaikokujin to no kyōsei shakai*. Incorporation is distinct from assimilation: local governments are not engaged in a process of Japanization.

The second caveat is that the incorporation programs are targeted only at documented migrants. Even the most progressive local officials in Japan feel bound to maintain the distinction between documented and undocumented migrants. Some are concerned about the undocumented migrants' presence, particularly in relation to their impact on health-care policy, but, in general, the local officials I interviewed believe that those not compliant with national immigration law cannot legitimately be included.[10]

By coordinating provision of social services to foreigners and linking such efforts to separate programs of international exchange between Japanese and foreign residents, International Offices create incorporation programs. One local official in Kawasaki explained how incorporation programs rest upon coordination:

> Well, at the same time that the number of newcomers in Kawasaki was increasing, the so-called "oldcomer" *Zainichi* Koreans were detecting problems of systematic discrimination in local administration and asking local government to reform. So, as each specific problem was discovered, they would say "please fix this" and "please reform that". Rather than have local government move bit by bit, within the course of performing duties separated between the various departments by each responsible official, they

wanted us to think about exactly what kind of problems existed where – all at one time, to act as a unified local government, thinking of all its various duties. And, just as the oldcomers were requesting a centralized office to make this kind of general policy, the newcomers were increasing. So, against this background, we decided, instead of fixing things one by one, let us clean it all up at once. And from this perspective it was decided that an International Office was necessary, and we created the International Office to skillfully link the two issues [of responding to oldcomers and newcomers] together.

(Interview 23 February 1996, Kawasaki City Hall)

In part, Kawasaki's commitment to a unified incorporation program is a response to the requests of the foreigners themselves, but most of the other cities' policies are a response to the bureaucrats' worries about cultural conflicts. Hamamatsu's annual report on its policies related to foreign migrants illustrates this underlying concern about social and cultural stability. Assumptions about the cultural threat are evident in the report's title: *An Outline Of Hamamatsu's Internationalization And International Exchange: Moving From A "Community Mixed Up By Foreigners" Towards "Community In Symbiosis With Foreigners."* The Japanese original is less awkward, but I have translated the phrase "*gaikoku-jin konjū shakai*" as "community mixed-up by foreigners" to convey the negative overtones of *konjū*. It has a connotation of mixed-breed and implies that the purity of the community has been spoiled by the presence of foreigners. Thus the International Office bureaucrats pursue coordinated incorporation programs because they want to preserve a united and cooperative community:

As the number of resident foreigners has rapidly increased in the last few years, differences in customs and culture, and misunderstandings based on language have brought many puzzles and issues of mutual misunderstanding to the attention of local government and the community. . .

In doing our best to ensure that local citizens accept foreigners as members of the community without delay, we have set up Japanese language classes and clubs for foreigners who use the City's International Exchange Center and neighborhood community centers in order to improve communication between foreigners and local citizens.

(*An Outline of Internationalization*)

Foreigners are assumed to be unfamiliar with the aspects of Japanese culture which regulate the interactions that comprise the fabric of daily life, for example, the expectation that neighbors will refrain from having too many guests or from entering and exiting homes too late at night so as not to disturb each other. Garbage disposal, proper behavior at public bath houses and bicycle parking are other examples of everyday behavior thought difficult to master without a feel for Japanese culture.[11] Foreigners are also assumed to suffer from lack of Japanese language capabilities which keep them from getting to know their neighbors or from obtaining necessary public information.

Many of the initiatives within incorporation programs are therefore targeted at overcoming the language barrier. Most city governments with a noticeable foreign-born population provide maps, information about local government offices, community newsletters and guides to daily life in Japan in a range of foreign languages. Japanese language instruction opportunities are also increasingly available through local government for minimal fees and the cost of instruction materials. In some cases, the classes are offered through the city's quasi-public International Exchange Association, and other classes are available at local city-run community centers. Many cities have both types of classes and, in either case, they are likely to be taught by volunteers who receive some training from the city.

Another increasingly popular way to overcome the language barrier is to offer consultation services to foreign residents. These services, either in person or over the telephone, are also typically dependent on volunteers who offer advice and introductions to the appropriate government offices for foreigners seeking assistance with problems concerning employers, health care, family law (marriage, divorce, birth certificates), residency status, immigration procedures, etc. Consultation is generally available in several different languages, depending on the city. In those cities which have seen rising numbers of foreign children enrolling in local schools, more extensive programs of supplementary classes and tutoring in Japanese language are being implemented. It should be noted, however, that these programs are generally run directly by the local Board of Education, with much less involvement on the part of the International Office than is evident in other services.

Even though these initiatives may appear rather uncontroversial, even the most seemingly benign of them are at odds with the official national immigration policy which is based on the premise of controlling foreigners as people who are a potential threat to the integrity of the nation. Teaching Japanese and offering information and assistance in gaining access to state services are actions inherently at odds with the "no immigration principle" underlying national policy. Furthermore, by targeting initiatives directly to foreign residents, local governments draw attention to their increased numbers and thus expose the inaccuracy of that principle.

The activities of the most progressive local governments go further in contradicting national rhetoric and official statements of immigration policy.[12] They have defined resident foreigners as local citizens who deserve the right to be in communication with their local government by virtue of their contributions to the community, payment of taxes and, more generally, because of their involvement in everyday life. The Local Government Act (*Chihō Jichi Hō*) is used as the ultimate justification for this stance. Although constitutional guarantees of social and civic rights are only extended to Japanese citizens (*Nihon kokumin*), the Local Government Act obliges local authorities to ensuring the safety, health and welfare of all local citizens (*jūmin*), including non-Japanese (Komai 1997, Jichirō 1991, Ebashi 1993).

This stance has led city governments to undertake extensive surveys and interviewing of these new constituents so as to better understand their living conditions, opinions and needs *vis-à-vis* local authorities. Kawasaki has even established a Foreigners' Advisory Council which enables representatives from the foreign population to participate in a regular ongoing forum with local bureaucrats and politicians. Other practical examples of this stance are the support of hundreds of local governments for efforts to grant the vote to long-term foreign residents at local level and the decisions by many local governments to abolish the nationality requirement (propagated by the national government) for most local administrative positions.[13]

Measuring differences between the four cities

Each of the cities is pursuing a different combination of these programs, as shown in detail in Tables 11.3 to 11.6. The differences in each of the cities incorporation programs are two dimensional, as shown in Figure 11.1.[14] Kawasaki and Hamamatsu have developed much more extensive incorporation programs than Kawaguchi or Shinjuku. The first dimension, which measures government to migrant relations, is simply the extent of initiatives undertaken by the city. This refers both to the number of programs and their scope: that is, how accessible they are to foreign residents and to what extent the actual needs of the foreign residents are taken into consideration. The second is the intensity of the effort to shape a broader community response to the changing demographic composition of the city. This dimension refers to whether the International Office is attempting to produce an active incorporation program which reaches across departmental jurisdictions within the city government as well as between the city and other governmental authorities. It also notes efforts to include Japanese residents in internationalization through lectures, classes, encouragement of volunteer activity and other forms of educational outreach.

First, let us consider the amount of information on the number and co-ordination of initiatives provided by each city to its foreign residents. (See Tables 11.3 to 11.6 for a detailed listing of specific activities.) There is little difference in the number of printed materials available in foreign languages. Each city offers materials in the array of languages appropriate to the resident foreign migrants.[15] Accessibility of counseling for foreign residents shows the greatest variation. Kawaguchi does the least: volunteers are only available one afternoon per week for four hours. Hamamatsu on the other hand provides well-advertised advice services over the telephone and daily consultations in Japanese, Portuguese and Spanish, with Chinese- and Tagalog- speaking counselors available one afternoon a week. Not surprisingly, Hamamatsu's information services reach more of the foreign community than do those in the other three cities.

Another aspect of the scope of cities' incorporation programs is the degree to which the city recognizes foreign residents as "local citizens", whether or not it seeks to ascertain their needs and to actively involve them in the community. Commitment of resources to surveying foreign residents is a key indicator here. Once again, Kawaguchi has done the least. Shinjuku conducted a small survey of foreign residents as part of a larger survey on the city's internationalization policy, but only 122 individuals participated. Hamamatsu and Kawasaki have done the most in this area. Both cities commissioned respected scholars to conduct extensive surveys of their foreign community. In Hamamatsu, there were 429 Brazilian and Peruvian *Nikkeijin* respondents. Kawasaki commissioned two surveys. The first of these had 1,146 respondents while the second, more intensive, survey interviewed sixty-eight documented and undocumented foreigners.

Table 11.3 Kawaguchi programs targeted at foreign residents, 1996

Foreign language publications	Daily life guide [E, C, K]. City maps [E, C, K]. Family safety checklist [E, C, K, P, S]. Natural disaster safety prevention chart [E]. Proper garbage disposal [E, C, K, P, S]. *Refreshing Life* (newsletter on family welfare) [E, C, K, P]. Handbook for guidance of foreign nationality students [E, C, K, P, S]. *Cupola* community newsletter [E, J]. Introduction to the city [E].
Public facility information in foreign languages	English translations of City Hall's information sign. Romanized versions of major street signs.
International Exchange Center/ counseling and advice opportunities	"International Exchange Corner" meets at a neighborhood community center from noon to 4 pm every Thursday. Sixty-three volunteers provide information primarily in English, also limited access to Chinese, Portuguese and six other languages.
Miscellaneous	Field trips to city facilities. Intended to deepen foreigners' understanding of safety, garbage disposal and provide a chance for interaction with Kawaguchi citizens. Several times a year.
Japanese language classes	General Affairs Dept. sponsors two-hour class on Saturday afternoon. Adult Education Dept. sponsors two two-hour evening classes that meet weekly. Supplemental Japanese language classes for foreign children enrolled in elementary and junior high schools. Weds. and Fri. from 3 pm to 5 pm.
Contact with local administration/ exchange activities within the community	Parties for foreigners and local residents.
Assistance for foreigners' unpaid medical expenses	When medical facilities have not received payment for treatment of foreigners after one year of billing, prefecture and city may reimburse the expense (50% each).
Survey and public opinion	Inclusion of two questions about attitudes towards internationalization activities in the city's public opinion poll. Survey of foreign residents in 1995 to determine who would like to receive the *Cupola* newsletter.
Training for Japanese residents or officials	Host "international understanding" lectures.
Communication between public offices	None.

Key for Tables 11.3 to 11.6

C	Chinese		E	English
G	German		J	Japanese
K	Korean		P	Portuguese
S	Spanish		T	Tagalog

Table 11.4 Shinjuku programs targeted at foreign residents, 1996

Foreign language publications	*Making the Most of Your Life in Shinjuku: Living Guide to Shinjuku City* [E, C, K]. *Shinjuku Town News* – community newspaper [E, C, K]. *Livelihood and National Health Insurance* [E, C, K]. Guide for individuals eligible for exemption of national insurance fees [E, C, K]. *Mother and Child Health Handbook* [E, C, K]. AIDS prevention leaflet [E, C, K]. Flyers for recycling program [E, C, K]. *School Life in Japan* [E, C, K]. *With a View Toward the Future: Education in Shinjuku* [E, C, K] Sports Festival flyers[E]. *Introduction to the Shinjuku Sports Center* [E]. *Keys to Shinjuku City* [E, C, G.].
Public facility information in foreign languages	Video providing basic information about living in Shinjuku, and local government services. Plays in the lobby of City Hall.
International Exchange Center/ counseling and advice opportunities	Counseling provided daily at City Hall. English available Mon–Fri; Chinese on Mon., Weds., Fri.; and Korean on Tues. and Thurs.
Miscellaneous	General Affairs Section administers a private grant which provides stipends of 240,000 yen yearly to as many as ten foreign college students who are nominated by their institution. Stipend of 6,000 yen per month given to resident foreign students attending foreign schools, on basis of financial need.
Japanese language classes	Special supplementary Japanese language classes and tutoring provided at three elementary and middle schools. (Board of Education). Classes for adults provided at a community center, fifteen sessions, from September through December. (Shinjuku International Exchange Association – SIEA).
Contact with local administration/ exchange activities within the community	Foreign City Government Monitors: Five resident foreigners are selected to act as "city government monitors" (Japanese citizens do likewise, separately), which gives them the opportunity to express opinions and communicate requests to the city government. (Public Relations Division). Invite foreigners to come to elementary schools, four times yearly, to interact with the children. Classes on Japanese culture offered to foreigners at community centers.
Assistance for foreigners' unpaid medical expenses	None.
Surveys and public opinion	1992 Survey for the Preparation of Policies aimed at the Internationalization of Shinjuku. Includes surveys of Japanese residents' opinions of internationalization, a questionnaire

(continued overleaf)

Table 11.4 (continued)

	distributed to registered foreigners, and other information about the City's internationalization programs.
Training for Japanese residents or officials	English, Chinese, and Korean language classes for city employees (Personnel Division) to increase communication abilities.
Communication between public offices	Twice yearly participation in meetings organized by the Tokyo Metropolitan Govt.'s International Affairs Division to exchange information on activities of the municipal governments in Tokyo.

Table 11.5 Kawasaki programs targeted at foreign residents, 1996

Foreign language publications	*Our Home Kawasaki: A Resident's Guide to the City* [E, S, P, C, K]. *How to Find Rental Housing.* *Watching Kawasaki* (intro to city). *Kawasaki International Association News.* *Kawasaki Ward's Guide to Daily Life* [E, C, P, K, S]. *Introduction to Elementary School* [K]. *Mother and Child Health Handbook* [E, K, C]. *Kawasaki Guide Map* [E]. *Public Health Care Centers* pamphlet [E, K]. *Conversation Guide to Nursery School Life* [E, C, K, S, P].
Public facility information in foreign languages	Signs at City Hall in English and Korean.
International Exchange Center/ counseling and advice opportunities	Multi-million dollar facility, the Kawasaki International Center (KIC), completed in 1994. Includes stages, library, small hotel facilities, classrooms, gardens, etc. Home to the Kawasaki International Exchange Association (KIEA). Counseling provided to foreign residents from 10 am to 4 pm daily, in English, Chinese, Korean, Portuguese, and Spanish (KIEA). Special counseling/advice meetings held twice yearly with regard to immigration procedures, employment, and other issues of particular concern to foreign residents (KIEA). Counseling at Public Health Care Centers in several foreign languages related to maternal and child health issues. City supports the "*Fureiaikan*" (Friendship Hall) community center. Managed by Zainichi Korean group, sponsors language and cultural classes and activities intended to increase understanding between Korean and Japanese residents.
Miscellaneous	Financial support of 10,000 per month for 200 foreign college students living in Kawasaki.
Japanese language classes	Three separate courses offered to adults at the KIC. Daytime course meets twice weekly for three months. Evening course meets once a week over a year. Advanced Japanese club meets once a week over a year. Other Japanese classes offered at ward community centers. KIEA sponsors a yearly Japanese language speech contest for foreigners.

Table 11.5 (continued)

Contact with local administration/ exchange activities within the community	Foreigners Advisory Board est'd in 1996. Regular meetings of this group of 50 foreigners, to provide a regular forum for their voices to be heard by the city government. KIEA hosts a variety of activities, including international festivals, lectures and clubs on Japanese and foreign culture, home visits and exchanges with Japanese students for foreign exchange students. Meeting with *Zainichi* Koreans to exchange opinions about urban planning, as background for the 2010 General Plan.
Assistance for foreigners' unpaid medical expenses	Program in cooperation with the Prefecture.
Surveys and public opinion	1992–3 *Survey of Opinions and Living Conditions of Foreign Local Citizens* (report issued in 1993). Extensive commissioned survey to determine the needs of resident foreigners with regard to medical care, working conditions, education, etc. 1994–5 *Interview Survey of Opinions and Living Conditions of Foreign Local Citizens*. Commissioned survey, with focus on newcomer foreigners. Extensive interviewing method. Surveys of Japanese residents which focus on "internationalization policy", notably the *10,000 Citizens* questionnaire.
Training for Japanese residents or officials	Lectures in English on the history and culture of foreign countries (KIEA). Lectures in Japanese intended to deepen understanding of other Asian countries (KIEA). Chinese, Korean, and Spanish language courses (KIEA). Training for volunteer Japanese language teachers (KIEA). Requests to local real estate agents to eliminate discrimination in renting to foreigners. Publication of two booklets explaining issues related to foreigners, and activities in the community targeted at helping them: *Questions and Answers : Living Together:* focus on the *Zainichi* Koreans. *Thinking About What It Means for Resident Foreigners and Japanese to Live Together As Local Citizens.*
Communication between public offices	1989 started the Committee for the Promotion of Foreign Local Citizens' Policy, which brings together the chief secretaries from each division of the city government. Liaison Consultative Council on Kawasaki's Foreign Local Citizens' Policy – this too brings together managers from various city government divisions, coordinated by the International Office. Forum for discussing how to implement the fifty-three goals established for the Foreign Local Citizens Policy. City participates in the Kanagawa Prefecture Consultative Council on the Resident Foreigners Problem. Participants include the prefectural police, Yokohama Immigration Bureau office, prefectural Labor Division, prefectural Employment Security Policy Section, Yokohama City officials.

Table 11.6 Hamamatsu programs targeted at foreign residents, 1996

Foreign language publications	National health insurance in Hamamatsu [P, S]. Simple conversation handbook [P, S, J]. Water and sewage guide [E, P, T]. Garbage disposal [E, P, S, J]. Natural disaster protection pamphlet [E, P, S, K, C, J]. Earthquake preparation [E, P, S, J]. Map for evacuation in natural disasters [E, P, S, J]. Tourist pamphlet [E, J]. Guide to entering nursery school [P, J]. *Living in Hamamatsu*: a guide book [E, P, J]. HICE guidebook map [E, P, J]. Citizens' English conversation handbook [E, J]. *Enshu Folktales* [E]. *HICE News* community newsletter [J, E, P].
Public facility information in foreign languages	Publication of *Sign-Writing Manual for Municipal Offices and Facilities* [E, P, S, D, F].
International Exchange Center/ counseling and advice opportunities	International Exchange Center (IEC) operates out of permanent facilities in cooperation with HICE. Employs staff for consultation in Japanese, Portuguese and Spanish Monday to Friday, in Chinese Tuesday afternoons, in Tagalog Thursday afternoons. Japanese language classes (see below) Collection and distribution of information for international exchange, implemented by volunteers, at least four of whom are present each day.
Miscellaneous	None.
Japanese language classes	IEC offers three sessions of classes yearly. Three levels of instruction are offered in two different time slots - two hours per week either Monday evenings or Thursday mornings. Board of Education runs the "Language Classroom" after school. In addition to Japanese, instruction is offered in the children's native languages.
Contact with local administration/ exchange activities within the community	Board of Education hosts a Friendship Group for foreign students. Board of Education twice a year exchange events for foreign and Japanese students and their parents. HICE hosts events like the Brazil Festa that focus on the foreigners in Hamamatsu.
Assistance for foreigners' unpaid medical expenses	None.
Surveys and public opinion	1992 commissioned *Survey of Living Conditions of Resident Foreigners*, published in connection with surveys of company attitudes towards employing foreigners, and local residents' attitudes towards resident foreigners. 1995 *Survey of Desired Conditions for Japanese Language Education* (in cooperation with the Cultural Affairs Agency, Ministry of Education).

Table 11.6 (continued)

Training for Japanese residents or officials	Board of Education holds Workshops on International Understanding Education for all related employees at the elementary and junior high schools. HICE trains volunteers to teach Japanese. HICE sponsored foreign language classes [E, P, S, other]. Portuguese language classes provided to Waterworks Dept. employees who deal with the public.
Communication between public offices	City Hall sponsors a Roundtable on Foreign Residents which brings together officials from the following organizations at least twice a year: Labor Standards Office, Public Employment Security Office, Social Insurance Office, Prefectural Commerce, Industry and Labor Policies Office, Prefectural Western Region Policy Center, Legal Affairs Bureau, Prefectural International Exchange Section, Police, Chamber of Commerce and Industry, Medical Association, Dental Association, Nagoya Region Immigration Bureau, HICE.

Kawasaki also actively tries to involve foreign residents in community politics. There are several ongoing, substantive forums for communication between the city government and foreign residents. The most innovative of them is the Foreigners' Advisory Board, which was modeled on similar councils in European cities. Another example of Kawasaki's initiatives in this area is the *Fureiaikan* (Friendship Hall), a community center dedicated to improving relations between the city's *zainichi* Koreans and Japanese residents as well as providing the *zainichi* with a place to explore and teach Korean culture and language.

The most dramatic differences between the cities' programs occur along the second the level of activity in the city's *uchi naru kokusaika*. For inward internationalization to have any lasting impact, the International Offices must

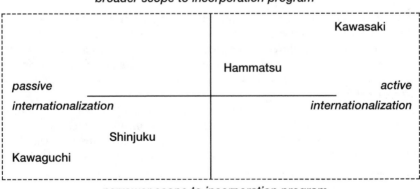

Figure 11.1 Comparison of intensity of incorporation programs

involve other institutions in their programs as they themselves tend to be marginalised and significant institutional and financial constraints mean that they often have little impact when acting alone.[16] Kawaguchi and Shinjuku's International Offices are very noticeably isolated from the mainstream of city government. Interviews with International Office officials revealed either a sense of resignation to this situation (in Kawaguchi) or the attitude that this was only natural, (in Shinjuku) suggesting that the officials themselves attached little importance to their activities.[17] In neither case are the officials trying to overcome this isolation.

Hamamatsu and Kawasaki's International Offices are exactly the opposite. In both cities, the International Offices occupy more prestigious places in the organization of City Hall. Kawasaki's International Office is in the Citizens Bureau and Hamamatsu's is in the Planning Bureau, whereas the offices in Kawaguchi and Shinjuku are located in the General Affairs Bureau. Both have established regular channels for communication with other public officials through which information relevant to the incorporation programs is exchanged. Such communication also presents the International Offices with the opportunity to bring other officials into the inward internationalization project by familiarizing them with its goals and explaining how they relate to the regular activities of other bureaux in city government.

Kawasaki and Hamamatsu have also done more to involve the general public in the internationalization project. Both cities have high profile quasi-public International Exchange Associations which interact regularly with a community of interested citizens who come to participate in volunteer activities, take classes and to attend lectures. Kawasaki has published a series of handbooks in Japanese explaining the city's official philosophy of inclusion for foreign residents and familiarizing citizens with the history of international migration to the city. Shinjuku also has a fairly active, if less visible, International Exchange Association.

The political sources of the policies

Bureaucracy and uchi naru kokusaika *as autonomous policy*

Now that we have discussed the content of incorporation programs at the local level, it is time to consider the political sources generating them. Moreover, we need to discuss how the different historical experiences of bureaucrats in the four cities combine with the current image of each city's foreign population to generate Kawasaki and Hamamatsu's comparatively more progressive view of internationalization.

There is a serious, if often overlooked, series of analyses emphasizing that local governments have a variety of resources at their disposal which allow them to make autonomous policies, despite the centralized nature of the Japanese state (Steiner *et al.* 1980, Samuels 1983, Reed 1986, Muramatsu 1988, Jain 1989). In the words of one frequent contributor to this debate:

> urban local governments in Japan affect the well-being of their residents,
> both Japanese nationals and foreigners, and . . . (have) displayed an extraor-

dinary capacity to generate policy change within a centralised system. This process of policy innovation and policy change continues unabated at the local level in Japan.

(Jain 1993)

Of the resources needed to support policy innovation, the one that has received the most attention is urban politics, that is, the expression of local preferences through citizens' movements and/or local electoral politics to influence local policy-making agenda. Local policies which challenge or contradict national policy have been primarily understood as an outcome of popular politics. Muramatsu convincingly demonstrates how the rise of *kakushin jichitai* (progressive local governments) in the 1960s and 1970s transformed the nature of inter-governmental relations in Japan and allowed the public to use local government as an outlet for its frustration with national policies and policy makers (Muramatsu 1988: 61–76).

One consequence of this transformation has been the strengthening of local bureaucracies. In the 1960s and 1970s progressive local governments increased the strength of ties between the public and local bureaucrats, thereby circumventing the older and more traditional local powers which had controlled city councils. The professionalization of local bureaucracies has consequently increased so that local bureaucrats are now thought to be more highly-skilled and knowledgeable than previously. The transformation in inter-governmental relations has led to a concurrent improvement in the quality of local administration (Kuwahara 1989). Kuwahara's study suggests that one lasting effect of these dual transformations has led to the acceptance of innovative policy-making at the local level to such an extent that it no longer need be based on widespread citizens' movements or even electoral politics.[18]

This historical background explains why the local bureaucracy itself is capable of launching new policies autonomously. However, bureaucrats still need room for political maneuver in which to develop policies. When electoral politics and citizens movements do not provide the opening, political spaces for one policy may be opened within another not obviously related policy area. Such is the relationship between incorporation programs and local internationalization. The nationally-sponsored local internationalization project became the place where bureaucrats could pursue their preferred solutions to the problems associated with the new international migration. In more formal terms, "several relatively independent streams" of problem definitions and solutions came together in a process of policy innovation described by the "garbage can" model of decision making (Cohen, March and Olsen 1972). Campbell, applying this model to Japanese politics, characterizes it as:

policy change as coincidence which is likely to occur. . . when goals are unclear (people do not know, or cannot agree on, what they want), means-ends relationships are uncertain (there is little knowledge of how to solve a problem or what the effect of some action might be), and participation is fluid (no rule governs who is active when).

(Campbell 1992: 31–2)

Specifically, incorporation programs developed into the embodiment of inward internationalization in the following manner. First, Japanese cities began to pursue international cultural exchanges. Separately, but at the same time, the Kawasaki and Hamamatsu City Governments tentatively formulated policies related to foreigners.[19] Second, several local internationalization projects were started by the national government. Third, Kawasaki and Hamamatsu's bureaucrats, located in the new International Offices, created proactive incorporation programs under the auspices of local internationalization and thereby implemented solutions to the newcomer problem that evolved from their previous experience with foreigners. We are currently witnessing the horizontal spread of their early innovations across local government as a whole.

Early internationalization of Japanese communities emphasized cultural exchange. In the early 1980s, Japanese cities were increasingly being invited to participate in sister city relationships. Local business communities favored the expansion of these relationships and their accompaniment of cultural activities for their public relations value (*Nihon Toshi Sentâ* 1995). At the same time, internationalization emerged as a hot new policy area, with national ministries competing to control it. Within a few years, the national government involved itself in the scattered local internationalization activities (*Kawasaki Chihō Jichi Kenkyū Sentā* 1991). The Ministry of Foreign Affairs was the first to attempt to take over local internationalization by establishing the Internationalization Advice Center in February 1986 to assist local governments interested in international exchange programs. The Ministry of Transportation and the Ministry of International Trade and Industry have also sought to manage local internationalization but the efforts of each of these ministries have been overridden by those of the Ministry of Home Affairs (MOHA).

MOHA's involvement, which began in 1986, led to a series of official notices establishing a framework for local internationalization projects. City governments were authorized to establish International Exchange Sections and quasi-public International Exchange Associations. Standards for MOHA certification of the Associations were established and those cities which met them were authorized to appropriate local bonds and transfer taxes for their administration. MOHA's prescribed mission for these new offices stressed sister city exchange, providing information about Japan overseas, cultural events and international festivals, assistance to small companies' exports, homestay programs and other types of cultural diplomacy (Jain 1993: 269–74) which basically share the characteristic of being targeted to local citizens of Japanese nationality (*Kawasaki Chihō Jichi Kenkyū Sentā* 1991: 7).

The original authorization for local International Offices was not intended to provide a base for the incorporation of foreign migrants. However, since growth in foreign population followed closely on the initial implementation of the centrally-approved local internationalization project, it was not much of an extension for local bureaucrats to include some services to new foreign residents, such as the publication of foreign language materials, in their agenda. Media coverage during this period defined increasing international migration as the third wave of internationalization: that is, as an internationalization of people following the earlier waves internationalizing trade and finance (Machimura 1990). This coincidence of timing is, perhaps, sufficient explanation for the limited activities pursued by Shinjuku and Kawaguchi. However, the incorporation programs of Kawasaki and Hamamatsu result from an alternative definition of internationalization.

By pursuing this alternative definition, Kawasaki and Hamamatsu's bureaucrats broadened the scope of programs under their jurisdiction and thus the importance of their own positions. Moreover, they have made their cities leaders in this policy area so that their ideas and initiatives are closely followed by other local bureaucrats throughout Japan working on internationalization. In Kawasaki and Hamamatsu the bureaucrats redefined local internationalization to include policy solutions reflecting their previous exposure to local events and problems facing foreigners living in Japan.

From the early 1980s, *zainichi* Koreans throughout Japan actively protested their treatment by Japanese society. The legal requirement that all foreign residents submit to fingerprinting when registering with local government became a symbol of oppression and many *zainichi* refused to submit to the requirement any longer. Local governments were at the center of the ensuing political scene since they were the ones required by law to report those refusing fingerprinting to the national government. Kawasaki was one of the local governments which refused to comply with the law. In February 1985, the mayor declared that the city would no longer report offenders. Kawasaki's *zainichi* community is particularly well-organized and has targeted the local government to support its goals for improving the situation of local *zainichi* (*Fureiaikan* interview, 9 December 1995). Many local bureaucrats have therefore come to know and respect the leaders of this movement and have been able to establish a cooperative relationship with them (*Kōminkan* interview, 16 May 1995).

The experience of working with the Korean social movement profoundly affected the bureaucrats' feelings about their own position. They were members of local government who were stuck between local community and national law. The Kawasaki bureaucrat quoted on pages 250–1 explained how working with the Koreans had been a powerful lesson:

> Well, one specific example, you had the fingerprinting problem, which the movement had spread throughout the entire country. Ultimately the Japanese people who supported them, in our case too – I was one of them myself – because we had direct experience with the job of foreigners' registration, during the day we did our job and were on the side taking the fingerprints, you know. And (laughing) at night we protested the fingerprinting system. After all, for bureaucrats in local government there is that element of actually hearing the voices of the people, but of course as part of an institution implementing national policy, even if you are unwilling, you have to do your job. It's (local government) a place with that kind of dilemma.
>
> (Kawasaki bureaucrat interview, 23 February 1996)

On the strength of a trusting relationship and their experience with the Koreans, a core group of Kawasaki's bureaucrats thus made policy decisions which set the stage for their move to redefine internationalization to include the incorporation programs which targeted the 1980s newcomers.

Hamamatsu's bureaucrats were also influenced by experiences pre-dating the newcomers' arrival. Hamamatsu was not one of the cities which sided with the social movements of the *zainichi* Koreans. Their *zainichi* community is comparatively low profile and less engaged in political action. I found no evidence of cooperation between the *zainichi* and City Hall. The early experiences leading to incorporation policy in Hamamatsu were based on the arrival of a small group of Vietnamese refugees in the early 1980s.

A religiously-based private association, which runs a hospital, hospice and provides many social services in the Hamamatsu region, had invited the Vietnamese to settle in the city in 1982 (*Seirei* interview 18 July 1995). Coincidentally, the precursor of today's Hamamatsu Foundation for International Communication and Exchange (HICE), which was staffed by city bureaucrats, was developing a small program providing English maps and information about the city to international business travelers who frequently visited Honda, Suzuki, Kawai and Yamaha, the large industrial corporations which dominate Hamamatsu's economic and social life. After the problems of the Vietnamese came to HICE's attention, it began to offer them Japanese language classes, instruction on the drivers' education examination and a video about daily life in Japan. These services were coordinated by HICE but financed largely with donations from individuals, the Rotary Club, etc. Volunteers did most of the work. Hamamatsu thus began its tradition of "homemade internationalization", defined in explicit contrast to the flashy ceremonies of other cities, international festivals and slick promotion of international tourism. Memories of these early, truly local efforts left a legacy so that those involved view the attempts of the City Government to reach out to resident foreigners as part of a natural progression of internationalization (City Hall interview, 17 July 1995).

Factors shaping the current policy environment

Differences in recent history partially explain why Kawasaki and Hamamatsu's bureaucrats actively pursue the goal of inclusive internationalization, while Shinjuku and Kawaguchi's are more quiescently reacting to broader changes in society. The policy environment is also shaped by two connected factors related specifically to the arrival of the newcomers in each city. First, outside interest in a city's experience with its newcomer population appears to increase a city's commitment to progressive internationalization. Second, when recent foreign migrants to a city have a generally positive image, it is easier to justify reaching out to them through incorporation programs.

Japanese academics have enthusiastically involved themselves in the debates about new international migration to their country. Many combine active research agenda with explicit support for specific policy programs. Those academics favoring the progressive internationalization agenda of increasing the openness of Japanese society often view local government as the best venue for realizing this goal. Their involvement with city officials contributes in several ways to an environment which is supportive of incorporation program initiatives. Their books, articles and research reports praise local governments' efforts to confront increased immigration more directly and creatively than the national government. This generates positive public relations material which is reported in the national media.[20] Moreover, their research on migrants in Japanese and foreign cities is a valuable source of information and policy ideas for city bureaucrats. Kawasaki has especially close, collaborative relationships with progressive intellectuals and has worked closely with them to develop the Foreigners' Advisory Council, for example. Hamamatsu has been the subject for a series of surveys on the *Nikkeijin* with dozens of Japanese and foreign academics descending on the city to study the patterns of *Nikkeijin* employment and their cultural adjustment to Japan. Most of these researchers have collaborated with city officials. Shinjuku and Kawasaki have not gone unnoticed by academic researchers, but there have been fewer studies of the foreign migrants living there, and very little contact between researchers and public officials.[21]

One of the reasons that academics who are interested in researching the conditions of foreign migrants living in Japan have found the situations in Kawasaki and Hamamatsu more attractive than those in Shinjuku and Kawaguchi is the respective image of the foreigners working and living in each city. Even though each city has comparable numbers of foreign residents who might make interesting subjects for these studies, there are many negative images associated with the growth of the foreign community in Kawaguchi and Shinjuku. Table 11.7 presents statistics on only those foreign nationals who are in compliance with the Foreigners Registration Act requiring registration with local authorities. In addition, each city has from one to three times as many undocumented migrants as registered foreigners. Shinjuku and Kawaguchi have received a great deal of attention in the national press for the numbers of undocumented foreigners. Researchers have a much easier time getting employers and the migrants themselves to cooperate with studies which target those legally in the country. This makes research in Hamamatsu, with its high percentage of *Nikkeijin*, and Kawasaki, with its *zainichi* Koreans and *Nikkeijin*, a much more attractive proposition.

Just as particular groups of legal foreigners are more attractive targets for research projects, they are also more attractive targets for activist incorporation programs. Attractiveness is more complicated than legality *per se*. As elsewhere, the Japanese react differently to foreigners living in Japan on the basis of their racial and/or national origins. Certain nationalities are closely identified with particular occupations and visa status and, thus, with perceptions of lawfulness or illegality. These factors combine to form an image of the foreign community living in each city.

Several practices of the national government reinforce the equation of foreigners' legality with their race and nationality. The most apparent of these is the existence of a discrete visa category for descendants of Japanese emigrants: the *Nikkeijin*. Granting legal sanction for employment of a distinct, racially Japanese group in unskilled occupations otherwise forbidden to foreigners has created a powerful image which has made the *Nikkeijin*, as a group, perhaps the most acceptable of the newcomers. An initial sense of cultural affinity with these ethnic Japanese also contributed to their positive image, although prolonged interaction has increased awareness of their foreignness by revealing substantial cultural and linguistic differences between the *Nikkeijin* and Japanese.

Another important practice is the way that official press releases and statements about enforcement of immigration statutes inevitably categorize foreign migrants on the basis of nationality. Mass media further popularizes the images consequently created around a given nationality. Thus the public is familiar with the *Japayuki* women from the Philippines and Thailand who work in bars and nightclubs, sometimes legally, but often as undocumented workers associated with the criminal underground.[22] Male Pakistanis, Bangladeshis and Iranians, most of whom overstay tourist visas and then work in construction and small manufacturing enterprises, are regarded as criminals for their violation of immigration statutes. These men are further despised because of reports of their compatriots' arrests for other crimes, of which selling fraudulent prepaid telephone cards and marijuana are the most frequent. Much government and press attention has been given to false refugees from China who, in hopes of working in Japan, arrive in rickety boats and claim to come from Vietnam. There has also been much talk of the increase in Chinese gang activity, much of which is centered in Shinjuku. The many Chinese who come to Japan as students are haunted by these images and by the fact that many of their numbers engage in work outside the restrictions of their visas.

Shinjuku and Kawaguchi both have reputations for high levels of foreign migrants engaged in illegal activities. Both cities have red-light districts which specialize in the sex-based entertainment industry, including prostitution. Kawaguchi's small factories are also known to employ large numbers of undoc-umented male workers. Stories about goings-on have been featured in national newspapers and magazine articles about the foreign worker problem.[23] For exam-ple, in the case of Shinjuku, the negative images of foreigners stem in part from the local merchants protesting about the visibility of prostitution by them. In June 1991, the local association of hotels and innkeepers decided to post signs deny-ing entry for foreign women to the area's dozens of love hotels.[24] The newspaper coverage of their initiative warned of prostitution zones being created by foreign women from South-east Asia and South America (*Mainichi Shimbun* 1991). (This was despite the fact that Shinjuku has been one of the most notorious cen-ters for the sex industry in Japan for years.)[25] Three years later, the Kabukicho (Shinjuku) Business Promotion Association organized citizens' patrols in con-junction with a police campaign to clean up the neighborhood of foreign prostitutes and Chinese mafia, following a six month period which had seen the murders of six Chinese, allegedly by Chinese gang members (*Nikkei Supōtsa Shimbun* 1994, *Mainichi Shimbun* 1994.[26] Meanwhile, Kawaguchi (and other cities nearby) were frightened by persistent rumors that foreign men ("South-east Asian") had raped and assaulted Japanese women. Bulletins from neighborhood associations and local employers' purchase of warning whistles for female employees fueled the rumors despite denials of their veracity from police (*Saitama Shinbun* 1991a, 199b).

Conversely, the legal foreigners in these cities are relatively invisible in com-parison to the *Nikkeijin* in Hamamatsu and the well-organized oldcomer Koreans in Kawasaki. Newspaper articles announcing the Kawasaki city government's decision to create an assembly for settled foreigners carefully noted the national-ities of those targeted for participation: "There are approximately 10,000 settled

Table 11.7 Nationality of registered foreign population as share of total foreign population, four case studies (in percent)

Year	Kawaguchi		Shinjuku		Kawasaki		Hamamatsu	
					1 October 1990			
1989	Korea	50.2%	Korea	42.4%	Korea	58.3%	Korea	63.0%
	China	26.6%	China	37.8%	China	14.6%	Philippines	9.4%
	Philippines	8.3%	USA	3.7%	Brazil	7.0%	China	9.0%
	Vietnam	2.4%	Philippines	3.3%	Philippines	5.3%	Brazil	4.7%
	Bangladesh	2.4%	France	2.4%	Peru	3.1%	Vietnam	3.9%
	Others	10.1%	Others	10.4%	Others	11.9%	Others	10.0%
1994	China	32.1%	Korea	40.1%	Korea	47.1%	Brazil	54.5%
	Korea	31.2%	China	35.0%	China	17.7%	Korea	16.9%
	Philippines	11.4%	Philippines	4.2%	Brazil	9.3%	Philippines	8.2%
	Brazil	7.3%	Myanmar	3.4%	Philippines	7.3%	China	6.4%
	Vietnam	2.3%	USA	3.3%	Peru	2.8%	Peru	5.6%
	Others	15.9%	Others	14.0%	Others	15.8%	Others	8.4%

Sources: 1995 versions of city statistics from each of the four cities. Current for the last day of the indicated year for Kawasaki and Shinjuku, Kawaguchi is 31 March of that year, Hamamatsu 1989 figures are for 31 March of that year, 1994 figures are current for the last day of the year.

Note: The statistics registering persons as Korean nationals deceptively unify three distinct groups. There are *zainichi* Koreans who have permanent residency in Japan, and register their nationality as from either the Republic of Korea (South) or The People's Republic of Korea (North). The third group are recent arrivals from the Republic of Korea, who come most often on either student or professional visas. The majority of Koreans in each city *except* Shinjuku are *zainichi* Koreans, according to my interviews with local officials. Although the city governments have statistical information on the breakdown of this category, they do not release it.

foreigners (*teijū gaikokujin*) in the city. About 9,000 of them are either South or North Korean, and there are also many *Nikkei* Brazilians and Peruvians." It appears that, owing to the identity of the intended targets, bureaucrats in Kawasaki and Hamamatsu have a much easier time justifying the appropriateness of their activities to themselves, other officials and the public at large than would the officials in Shinjuku and Kawaguchi.

The absence of an "urban politics" story

I have argued that bureaucrats play the most important role in shaping the initiatives for the activist incorporation programs in Kawasaki and Hamamatsu, based in part on their direct relations with community members and intellectuals but without the involvement of politicians, political parties or even widespread social movements. The initial catalysts for establishing relations between city government and foreign residents originate in the community with the bureaucrats setting the policy agenda and thereby shaping the response to the increase in newcomers. Although there are informal networks of community members who are involved in these programs – primarily the volunteers who teach the Japanese classes, staff the consultation services, etc. – their participation is largely in response to the needs of the incorporation programs as defined by the bureaucrats. This is equally true in Hamamatsu, Kawaguchi and Shinjuku. Only the *zainichi* Koreans in Kawasaki are engaged in regular discussions with local officials about the incorporation programs and they are, for the most part, uninterested in the aspects of those programs which are targeted at the newcomers (*Fureiaikan* interview, 9 December 1995).

There are three groups of private, or community-based, groups who might be expected to contribute to the framing of local incorporation programs but are not doing so. The first is the foreign migrants themselves. Although the oldcomer *zainichi* Koreans are well organized in some places, newcomer foreigners have yet to form political organizations representing their own interests. Much of this is due to the fact that they have only just arrived. Many of the newcomers are in cycles of migration, working for half a year, a year or longer before returning to their home country for some time, and then coming back to Japan. Even those who have been in Japan continuously for five years or longer have, on the whole, yet to organize formally. In light of the experiences of migrants in other countries, it is reasonable to expect that they will become more politically oriented in the coming decade (Ireland 1994).

The second group is local business. Since local demand for labor is implicit in the growth of the foreign population in each of these cities, I expected businesses and their associations to participate in framing a public response to their presence. Businesses are certainly critical in shaping the experiences of foreign migrants but, for the time being at least, their influence takes place privately. The businesses are not contributing to the shaping of incorporation programs. It has been suggested that some cities with active incorporation programs, including Hamamatsu, are promoting these programs because "foreign workers have become an integral part of local labor markets" (Ebashi 1993: 17–21). However, my interviews suggest that to the extent that it is true it is because the bureaucrats are blindly assuming that their programs will promote local industry in some unspecified manner. Of the four cities, Kawaguchi is the only example of sustained cooperation between local bureaucrats and the business community in the field of increased international migration. The iron-casting industry there has negotiated with City Hall to receive modest financial support for programs bringing (perhaps fifty per year) Chinese to work as trainees in their firms. Support for trainees is included in Kawaguchi's internationalization budget. Even there, however, the involvement of business in the overall incorporation programs is limited to this one initiative. Interviews with local Chambers of Commerce, sub-contractor associations and businesses in the four cities indicated that, in general, very few employers are so dependent upon foreign labor that they have any material interest in facilitating foreign migrants' integration into the community. Most employers of foreign migrants simply wish to get on with their business and have as little as possible to do with local authorities. As long as employers avoid flagrant violations of the labor laws and their employees do not disturb their neighbors, city officials are willing to leave them in peace.

The other seemingly missing participant is community groups. There are community members who volunteer to participate in the various city's incorporation programs. In some cases they have formed clubs of like-minded individuals – most frequently to teach Japanese. These groups, however, follow the lead of the bureaucrats. This is not true for a second type of civic group, which has been organized independently of city programs. These non-governmental organizations, or "solidarity groups" to borrow a term from Patrick Ireland (1994), are an important source of local responses to increased international migration. They are organized in a way that ignores city boundaries. NGOs tend to address the needs of foreign migrants living in districts and organize themselves on either a neighborhood basis or across several cities. They do not identify with cities nor do their activities fit within a framework of urban politics which takes account of the role of local government. The NGOs and city governments tend to be aware of each other's attitudes and practices but interaction is so limited that it would be mistaken to analyze them within the same framework.

Conclusion: the consequences of local incorporation policies

There are two points to be made about the broader significance of city governments taking the initiative in attempting to integrate the foreign migrants into Japanese society. The first relates to the long-term prospects for the incorporation of foreigners. The second concerns the ongoing discourse on Japanese national identity.

Even in their most expansive forms, the incorporation policies of local governments outlined in this chapter, are the target of much criticism from Japanese NGOs that work with foreigners, as well as from many scholars. This chapter is not intended to argue that they are successfully resolving the problems associated with international migration. However, given the history of Japanese policies towards foreigners, it is truly remarkable that local governments are even talking about foreigners as community members let alone pursuing measures to realize such goals. Fifteen years ago, there was scant interest in these matters amongst local authorities. The only national policies dealing with the question of incorporating non-Japanese have sought complete assimilation and denial of difference. Local governments, with a few exceptions, used to comply with central efforts to marginalize the *zainichi* minority. This policy was so successful that most Japanese believe that the last decade is the first time that there have been foreigners in their midst.

There are limitations to the long-term prospects of current incorporation policies. It is questionable how many foreigners will seek to avail themselves of the culturally-oriented programs. For the time being, most foreigners may be satisfied with opportunities to learn Japanese and receive information in their native languages. The experiences of other countries suggests that, in the long-term, access to good jobs, health care, education for their children and political partici- pation will be more important. There is no doubt, however, that actions currently being taken by local officials will help shape future concerns and strategies of the foreigners themselves and, therefore, their long-term relationship with Japanese society. This may or may not represent a positive contribution to Japanese democracy, since Japanese citizens and their political representatives have yet to express their opinions about how the nation should respond to international migration and foreigners in their neighborhoods and workplaces. Should these issues ever reach the electoral agenda, all groups will have to contend with the course of action being decided upon by today's small group of policymakers.

The second point is that the actions being taken by local governments contribute to the ongoing debate about Japanese national identity. As we have seen, many of the initiatives involved in local incorporation programs are intended to resolve small problems of miscommunication and cultural misunderstanding, and to pre- vent them from developing from minor tensions to outright conflict and violence. However, discussions of these issues are a route to more profound discussions of the flexibility of Japanese culture and society. Local bureaucrats are asking how this process of internationalization is affecting the common understanding of com- munity membership. This is evident in the changing vocabulary used to discuss these issues: as the Hamamatsu report on incorporation noted, there is a shift from a community mixed-up by foreigners to one living together with them. These poli- cies contribute to discussions of a multicultural Japan. The documents, articles and books written about the role of local government in immigration politics are offer- ing alternative visions of what it means to be Japanese in an era of internationalization.

Notes

This research was made possible thanks to generous support from the Japan Foundation. Thanks also to Mary Brinton, Michael Dawson, Ann Kaneko, David Leheny, Elizabeth McSweeney, Christiana Norgren, Joshua Roth, Susanne Hoeber Rudolph, and Bernard Silberman for their helpful comments on earlier drafts of this paper.

1   Two hypotheses guided the selection of the four cities. First, the identity, indicated by nationality, of the foreigners living in a city was expected to shape the responses of city government to increased international migration, in that various racial/national groups are believed to be more or less different or threatening. The distinction was drawn between cities where *Nikkeijin* (descendants of Japanese emigrants, mostly of Brazilian or Peruvian nationality) are the largest newcomer population, and those where some other nationality is larger. The expectation was

that the "*Nikkeijin* cities" would have more open and accommodating policies. Second, I expected employers, through business and industy associations, would participate in framing the public response to international migration since they stand to benefit from the consequent loosening of the labor market. Because local governments in Japan have historically cooperated with manufacturers on local industrial policies (Hill 1990), a distinction was drawn between cities where manufacturing is the most important sector of the local economy and those where the service sector is more important, in the expectation that different patterns of relations with local government might be reflected in policies towards foreign migrants. Manufacturing cities were expected to take a more proactive approach to immigration-related policy making.

2   This theory has become commonly accepted by many social scientists and government officials in France who borrowed the concept from Amercian sociologists' analyses of black migration into white neighborhoods. It holds that 'beyond a certain 'threshold (which . . . [varies] at anything between 5 percent and 20 percent of the population)' the French react against a foreign presence in their midst. See Grillo (1985) for a discussion of the impact of this theory in France. Similar assumptions that immigrants necessarily disrupt social order underlay the political and social science arguments about the costs and benefits of international migration to specific communities.

3   Several such incidents are reported in, for example, *Chunichi Shimbun*(1992) and *Asahi Shimbun* (1993a, 1993b).

4   The same constraints apply to the range of community-based government offices administered by the prefecture which might otherwise conceivably provide an institutional home to foreigner policies. This includes organizations such as the Public Employment Security Offices, Labor Standards Offices and Social Insurance Offices.

5   This is truly a relative freedom from central administration. Generalist departments, like all others, remain responsible to the Ministry of Home Affairs which oversees all local administrations in Japan.

6   At this time, the individual bureaucrats assigned to these offices generally do not have any previous experience with foreign residents nor issues of international exchange. Most are simply rotating through various city departments.

7   As the incorporation programs become more widespread, the original ideological impact of *uchi naru kokusaika* is being diluted. The Ministry of Home Affairs, following the lead of local government initiatives dealing with foreign residents, now favorably promotes the concept of inward internationalization in *Jichitai Kokusaika Foramu* (Local Governments Internationalization Forum), a magazine it publishes and distributes to local government officials.

8   There is also a "conservative" or nationalistic conceptualization of internationalization, which seeks to expand Japanese influence overseas (Befu 1993). See also Tegtmayer Pak (1998).

9   Foreign residents' eligibility for such services is typically of recent vintage. During the 1980s, as Japan signed UN accords on human rights and refugees, long-standing barriers to resident foreign nationals' participation in welfare state programs were eroded (Ebashi 1993, Jichiro 1991).

10   This is not absolute, as there is always room for flexibility during implementation. Even if incorporation policies' stated targets are documented migrants, in practice, undocumented individuals may be able to receive a given service. Access to education (for children) and National Health Insurance, for example, are sometimes provided to individuals who are not eligible due to their legal status. City governments that are more flexible in their implementation are not willing to publicly advertise the fact for risk of attracting unwanted attention from the national government.

11   All of the above cultural understandings are frequently violated on a regular basis by Japanese living in urban neighborhoods, with the possible exception of behavior in

public baths. Their violation is likely to generate complaints, which might be dealt with by neighborhood councils. Only when the offender is foreign are such issues considered important enough to warrant the involvement of the city government.

12   Although this chapter discusses city governments, prefectures have also been involved in creating incorporation programs. In fact, several prefectural level governments, notably those in Tokyo, Kanagawa, Hyogo, Osaka and Saitama, have been leaders in addressing these issues. To varying degrees, they may offer encouragement and assistance to their constituent municipal governments. See Takahashi (1992) for more on Kanagawa, and Tani (1997) on Osaka.

13   These last two examples of incorporation policy are rooted in the efforts of the *zainichi* Koreans to improve their standing in Japanese society. As such, they predate the increase in newcomers which is the main focus of my research. Nevertheless, the issues are inextricably intertwined in Japanese debates. See Ebashi (1993), and the articles in the July 1992 issue of *Toshi Mondai* on the "Participation of Alien Residents in Civic Government."

14   Although these four cities fall into only two quadrants in this figure, I believe that it would also be possible that other cities fit in the upper left-hand quadrant. In the near future, one might reasonably expect to see a city with the broader scope to its incorporation program, due not to an internal activist orientation, but rather as a consequence of the policy menu of the most activist cities spreading horizontally to other cities throughout Japan. It is harder to imagine how a city might fall in the lower right hand quadrant but perhaps a smaller town might have an activist orientation without having the resources to engage in a broad incorporation program.

15   That these materials are available in languages other than English is proof of increasing sensitivity to the needs of recent migrants. In Japan foreign language education overwhelmingly means English instruction. It is no surprise that the initial attempts to provide information to foreigners were heavily biased towards English. Increased sensitivity to the irrelevance of English for communication with the vast majority of foreign migrants in Japan, and the consequent expansion to other languages, demonstrates a greater change in thinking about relations between Japanese and foreigners than may be immediately evident to Americans and other Westerners accustomed to the demand for information in multiple languages.

16   International Offices after all are quite marginal within the overall scheme of city government. There are significant institutional and financial constraints on the impact that they can have acting alone.

17   Kawamura (1997) makes passing reference to the Shinjuku city government's intention to disband its International Office (the Peace Events and International Exchange Promotion Division of the General Affairs Section) in 1997. It is not clear to me whether their task of coordinating information about foreigner-related policies has also been abandoned, or merely transfered to another section. See Kawamura (1997: 273).

18   Kuwahara's (1989: 52–3) survey of participants in local government argues that municipal bureaucrats are very active in the policy process and are perhaps second only to mayors in their ability to set local policy agenda.

19   This is not to say that Kawasaki and Hamamatsu were the only local governments in Japan exploring foreigner policy but I am describing the process in the context of this project's focus on four cities.

20   Examples of such research include Ebashi (1993), Komai and Watado (1997), and Tezuka *et al.* (1992).

21   The research on Shinjuku and Kawaguchi has a less prescriptive orientation. For example, Okuda and Tajima's 1993 study of Shinjuku, the most thorough of that city, is primarily interested in ethnographic documentation of recent migrants' experiences. Unpublished research on Kawaguchi focuses on demand for foreign labor. Local government policies are not discussed.

22 *Japayuki* (literally "going to Japan") refers back to the term *karayuki* that labeled poor, young Japanese women sold by their families to brothels throughout Asia in the first decades of this century. Today, Thais and Filipinas most frequently fall into this category but women from Korea and Taiwan also featured in the early 1980s.

23 See the *Asahi Shimbun* series *Dekasegi Burusu* (Migrant Blues) which ran in April 1988 and featured stories about the experiences of undocumented migrant workers from Pakistan and Ghana in Kawaguchi.

24 Love hotels charge by the hour or for the night and are frequented by many couples seeking more privacy than small Japanese homes generally allow, as well as by prostitutes and their clients.

25 Kawamura notes that Shinjuku's Mayor and Deputy Mayor participated in the September 1994 start of this "campaign."

References

Asahi Shimbun (1993a) "Komoro Hotel Ignores Ministry of Justice's Suggestion to Remove Notices Prohibiting Illegal Aliens from Entering Baths," 2 March.

—— (1993b) "'Expel the Foreigners' Banners appear throughout Tokyo and Saitama: Neo-Nazis," 7 April.

Befu, H. (1993) "Nationalism and Nihonjinron" in H. Befu (ed.), *Cultural Nationalism in East Asia: Representation and Identity*, Berkeley, Calif.: Institute of East Asian Studies, Research Papers and Policy Studies, University of California.

Body-Gendrot, S. and Schain, M. A. (1992) "National and Local Politics and the Development of Immigration Policy in the United States and France: A Comparative Analysis," in D. L. Horowitz and G. Noiriel (eds) *Immigrants in Two Democracies: French and American Experience,* New York: New York University Press.

Chunichi Shimbun (1992) "Foreigners Go Home! Warning Fliers on Electricity Poles in Kosai," 31 October.

Campbell, J. C. (1992) *How Policies Change: The Japanese Government and the Aging Society,* Princeton: Princeton University Press.

Cohen, M. D., Marsh, J. G. and Olsen, J. P. (1972) "A Garbage Can Model of Organizational Choice," *Administrative Science Quarterly* 17, 1 (March).

Ebashi, T. (ed) (1993) *Gaikokujin wa Jūmin desu: Jichitai no Gaikokujin Jūmin Shisaku Gaido*, Tokyo: Gakuyo Shobo.

Grillo, R. D. (1985) *Ideologies and Institutions in Urban France: the Representation of Immigrants,* Cambridge: Cambridge University Press.

Hill, R. C. (1990) "Industrial Restructuring, State Intervention, and Uneven Development in the United States and Japan." in J. R. Logan and T. Swanstrom (eds) *Beyond the City Limits: Urban Policy and Economic Restructuring,* Philadelphia: Temple University Press.

Ireland, P. (1994) *The Policy Challenge of Ethnic Diversity: Immigrant Politics in France and Switzerland,* Cambridge, Mass.: Harvard University Press.

Jain, P. (1989) *Local Politics and Policymaking in Japan,* New Delhi: Commonwealth Publishers.

—— (1993) "Subsidiary, Supporter, or Challenger? Local-National Relations in Japan," *Local Government Studies* 19, 2.

Jichirō Jichiken Chūō Suishin Iinkai (1991) *Gaikokujin wa Jūmin desu*, Tokyo: Jichiro Jichiken Chūō Suishin Iinkai.

Kanagawa Shinbun (1997) "Plans for a 'Representative Council' Giving Settled Foreigners a Voice in Policy – Kawasaki sets up an Investigatory Commitee – The First Attempt by Domestic Local Government", 19 October.

Kawamura Chizuko (1997) *"Shinjuku-ku: Kyōsei no Mainasu-men wo Purasu ni Kawaeru*

Machizukuri" in H. Komai and I. Watado (eds) *Jichitai no Gaikokujin Seisaku: Uchinaru Kokusaika he no Torikumi*, Tokyo: Akashi Shoten.

Kawasaki Chihō Jichi Kenkyū Sentā (1991) *Kawasaki-shi no Kokusaika ni Tsuite*, Kawasaki: Kawasaki City Government Document.

Komai, H. (1997) "*Hajime ni – Uchinaru Kokusaika ni yoru Tabun Kyōsei Shakai no Kochiku*," in H. Komai and I. Watado (eds) *Jichitai no Gaikokujin Seisaku: Uchinaru Kokusaika he no Torikumi*, Tokyo: Akashi Shoten.

Kuwahara Hideaki (1989) "*Toshi Gyōsei Kan no Ishiki to Kyōdō: Kikaku, Zaisei, Jinji Kacho Chōsa kara*," *Toshi Mondai* 80, 3 (March): 43–54.

Layton-Henry, Z. (1992) *The Politics of Immigration: Immigration, 'Race' and 'Race' Relations in Post-war Britain*, Oxford: Blackwell.

Machimura, T. (ed) (1990) '*Kokusaika' no Fūkei: Media kara mita Nihon Shakai no Henyō*, Tsukuba, Japan: Kokusaika to media Kenkyukai, Tsukuba University Department of Sociology.

Mainichi Shimbun (1991) "No Entrance to Foreign Women: Business Owners Protest the 'Prostitution Game' with Posters in Shinjuku's Love Hotel District," 18 June.

Miller, M. J. (1994) "Preface," *Annals of the American Academy of Political and Social Sciences*, 534: 8–16.

Mouer, R. and Sugimoto, Y. (1983) "Internationalization as an Ideology in Japanese Society," in H. Mannari and H. Befu (eds.), *The Challenge of Japan's Internationalization: Organization and Culture*. Nishinomiya, Japan: Kwansai Gakuin University.

Muramatsu, M. (1988) *Chihō Jichi: Gendai Seijigaku Sōsei*, Tokyo: Tokyo University Press.

Nihon Toshi Sentā (1995) *Toshi Gaiko: Jichitai no Kokusai Koryu Senryaku*, Tokyo: Kyosei.

Nikka Supōtsa Shimbun (1994) "Shinjuku's Street Girls: Hanging Around has Ended. Down to Less than 10 percent of 400 People," 10 September.

Okuda, M. and Tajima, J. (eds) (1993) *Shinjuku no Ajiakei Gaikokujin: Shakaiteki Jittai Hōkoku*, Tokyo: Mekon.

Reed, S. R. (1986) *Japanese Prefectures and Policymaking*, Pittsburgh, Pa.: University of Pittsburgh Press.

Saitama Shimbun (1991a) "Rumor Defiles Town: Bulletin and Warning Whistles – It Might be a Lie, But if By Chance," 28 November.

—— (1991b) "Town Filled with Rumors: Warning Whistles for Self-Defence," 29 November.

Samuels, R. (1983) *The Politics of Regional Policy in Japan: Localities Incorporated?* Princeton: Princeton University Press.

Steiner, K., Krauss, E. S. and Flanagan, S. C. (eds) (1980) *Political Opposition and Local Politics in Japan*, Princeton: Princeton University Press.

Takahashi, S. (1992) "The Internationalization of Kanagawa Prefecture," in G. D. Hook and M. A. Weiner (eds) *The Internationalization of Japan,* London: Routledge.

Tani, T. (1997) "*Osaka-fu: Kyūrai Gaikokujin-gata Jichitai no Gaikokujin Seisaku to Saikin no Ishiki Chōsa*" in H. Komai and I. Watado (eds) *Jichitai no Gaikokujin Seisaku:* Uchinaru Kokusaika he no Torikumi, Tokyo: Akashi Shoten.

Tezuka, K., Miyajima, T., To, T., and Ito, S. (1992) *Gaikokujin Rōdōsha to Jichitai,* Tokyo: Akashi Shoten.

Tokyo Metropolitan Government, Bureau of Citizens and Cultural Affairs, International Affairs Division (1994) *Kokunai Jichitai no Kokusaika Shisaku Chōsa: Kokunai 29 Jichitai.*

Tokyo Metropolitan Government Thinktank (1996) *Tokyo-to Shokuin Kenshu-sho Chōsa Kenkyū-shitsu Ho* 24, (25 January).

Toshi Mondai (1992) Special Issue on "*Gaikokujin no Shisei Sanka*" 83, 6 (June).

12 NGO support for migrant labor in Japan

Glenda S. Roberts

As the numbers of foreign workers has increased, so have NGOs sprung up to support them. In this chapter I will concentrate on how undocumented migrant workers are served by non-governmental organizations in the greater Tokyo/Yokohama area.[1] By examining these organizations and their activities, we can see the importance of gender in the migration process. In other words, the demand for certain categories of employment is highly gender-specific, with most undocumented male workers entering construction and factory work,and a majority of undocumented women workers as well as "entertainers" with legal visas entering the so-called "water trades."[2] This differentiation leads to major differences in men's and women's experiences of migration. Most importantly it affects the degree to which they can control their daily lives, and the degree to which they can seek redress for violations of their human rights when these occur. This chapter also provides an example of how NGOs uphold human rights and advocate fair treatment of foreign residents within Japan.

These support groups' position as mediators for outsiders in their own society has also been the catalyst for NGOs themselves to question the premises of gender relationships in Japan, and while placing Japanese gender relationships within an international and historical framework of gendered migration, to advocate changes in those relationships.

My research focuses on support groups formed by Japanese citizens to assist foreign residents who are often most disadvantaged: those who have overstayed their visas, those who are working without authorization from the state, people who have entered the country on falsified documents, or people whose documents have been confiscated by *yakuza* brokers when they entered Japan. These are the people the government refers to as illegal workers, but whom people in support groups call simply foreign migrant workers, undocumented workers, or overstayers.[3]

In a 1992 study of structural diversity in the United States, Louise Lamphere and her co-authors ask whether and how new immigrants are being integrated into the major structures of urban life. They concentrate their study on the inter-relationships between mediating institutions, and question the nature of interactions between mediating institutions, migrants, and established residents (Lamphere 1992). The work of the support groups I am studying can also be seen as mediating work, but one step removed. These groups assist foreign migrants, whether they are legally or illegally in Japan, in learning how to make use of the social institutions available to them, and even how to push to open those that are closed to them.

Basically, there are two types of non-governmental support groups for foreigners in Japan. One is a volunteer-based citizen's action-oriented organization, financially supported through donations and, in some cases, grants from foundations or local governments. Many such groups are affiliated with Christian or Buddhist churches, while others are purely secular. The other type is the local labor union, financially supported through membership dues and a percentage of revenues from successful cases, as well as through affiliation with national-level unions. Both types are active in supporting migrant's human rights and in utilizing the Labor Standards Law to redress migrant workers' problems. Non-union groups have developed substantial expertise in problems encountered in daily life, such as medical access problems, family relationship problems, education, housing, immigration status-related issues and re-settlement in the home country. The unions focus somewhat more narrowly, although not exclusively, on labor issues. There is much dialogue and mutual assistance between the two types of groups, and they have formed a national umbrella organization for action, which is outlined at the conclusion of this paper.

The ethnicities and nationalities of migrants assisted by these organizations differ according to locale and the particular expertise of the group, but in this paper I concentrate on groups in the Tokyo metropolitan area, and on shelters and unions that concentrate on undocumented workers. Hence, such groups receive few inquiries for assistance by *Nikkei*, whose largest concentrations of populations are found in Shizuoka, Gunma and Aichi, and who are legal workers. This is not to say that the *Nikkei* population has no need to seek help from NGOs, nor that NGOs do not assist them. It is simply that the NGOs discussed in this study happen not to have large constituencies of *Nikkei* people.

Given the illegality of undocumented workers' presence in Japan, it is difficult to obtain accurate accounting of how many people there are in this situation.[4] If we look at the immigration office estimates on foreign entrants (Table 12.1) who have overstayed their visas, we can see there was a steady increase until 1993, followed by a slight decline.

In 1997, the majority of overstayers were from South Korea, 18.5 percent (52,387); the Philippines, 15 percent (42,547); Thailand, 14 percent (39,513); mainland China, 13.5 percent (38,296); with the next largest tier being Peru, 4.6 percent (12,942); Iran, 4 percent (11,303); and Malaysia, 3.7 percent (10,390). Other overstayers come from Taiwan, Bangladesh, Myanmar (formerly Burma), Pakistan and various other countries unnamed in the statistics. Amongst overstayers from South Korea, the Philippines, Thailand, and Taiwan, women outnumber men. However, these statistics vastly underestimate, since they are taken from those foreigners who were found to have overstayed when leaving Japan.

While national government policy does not recognize or welcome the settlement of foreign migrants in Japan, NGOs have been addressing their presence and assisting them in their daily lives for over a decade. By 1997 there were 145 NGOs supporting migrant workers throughout Japan (Catholic Diocese

Table 12.1 Total estimated number of overstayers

Year	Number
1986	28,000
1989	100,000
1991	159,000
1993	298,646
1995	286,704
1996	284,500
1997	282,986

Source: Homusho, Nyukokukanrikyoku, (eds) in *Kokusai Jinryū*, September 1996: 21, and May 1997: 30.

Note: Figures for 1991–6 were from the month of May; 1997 figures are from the month of January.

of Yokohama Solidarity Center for Migrants 1997). The trends which can be discerned from the cases dealt with by support groups for foreign migrants certainly belie the official stance that Japan has entrants, but no migrants.[5] Foreigners not only enter Japan, but they work there for many years, with increasing numbers marrying and raising children.[6] There are many human consequences of their presence in Japan for the migrants themselves, their children, and for the Japanese people. While migration is a fact, however, responses to questions about the extent to which migrant workers should be incorporated into Japanese society are extremely varied. For instance, a 1995 nationwide random sample survey of 703 people by the *Raifu Dezain Kenkyūsho* (Life Design Institute) revealed that while 52.8 percent of those polled considered the presence of illegal foreign workers "undesirable," 40.7 percent saw it as "undesirable, but unavoidable," 2.8 percent responded "It doesn't bother me" and 0.6 percent responded "It's a good thing."[7] Furthermore, in the same poll, about 80 percent of respondents felt that illegal workers should have medical coverage and labor accident compensation provided, and another 40 percent responded that there should be no discrimination in housing, and that illegal workers should have access to public education (*Raifu Dezain Kenkyūsho* 1997: 121, 122). Although the general public is not convinced of the benefits to Japanese society of migrant labor, the NGOs with whom I have had contact over the past three years are remarkable in their willingness to take on the problems of outsiders, and work toward solutions.

The best way to gain an understanding of the scope of NGO support for undocumented foreign workers is to examine their activities in detail. Let us begin by surveying *Zentōitsu*, a local labor union in Tokyo's Ueno district.

Zentōitsu

Zentōitsu is located in an aging office building off a main thoroughfare, near the Okachimachi station. It was founded in the late 1960s with the purpose of organizing the many small- and medium-sized enterprise workers who populated the area. Organizers from the General Council of Japanese Trade Unions (*Sōhyō*), were despatched to form the union, but *Zentōitsu* was not strictly affiliated with any larger union or political party.[8] This changed in the fall of 1994, when *Zentōitsu* joined the Zenrōkyō, the National Trade Union Council, an independent (non-*Rengo* affiliated) labor union with over 300,000 members.[9] One condition under which *Zentōitsu* agreed to join Zenrōkyō was that Zenrōkyō would promote foreign workers' issues.

Zentōitsu's Foreign Workers' Branch (FWBZ) began in 1992, with twenty Bangladeshi, Iranian and Pakistani workers. *Zentōitsu* had begun to see the need for a foreign workers' branch the previous year, when its leadership encountered several foreigners with serious injuries from labor accidents. The number of cases from foreign workers grew by word of mouth. By January 1998, there were 1,449 members in FWBZ, far surpassing the 550 Japanese workers in the union. Bangaladeshi men make up 50.6 percent, followed by 23.7 percent Pakistani, 6.9 percent Indian, 5.6 percent Senegalese and from other parts of Africa, 5.4 percent Iranian, 1.9 percent Sri Lankan, and the remaining 5.9 percent from other countries. About 80 percent of the cases taken on have been settled, and currently 300 cases are in progress.

Zentōtitsu has close ties with two occupational safety and health centers (the *Zenkoku Anzen Sentā*, the Japan Occupational Safety and Health Resource Center, and the local Tokyo Eastern District Occupational Safety and Health Center, or *Tōbu*. These provide useful advice for *Zentōitsu*u while also offering venues for international linkages *vis-à-vis* labor conferences. In turn, *Zentōitsu* is a kind of laboratory for these occupational health and safety organizations. *Zentōitsu* also has ties with other local unions which support foreigners, and is a joint member of the Foreign Workers Executive Committee. This includes three other local unions that organize foreigners in the greater Tokyo area – the National Union of General Workers Tokyo South District (NUGW), *Zenkoku Ippan* Foreign Laborers' Union, and the Kanagawa City Union – as well as *Tōbu* and the *Kenri Shuntō* (Capitol Liaison Council for Rights). The NUGW comprises approximately 500 foreign members, mostly English teachers from the USA, England, Canada and Australia. *Zenkoku Ippan* has 200 members, previously mostly manufacturing workers from Bangladesh and Iran, but now 60 percent *Nikkei* Brazilians.[10] Kanagawa City Union has 586 members, mostly in manufacturing and construction, of whom approximately half are Japanese, 40 percent are Korean newcomers, and 7 percent are *Nikkeijin* from South America. Their joint activities include publishing a White Paper and other materials on the problems of migrant workers, rallies for migrant workers' rights, joint strategy and problem-solving meetings, plus joint attendance at international conferences on such topics as migrant workers and human rights, or migrant workers' response to Asian Pacific Economic Cooperation Organization (APEC).

The Executive Secretary of *Zentōitsu*, Mr Torii, also holds executive office in *Tōbu*. It is, in turn, responsible to the *Zenkoku Anzen Sentā* (Japanese Occupational Safety and Health Resource Center, or JOSHRC), which is located in Mita. Mr Torii told me that *Zentōitsu* is a kind of testing ground for their ideas, as it affords them access to small companies. Because of his affiliation with these two groups, Mr Torii noted he is known as the *Anzen Kenkō no Torii*, or Safety and Health Torii. He has represented the JOSHRC at European Work Hazards

Conferences, and has a comprehensive awareness of workers' problems worldwide. Indeed, *Zentōitsu* sent a member to support US workers in their strike against Bridgestone in 1996, and to Korea to support the massive strikes there in January 1997. Communication with other small labor unions in the Tokyo area is extensive, and they frequently band together to hold rallies on behalf of foreigners, such as the Day for Migrant and Immigrant Workers' Rights, which has been held yearly since March 1993.

Zentōitsu *and foreign workers*

It was at the request of the *Minatomachi Shinryōsho* Medical Clinic in Yokohama that *Zentōitsu* first began accepting foreign workers, in the summer of 1991. The Clinic had been called upon to assist a Ghanian man who was suffering from lung cancer. He had worked for a year and a half at a plastics factory in Chiba, but had not been paid. He wanted to return to Ghana, so *Zentōitsu* assisted him by negotiating with his company. They succeeded in getting the company to pay this worker the five million yen ($50,000 at 100 yen/$1) he was owed in back wages. As he had to repatriate before receiving the settlement, *Zentōitsu* wired it to his bank account in Ghana.

Then came another call, this time about a Mr Rana from Bangladesh who had lost three fingers in a press at the factory in Chiba where he was employed. The factory was a subcontractor for Honda Motors. *Zentōitsu* has three branches in the city where the factory is located, so they agreed to take on this case (which I will detail later). By visiting the injured worker at the large general hospital where he was being treated, Mr Torii became aware of the seriousness of foreign workers' problems, as the waiting room was full of foreigners who had been injured on the job. He ended up talking with these men, some of whom eventually became members of *Zentōitsu*. Through word of mouth, more and more foreign workers began calling *Zentōitsu*. This led to the establishment of the FWBZ. It began in April 1992 with twenty Bangladeshi, Iranians and Pakistanis, marked by a barbecue party at Noda City Park.

By July 1994 there were 500 Japanese and 570 foreigners enrolled in *Zentōitsu*. By the end of 1994, the total number of foreigners was 591. *Zentōitsu*'s foreign workers' branch is supported by union fees of 3,000 yen per month per member, plus funds received from the *Kyōdō Kumiai Hoken* (Cooperative Union Insurance). It receives half of its operating expenses from the latter insurance schemes. Each foreign worker pays a membership fee of 4,000 yen upon joining. Thereafter, monthly dues are 3,000 yen, one-third of which is allotted to a cooperative insurance scheme (*Zen Rōsai Hoken*), one-third to a labor bank and recoverable when the worker leaves the union, and one-third towards union overhead fees. The union also takes approximately 10 percent of any settlement negotiated under the auspices of the union on behalf of a member. When I interviewed Mr Torii in July 1994, he said that he would like to increase the scope of their movement and make it a national center for foreign workers, but *Zentōitsu* lacks the funding. They are prohibited by law from accepting donations.

Workers usually join local unions after there has been a serious breakdown in employer/employee relations, so as to seek the union's expertise as a negotiating agent. The three most typical problems which bring in members are unpaid wages, sudden dismissal and labor accidents. These sorts of problems are nothing new to local unions, which organize workers in the most vulnerable sector of the economy, where wages go unpaid because many small firms operate on the edge, workers are dismissed suddenly for the same reason, and they are not compensated as the law requires. Labor accidents are likely the smaller the company, as firms neglect to use safety devices in order to increase production.[11] Japanese workers themselves find difficulty in resolving these problems without the assistance of a union, but foreigners, because of language difficulties, the vulnerability of their undocumented status and their lack of knowledge, would be unable to utilize the system without the expertise and advocacy of the union. The following three cases, related to me by Mr Torii, represent typical problems that are brought to the union by foreign workers.

Company H: unpaid wages

Company H, a chrome-plating manufacturer in Saitama, employed twenty people including non-regular workers, among them fourteen Bangladeshi and South Indians. On 17 February 1993, the owner of the company committed suicide. Apparently the financial condition of the company was worsening, and people who seemed to be loan collectors were coming on a daily basis to press him. The workers, including the Japanese workers, had not been paid for between two and four months. Amongst these were three men whose checks for September and October's salary, which they had received in December, bounced.

The workers – both foreign and Japanese – came to *Zentōitsu* for help after the owner committed suicide. Meanwhile, the company was transferred to someone else. The union decided to file with the Labor Standards Office under the Payment System for Unpaid Wages clause of the Law Securing Wage Payments. Under this system, the Labor Social Welfare Group (*jigyōdan*) pays 60 percent of the unpaid wages for those laborers who became unemployed due to the bankruptcy of their companies.

The problem with these men making use of this law, as is the case of most foreign workers, is that most of them were not in possession of the necessary documents (such as wage slips, time cards, wage statements, and so on), to prove their cases. Upon investigating the company, the Labor Standards Office (LSO) found these documents missing. Mr Torii noted that, perhaps because the authorities want to make it difficult to utilize the system, it requires quite a strict investigation and evidence, so it was unclear as to whether *Zentōitsu*'s claim would be recognized. Fortunately, one of the union members knew the home telephone number of the factory head, and when the LSO contacted him, they found that he had taken charge of the relevant documents. Thus the work toward authorization was able to go ahead, and both the Japanese laborers' and the foreigners' applications were processed. All procedures were completed by the middle of September, apart from those of a few laborers with whom *Zentōitsu* had lost contact, and payment was expected in November. It should be noted here that during negotiations with the Labor Ministry, termed the Day-long Action for the Livelihood and Rights of Foreign Workers, *Zentōitsu* proposed that the Labor Ministry should reform the payment system for unpaid wages to make it more accessible. (Handling procedures are currently troublesome and must be completed within six months of the beginning of unemploymen. Because of this there are many cases which cannot be handled, particularly but not exclusively among foreign workers). Nothing has come of *Zentōitsu*'s proposal yet.

The case of Company K in Saitama: sudden dismissal

At company K which manufactures metal parts for toys, two Bengali workers who had protested a lowering of their wages were dismissed without warning in June 1993. *Zentōitsu* gave notice to the firm several times, and the Kasuga Labor Standards Office first urged and then directed them to comply. Although they did make a few improvements on their safety measures, the manager continued to strongly reject payment of *kaiko yokoku teatekin* (supplemental wage for notification of dismissal).[12]

On 1 April, as a one-day action, *Zentōitsu* went to pay a call on the K company. The same day, twenty *Zentōitsu* members put on armbands and, hoisting a banner, drove up to and surrounded the company president's residence. Mr Torii noted that the president finally gave in and responded to *Zentōitsu*'s demands, although he still repeatedly protested that he had no money.

Company S in Chiba: labor accident

At the introduction of a Ms I, who works at a pharmacy in a city in Saitama where small factories which hire many foreigners are concentrated, Mr Rana, a young man from Bangladesh, first appeared at *Zentōitsu* on 14 November 1991. Ms I receives many requests for advice from foreign workers who cannot go to a clinic because they lack medical insurance.[13] Mr Rana had lost three fingers. When Mr Torii found that Rana had met the accident working for a company in a district of Chiba where *Zentōitsu* is active, he agreed to take on the case.

The company was a metal press factory, sub-contracting for Honda, mostly manufacturing metal molds. Besides the company president, there was only one other Japanese employee, and two foreign employees, Mr Rana and his cousin: typical of very small enterprises. One week after he began employment at that factory, Mr Rana lost the three middle fingers of his right hand while he was operating the press. It was a disability of the eighth grade, which, according to the Workmen's Accident Compensation Insurance Law, requires compensation of the lump sum equivalent to 503 days of basic daily benefit.

The accident had taken place on 7 September, two months before Mr Rana's visit to *Zentōitsu*. The safety mechanism was not on the machine. Mr Torii noted that, after hearing about the pattern of the accident and the sound of the machine in operation, it seemed that there was a strong possibility that the press came down twice (rather than once as it should have), which was indicative of equipment failure.

Immediately after the accident the company president declined to file labor accident papers for Mr Rana, citing his overstayer visa status as an excuse.[14]

Instead, he told him, "I'll give you $10,000 (1,000,000 yen) if you return home immediately." He did eventually begin the enrollment procedures for labor accident insurance, but used his own company bank account number as the account to which unemployment payments should be made. It was at this point that Mr Rana decided to act. After *Zentōitsu* heard Rana's story, they decided to negotiate immediately with the company, and together with the East District Occupational Safety and Health Center, they undertook investigations at the clinic where Mr Rana was being treated, and at the company.

This was a small factory in the midst of the fields, in a residential district. Mr Torii doubted that it had ever occurred to the company president that a labor union might pursue the case. According to Mr Torii, the president appeared to be in shock, and kept repeating the company's version of the incident. None the less, he admitted that the safety mechanism had not been attached to the press.

Zentōitsu drew up a memorandum of agreement (*kyôteisho*) which they then confirmed. Labor Accident Insurance procedures would be begun immediately, the payment address for unemployment and the one-time compensation for injury would be changed to Mr Rana's own account, and henceforth the company would negotiate with *Zentōitsu*.

After this, Mr Rana continued to be treated, and received certification of disability on 22 January 1992. *Zentōitsu* then went to the president to begin discussions about additional compensation payments. The president held out, stating he could not pay more than one million yen. Mr Torii noted that he expressed no regret whatever concerning his company's responsibility for this accident. In response, *Zentōitsu* withdrew from negotiations, and on 13 March 1992, filed a legal suit against the company seeking reparation for injury.

When the case opened, the company president began telling the judge an entirely different story from the one he had told *Zentōitsu* during negotiation. He asserted that there had been a safety mechanism on the press at the time of the accident, and he intimated that Mr Rana had deliberately injured himself. The judge of the Twenty-Seventh Tokyo District Civil Court then expressed publicly his opinion that disability compensation payments to foreigners should be settled according to the wage level of the foreigner's home country. This was even before the company itself had made such an argument. In response, *Zentōitsu* put on a one day action on 8 March 1993, lodging a protest document with the Twenty-Seventh District Civil Court.

By October 1994, probably due to *Zentōitsu*'s protest, the case was re-assigned to a collegiate court of three judges, with the Chief Judge of the Twenty-Seventh District Civil Court as the head. The case entered conciliation, and in December 1994, the parties reached a settlement of 6,000,000 yen ($60,000).

Mr Torii said that, through Mr Rana's case, *Zentōitsu* discovered many of the obstacles to realization of foreign workers' rights: the inadequacy of the court translator system, the unhelpful attitude of the Labor Standards Office, the pro-company bias of many judges, the difficulty for foreigners of opening a bank account, and problems in matching prostheses to skin color in a country where the only prostheses available are manufactured to match the Japanese skin tone spectrum.

While this advocacy work is personally rewarding, it is also risky. In 1993, Mr

Torii was incapacitated for several months when a company manager responded to his lodging a complaint by dousing him with gasoline and igniting it. In 1995, another local labor union leader was injured when he was assaulted by gangsters who were attempting to stop him from assisting a Korean worker against whom they held a grudge.

Future prospects

Despite their ability to unite over perceived injustices, foreign workers are unlikely to form their own fully foreign-staffed branch union in the near future, as hoped for by some Japanese union activists. Only workers with legitimate visa status could safely take on the role, which resticts the field to foreigners married to Japanese citizens. While economic feasibility is among the problems, it may not be the most difficult to overcome.

The most important obstacle noted by Mr Torii is the factionalism among the constituents that arise from ethnic and class differences. The local unions involved in foreign workers issues tend to vary in ethnic make-up as well as the nature of the jobs which the majority of their workers are performing. While Kanagawa City union is overwhelmingly composed of members who are Korean newcomers, the Nanbu union is European, American, Canadian and Australian. Within its own ranks, *Zentōitsu* has had problems keeping peace between Iranians on one hand, and Pakistanis and Bangladeshi on the other. Mr Torii observed that people bring the political views of their origins with them, and nationalism becomes an issue.

Tension also stems from the philosophical basis of the different unions. Mr Torii noted that the *Zenkoku Ippan* FLU consists mainly of former Japanese activists, rather than labor organizers. In his view, FLU is more like a volunteer group, interested in a wide assortment of human rights and political problems such as nuclear testing. He voiced doubt that disparate unions could unite. Although the Nanbu union does cooperate with the other unions, its agenda is markedly different, owing to the nature of the work its members perform. While workers in the other unions are fighting for just remuneration for injury, medical coverage and safe working conditions, workers in Nanbu are fighting for job tenure, improvement and standardization in work conditions and salary schedules, workman's compensation, and so on. Foreigners who have contracts to teach their native language and a proper working visa have protected and respected status, compared with undocumented foreigners performing blue-collar work. The former group see benefit in forming a union, as they are just as vulnerable to rationalization as are other workers, but nevertheless, among foreign workers, they occupy a favored status. Some foreign workers who perform blue-collar jobs recognize and resent this. They regard Westerner union members with disdain, viewing them as self-important. They point to some Westerners' inability and/or refusal to try to speak Japanese as the sign of their general lack of willingness to adapt to Japan or, more immediately, to make efforts at solidarity with non-Western foreigners who cannot speak English.

There are also arguments among these unions *vis-à-vis* how to solicit new membership. Should this be through study groups on Marxism and exploitation, or through analysis of daily experience (this is your problem; this is how you can go through the union to solve it). Furthermore, while they have achieved some success in expanding membership, the unions have difficulties in collecting dues regularly. Many foreign workers join only when they have a problem, and then pay dues until it is solved, or they join and cease paying dues until a problem occurs, and then begin paying again. One foreign staff worker lamented that some see the union as a company providing services rather than as a social movement which needs their allegiance and support. This attitude may change as workers increasingly settle in Japan, and see the benefits of long-term membership.

Finally, Mr Torii noted that the more his volunteer staff working on behalf of their compatriots associate with Japanese and other professionals, the more they forget their real purpose, and who their constituency is. They become "office workers," proud of being able to disassociate themselves from manual work. Indeed, for some of these workers, their jobs in Japan are their first manual jobs, as their backgrounds in their home countries are middle-class.

Zentōitsu and other local unions have been able to negotiate workers' cases successfully, taking the employers to court when necessary, so as to secure the compensation the worker was entitled to under the Labor Standards Law. Their mission is a familiar one: labor safety, job security, wage assurance, a decent livelihood for workers. These unions see their activities for foreigners as the same as those for Japanese workers: protecting the legal rights of those in the most vulnerable industrial sector, the very small manufacturing and construction firms. They are backed by the Labor Standards Law which, though not without bureaucratic difficulties, is effective, and prohibits any form of discrimination against workers because of their nationality (Hirowatari 1993). While FWBZ clientele are undocumented, their work itself is legitimate and unstigmatized from the legal and social viewpoint. FWBZ members are, by and large, free agents. Their jobs are often dangerous and unpleasant, their working conditions unstable. They come to Japan largely on their own auspices, finding jobs through word of mouth from their countrymen. They join the union openly, attend union activities, get together on Sundays to share information, or take advantage of the very inexpensive medical clinic sponsored by the union and a medical NGO. They may also join the Japanese language lessons offered at *Zentōitsu*.

None of the local unions mentioned has more than a handful of women members, apart from the NUGW South, which organizes language instructors and some office workers. This reflects largely the gendered segmentation of the labor market for undocumented workers which has been mentioned earlier. Support groups for undocumented women workers are found in women's shelters.

Another view of gendered migration: women's shelters

Women's shelters, in contrast to local unions, deal with problems for which there are often no effective remedies in place: forced or exploitative prostitution, domestic violence, irreparable or even fatal health damage. As foreign women stay increasing lengths of time in Japan, problems related to pregnancy, marriage, divorce, residency status, and the nationality of children are also prominent.

The legal apparatus for upholding the rights of many foreign migrant women is either absent or inaccessible. Why? The reason is that many foreign women end up coming to Japan to work in sectors which fit under the gendered category which Thanh-Dam Truong (1996) refers to as "reproductive labor," such as sex worker or mail-order bride. Domestic worker is another, but for reasons I shall not elaborate on here, this is not a large category for foreign migrant women in Japan (see Douglass, ch. 5). These jobs are open because, with the increasing affluence of the society, the supply of Japanese women willing to enter them has declined. The entertainment industry grew with the bubble economy, and Japanese sex tours to Thailand and the Philippines had been curtailed due to a protest campaign in the 1970s. These factors set the conditions for the importation of women from abroad, explicitly supported by immigration policy, which contains a legal "entertainer" category of worker to fill this need (Yamanaka 1993).

Gender, as it is tied in with the kinds of labor in demand, and the social legitimacy of such labor, does matter in the experience of migration to Japan. Women in the sex industry are often duped into coming to Japan by networks of wily and vicious brokers who are connected with, if not themselves members of, the *yakuza*. Once they arrive, they are often forced into debt bondage to be 'repaid' by sex work. In the worst cases their movements and even food intake is restricted, they have no control over changing jobs, and many operate in isolated situations under virtual slavery (Oshima and Francis 1989, Matsuda 1992, Babior 1993). The conditions in the sex industry are such that these women often find their actions and movements severely curtailed by brokers and bar owners.[15]

While male workers in construction and factory work are in the peripheral sector of the legitimate economy, women in the sex industry are beyond the framework of socially legitimate work. Male workers have at least a small likelihood of seeing their labor grievances addressed, while female sex workers' injuries go uncompensated and unnoted, except in the danger they are perceived to pose to the customer.

As Robyn Rowland in her work on human rights theory (1995) has pointed out, choices are constrained by such factors as economics, social ideologies, personal convictions, and gendered power relations. She further states that human rights are differentially structured around race, class, age, marital status, sexuality, religion, culture, and able-bodiedness. Women, she notes, have more constraints. In Japan, these constraints are evidenced in the total ineffectualness of the legal framework (including the Prostitution Prevention Law of 1956) to redress the problems of women in the sex industry (Herbert 1996: 30). This situation is in no way specific to Japan. Truong and del Rosario note:

> In their attempt to control the traffic in sex workers and mail order brides, European Union states have mainly placed their control on the women who therefore have to bear the main burden of proof. In this practice, state practices buttress the interests and power of individual men as husbands, fiancées, or pimps.
>
> (Truong and del Rosario 1995: 53)

As in Japan, women are deported and criminalized for violating prostitution laws, and the customers walk away unscathed.[16]

In 1994, there were seven privately-run shelters for women in the Tokyo/Yokohama metropolitan area.[17] The three with which I have had contact are *Saalaa, Mizura* and HELP. The services provided by these shelters are diverse, ranging from housing and meals to medical and legal referral, counseling, negotiation with public offices such as the social welfare and immigration offices, day-care advice, and provision of information on all manner of issues surrounding residency in Japan. In 1996, the shelters I studied reported increasing numbers of women seeking assistance with problems related to their efforts to remain living in Japan, with many seeking to legalize or nullify relationships with Japanese men or other partners, establish citizenship for their children, gain entrance to public day-care or education systems, and so on. This contrasts to only a few years ago where most women coming to shelters sought assistance in leaving Japan to return home. As a staff member of one shelter put it, "We used to provide *kikoku enjo*; now we provide *seikatsu enjo* [livelihood support]."

The numbers of women with babies and small children coming to shelters is also on the rise, and staff at *Saalaa* note that they are unequipped, financially and in terms of space, staffing, and training, to handle this new development. While staff seek public welfare funds for women who have resident status, their hands are tied when it comes to women who are undocumented.

In 1995 the House of Emergency in Love and Peace (HELP) reported a rise in the number of women with mental health problems, developed over increasingly long periods of stay in the sex industry. Meeting the needs of migrant women, and empowering them to get back on their feet takes an enormous amount of effort and commitment on the part of the shelter staff and volunteers. Shelters experience staff turnover when new volunteers lose their enthusiasm upon realizing that the women whom they had considered pitiable and in need of assistance did not want the kind of assistance they were ready to offer, or upon realizing indignantly that some migrants leave Japan once only to return again to the sex industry, or that they marry men with whom even minimal communication is lacking.[18] Volunteers also quit when they realize the amount of energy needed.[19]

There are significant differences among the three shelters discussed. I shall take a closer look at each institution.

HELP

The House of Emergency in Love and Peace (HELP) has been in operation since 1986. As the women seeking shelter are sometimes running away from people who have a high stake in keeping them captive, safety is a constant concern. As HELP, unlike other shelters in the area, combines offices and housing space in the same building, such precautions are entirely necessary. There are no signs proclaiming its presence, nor do HELP personnel give out their address to strangers, but instead arrange to meet them at the train station and escort them to the office. One cannot help but feel cautious when approaching the office. A warning bell rings sharply when one treads on the stairway leading to the entrance.

By 1997 2,050 foreign women had been sheltered, over two-thirds of them from Thailand. HELP reports that 90 percent of the foreign women sheltered have been working in *mizushōbai*, the term used in Japan to refer to the nightlife industries of entertainment and sex, found in bars, clubs, hostess clubs, "soaplands" and so on (Allison 1994: 7). In 1998, about one-quarter of the women sheltered say that they had been sex workers prior to seeking shelter. The average stay at HELP is twelve days. The overwhelming majority of foreign women seeking shelter are from Thailand and the Philippines, but the ratios have changed over time. In 1986 eighty-three Filipinas and no Thais sought shelter; in 1987, ninety-nine Filipinas and nine Thais sought shelter. This changed dramatically in 1988, when 144 Thai women were sheltered and fifty-two Filipinas. Ever since then, Thai women have outnumbered Filipinas by far.[20] From 1986 to 1997, 2,050 foreign women and 189 children were sheltered. (See Table 12.2.) Besides being a women's shelter, HELP is an information and referral service. Unlike the government welfare offices, its telephones operate around the clock, and receive over 4,000 calls per year, up from about 2,000 calls in 1994.

Thai women predominate among foreign women in two other women's shelters in Kanagawa prefecture, *Mizura* and *Saalaa*. *Mizura* is open to all women, foreign or Japanese, while *Saalaa* shelters only foreign women. (See Table 12.3.)

According to the director of *Mizura*, the Thai government estimates there are approximately 70,000 Thai women overstayers in Japan. She believes that about 50–60,000 of these women are in forced prostitution. Women from Thailand tend to have the fewest support resources available to them once in Japan. They lack the solidarity or networking benefits which Filipinas may share from frequenting Mass at the Catholic Church, they are illiterate in Japanese and English, and many have had little education in Thailand. Some of them are barely teenagers. Moreover, the only visa available to most Thai women is the tourist visa, so they are not covered by even the minimal contractual benefits which the entertainer visa status carries.[21]

Origins

Many support organizations spring from religious institutions. HELP has its origins in the Japan Women's Christian Temperance Union, which was founded in Tokyo by Yajima Kajiko in 1886, and which consolidated a number of locally-based organizations of the Tokyo Women's Reform Society (Babior 1993: 86). According to Japan WCTU literature, HELP was started "because we wanted to try to put into practice Christ's teachings to love they neighbor." They note another motive: that it would be "a stimulant and a hope to return to our founding spirit." They also wanted it to be a sign of repentance for sins which Japan committed in its past and today (*Nihon Kirisutōkyō Fujin Kyōfukai* 1988: 33). Although the latter document does not elaborate on these "sins," it may refer to the JWCTU's historical role in lobbying for the repatriation of Japanese *karayuki san*, who were sold into prostitution and worked throughout Asia in the early twentieth century.[22] Their rationale for this effort stemmed not from humanitarian concerns for the *karayuki san*, but from the conviction that *karayuki san* cast shame on Japan's international image (Oshima and Francis 1989: 189–90, Babior 1993: 107). Nevertheless, the JWCTU saw the need for providing means for a living for the *karayuki san* and other women in need of employment, and established a dormitory and training center for them. Garon argues that the JWCTU

Table 12.2 Women sheltered at HELP, 1986–97

Year	Filipinas	Thais	Other foreigners	Japanese
1986	83	0	5 (2)	74 (23)
1987	99 (4)	9	7 (4)	140 (41)
1988	52 (4)	144	7 (1)	80 (35)
1989	13 (2)	131	8 (2)	62 (28)
1990	16 (1)	119	8 (4)	55 (22)
1991	10 (2)	270 (1)	19 (3)	33 (18)
1992	14 (7)	210 (3)	47 (8)	23 (15)
1993	25 (7)	220 (9)	17 (5)	39 (14)
1994	14 (14)	160 (11)	16 (4)	54 (15)
1995	9 (5)	106 (10)	16(4)	60 (25)
1996	20 (26)	47 (12)	25 (8)	84 (35)
1997	8 (6)	40 (7)	46 (13)	0
Total	363 (78)	1,456 (53)	231 (58)	704 (271)

Source: HELP Newsletters.
Note:　Grand total 1986–97: 2,050 foreign women and 189 children sheltered.　Numbers in ( )
refer to children sheltered. * Figures for the number of Japanese women and children sheltered were not available for 1997.

Table 12.3 Women sheltered at *Saalaa*, September 1992–December 1997

Date	Thais	Filipinas	Chinese	Korean	Others	Total
September 1992 – March 1993	40	2				42
April 1993 – March 1994	72	5	1		1	79
April 1994 – March 1995	52	6	3	4	2	67
April 1995 – March 1996	17	13			2	32
April 1996 – March 1997	7	12	1		8	28
April 1997 – December 1997	5	7	1	1	3	17
Total	193	45	6	5	16	265

Source: *Saalaa* Newsletters.
Note:　Ninety-one children have accompanied seventy-one women from September 1992 until
December 1997, their numbers increasing steadily since Saalaa's inception: 1992–3: (1),
1993–4: (10) 1994–5 (12), 1995–6 (21) April 1996–March 1997 (30) April 97–December
1997 (17). Cases concerning divorce and domestic violence have increased since the third
year, accompanied by much longer stays at the shelter.

and other moral reform groups were influential in government policy-making at this time:

> Committed to a small, inexpensive bureaucracy, the inter-war Japanese government actively supported and sometimes subsidized the efforts of Christian social work organizations, notably the Salvation Army and the WCTU. These organizations in turn served the government, operating shelters for the poor and rescue missions for ex-prostitutes.
>
> (Garon 1997: 112)

Indeed, this trend is still visible, in the sense that NGOs tackle the problems of migrant workers largely invisible to official government assistance.

HELP's main financial contributors at its inception were the Ichikawa Fusae Foundation, the JWCTU (which donated building space plus funds), privately solicited contributions, and feminist groups (Babior 1993: 306). By 1992, it had become almost self-supporting, through private donations, and grants from the Tokyo municipal government. How much does the JWCTU affiliation influence HELP's mode of operations? It would probably be inaccurate to say not at all, since the WCTU connection remains, and some of the staff and many of the volunteers are Christian. But when I questioned HELP's director, Ms Mizuho Matsuda, about this, she responded that it is her policy not to exert religious influence on the women who seek shelter.[23] Although there are no doubt people within the WCTU who would like to convert HELP's clientele, Matsuda said that she would not hire them as staff members. She commented that one reason it is so difficult to find capable staff is that she excludes the evangelists, who are likely to seek out such work. To Ms Matsuda, HELP's basic policy is to respect the will of the person who is seeking assistance, support her independence, and to treat her with equality.[24] She also noted it is important not to foster dependency.[25]

Ms Matsuda, who built her career in administration and counseling work in Pakistan and Singapore for the World Christian Student Federation and the Christian Conference, took over from Ms Oshima as Director of HELP in 1988. In July 1994 I asked her how HELP had changed since she first arrived. She responded that, under her guidance, HELP had been given a facelift, and had been transformed from a very dreary and institutional setting to one which boasts color, comfortable albeit worn furniture, flowers, and a television. For women who have been living under great duress, a warm environment is reassuring. Ms Matsuda told me she wants the women who stay at the shelter to feel at home. Although HELP has not completely discarded its institutional style, redecorating seems to have been an important marker of Matsuda's philosophy. However, HELP is constrained by space and budget in the extent to which it can change its surroundings.

Ms Matsuda's comments also illustrate a process of increasing professionalism as HELP staff learned how to deal with the problems encountered in running a shelter. At first, she said, they did not know how to care for the women who sought their assistance. They only thought of them as pitiable (*kawaisō*), and ended up trying to help them without obstructing their independence. As an example, she told me that one of the women staying at HELP was marking up the furniture, but the staff had no idea how to handle this behavior. They eventually realized that this woman was having psychological problems, and referred her to a mental health professional. Ms Matsuda noted that every NGO has similar problems at first, of not knowing where to begin, or how to actually carry out their objectives, especially if the staff consists of new volunteers. She estimates that the move towards professionalism has been the biggest change in HELP since she took over. She noted ruefully that this is probably also why some people see HELP as *tsumetai* (cold, unfeeling).

In the autumn of 1996, HELP had six full-time, regular employees, including two resident housekeeping staff and a member of staff from Thailand. There were also three part-time workers including one from the Philippines. Ten volunteers assisted with babysitting.

Since 1990, HELP has received $80,000 annually in general support from the Tokyo municipal government. Its total yearly expenses amount to about $400,000. While some support groups are opposed to receiving government support as they view it as hypocritical, Ms Matsuda is of the opinion that it has been of use since the economic downturn, and has given them flexibility in operations, but if they were not receiving it, they could manage by fundraising. She noted, too, that being a recipient of public funds has also aided other such NGOs in obtaining funds. Until 1989, HELP charged its lodgers 3,500 yen per day for room and board. Since then, however, Ms Matsuda decided not to charge the women from foreign countries, regardless of their financial resources. In principle, at HELP, Japanese women have to pay the daily fee themselves, or the social welfare office will pay for them. In 1986, the Shinjuku Social Welfare Office signed contracts with HELP to provide temporary shelter for women with nowhere to stay.

As HELP receives municipal funding, it is required to keep strict financial accounts which are made open to the public. Every three years, HELP's books are audited by a public accountant. Hygiene must also be carefully maintained, as this too is under inspection.

Just as a union card offers some legitimacy to foreign workers, a grant from the city government lends a sufficient cloak of respectability to HELP so that the Immigration Office treats them less harshly than previously, and the police no longer press as sharply for answers as to the whereabouts of women who had stayed at the shelter (which HELP staff do not divulge). In terms of changes in operating procedures since receiving funding, Ms Matsuda noted only that the report-writing requirement of government funding is time-consuming.

Mizura and *Salaa*

HELP has the longest history of the women's shelters in the area. It is useful to compare its operational style and programmatic thrust to similar organizations which have followed. I look now at Kanagawa Women's Space *Mizura*, a telephone counseling hotline, women's shelter, and women's labor union founded in 1990, and *Saalaa* (literally, a place to stay), which opened in 1992 and operates a women's shelter.

Organizational style

HELP seems more strictly run than these other two shelters. Part of the difference undoubtedly lies in the substantial influence and resources of the long-standing

Japan WCTU. HELP's facility, which is owned by the JWCTU, contains its offices as well as kitchen, dining room and shelter lounge all on one floor, although the lodgings are separate. The staff have worked hard to improve the comfort of the shelter and to maintain the privacy of the lodgers by keeping the public and most volunteers out except for defined hours. Nevertheless, it is not the same as having offices and shelter space totally separate, as at *Mizura*. Furthermore, the *Mizura* apartment has no curfew and no overnight staff. Moreover, while HELP allows its residents to cook ethnic dishes for the evening meal if they want to cook, it also employs a cook who provides hot meals so that women who do not wish to cook, or who cannot cook, can still eat. Because HELP contracts its services with government welfare offices, it is obliged to provide clean sheets, regular meals, and so on. *Mizura* is not bound by such contracts, and dwellers are responsible for cooking, cleaning, and so on, themselves. The *Mizura* Director, Abe Hiroko, remarked that the staff assume that whoever stays at *Mizura*'s apartment knows how to take care of a place inasmuch as they have lived in Japan up to now. On the other hand, if the person could not take responsibility for herself, *Mizura* would refer her to *Saalaa*, which does have overnight staff.

Mizura was founded in 1990 by a group of women who were dissatisfied with the Equal Employment Opportunity Act of 1986. They began as a hotline with an unrestricted remit. Finding that many of the women calling in were in need of a shelter, whether they were foreign women fleeing from forced prostitution or spousal abuse, or Japanese women seeking shelter from dysfunctional relationships, they then acquired an apartment for this purpose. A fundamental difference between *Mizura* and the other women's shelters is that *Mizura* is also a registered local union which specializes in women's employment problems, such as sexual harassment, dismissal, and so on. Ms Abe, like Ms Matsuda, is a seasoned professional activist, although her roots are in the student and labor organizing movements, rather than the Christian social activist movement. She says that she emphasizes practical, not theoretical, feminism, and that while some of the group would identify themselves as feminists, others would not. She said they didn't waste much time discussing this issue. *Mizura*'s funding comes mainly from donations and membership dues, but they also received one-off donations of $20,000 from the Toyota Foundation and $10,000 from the Niwano Foundation. Furthermore, the union takes 10 percent of whatever is received as compensation when they negotiate with a company on a woman's behalf, and it charges 1,000 yen per month in dues. Even so, this is not sufficient to keep them financially afloat, and they have a deficit.

The same problem confronts *Saalaa*, which also operates on donations from individuals and the Catholic diocese. In 1996, *Saalaa* reported increasing financial pressure as fewer single women sought shelter, while mothers with children were becoming commonplace. They had no room in the budget for the cost of baby food and diapers, and fundraising was proving difficult. One staff member noted the general populace could not see the need for sheltering foreign women and children, and asked why *Saalaa* did not just send them back to where they came from.

Although the organizational styles between the two groups are quite different, their basic policy toward the women who use their shelters is similar. Like HELP,

Mizura also seeks to get women to make their own decisions. *Mizura* is also involved in support activities for women who want to stay in Japan, while to my knowledge, HELP sees its mission more strictly as a shelter, a facilitator for women who wish to leave Japan, and as an advocate for human rights for women on the national and international levels. *Mizura*, noting an increase in cases dealing with marital problems of foreign women and Japanese men, is planning to create a group to help foreign women learn to understand and negotiate the school system. Once one group learns, Ms Abe remarked, they can then pass on their knowledge to others. In July 1995 *Mizura* noted an increase in cases of problem marriages, over 90 percent of them being between Japanese men and foreign women. *Mizura* has negotiated with the city social welfare office to allow foreign women's children into daycare facilities even if the women are overstayers. When I asked Ms Abe how she managed to negotiate for overstayers when I had had to show my passport when applying for public daycare services, she replied that she points out to the social welfare official, "You are not the Immigration Office." Ms Abe's long experience as a union organizer probably stands her in good stead when dealing with bureaucracy.

There are limits to the programs *Mizura* and *Saalaa* can provide their clientele, because of their tight funding. *Mizura* reported they would like to have a foreign staff member trained in counseling, but they cannot afford to hire one. Ms Abe commented that *Mizura* is too busy trying to satisfy daily needs to do much else. *Saalaa* is in the same situation.

Role vis-à-vis government institutions

Municipal government offices such as the Women's Counseling Office in the Social Welfare Bureau maintain lines of communication with women's shelters, making referrals to and seeking advice from them. Because of the official policy regarding overstayers, they do not allow undocumented foreign women to stay in the shelters which they manage, but they send them on to HELP, *Mizura* or *Saalaa*. When I attended a public meeting of *Saalaa*, I found that some staff of a Yokohama City Women's Counseling Office had come in an unofficial capacity. During the discussion period, one of them spoke at length, urging NGOs to press the government to make facilities, services and moneys available to foreigners, whether documented or undocumented. She said the money is there, the need is there, and people should press for the necessary funding. Later, a male staff member of a Yokohama City Women's Counseling Office told me that some from his office might not like his involvement with and interest in the shelter, but others want to lend a hand. By the summer of 1995, *Saalaa* had an official from the Yokohama City Office on its Board of Directors. This person's practical information and know-how about how the government operates is reportedly quite useful to the shelter.

A staff member at one shelter remarked that some people from these local government offices are tired of not being able to help people, so they send their staff to NGOs to learn how to circumvent the bureaucracy. Local self-governing agencies and the Social Welfare Ministry send staff to HELP for brief training, and the staff usually take them to the Immigration Office so that they can see for themselves how tough it is. A general critique voiced by shelter staff of government agencies is that they foist as much work as possible on to NGOs.

How productive are these informal relationships in the final analysis? They are not systematic nor can they be counted on to establish lasting precedents. One shelter staff noted in exasperation that in wealthier districts there are still personnel running the social welfare office reception who do not understand why a foreign woman might not be in possession of a passport, or why someone who obtained a divorce from her Japanese spouse did not desire to return to her home country.

One reason for this disparity in knowledge on the part of public officials is that some districts see many foreigners come through and become adept at handling their problems, or at least they show consistency, while other districts see few undocumented foreigners and are unaware of the problems. Furthermore, personnel are frequently shifted to different jobs, which means the loss of expertise in these issues. Most important, however, is a lack of transparency in the system, and the arbitrariness of the officials. For instance, if a foreigner who has overstayed her visa wishes to register her marriage to a Japanese citizen, she will usually be turned away at the registration bureau, with demands for valid documents. However, if the couple presses, it is possible to register the marriage, and then apply for a spouse visa. The process takes at least three years – the amount of time is not specified – and the couple must pay a kind of guarantee money for the overstaying spouse. This fee varies from 50,000 to 3,000,000 yet HELP's assistance and expertise with the system, most couples in this situation would become discouraged from registering the marriage at the first attempt. [26]

At the national level, the immigration law and enforcement procedures rigidly penalize foreign migrants, while NGOs handle the problems that these policies create, functioning as buffers for municipal agencies, handling cases they refuse, answering calls during hours that public agencies are closed. Shelters also push the local, prefectural, and national police to crack down on sex traffickers and brothel owners, and lobby them to make their arrest and detention procedures for foreign women less traumatic.

Public education

HELP provides public education mainly through offering monthly lecture tours of its facility, and the lectures which Ms Matsuda gave at national and international conferences such as the AIDS conference held in Yokohama in August 1994, and at local gatherings other NGOs sponsor. HELP is also active in AIDS education, and has assisted in carrying out a survey of condom use among sex workers. From my observation, of the three women's shelters, *Saalaa* appears to have the most public-oriented education function.[27] Until 1996, *Saalaa* held monthly open meetings which were well attended by the public, but they were canceled because they proved very time-consuming for the staff.

The human consequences

Shelters are faced with the problems that arise from migration patterns based on economic structural inequalities between Japan and its regional neighbors. These are combined with socio-cultural factors such as a strong division of labor by sex, a double standard in sexual morals and behavior, and a corporate culture that reinforces the notion that corporate warriors (*kigyō senshu*) find reward and release in purchasing sex (Abe 1994, Matsuda 1992, Allison 1994, Kanematsu 1992, Kasama 1996). These factors contribute to a strong sex and entertainment industry, and simultaneously stigmatize and criminalize those who work in it. As Kasama observes, unless the socio-cultural institutions which underlie this system of gender relations change to become more equal, Japanese women's social status will remain fragile (Kasama 1996: 176).

Some shelters are grappling with these issues by recognizing that the problems of others in Japan are indeed their own problems, and they hold meetings or seminars where these ideas are examined. For instance, *Saalaa* has held and published seminar series in which professors, activists, counselors, sex workers, and others have given talks on a wide range of thought-provoking topics, such as the nature of masculinity in Japanese society, male sexuality and aggression, the history of the sex industry in Japan and its relationship with the Korean Comfort Women (*jūgunianfu*), gender roles in the family, and so on. Through such seminars, *Saalaa* challenges the audience to re-think their assumptions about gender, sex, and family relationships.

If these challenges bear fruit in the minds and actions of individuals, this will be another human consequence of migration to Japan. While there is change in individual lives, however, the question remains how to reach a much broader audience with these messages. NGOs have great difficulty in maintaining their present size of operations, much less expanding their bases of their support. Since 1997, HELP's government support has been cut 10 percent along with government support to other NGOs. Donations from individuals have kept up, but at lesser amounts. HELP may run a budget deficit for the first time in 1998.

Conclusion

One volunteer remarked to me that his place of employment is a small factory in a conservative neighborhood. When, on occasion, he cannot stand the tension that comes from keeping his views on life to himself, and confides in his co-workers, they tell him he sounds like a college student and that he should grow up. Along the same lines, at a symposium in 1997, an attorney for *Saalaa* remarked that as long as foreign women returned home after a stay at *Saalaa*, the public was willing to see them as pitiable and give *Saalaa* donations, but now that many women come to *Saalaa* as a way out of a broken marriage to a more stable situation with the intent of residing permanently and independently in Japan, the public has lost interest in funding them. No one is more keenly aware of this gap in consciousness between the public and the NGO staff and volunteers than the support group personnel themselves. Given the lack of substantial support, what are the future prospects for these NGOs? Can they succeed in making more than a piecemeal impact?

While they are certainly a minority, their core is highly dedicated as well as knowledgeable in working the system. On 29 April 1997, representatives of support groups nationwide, including *Zentōitsu* and HELP, met in Nagoya to organize the National Network for Solidarity with Migrant Workers. With sixty-six groups and seventy-two individual members, this group seeks to lobby the national government to improve the situation of migrant workers and their families. As its first public action, on 2 December 1997, the group met officials from the Ministry of Labor and handed them a list of questions on migrant workers' problems to which the Ministry officials responded verbally. While this initial meeting had little immediate effect on the bureaucracy, it did serve to announce the Network's presence, and open up a channel for further communication and interest representation within the bureaucracy.

Plans for concrete future actions and campaigns are now underway, including the creation of a counter-report to the government's Fourth Periodic Report to the United Nations on human rights in Japan, which it submits in keeping with the International Covenant on Civil and Political Rights. Japan's migrant advocacy groups are well-informed on the international discourse on human rights, and try to utilize it to improve and legitimize their position, much as those groups mentioned by Soysal who "appeal to dominant human rights principles and develop discursive and organizational strategies around them"(Soysal 1994: 44).

By way of their protests, appeals, conferences, and presence, Japan's NGOs encourage citizens to examine their relationships to the foreigners who are building their roads, producing their factory goods, serving them in restaurants or servicing their fantasies. They have made inroads in upholding the rights of male and female foreign migrants. While none of these groups carry the consensus of Japanese society, their efforts make a positive difference to the lives of those with whom they work, and speak to a society more open to the possibility of multi-culturality and multi-ethnicity.

Notes

With the financial support of the University of Hawaii Japan Endowment Fund, I spent three months researching this topic, from May to July 1994, when I interviewed the Directors of HELP, the *Zentōitsu* Workers' Union, *Mizura,* and a *Saalaa* staff member and founding member, and collected unpublished documents from them. I also volunteered at HELP, tabulating case intake information. I presented a draft of this paper at the Association for Asian Studies Annual Meeting in Washington, D.C. in April 1995. This revised edition benefits from additional input from the relevant organizations, to whom I showed the previous paper, and from additional data collection while I was in Tokyo in June and July, 1995, and during a Visiting Associate Professorship at the Institute of Social Science, University of Tokyo, from June 1996 to January 1998. I would like to thank Lonny Carlile, Mike Douglass, Keiko Yamanaka and Jim Nickum for their comments on drafts of this paper.

1 I am using this term broadly to include foreigners who are working without a proper working visa as well as those who are working in jobs where they perform tasks outside of their legal visa classification (such as an entertainer who is working as a hostess or sex worker), and overstayers. Some undocumented migrants wish to stay in Japan as long as possible, others go home and return again on false documents, some return home for good, while yet others marry Japanese citizens and eventually settle in as legal residents.

2 The Japanese term is *mizushōbai.* This industry runs the gamut from entertainment (dancing, singing, playing music, etc.) to bar hostessing (serving drinks and making conversation with customers, possibly also dancing with customers) to massage parlors, to prostitution. The entertainment visa is often used as a window by brokers

to bring foreign women to Japan to work legally, while actually coercing women to work as hostesses or prostitutes. Some women come on these terms fully aware of the working conditions, while others learn after arrival.

3 These support groups also advise foreigners who legally reside in Japan, and Japanese citizens who seek assistance, but their initial *raison d'être* was to improve conditions for migrants.

4 Herbert reports that in January 1988, government officials who were approached for assistance by illegal foreigners were directed by an ordinance to notify the Immigration Control Bureau. This was relaxed for the newly-created Offices for the Human Rights of Foreign Workers, which were established in August 1988. Eventually "the strenuous efforts of organizations for the protection of the rights of migrant workers . . .led Labour Offices also to loosen their reporting practices" (Herbert 1997: 98). Nevertheless, as workers cannot strictly be assured that the Labor Standards Office or other government office would not turn him in, they generally stay clear of such places. Also see Patel, "The Role of the Bureaucracy in the Enforcement of Human Rights," in Goodman and Neary (eds) 1996: 27–50. In a related vein, I recently took advantage of a visit by my neighborhood policeman (who had heard a foreigner had moved in and wanted to know our particulars, including our visa status and so on), to inquire what he would do if I were an overstayer. He told me that he sees a number of such people, and, though he used to report them, Immigration is now far to busy to handle the overload, so the police no longer bother unless the foreigner has caused trouble.

5 By 1995, Japan had accepted 8,679 refugees from Indo-China as permanent residents in Japan, and from 1982 to May 1995, 208 of 1,141 people who applied for political asylum were recognized as refugees (Weiner and Hanami 1998: 432–3).

6 According to government statistics, in 1995, 3.5 percent of all marriages in Japan were between a foreigner and a Japanese citizen. In 1970, the percentage was 0.5 per cent. Of these, the majority (2.6 percent) are between a Japanese man and a foreign woman. The breakdown by nationality of the foreign wives in 1995 was the Philippines, 34.6 percent, China 24.9 percent, South and North Korea 21.7 percent, Thailand, 9.2 percent, Brazil, 2.8 percent . In 1995, 20,254 children were born to couples where one partner was Japanese, as compared with 10,022 in 1987 (*Kokusai Jinryū* February 1997: 37, 39).

7 An additional 0.4 percent had "other" answers, and 2.7 percent did not reply. The sample consisted of 325 men and 361 women.

8 At this time, *Sōhyō* was the main left-wing union, dominated by the Japan Socialist Party.

9 In 1989 *Sōhyō* as such disbanded and merged with the *New Rengo*, which had absorbed three other former national union centers, *Dōmei, Chūritsu Rōren* and *Shinsanbetsu*. At this point, Tabata (1997: 106) remarks, "'class-based' (and left-wing) labour unionism was virtually confined to two newly created but small labor federations, *Zenrōren* and *Zenrōkyō*, both composed largely of civil servants and unions in small and mid-sized enterprises."

10 The union notes that this change is due to an increase in Iranian and Bangaladeshi men getting caught by the police and returning home, and increases in the numbers of Brazilian Japanese coming to work in manufacturing.

11 I have heard this many times since 1996 when I began attending the Foreign Workers Executive Committee meetings. Mori Hiromi also notes this situation in his book, *Immigration Policy and Foreign Workers in Japan*. In particular, he cites Mori Hiromasa (1994), who states that "almost 60 per cent of accidents clandestine workers encounter are reported to have happened within three months of their initiation of work" (Mori 1997: 195, 197).

12 According to the Labor Standards Law, Article 20, Section One, an employer is obliged to provide an employee with thirty days' notice. If he fails to do so and tries to summarily dismiss an employee, he must pay the employee more than thirty days'

worth of his average pay (this is referred to as *kaiko yokoku teate*, or warning of dismissal allowance) (*Tōkyō-to Rōdō Keizai Kyoku Rōseibu Rōdō Kumiai ka* 1994, *Gaikokujin Rōdōsha to Rōdōhō* (Foreign Workers and the Labor Law), Tokyo: *Tōkyōto Rōdō Keizai Kyoku Rōseibu Rōdō Kumiai ka*).

13 The vast majority of clandestine foreign workers are covered neither by Health Insurance, which applies to employees in firms, nor by National Health Insurance, which is managed by local governments designed for those not covered by Health Insurance. For a thorough analysis of the medical insurance system and the problems of coverage for foreign workers, see Mori 1997: 197–202.

14 This is fairly common behavior on the part of shop owners. Some fear being fined or incarcerated for having hired an undocumented worker, or they are reluctant to call attention to the unsafe working conditions in their shops. Others are simply unsympathetic.

15 In 1997, the debt price on the heads of Thai women who have sought shelter at HELP was on average 4,500,000 yen. Furthermore, working conditions for women in the sex industry are worsening with the advent of mobile units, where women literally live in a van and are shuttled to customers' locations. It has also become more common for gangsters to have women of the same nationality as the sex workers act as the *mama-san* managers of the brothel, with the outcome that it is more difficult for women working there to plot escape in a group. Lastly, *yakuza* have begun to put a bounty on the heads of women who have escaped, and they take wanted posters to women waiting in line at the embassies to see if they can get countrywomen to betray each other (Interview with the director of HELP, 20 January 1998). For further discussion on the situation of women in the sex industry, see Herbert1996: 27–38.

16 Yamazaki Keiko comments:

> The focus of Japanese anti-prostitution measures seems to be to deport foreign women accused of prostitution . . . more than anything else, I want to emphasize that we need to put an end to this system in which women are punished for prostitution but the brokers go free, and no one even mentions the customers' role.
>
> (HELP's *Network News*, no. 30, December 1997)

17 In order of establishment, they are *Micaela* (1985) HELP (1986), *Daruku Josei Hausu* (1990), *Furendoshippu Ajia Hausu Cosumosu* (1991), *Saalaa* (1992), *Mizura* (1993), and *AKK Josei Sherutâ* (1993) (Yokohama shi Josei Kyōkai 1995) (Yokohama City Women's Assocation).

18 I do not intend to give the impression that the majority of marriages between foreign women and Japanese men end up disfunctional. Shelters see the worst cases. Case workers have told me that many of them women seeking to marry or seeking asylum from their husbands have only the most rudimentary grasp of the Japanese language, and see marraige as an economic refuge; the Japanese husbands are often involved in gangster activities and are out to exploit their partners, and such marraiges have little prospect of succeeding from the start.

19 Working in a shelter becomes an education in itself. Whatever motive brings a person to initially volunteer or work on the staff, she comes over time to see the complexities of the reasons behind women's work in the sex industry, or reasons for the abusive relationships from which they run. A sex worker may have come to Japan well aware of the conditions she might meet, and she might be willing to return again if she thinks she can turn the system to her advantage the next time around. A staff worker told me that women from third world countries, when "choosing" to come to Japan as sex workers, are not exercising choice in the same way as Japanese sex workers, who have many other options. Women from the third world, she noted, are constrained by the North/South economic differential, as well as by Japan's restrictive immigration policy, which does not allow unskilled women to work. Volunteers and staff who follow this logic are more able to handle seeing repeat cases than

those who hope to "rescue" victims and send them home for good. In a similar vein, Naiyana Supapung, a Thai attorney for the women's NGO *Foiwa*, remarked at a 1995 conference at Meiji Gakuin University in Tokyo that Japan's NGOs need to be active in persuading the government to open the door to legal unskilled work, so that women would have more alternatives than the sex industry. For a thorough explication of her views on the situation of Thai migrant women in Japan, see Supapung 1997.

20 By the end of 1997, the number of Filipina women – eight – equaled that of Taiwanese and Chinese women who came to HELP; and the number of Colombian women increased to nine. HELP's Director noted that the drop in Filipinas seeking shelter is due to a tightening of the requirements for issuing the entertainment visa (interview, 20 January 1998).

21 The 1997 *Keisatsu Hakusho* (Police White Paper) confirms that brokers are involved in trafickking women to the sex industry, and that there are some among the trafficked who are made to assume large debts, forced into prostitution without receiving any remuneration, and are working in terrible conditions. They also note that of the 934 women arrested in 1996 for prostitution-related offenses, Thai women accounted for just over one-third of the total (316), while women from Korea (189), Colombia (155), Taiwan (99), and the Philippines (89) made up the next most numerous groups. There were 86 from "other" nationalities (Keishicho 1997: 232).

22 JWCTU members helped to organize the Association for the Prevention of Prostitutes in 1919, and the founder of the JWCTU, Yajima Kajiko, was among those petitioning for the Bill to Regulate Overseas Prostitutes, which was adopted in 1921 by the Forty-Fourth Diet (Ohshima and Francis 1989: 187).

23 Matsuda Mizuho was the Director of HELP from 1988 to 1996, and my interviews and conversations in the summers of 1994 and 1995 were with Ms Matsuda. Ms Matsuda left HELP in March 1996 to become the director of the Asian Women's Fund. Shoji Rutsuko became HELP's director in 1996, and my information on HELP from this date comes from conversations with Mrs. Shoji in 1997 and an interview in January 1998.

24 When I sat in on a monthly public meeting on HELP's activities, I found that there are some people to whom this policy comes as a surprise. During a question and answer session at the end of Ms Matsuda's talk, a pastor from a local Protestant church asked whether HELP requires its residents to have physical examinations. Matsuda replied that HELP does not force women to do anything, whether it be listen to a lecture on sexually transmitted diseases or to return to their home countries or go to the doctor, or whatever. She noted that many Japanese like to do things for others without asking the people first whether or not that is what they wish. She said that she does not want to presume things on behalf of others. The pastor appeared to be quite astonished. Another pastor asked whether HELP takes any special measures regarding AIDS, since many of the women coming to shelters surely have caught it. Ms Matsuda replied that AIDS is the least of her worries, since it is difficult to transmit, unlike hepatitis, for instance.

25 Here we can see that HELP's basic philosophy has remained, even with the change of Directors. Babior (1993: 185) noted, "The HELP shelter is remarkable in that it avoids blaming women for their problems, and respects and encourages women to make decisions based on their own best interests." For an in-depth analysis of sexual violence and abuse in Japanese society, from an ethnographic portrayal of HELP at its inception and its years with Oshima Shizuko as Director, see Babior (1993).

26 Interview with HELP's director, 21 January 1998.

27 At an evening meeting which I attended in July 1994, *Saalaa* staff distributed short case studies of women who had come to the shelter. The staff then asked the audience to figure out how we would handle these women's problems. It was an excellent method for breaking the ice, and for getting us to understand the com-

plexities of the cases. The staff members were frank in their assessment of what they can accomplish, noting that some women have worked in Japan previously, and, although cognizant of the exploitation which might occur, take the risk and return again. Furthermore, they reported that other women marry Japanese men without the least basis for compatibility. *Saalaa* staff want the public to realize that whatever the motive that brought a migrant worker to Japan, whether they were duped or not, they should not have their human rights violated. The job of the shelter is to deal with each case.

References

Abe, H. (1994) *"Josei Sherutā wa Ima"* (Women's Shelter Now), in *Taminzoku, Tabunka, Kyōsei* (Multiethnic, Multicultural, Living Together), Yokohama: Kanagawa Jinken Sentā (Kanagawa Center for Human Rights): 16–29.

Allison, A. (1994) *Nightwork: Sexuality, Pleasure and Corporate Masculinity in a Tokyo Hostess Club,* Chicago: University of Chicago Press.

Babior, S. L. (1993) *Women of a Tokyo Shelter: Domestic Violence and Sexual Exploitation in Japan,* Ann Arbor: University Microfilms International.

Catholic Diocese of Yokohama Solidarity Center for Migrants (1997) *Manual for Migrants Living in Japan: Information for Living in your Community,* Yokohama: Catholic Diocese of Yokohama.

Garon, S. (1997) *Molding Japanese Minds: The State in Everyday Life,* Princeton: Princeton University Press.

Hirowatari, S. (1993) 'Foreigners and the 'Foreign Question' Under Japanese Law," in *Annals of the Institute of Social Science,* University of Tokyo.

Herbert, W. (1996) *Foreign Workers and Law Enforcement in Japan,* London and New York: Kegan Paul International.

Hōmushō Nyūkankyoku (eds) (1997) *"Honpō ni okeru Fuhō Zanryūsha Kazu"* (Numbers of Illegal Overstayers in the Country), *Kokusai Jinryū* 97, 5: 29–33, Tokyo: Zaidan Hōjin Nyūkan Kyōkai (Japan Immigration Association).

Kanematsu, S. (1992) *"Sei o Uru Genba kara Mieta Mono"* (What was Viewed from a Place where Sex was Sold) in *Daini Josei no Ie Sālā Renzoku Seminā* (Second in a Continuing Series of Seminars at Sālā, *"[Sei] ga Urikai Sareruwake – Ima Towareru Sei Ishiki"* (When 'Sex' is Bought and Sold – Questioning Sexuality in the Present), Yokohama: Sālā.

Kasama, C. (1996) *"Tainichi Gaikokujin Josei to 'Jendā Baiasu': Nihonteki Ukeire no Issokumen to Mondaite"* (Gender Bias and Foreign Women in Japan: One Side of the Japanese Style of Reception and its Problems), in T. Miyajima and T. Kajita (eds) *Gaikokujin Rōdōsha kara Shimin he* (From Foreign Workers to Residents), Tokyo: Yūhikaku.

Lamphere, L. (1992) *Structuring Diversity: Ethnographic Perspectives on the New Immigration,* Chicago and London: University of Chicago Press.

Matsuda, M. (1992) "Women from Thailand," *Ampo* 23, 4: 16–19.

Mori, H. (1997) *Immigration Policy and Foreign Workers in Japan,* New York: St. Martin's Press.

Nihon Kirisutokyō Fujin Kyōtūkai (Japan Women's and Christian Temperance Union) (ed.) (1998) *Me de Miro Hyaku Nen Shi: Nihon Kirisutokyō Fujin Kyōtūkai, 1886 Nen Sōretsu* (A Hundred Year History Through Our Eyes: JWCTU, Established in 1886), Tokyo: Nihon Kirisutokyō Fujin Kyōtūkai.

Ohshima, S. and Francis, C. (1989) *Japan through the Eyes of Women Migrant Workers,*

Tokyo: Japan Women's Christian Temperence Union.

Patel, J. (1996) "The Role of the Bureaucracy in the Enforcement of Human Rights," in R. Goodman and I. Neary (eds) *Case Studies on Human Rights in Japan,* Richmond, Surrey: Japan Library, Curzon Press.

Raifu Dezain Kenkyūsho (eds) (1997) *Seikatsusha Ishiki Deita Shū, '98* (Databook on People's Lifestyles and Opinion Surveys), Tokyo: Raifu Dezain Kenkyūsho.

Rowland, R. (1995) "Human Rights Discourse and Women: Challenging the Rhetoric with Reality," in "Symposium: Human Rights And The Sociological Project," *ANZJS* 31, 2 (August): 8–25.

Soysal, Y. (1994) *Limits of Citizenship: Migrants and Postnational Membership in Europe,* Chicago and London: University of Chicago Press.

Supapung, N. (1997) "Thai-Japanese NGOs' Cooperation to Assist Thai Female Migrants: Progress and Problems in Terms of Networking and Human Rights," in International Peace Research Institute, Meiji Gakuin University (ed.) *International Female Migration to Japan: Networking, Settlement and Human Rights,* Tokyo: International Peace Research Institute.

Tabata, H. (1997) "Industrial Relations and the Union Movement," in J. Banno (ed.) *The Political Economy of Japanese Society, Volume 1: The State or the Market?,* New York: Oxford University Press.

Tokyo-to Rōdōkeizai Kyoku Rōseibu Rōdōkumiai Ka (Tokyo Prefecture, Labor Economics Bureau, Labor Administration Divison, Labor Union Section) (1994) *Gaikokujin Rōdōsha to Rōdōhō* (Foreign Workers and Labor Law), Tokyo: Tokyo-to Rōdō Keizai Kyoku Rōseibu Rōdōkumiai Ka.

Truong, T. D. (1996) "Gender, International Migration, and Social Reproduction: Implications for Theory, Policy, Research and Networking," *Asian and Pacific Migration Journal* 5, 1.

Truong, T. D. and del Rosario, V. O. (1995) "Captive Outsiders: the Sex Traffik and Mail-Order Brides in the European Union," in J. Wiersma (ed.) *Insiders and Outsiders,* Kampen, Netherlands: Pharos.

Weiner, M. and Hanami, T. (eds) (1998) *Temporary Workers or Future Citizens? Japanese and US Migration Policies,* Basingstoke and London: Macmillan.

Yamanaka, K. (1993) "New Immigration Policy and Unskilled Foreign Workers in Japan." *Pacific Affairs* 66, 1 (Spring): 72–90.

Yokohama-shi Josei Kyōkai (Yohohama Women's Association) (1995) (ed.) *Minkan Josei Sheruatā Chōsa Hōkokusho 1* (Report on a Survey of Private Sector Women's Shelters, 1) Yohohama: Yokohama Women's Assocation, Forum Yokohama.

Zaidan Hōjin Nyūkan Kyōkai (ed.) (1996) "*Kokuseki (Shusshinchi) Betsu, Seibetsu Fūhō Zanryūsha Kazu no Suii*" (Number of Illegally Overstaying Foreigners, by Nationality (Place of Origin) and Sex), *Kokusai Jinryū* 96, 9: 18–21, Tokyo: Zaidan Hōjin Nyūkan Kyōkai (Japan Immigration Association).

Index